Accession no.
00956587

KU-302-327

SPECIMEN,

LIBRARY
Library

CHESTER
COLLEGE

This book is to be returned on or above
the last date stamped below.

CANCELLED
CANCELLED
CANCELLED
CANCELLED
CANCELLED

14 OCT 1996

22 OCT 1996

26 NOV 1996

- 5 DEC 1995

2 2 JAN 1996

2 MAY 1996

1 3 DEC 1996
- 6 JAN 1997

1 5 OCT 1997

CANCELLED 1997

2 5 MAR 1997

CANCELLED

UCC LIBRARY
CANCELLED 2001
2 1 FEB 2001

UCC LIBRARY

2 7 MAR 2001

UCC LIBRARY

1 2 NOV 2002

CANCELLED

One
Week
Loan

Dedicated to the memory of
Dr. Tom Waddell,

Olympic decathlete, healer, and visionary
founder of the Gay Games,
1937-1987

Library of Congress Cataloging-in-Publication Data
Sport, men, and the gender order : critical feminist perspectives /
   Michael A. Messner, Don F. Sabo, editors.
      p.   cm.
   Includes bibliographical references.
   ISBN 0-87322-281-4
   1. Sports--Psychological aspects.   2. Sports--Social aspects.
   3. Masculinity (Psychology)   4. Identity (Psychology)   5. Sex role.
   6. Feminism.   I. Messner, Michael A.   II. Sabo, Donald F.
   GV706.4.S66   1990
   796'.01--dc20   90-31880
                                                                         CIP

ISBN: 0-87322-281-4 (case)
         0-87322-421-3 (paper)

Copyright © 1990 by Don Sabo, PhD and Michael Messner, PhD

All rights reserved. Except for use in a review, the reproduction or utilization of this work
in any form or by any electronic, mechanical, or other means, now known or hereafter
invented, including xerography, photocopying, and recording, and in any information
storage and retrieval system, is forbidden without the permission of the publisher.

Acquisitions Editor: Richard Frey, PhD
Developmental Editor: Holly Gilly
Assistant Editor: Timothy Ryan
Copyeditor: Julie Anderson
Proofreader: Dianna Matlosz
Indexer: Barbara Cohen
Production Director: Ernie Noa
Typesetter: Angela K. Snyder
Text Design: Keith Blomberg
Text Layout: Denise Lowry and
   Kimberlie Henris
Cover Design: Tim Offenstein
Illustrations: Denise Lowry
Interior Photos: Photo on page 17 from
             the Amateur Athletic
             Foundation of Los
             Angeles; photo on page
             171 © CLEO
             Photography.
Printer: United Graphics

Printed in the United States of America

10 9 8 7 6 5 4 3 2 1

Human Kinetics Publishers
Box 5076, Champaign, IL 61825-5076
1-800-747-4457

Canada Office:
Human Kinetics Publishers
P.O. Box 2503
Windsor, ON   N8Y 4S2
1-800-465-7301 (in Canada only)

Europe Office:
Human Kinetics Publishers (Europe) Ltd.
P.O. Box IW14
Leeds LS16 6TR
England
0532-781708

Australia Office:
Human Kinetics Publishers
P.O. Box 80
Kingswood 5062
South Australia   374-0433

Contents

Preface   v

Acknowledgments   vii

Introduction: Toward a Critical Feminist Reappraisal of Sport,   1
Men, and the Gender Order
Michael A. Messner and Donald F. Sabo

Part I: Theoretical and Historical Foundations   17

Chapter 1: Sport in the Social Construction of Masculinity   19
David Whitson

Chapter 2: The Men's Cultural Centre: Sports and the Dynamic   31
of Women's Oppression/Men's Repression
Bruce Kidd

Chapter 3: Masculinity, Sexuality, and the Development   45
of Early Modern Sport
Todd Crosset

Chapter 4: Baseball and the Reconstitution   55
of American Masculinity, 1880-1920
Michael S. Kimmel

Chapter 5: Rugby in the 19th-Century British Boarding-School System: 67
A Feminist Psychoanalytic Perspective
Philip G. White and Anne B. Vagi

Part II: Contemporary Research   79

Chapter 6: An Iron Man: The Body and Some Contradictions   83
of Hegemonic Masculinity
R.W. Connell

Chapter 7: Masculinities and Athletic Careers: 97
Bonding and Status Differences
Michael A. Messner

Chapter 8: Cool Pose: Black Masculinity and Sports   109
Richard Majors

Chapter 9: Football Ritual and the Social Reproduction **115**
of Masculinity
Donald F. Sabo and Joe Panepinto

Chapter 10: Little Big Man: Hustling, Gender Narcissism, **127**
and Bodybuilding Subculture
Alan M. Klein

Chapter 11: Gay Jocks: A Phenomenology of Gay Men in Athletics **141**
Brian Pronger

Chapter 12: Male Cheerleaders and the Naturalization of Gender **153**
Laurel R. Davis

Chapter 13: Women Coaching Male Athletes **163**
Ellen J. Staurowsky

Part III: Challenges, Changes, and Alternatives **171**

Chapter 14: Challenges to Male Hegemony in Sport **173**
Lois Bryson

Chapter 15: Women of Color, Critical Autobiography, and Sport **185**
Susan Birrell

Chapter 16: Warriors or Wimps? Creating Alternative Forms **201**
of Physical Education
Barbara Humberstone

Chapter 17: Addressing Homophobia in Physical Education: **211**
Responsibilities for Teachers and Researchers
Pat Griffin and James Genasci

Chapter 18: How Should We Theorize Gender
in the Context of Sport? **223**
M. Ann Hall

Epilogue **241**
Carole Oglesby

Notes 247

References 257

Supplemental Readings 279

Index 281

About the Authors 285

Preface

This book aims at forging new understandings of the old relationship between men and sport. Scholarly scrutiny of men and sport is not new. Indeed, until quite recently, almost all sport research focused on men, not on women. By the early 1970s, a multidisciplinary sport studies had blossomed and had succeeded in illuminating the relationships between sport and racism, class inequality, nationalism, violence, drug use, and other social issues. However, the concept of gender was conspicuously absent from most analyses of sport. The fact that the institution of sport, in its dominant forms, was constituted from the very beginning as an exclusive arena of *male* experience and *male* relations was ignored or taken for granted as "natural." Indeed, that women were excluded from sport research shows that like the rest of the populace, sport sociologists saw sport as a male activity, not a female or human activity. This blind spot concerning the fundamental relationship between sport and the social construction of gender resulted in a very incomplete—sometimes distorted—analysis of the historical and contemporary importance and meaning of sport.

The articles in this volume, by sport researchers and theorists from Canada, Australia, the United States, and England, represent an emergent trend that is inspired by feminism and given shape by new perspectives on men and masculinities that are being constructed by feminist men's studies scholars. First, these articles demonstrate that in order to fully understand the historical and contemporary meaning of sport, we must utilize gender as a fundamental category of analysis. Second, these studies show that not only women are "gendered." The utilization of critical feminist perspectives in examining *men's* relationships to sport reveals fascinating insights and new research questions. Third, concrete studies of men's historical and contemporary relationships to sport suggest that sport tends to unify men in the domination of women and that women's movement into sport is thus a challenge to male domination. Yet these studies also demonstrate that different groups of men may have different stakes in the types of masculinity that sport constructs and celebrates. Specifically, how do gay men's, ethnic minority men's, and working-class men's experiences and relationships with sports differ from those of middle-class, straight, and/or white men? No single article in this volume answers all of these questions. But together, the articles demonstrate that by exploring the links between sport and gender, we can better understand sport customs and beliefs; the lives of individual athletes; the structures and workings of sport organizations; and the changing relations between and within the sexes in sport.

CHESTER COLLEGE

ACC. No.   DEPT.
00956587   SWIN

796. 01   MES

LIBRARY

WITHDRAWN

v

The scope and uniqueness of this book will appeal to a wide variety of scholars within the general areas of sport sociology, sport psychology, and physical education. This volume has particular relevance for the growing number of researchers and scholars interested in the general area of sex and gender in sport and physical education. It will make for engaging reading in courses dealing with women and sport, gender and sport, and sport and society. Because of this book's challenging theoretical discussions, it will also prove useful to master's and doctoral students engaged in gender-related research. Finally, feminist theorists and critical theorists outside sport research and physical education will find that this volume can make a contribution to the women's studies and men's studies literatures.

This book is organized in three parts. Part I lays out theoretical and historical conceptualizations of sport and the gender order. The articles in this section represent not so much an attempt to hammer out "the" theory of gender and sport as an attempt to promote dialogue among and between various critical and feminist theories. Part II consists of several examples of current research on sport and gender. And in Part III we look to the future, in terms of pragmatic strategies both for challenging oppressive aspects of sport and for developing more systematic and inclusive theories with which to inform that social practice. Finally, the book concludes with a combined bibliography, which should be useful to researchers of gender and sport.

Acknowledgments

We would like to thank the authors who contributed to this book. Without their thoughtful work and their determination amidst revisions and delays, this book would have not been possible.

We gratefully acknowledge the contributions to the development of this book by our editors at Human Kinetics Publishers, Rick Frey and Holly Gilly. Anonymous readers also provided valuable feedback on early versions of the manuscript.

The women's movement has been responsible for creating the social and intellectual context within which this book was created. More specifically, the feminist scholars of the past 15 years or so who put gender on the sports studies agenda paved the way for this book. Special debts are owed to Eva Auchincloss, Bonnie Beck, Susan Birrell, Cheryl Cole, Margaret Carlisle Duncan, Kari Fasting, Susan Greendorfer, Pat Griffin, Ann Hall, Dorothy Harris, Susan Curry Jansen, Carole Oglesby, Nancy Theberge, and Beth Vanfossen.

While working on this book we have benefited from our affiliations with our institutions. Mike's colleagues in the Program for the Study of Women and Men in Society and in the Department of Sociology at the University of Southern California were supportive throughout this project. Don's energy has been amplified by colleagues at D'Youville College and especially by the network of persons who comprise the Women's Sports Foundation.

Various friends and family members contributed, directly and indirectly, to our work on this book. For Mike, Pierrette Hondagneu-Sotelo has always offered loving support and encouragement as well as helpful editorial and intellectual feedback. Don has depended on Linda Weisbeck Sabo for intellectual and emotional support throughout the life cycle of this project. Finally, the book has brought its two editors closer together, despite some 3,000 miles and a mountain range of traditional gender socialization that separate us.

Introduction

Toward a Critical Feminist Reappraisal of Sport, Men, and the Gender Order

Michael A. Messner
and Donald F. Sabo

In the early and mid-1970s, an academic revolution of sorts was taking place that began to challenge the androcentric blind spots and biases of the social sciences and the humanities (Spender, 1981). By the end of the decade, feminism had made important inroads into many areas of scholarship and had even begun to participate in defining the terrain of discourse in others. The term *feminism* resists handy definition. There is no single feminist school of thought but rather a multifaceted mosaic of feminist visions and practices. Here we generally refer to feminism as a movement to end sexist oppression (Hooks, 1984).

Today, feminist scholarship prospers. Feminist writings have proliferated in Canada, the United States, Western Europe, and Australia. Contrary to traditional social science, which displays a general indifference to the fact that social groups are composed of gendered individuals, feminist analysis centers on the study of relations between the sexes. Within the incipient feminist paradigm, gender is considered a key dimension of overall identity and a determinant of behavior. Gender stereotypes are scrutinized and their influences on socialization are evaluated. The ties between sex inequality and other institutional processes are diligently studied. Sex-based status differences and patriarchal values are discerned and

1

described, and their significance for social control and culture maintenance is explored. And feminism is yielding new interpretations of social history and of the nature of social scientific knowledge itself (Harding, 1986; Roberts, 1976; Safilios-Rothschild, 1977). Sport, among the most masculine of social institutions, has not been immune to these sorts of feminist challenges.

FEMINIST THEORIES
AND THE STUDY OF SPORT

Feminist analysis of sport has a very short history. One is hard put to find any consideration of sport in mainstream feminist classics written before the 1980s. For example, there is no substantive treatment of sport in Simone de Beauvoir's *The Second Sex* (1952), Susan Brownmiller's *Against Our Will* (1975), Kate Millett's *Sexual Politics* (1970), Juliet Mitchell's *Woman's Estate* (1973), Mary Daly's *Gyn-Ecology: The Metaethics of Radical Feminism* (1978), or Betty Friedan's *The Second Stage* (1981). Similarly, the feminist leadership of the 1978 First National Women's Conference in Houston had little understanding of women's issues in sport. Efforts by leading women's sport activists Eva Auchincloss and Carole Oglesby to include a platform statement endorsing women's athletic rights were to no avail; no official recommendation regarding women's athletic rights was included in the *Official Report to the President, the Congress, and the People of the United States* (The Spirit of Houston, 1978).

Despite the lack of recognition of gender issues in sport within the wider women's movement, by the late 1970s feminists in academia began to develop a critique of sport "as a fundamentally sexist institution that is male dominated and masculine in orientation" (Theberge, 1981, p. 342). A multifaceted analysis of women, gender, and sex inequality in sport was developed by pioneers such as Dorothy Harris (1972), Ann Hall (1972, 1978, 1981, 1984), Susan Greendorfer (1974, 1978), Mary Duquin (1978, 1984), Susan Birrell (1978), Carole Oglesby (1978), Jan Felshin (1974), and others. The impressive outpouring of research and theory was collected in several texts and anthologies (Boutilier & SanGiovanni, 1983; Gerber et al., 1974; Oglesby, 1978; Twin, 1979). Feminist analyses uncovered a hidden history of female athleticism, examined sex differences in patterns of athletic socialization, and demonstrated how the dominant institutional forms of sport have naturalized men's power and privilege over women. The marginalization and trivialization of female athletes, it was demonstrated, serve to reproduce the structural and ideological domination of women by men. In the decade that has followed, the feminist critique both of the institution of sport and of the androcentric biases in sport studies has had a profound impact. Feminism now makes a major contribution to defining the terrain of scholarly discourse in sport studies (Hall, 1987a, 1988; Melnick & Sabo, 1987).

Feminism's Inherent Struggle

Yet the full contribution that feminism is capable of making is still to be felt. As Stacey and Thorne (1985) have noted, the marginalization of feminist theory is due both to the institutionalized sexism built into the larger disciplines and to the shortcomings of feminist theory itself. Within sport studies, feminist scholars have often found themselves marginalized and ghettoized for similar reasons. There has been resistance to the new perspectives introduced by feminist scholars. And feminism is still struggling to develop into a more mature, fully developed paradigm.

A large part of that struggle lies in the need to come to grips with internal political cleavages within feminist theory itself. Josephine Donovan (1985) identifies six distinct schools of feminist theory: liberal feminism, cultural feminism, socialist feminism, psychoanalytic feminism, existentialist feminism, and radical feminism. Rosemary Tong (1989) adds a seventh category: postmodern feminism. Though, there are often important points of overlap (e.g., Chodorow's [1978] psycho-analytic feminism is developed, implicitly, within a socialist-feminist macro-perspective), there are important, often conflictual differences between these various perspectives. In feminist sport studies, the major cleavage has fallen between liberal feminism and variants of radical or socialist feminism. At the risk of oversimplifying these differences, we will briefly outline these perspectives.

Liberal Feminism. Liberal feminism is a direct descendant of Enlightenment thought, wherein political philosophers argued that individuals possessed certain inherent rights such as life, liberty, and the pursuit of happiness. Nineteenth-century women such as Mary Wollstonecraft (1975) and abolitionist Sarah Grimkè (1970) as well as a handful of men like John Stuart Mill (1970) argued that women had the same inalienable rights that men had. Women's rights activists stressed the similarities between the sexes, embraced a fundamental individualism, and pressed for equal opportunity for women in education, government, and the economy. In the late 1960s and into the 1970s, this liberal individual rights and equal opportunity agenda was taken up by the mainstream of the modern feminist movement (especially in the United States). And in the 1980s, the language of individual rights continued to dominate most discussions of gender politics, from abortion to sport participation.

Radical Feminism. Radical feminists criticize liberal feminists for their emphasis on individual equal rights, especially to the extent that liberals tend to uncritically assume that our social system is fairly innocuous. To the contrary, radical feminists argue that equal opportunity for women within the present society is impossible, because the system itself is fundamentally patriarchal in structure. Radical feminists see the original oppression of women by men in the patriarchal family as a proto-type of other forms of oppression that exist in sexual relationships, class and race relations, and political and economic institutions. Theorists like Kate Millett (1970) and Mary Daly (1978) argue that the state and women's castelike subjugation within it are maintained by the threat or application of force and through social-ization of both sexes to patriarchal ideologies. Radical feminists advocate the destruction of patriarchal ideologies and the abandonment of hierarchical, patri-archal institutions and relationships—not "equal opportunity" for women within these oppressive structures.

Socialist Feminism. Like radical feminists, socialist feminists are very critical of liberals' emphasis on individual equal rights and their generally uncritical stance toward the existing social structure. In particular, socialist feminists believe equality for women cannot be achieved within a capitalist system. Yet socialist feminists go beyond traditional Marxism by arguing (based on observations of the persistence of patriarchy in "socialist" societies such as Cuba, China, and the Soviet Union) that the establishment of socialism is necessary but not sufficient for the establishment of freedom and equality for women (Stacey, 1979). Socialist feminists draw from the radical feminist conception of patriarchy and ground it in a Marxian historical materialism. In fact, they argue, capitalism transformed patriarchy in fundamental ways, especially in the creation of a gendered public/domestic split. Understanding (and acting to overcome) women's oppression, then, means developing a "dual systems" theory that illuminates the sometimes consistent, sometimes contradictory ways that capitalism and patriarchy interact (Eisenstein, 1979).

Integration of Feminist Factions

Within feminist sport studies there has been an uneasy coexistence between these different feminisms. Liberal feminists, as scholars and as change agents, have argued for—and have partially achieved—greater opportunities for girls and women in sports. Radical and socialist feminists have developed historical and theoretical critiques of the deeply gendered structure and values of the sports world. These feminists argue that because sport is an important institution in the construction of patriarchy (or capitalist patriarchy), women may be contributing to their own oppression by uncritically participating in this institution rather than attempting to transform it or construct alternative feminist sports structures (Beck, 1980).

Two points should be made here. First, though some liberal feminist ideas are represented here, the editors and the majority of the authors in this book work primarily within radical and/or socialist feminist frameworks. But second, though we do not want to minimize the fundamental differences that exist between liberal feminism and its radical and socialist counterparts, some evidence suggests that the differences have been overstated. For instance, radical and socialist feminist sport scholars have argued that the dominant forms that sport has taken have served to exclude women from public life and to support the construction of (and ideological naturalization of) women's subordinate status in domestic life and mothering (Lenskyj, 1986; Messner, 1988). Yet, liberal feminist activism over the past 2 decades has been fairly successful at gaining increased funding, more programs, and thus greater opportunities and social legitimacy for female athletes. In the United States, since the passage of Title IX in 1972 (a decidedly liberal initiative), female athleticism has grown rapidly: Athletic participation of school-age girls increased from 294,000 (4% of the female school-age population) in 1972 to 1.8 million (26% of the female school-age population) in 1987 (Sabo, 1988).

If it is indeed true, as feminist scholars have argued, that sport participation prepares males for participation in public life (Lever, 1976), then we can expect that increased female athleticism will result in a sense of empowerment and increased self-actualization for female participants (Oglesby, 1978; Theberge, 1987). Thus, female athleticism (and increased participation by women in other areas of public life) might become a means of women's challenging the gendered public/domestic split that is an important basis of men's continued power and privilege over women. In short, it is conceivable that, to paraphrase Zillah Eisenstein (1981), there is a "radical future to liberal feminism." Sometimes, radical theorists inside academia tend to ignore or look down their noses at reformism, while remaining theoretically pure (and possibly irrelevant). Meanwhile, liberal activists are bringing about actual changes that may serve as the basis for more fundamental, radical transformations. We do not want to imply that radical feminists are strangers to nitty-gritty social reform. Many grass-roots organizations have been spearheaded by radical feminists' energies and visions (e.g., halfway houses for battered women, alternative health care services, women's bookstores, and alternative women's sports organizations). The point is that radical and liberal feminists in sport would probably benefit from increased dialogue about social change and transformative action. Moreover, divisiveness among women in sport, whether it is theoretically or politically inspired, ultimately serves the interests of masculine hegemony.

Limitations of the Liberal Feminist Agenda

Still, there are important limitations to the liberal feminist agenda. The language of individual rights tends to inhibit the development of movements that aim to transform capitalist and patriarchal structures. As some women gain access to compete within previously male-dominated institutions, these women may adopt the competitive, meritocratic (and patriarchal) values and consciousness that form the basis of these institutions. As a result, increased female participation does not translate into a movement for greater equality. In sport, this paradox is best demonstrated by the fact that as women have dramatically increased their participation in recent years, they have simultaneously lost their control of women's sports to men. In the 1920s, for instance, as the dominant sport world blossomed as an unambiguously masculine world, female athleticism increased as well, mostly in women's colleges. And as long as women's athletics was clearly marginalized and easily ignorable (and thus not a challenge to masculine hegemony), women's athletics remained mostly under the control of women (Beck, 1980; Lenskyj, 1986; Twin, 1979). Yet as budgets for women's athletics increased in the 1970s and 1980s, and especially after the NCAA took control over most women's college athletic programs and the women-controlled AIAW all but disappeared, the number and proportion of women athletic directors and women head coaches declined dramatically (Acosta & Carpenter, 1985; Birrell, 1987/88; Uhler, 1987).

It is clear, then, that a single-minded liberal feminist push simply to increase individual opportunities for women within sport (or any other masculine-dominated institution) will not automatically result in increased freedom, equality, and social empowerment for women. In fact, the contrary can occur, as we have seen from data that show how increased labor participation for middle-class women has left many of them with a double workday. But Rosemary Tong argues that more and more liberal feminists are aware of the limits of a strategy of individual equal opportunity within the present social structure:

> An increasing number of liberal feminists are willing to concede that individual actions *and* social structures prevent many, if not most, women from securing full liberation. . . . Sexual equality cannot be achieved through women's willpower alone. Also necessary are major alterations in the deepest social and psychological structures.'' (Tong, 1989, p. 38)

In fact, though we do not want to minimize the depth and importance of the differences between these various feminisms, we see a similar sort of convergence among feminist theories within sport studies. Many liberal feminists are not ignorant of the need for fundamental transformations of sport and other social institutions. And many radical and socialist feminists are supportive of, even working for, what are clearly reformist liberal changes. What is clearly necessary, from our (the editors') perspective, is that as we push for athletic reforms or experiment with new athletic structures, our efforts must be couched in a broad, critical feminist theory. And it is to the task of constructing such a theory that we shall next turn. We will first discuss the major limitations of feminist sport studies thus far and the emergent tendencies that we see as having potential to transcend these limitations. Then, we will argue that two promising developments have recently begun within feminist scholarship: (a) the movement away from reductionist theories of patriarchy toward more inclusive theories that analyze the relationships between various forms of domination (e.g., gender, race, class, and sexuality) and (b) the movement away from an essentially static sex-role paradigm toward a more dynamic and relational conceptualization of gender. We will argue that a key element of these movements in feminist theory involves the development of concrete critical examinations of masculinities.

BEYOND "PATRIARCHY" AND "SEX ROLES"

Much early feminist scholarship aimed at filling in the gaps in historical, literary, and social-scientific knowledge. The basic recipe was to add a focus on women to the analytic concerns of existing disciplines. The successes of this "additive" approach were limited, though, by two theoretical frameworks that most feminists utilized. First, at the macro level, the concept of patriarchy was developed as a basic theoretical category to explain the seemingly universal domination of women by men. And second, many feminists adopted mainstream social-scientific role theory to provide a social explanation for perceived differences in the personalities of men and women. We will discuss the limitations of these two theoretical frameworks separately.

Patriarchy

The concept of patriarchy has been a powerful tool in illuminating the many layers of male domination, yet it has been criticized for two general reasons. First, it is criticized as a transsocial and ahistorical concept that ignores varying forms of male domination as well as the myriad ways in which women have resisted male domination and carved out spheres of influence, control, and power within male-dominated societies (Kandiyoti, 1988). As feminist sport theorist Jennifer A. Hargreaves argues, "The concept of patriarchy implies a fixed state of male oppression over women, rather than a fluid relationship between men and women which is complex and moves with great speed at times" (1982, p. 115). Second, patriarchy as a theory of social domination has been criticized as reductionist. Feminism, in the industrialized societies, has been essentially a movement of and by white, middle-class women who have tended to falsely universalize their own issues and interests as "women's" issues and interests. This has contributed to the marginalization and alienation of working-class women and women of color from feminism (Davis, 1981; Hooks, 1981). The initial response of feminist scholars to the criticism of their class and race biases was to conduct more studies of working-class women and women of color. Yet many of these studies still utilized a theoretical framework that a priori privileged gender oppression over other forms of oppression. As a result, as Maxine Baca Zinn and her coauthors (1986) pointed out in an influential *Signs* article, women of color still felt that their experiences and needs were being falsely subsumed under the rubric of a middle-class feminist agenda. The experiences and life chances of poor and minority women are, the critics argued, at least as much shaped and limited by class and race domination as they are by gender domination. Feminist activists and scholars have often felt confused by minority women's insistence that their interests might best be served through alliances with men, waged against race and class oppression; poor and minority women have often felt uneasy being lumped together with white, privileged women as mutual victims of "patriarchy." Clearly, what is needed is a conceptual scheme that theorizes the varied and shifting manifestations of male domination as they interact with other forms of social domination.

Social-Scientific Role Theory

The development of a more relational and inclusive feminist theory was also impeded by the largely uncritical adoption of social-scientific role theory. Role theory, scholars now are recognizing, inadvertently simplifies the complexities of gender (Connell, 1987b; Gerson, 1986; Harding, 1986; Stacey & Thorne, 1985). First, though role theory aims at identifying the social basis and thus the malleability of personality, role theory's tendency to insist on the existence of "a male sex role" and "a female sex role" inadvertently legitimizes and normalizes dominant forms of masculinity and femininity while marginalizing others. (This, incidentally, makes role theory a curiously consistent microlevel partner with patriarchy's false universalization of white middle-class women's lives.) Second, role theory often assumes a false symmetry that ignores the existence of power inequities between women and men. In defining masculinity and femininity as separate (and often complementary) social scripts, role theory ignores the extent to which gender is a dynamic relational process through which unequal power relations between women and men are constantly constructed and contested.

Most early feminist work on sport suffered from the same limitations that feminist scholarship (especially in the United States) exhibited—a tendency to meticulously measure and compare male and female experiences, attitudes, and athletic performances without a broader contextual framework that situates these attitudes and actions in a theory that emphasizes process, change, and power. As a result, a collection of empirical studies accumulated that had been sensitized to utilize the concept of gender as a variable but did not deal with the more classical social-scientific questions of freedom and constraint, structure and agency. Recently, some feminist scholars of sport have begun to historicize their conceptions of gender, and many of these scholars are looking to critical neo-Marxist theories of sport.

CRITICAL SPORT SOCIOLOGY AND FEMINISM

In the 1970s Western Marxism, which had suffered from the limitations of a simplistic and mechanistic economic determinism, had new life breathed back into it with the discovery (or recovery) of more dialectical historical perspectives that were based on the works of the young Marx, Hegelian Marxists, and theories of hegemony begun by Antonio Gramsci. In sport studies this shift is reflected in the movement from Paul Hoch's (1972) economic reductionist critique of sport to Richard Gruneau's (1983) more dialectical examination of sport. Sport, Gruneau argues, does reflect capitalist relations, but not in a simplistic or one-dimensional manner. Culture (of which sport is one expression) is a space in which dominant classes attempt to ideologically legitimize their power. But the hegemony established by the dominant classes is always incomplete. Sport may be a cultural sphere that is dominated by the values and relations of the dominant class, but it does not fully strip working-class participants of the abilities to think critically and to reshape (at least in part) and redefine sport in such a way that it meets their needs or even becomes an arena of resistance. Sport, then, is conceptualized as a cultural terrain in which meanings are always subject to contest and redefinition. In essence, dominant classes place structural and ideological constraints around people's thoughts and actions, but these constraints do not fully determine the outcome—people retain the ability to act as historical agents, thinking critically and acting transformatively.

The major problem with the new critical sport studies is its tendency toward class reductionism. Just as with traditional Marxism, all other forms of social domination (such as race and gender) are, in the final analysis, viewed as manifestations of social class dynamics. For instance, John Hargreaves's (1986) analysis of the development of sport in Britain makes an important contribution to our understanding of how working-class masculinity, as expressed through organized sport, played an important role in the recomposition of a working class that ultimately solidified bourgeois hegemony. Yet this is not a feminist analysis—it is a Marxism that is sensitized to how gender "fits into" a class dialectic. To move beyond its tendency toward simplistic (though more sophisticated in its

Gramscian leanings) economic reductionism, the new critical sport studies will benefit greatly from a dialogue with feminist theory.

And it is clear what feminist sport studies can gain through a dialogue with critical sport studies. Some feminists have already recognized the importance of the concept of hegemony and have turned it to an examination of gender relations (Bryson, 1987a; Hall, 1987a; Messner, 1988; Sabo, 1987). Sport, it is argued, is an institution created by and for men. As such, it has served to bolster a sagging ideology of male superiority and has thus helped to reconstitute masculine hegemony in the 19th and 20th centuries. Yet women's movement into sport (as athletes and as spectators) has challenged the naturalization of gender difference and inequality, which has been a basic aspect of the institution of sport. The dialogue between feminist and critical sport sociologists is promising. Yet many feminists approach this sort of dialogue cautiously, knowing from their 1970s experiences with socialist feminism that the "marriage" between these two political theories has often been an unhappy one, fraught with contradiction (and with "feminist" often becoming swallowed up by "Marxist" categories) (Hartman, 1981).

SPORT AND THE GENDER ORDER

Today more and more feminist scholars are making conscious efforts not to fall into a gender reductionism that ignores varied systems of domination. Indeed, as a more dynamic and relational conception of gender begins to emerge, one of the major questions facing the development of feminist sport studies involves how to integrate a critical examination of a contested male domination with an analysis of contested class and race relations. We will argue here that a more dynamic and inclusive conceptualization of the sport/gender relationship can be developed through the utilization of a nonhierarchical theoretical framework that takes the historical dynamic of structural constraint and human agency as its center. Many of the articles in this volume represent preliminary efforts to develop and utilize such a framework.

A major reason behind the reductionism of much Marxist and feminist theory has been the continued insistence, based on Enlightenment thinking, that there must be one fundamental dynamic (e.g., class or gender) driving history and thus one fundamental historical subject (e.g., the working class or women). In contrast, Sandra Harding (1986) argues that the fractured nature of social reality, and indeed, the fractured nature of contemporary identity even among feminists (e.g., Black women, Asian women, Native American women, working-class women, and lesbian women) should serve as a warning sign against the development of theories that privilege one form of social domination (and identity) over others. Instead, Harding argues,

We should explicitly recognize the ambivalences and contradictions within both feminist and androcentric thinking, and learn how to cherish beneficial tendencies while struggling against the social conditions that make possible regressive tendencies in both. I am not suggesting that we should *try* to produce incoherent theories, but that we should try to fashion conceptual schemes that are more alert to the complex and often beneficial ways in which the modernist world is falling apart. (pp. 163-164)

Developing a Nonhierarchical Theory

We agree with Harding that the major task of social theory today is the development of a nonhierarchical theory and that this does not mean the acceptance of a sort of watered-down relativism or theoretical anarchy. This task involves the development of theories that allow us to conceptualize varied and shifting forms of domination in such a way that we do not privilege one at the expense of distorting or ignoring the others. In Figure I.1, we outline the basic principles of just such a conceptual scheme, which we see now emerging in the literature, largely inspired by feminism.

The image of a wheel indicates a commitment both to a theory that does not privilege one form of social domination over others and to a theory that can examine and facilitate change. At the hub, constantly keeping the wheel in motion, is the historical dynamic of structural constraint (which includes structural, ideological, and characterological oppression) and human agency (which includes crit-

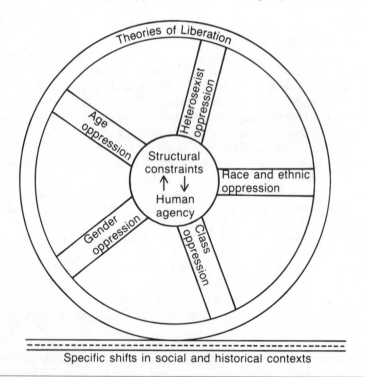

Figure I.1   The wheel model.

ical thought and resistant, transformative action). The spokes of the wheel represent varied forms of oppression: class, race, gender, age, and sexual preference (others certainly can be added). The rim of the wheel represents social theories of liberation, whose role it is to link the spokes in such a way that the hub can move the wheel. The fact that the spokes of the wheel are linked to one another at the hub and at the rim of wheel shows that all forms of oppression, although relatively autonomous, are still dynamically interdependent. Finally, because we should view the wheel as always in motion, it is clear that at any given moment one or two spokes may carry the majority of the weight of the entire system, yet they retain their overall interdependence with the other spokes.[1]

The role of theory, then, might be to identify which dynamic of structural constraint and human agency is most salient at a given historical moment without losing sight of the connections to other dynamics. Out of such an analysis could emerge a theoretically informed politics along the lines of what Jeffrey Weeks (1985) called "radical pluralism." This kind of theory allows us to examine social institutions such as sport within specific historical contexts without always assuming that one dynamic is universally fundamental. For instance, it may be that during the industrial revolution and its immediate aftermath, the most salient dynamic in the development of organized sport was social class, whereas gender and race remained crucially important subtexts. In the 1960s, we might argue, race relations in the United States moved to the forefront in the politics of sport. And since the 1970s, we could argue, gender is the most salient dynamic in the contemporary meaning of organized sport (though the interplay with race and class continues to be essential). Indeed, Connell (1987b) argues more generally that though it is probably wrong to assume (as have some radical feminists) that gender is transhistorically the sole basis of culture, gender may be the most salient dynamic today:

> The scope of gender relations is historically variable, and their power to determine cultural processes must be variable too. But a more limited strategic claim may be right. There are likely to be historical moments where the possibilities of general change in consciousness and culture depend more crucially on the dynamic of gender relations than on any other social force. It can be argued that we are in such a moment now. (p. 253)

Gender Order Framework

We agree that the current salience of gender merits special theoretical attention. (This claim, however, probably does not hold for Third World nations, where race and class dynamics are probably more salient.) We also find that the use of the concept of the gender order (Carrigan, Connell, & Lee, 1985; Connell, 1987b) is a useful theoretical framework with which to examine the meaning of sport and its shifting relation to the wider array of systems of domination that comprise the modern political economy.

Briefly, the concept of the gender order begins with the assumption that gender is better conceptualized as a process than as a "thing" that people "have." The gender order is a dynamic process that is constantly in a state of change. It is "a historically constructed pattern of power relations between men and women and definitions of femininity and masculinity" (Connell, 1987b, pp. 98-99), relations that unfold within changing structural contexts. Moving beyond static sex-role theory and reductionist concepts of patriarchy that view men as an undifferentiated group that oppresses women, Connell argues that at any given historical moment, there are competing masculinities—some hegemonic, some marginalized, and some stigmatized. Hegemonic masculinity is constructed in relation to various subordinated masculinities as well as in relation to femininities, and work by and about gay men has been a key to the development of this insight. What this all means is that the project of male domination of women may tie all men together, but men share very unequally in the fruits of this domination (just as women are differentially oppressed by male dominance).

THE STUDY OF MASCULINITIES AND SPORT

As we (the editors) began to read the papers submitted for this book, we realized that the implications of Connell's insights are already being recognized as keys to the expansion of the study of gender and sport (which has mostly meant, up until recently, the study of women and sport) to the study of men's relationships to sport. The earliest feminist critiques of sport and patriarchy in the 1970s led to a certain amount of reflection by men concerning their relationships to sport. A number of "radical critics" of sport included some treatment of gender issues in their overall class or racial analyses: Hoch (1972) labeled sport a "school for sexism," whereas Naison (1972) saw sport as an institutional source of the "ideology of male domination." The writings of Scott (1971) and Edwards (1973) focused on unraveling the links between sport ideology, class relations, and race inequality, yet these writers also discussed sex segregation and inequality in sport. Other writings, inspired by the mid-1970s "men's liberation movement," also appeared. Farrell's (1974) analysis of the cultural significance of the Superbowl drew connections between sport, masculinity, sexism, and militarism. Fasteau (1974) and Townsend (1977) focused on the negative emotional consequences of men's athletic training for aggression and excessive competition.

In 1980, Sabo and Runfola published a consciously profeminist analysis of sport that attempted to prompt "men to understand themselves individually as victims of sexual inequality without losing sight of why they are the collective oppressors of women" (p. 337). This represented an important departure from the analyses presented both by the radical critics, who tended to continue to collapse gender issues into a race or class dynamic, and by the men's liberationists, who tended to focus on the "costs" *to men* of narrow definitions of masculinity, while downplaying or ignoring how sport fit into the construction and legitimation of male privilege. Sabo and Runfola were motivated by feminist concerns and an incipient belief that feminist analysis could somehow further an understanding of men and sport. Yet the volume was limited by the reality that no systematic feminist theory outlining the relationships between men, sport, and gender relations had yet been developed. It might be said that on a more general level, feminists had raised "the man question," yet systematic studies of men and masculinity were not yet on the agenda, impeded in part by the more immediate task of developing a body of research on women and by the simplistic conceptualization of men as an undifferentiated oppressor class.

By the 1980s, feminists had recognized the need for the development of a more relational theory of gender. They recognized that various theories of oppression and liberation have often suffered from a certain irony. Marxists have done myriad studies of the working class but very few studies of the upper classes; likewise, ethnic studies scholars focus their analytic attention mostly on minority communities, almost never on the white majority. Similarly, feminist studies have focused almost exclusively on women, rarely upon men (except as an abstract category). This is not surprising, because one of the major goals of these theories of liberation is to illuminate that which has been pushed to the margins: the experiences, thoughts, and actions of oppressed groups. Yet an ironic result of this focus is that the dominant groups are posited as the norm: Only the working class are analyzed within a class framework, only ethnic minorities appear to have racial and ethnic identities, and only women appear to be gendered beings. When feminist theory focuses almost exclusively on women's experiences, the conception of gender as a relational process is lost (Gerson, 1986; Kimmel, 1986). A relational conception of gender necessarily includes a critical examination of both femininity and masculinity as they develop in relation to each other within a system of structured social inequality.

Recently, feminist scholarship has germinated what some are calling a new "men's studies" (Brod, 1987; Kaufman, 1986; Kimmel, 1986). Men's studies scholars see in feminism a critique, theory, or paradigm that holds the potential of liberating men as well as women from the limitations of sexism. Yet men's studies cannot be a simple mirror image of women's studies. Though equally normative and ideological, men's studies cannot simply be presented as an advocate for male interests. Men's studies scholars start from the premise that existing gender arrangements entail various costs for men (e.g., low life expectancy, emotional inexpressivity, and relational problems), yet males also enjoy significant privileges as a result of these arrangements. A feminist study of men and masculinity, then, aims at developing an analysis of men's problems and limitations compassionately yet within the context of a feminist critique of male privilege. From this insight, theoretically informed studies of men, masculinity, and sport began to emerge in the mid-1980s (Kidd, 1987; Messner, 1985a, 1987a; Sabo, 1985).

A FINAL WORD ON THIS BOOK

The essays in this book, although mostly about men and sport, are not written exclusively by men. This reality represents a political position by the editors. Some have argued that research and writing about women can only be legitimately done by women (and Black women by Black women, lesbians by lesbians, etc.).

Advocates of this position argue that the subjective experience of being a member of an oppressed group gives one a privileged standpoint from which to appreciate the reality of that group in ways that will counter the traditional distortions of that reality by social scientists and commentators from the dominant groups. We think that there is something to this argument, but it does not follow that only men should write about men. A brief discussion of our own personal and scholarly connections to our subject matter, men and sports, will illuminate this seeming contradiction.

As boys, both of us were initiated into the world of sports by men and into the world of men through sports. For both of us, our experiences in sport have always had a joyous upside and a very limiting, often painful downside. For Mike, there has always been a certain existential high in putting a basketball through a hoop, a feeling of transcendence unmatched in other aspects of life. And from an early age, he found that sports participation was the key to his relationship with his father and eventually with same-aged male peers. But as he passed through adolescence and into adulthood, he became increasingly aware of how the athletic role, because of its narrow definitions of success and failure, limited the foundation upon which his self-image was constructed. And though sports formed the basis for relationships with other males, he became aware of how the competition, homophobia, and misogyny in the sports world limited his ability to develop truly intimate relationships with women and with other men.

Like Mike, Don's athletic experiences have shifted between joy and misery, healthful release and personal harm. As a fourth grader in western Pennsylvania, he discovered organized football and went on to play and love the game throughout his college years. Football provided a vision of athletic excellence that harnessed his adolescent energy and longings. The game was a vehicle for making friendships and building self-confidence, and it ultimately became a ticket out of the steel mills and into a university. The "patriarchal piper" demanded his pay, however, and the hypermasculine and physically brutal aspects of the "game" took their toll. The women's movement eventually taught him that there were more fulfilling ways to live life than that prescribed for him by the linebacker image. Six years of chronic back pain and a resulting lower lumbar, double-level, spinal fusion also prompted him to critically rethink the beliefs and practices that inform traditional men's sport. Today, he works closely with the Women's Sports Foundation in an effort to redefine and restructure sport in more humane ways that emphasize its beauty and benefits and extend them to women as well as to men.

To return to the question of whether men, by virtue of our "privileged standpoint" in relation to the world of organized sport, should analyze masculinity and sport, it is clear that our own experiences as men and as former athletes give us knowledge, insights, and a certain privileged entrée as researchers into the world of men and sports. Mike's experience as an athlete led him to focus on "the meaning of success" to male athletes (Messner, 1987c). And Don's experiences have inspired and informed research on the relationship between masculinity, sports, and what he calls "the pain principle" (Sabo, 1986). Yet it is crucial to recognize that we began to conduct critical research about masculinity and sport because feminist women had created new frameworks of meaning through which we could examine our own experiences. We are certain that had the women's movement and feminist theory not developed in the 1970s, we as men and as former athletes would not today be examining the masculinity and sport relationship. It would never have crossed our minds.

In short, the feminist elucidation of women's marginal status has created an epistemological standpoint with which men can examine our own experiences not "as paradigmatically human," but rather, critically, as "typically masculine" (Flax, 1983, p. 627). Thus, it is not simply that men's studies is too new to stand on its own. In fact, we take it as a basic principle that so long as male privilege exists, men's studies scholars should consciously couch our work within feminist theoretical frameworks. If we fail to do so, men's studies will, at best, fall into abstracted empiricist irrelevance; at worst, men's studies will become a "scientific" ideological tool for antifeminist backlash.

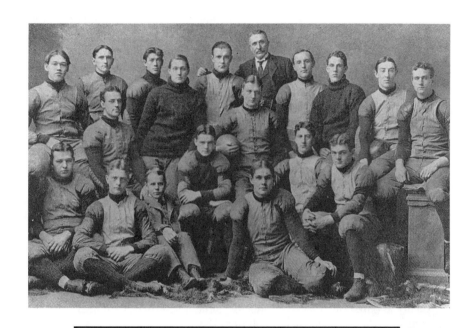

PART I

⚥

Theoretical and Historical Foundations

The first task in building a critical scholarship of sport, men, and the gender order is to situate the sport/gender relationship theoretically and historically. The institution of sport must be viewed as a gendered cultural space. This does not mean, as several of the articles in this section demonstrate, viewing sport simply as an arena of gender relations. Economic structures, urbanization, race relations, sexuality, and nationalism are also fundamentally important aspects of the structure and ideology of organized sport. Viewing sport as a gendered cultural space does mean that gender, as a dynamic, relational process, is taken as a fundamental theoretical category in understanding the historical and contemporary importance and meaning of sport. Together, the articles in this section make an important contribution toward this end.

The first two articles lay out many of the important themes of this book. First, David Whitson, drawing from R.W. Connell's idea of sport as a "masculinizing practice," traces how sport as a social institution helps to construct men's power over women as well as heterosexual men's privilege over gay men. Despite women's recent movement into sport, Whitson argues, sport continues to bolster hegemonic masculinity by ritualizing and embedding aggression, strength, and skill in the male body and linking it with competitive achievement. Bruce Kidd's article further examines and illustrates this process. He uses historical and feminist theoretical frameworks to examine developments in athletics, like Toronto's "men's cultural centre." Kidd deconstructs the "naturalness" of the sport/ masculinity relationship and argues for the development of more humane sporting practices.

The next three articles use feminist and critical perspectives of gender to reexamine the meaning and importance of the rise of sport in particular historical eras. First, Todd Crosset offers insights into why sport, an essentially purposeless activity, blossomed in the increasingly rational 19th century. Drawing from Foucault, Crosset argues that this seeming paradox can be explained by examining how, in an era when men's power and privilege over women were being eroded and challenged, men used sport to naturalize ideological conceptions of male sexuality as superior to female sexuality. Similarly, Michael Kimmel examines the rapid growth of American baseball from 1880 to 1920 as a phenomenon arising from a crisis of masculinity (especially among white middle-class men), brought about by urbanization, industrialization, and women's push for equality in public life. And Philip White and Anne Vagi, utilizing psychoanalytic insights, see the masculine rugby culture that developed in 19th-century British boarding schools as an institutional context in which boys and men could express their deep psychological ambivalences concerning intimacy and connection with others.

Though the authors in this section share a great deal—especially their commitment to a feminist reconceptualization of sport—there are clearly tensions, contradictions, and ambivalences between and within the approaches developed here. For instance, whereas Vagi and White utilize feminist object relations theory to explain men's attraction to organized sport, Whitson and Kidd prefer to view sport as an arena of power relations. This kind of theoretical tension is not necessarily a bad thing; indeed, it would be a grave mistake to attempt to subsume all of these approaches under the rubric of one "grand theory." As Sandra Harding (1986) has written of the strains and tensions within contemporary feminist theory,

> Coherent theories in an obviously incoherent world are either silly and uninteresting or oppressive and problematic, depending upon the degree of hegemony they manage to achieve. Coherent theories in an *apparently* coherent world are even more dangerous, for the world is always more complex than such unfortunately hegemonious theories can grasp. (p. 164)

Indeed, the diversity of the theoretical approaches that are drawn upon in these articles—critical neo-Marxist, Foucaultian, radical feminist, socialist feminist, psychoanalytic—underline the complex, multifaceted, often fractured reality that organized sport is. What links these approaches is a shared commitment to the development of a feminist analysis of sport that opens up new avenues for research and moves us closer to a liberating theory and transformative practice.

Chapter 1

Sport in the Social Construction of Masculinity

David Whitson

Sport has become, it is fair to suggest, one of the central sites in the social production of masculinity in societies characterized by longer schooling and by a decline in the social currency attached to other ways of demonstrating physical prowess (e.g., physical labour or combat). Indeed, demonstrating the physical and psychological attributes associated with success in athletic contests has now become an important requirement for status in most adolescent and preadolescent male peer groups. Boys who are good at sports have happily profited from this fact (Oriard, 1984) and often come to think of it as natural. Meanwhile, other boys—small or awkward boys, scholarly or artistic boys, boys who get turned off from sports (or who never develop any interest in sports)—have to come to their own terms with sport and find other ways to stake their claims to masculinity.[1]

However, despite this, and despite the increasing attention that feminism has brought to the study of gender relations, theoretically informed studies of the place of sport in the social construction of masculinity remain exceptional and isolated, not forming part of a focussed scholarly dialogue. Certainly the sociology of sport, which was for too long simply the sociology of male sport, has seen an explosion of work on women and sport. At first, what Hall (1987a) describes as the "add women and stir" phase simply registered the growth of women's sport, as well as some of the constraints that women have had to overcome in their pursuit of sporting excellence. *Woman* was treated unproblematically as a biological category, and the history of sport was not systematically connected to theories of gender relations (i.e., of institutionalized relations between men and women). Later, however, influenced by feminist scholarship, women began to develop a critical analysis of male sport, including its effects on women, and of the contributions of male sport to the reproduction of male hegemony in society.

Encompassed in the latter concept are usually two claims. First, sport is named as a male institution, not just in the numerical sense that many have pointed to but, more importantly, in the values and behavioural norms it promotes and ultimately naturalizes, both on the field and in organizational hierarchies. Second, and following from this, it is argued that the social attention and indeed acclaim that thereby are given to male "ways of being" help to confirm patterns of male privilege and female subordination (and indeed structures of domination) that exist outside sport. The feminist literature has thus reformulated what were once seen as distributional issues within sport—issues concerning the relative absence of women at different levels of sport, which are resolvable (albeit not without resistance) within a reformist politics—as relational issues, with much broader implications.

SYSTEMATIC EFFECTS OF GENDER RELATIONS

This concept refers us to the systematic effects of the ways in which male-female relations are structured within most social institutions. Connell, Ashenden, Kessler, and Dowsett (1982) suggest that three points are important in understanding gender relationally. First, we need to recognize that relations between men and women are constituted cumulatively, in a system of mutually reinforcing structures. Norms for family relations, for work-place behaviour and promotion, and for teenage social life are all related. Indeed, "they mesh with each other to make an overall pattern, one of the most general and powerful structures in our society" (Connell et al., 1982, p. 72). Second, this structure is one of male privilege and power and female disadvantage and subordination. This is true in virtually every social institution we can think of, and "it is important to recognize that it persists as an overall pattern despite being reversed in particular instances" (Connell et al., 1982, p. 72). Yet, third, the structure can and does change as a result of intellectual and political struggle. The recent history of change and tension in male-female relations underlines this.

Sport is therefore beginning to be interrogated for its contributions to historical patterns of male empowerment and female disadvantage, and feminist analysis seeks to explicate the role of sport in the reproduction and/or transformation of contemporary relations between (and indeed within) the sexes. Such relational questions are of more far-reaching significance, both theoretically and in practice, than the distributional issues (though they are not, of course, disconnected). Their resolution, moreover, points to a politics whose implications are recognized to include sport but also to stretch beyond it.

This chapter seeks to explore the place of sport in the social construction of masculinity. Two main lines of argument will be developed. The first emphasizes connections between manliness and the body; it argues that learning to use the body in "forceful and space-occupying ways" (Connell, 1983) through the practice of sports, and learning to associate such behaviour with being a man, have for many boys constructed their expectations of themselves in social relationships with women and with other men. Second, it will be argued that sport as a "male preserve" (Dunning, 1986) has served as an important site in the construction of male solidarity, an institution that encourages men to identify with other men and provides for the regular rehearsal of such identifications. It is proposed that together, these dynamics point to a powerful role for sport in the reproduction of male hegemony.

MASCULINITY, MANLINESS, AND THE BODY

Our concern in this section is with how masculinity is constructed in a society and how the particular way of being male that we know as manliness has achieved and maintained its privileged position in Western societies. Arguably, sport has played an important part in this, at least since the middle of the 19th century. Analyses of the prominent place of sport in the programmes of the elite English boys' schools are replete with references to manliness and to official belief in the capacity of sport to "turn boys into men" (Mangan, 1981). Certainly, Olympics promoter de Coubertin appears to have been among those convinced that the lessons learned on these private-school playing fields were an important factor in the ascendancy of Victorian England; he is described as a vigorous advocate of the introduction of "English games" into the elite French lycées, arguing that the training these games provided in "manliness" could reverse the decline of a French upper class grown weak and effete (Weber, 1970). Meanwhile, in America, the founders of the playground movement were making a somewhat different but not dissimilar case for organized sports in teaching boys (this time working-class boys) to be appropriate kinds of men (Cavello, 1981).

Muscles and Morality

Several themes recur in this literature that are appropriate to our own discussion. The first is the equation of physical prowess with moral strength. In the "muscular Christianity" espoused by the leading English headmasters and their counterparts abroad, athletic fields were places where the development of physical presence, stoic courage in the endurance of pain, and judgement under pressure was portrayed as simply part of the achievement of manhood. The second theme is a clear concern to maximize and (among men) to celebrate the differences between men and women. This underlines Craib's (1987) observation that masculinity is often organized not as a positive construct but rather as that which is "not feminine, or, more bluntly, not effeminate" (p. 721). We have previously observed that de Coubertin's keen promotion of sport in France was related to his concern that Frenchmen of his class had grown effete; indeed Mangan's (1981) account suggests that a similar concern was an important dimension of the ideology of manliness in the English schools themselves. In the contemporary era we can see the same urgency about boundary maintenance in behaviours such as the vituperative attacks on longhaired male athletes in the 1960s (Scott, 1971) and in protests that ice hockey as "a man's game" is somehow ruined by enforcement of the rules against physical intimidation and violence.

Boys Becoming Men

Finally, it is important to register just how much time, effort, and institutional support is given over to *masculinizing practices* (Connell et. al., 1982). It is also important to understand just how much urgency is usually attached to the success or failure of such projects—by parents and indeed by the boys themselves. What such effort and concern immediately belie is any notion of biological destiny. If boys simply grew into men and that was that, the efforts described to teach boys how to be men would be redundant. We can suggest, then, that "becoming a man" is something that boys (and especially adolescent boys) work at. We can also suggest, however, that although this work takes place in the context of considerable pressures from adults and peers alike, a personal way of being a man must be constructed out of each boy's own body and desires. Indeed, Connell (1983) suggests that for some years, as the adolescent tries out different ways of being himself, there is much unsettled about the kind of man he will become.

Therefore, we have to develop an understanding of the formation of masculine identity that registers the effects of the external pressures and rewards that are constructed by the masculinizing projects of schools and parents as well as by the less direct influence of many other "normal" role models. However, in discussions of sex-role socialization, there is seldom sufficient recognition that male "norms" of mental and physical toughness are themselves historical constructs, as described previously. Specific socialization practices, in other words, need to be seen not as natural but rather as collective (and mutually reinforcing) practices, through which patterns of empowerment, habits, and self-expectations of domination are encouraged in successive generations of boys, and through which structures of gender relations are thereby reproduced.

At the same time, though, we also need to recognize the force of internal desires and conflicts—for example, in boys who apparently "choose at some level" (Connell et al., 1982, p. 77) to be not quite like their competitive and successful fathers. This is a force that the language of social learning theory (i.e., of role learning and socialization) has notorious difficulty in crediting. Craib (1987), in arguing for a theory that can encompass the realities of deviance and contradiction in masculine identities more satisfactorily than can socialization theory, proposes that theories that emphasize the inexorable effectiveness of external forces "cannot do credit to the centrality of gender identity to a person's sense of self, or to the complexity of the internal conflicts which surround gender identity" (p. 725).

Body Knowledge, Gender Identity, and Sport

This leads us, then, to the importance of the body (and how we come to know our bodies) in the formation of gender identity, and from there to the importance of sport, especially in the childhood and adolescent years. Merleau-Ponty (1962) has presented the fullest argument that our experiences of our bodies are central to our senses of who we are and how we relate to the world and thereby to other people. However, Connell (1983), in an important argument that body sense is crucial to the development of male identity, suggests that to learn to be a male is to learn to project a physical presence that speaks of latent power. He argues that sport is empowering for many young males precisely because it teaches us how to use our own bodies to produce effects and because it teaches us how to achieve power through practiced combinations of force and skill.

Certainly Oriard's (1984) discussion of the importance of football in his (and his friends') learning to be a man illustrates the force of the belief that "what it means to be masculine is, quite literally, to embody force, to embody competence" (Connell, 1987b, p. 27). Especially among adolescent males, for whom other sources of recognized masculine authority (based on earning power, adult sexual relations, or fatherhood, see Note 1) are some ways off, the development of body appearance and body language that are suggestive of force and skill is experienced as an urgent task. This explains boys' embarrassment at weakness or lack of coordination as well as the energy they invest in many forms of exercise, in cults of physicality and martial arts, and especially in sport.

The Empowerment Experience

It is worth observing that the experience of force and skill coming together, however briefly, in the long home run, the perfectly hit golf shot, the crosscourt backhand, or "flow" in a cross-country run, is a great part of what makes sport so popular. Such moments afford enormous satisfaction and pleasure, even to the normally moderate athlete, and indeed to the spectator who understands and appreciates what has been achieved. The experience of empowerment, however temporary, is captured by former hockey player Eric Nesterenko:

> You wheel and dive and turn, and you can lay yourself into impossible angles that you never could walking or running. You lay yourself out at a forty-five degree angle, your elbows virtually touching the ice . . . Incredible! It's beautiful! You're breaking the grounds of gravity. (Terkel, 1974, p. 386)

Nesterenko is talking here about how much he loved the physicality of sport, and arguably it is precisely this physicality, this potential for the sensuous experiencing of strength and skill, that makes many kinds of sport (including the noncompetitive pursuit of sports like swimming and skiing) so appealing, especially among those whose daily lives do not otherwise afford such experiences of completeness and competence.

If Merleau-Ponty and Connell are right, then, in contending that our sense of who we are is firmly rooted in our experiences of embodiment, it is integral to the reproduction of gender relations that boys are encouraged to experience their bodies, and therefore themselves, in forceful, space-occupying, even dominating ways. It may be suggested that masculinizing and feminizing practices associated with the body are at the heart of the social construction of masculinity and femininity and that this is precisely why sport matters in the total structure of gender relations. We are suggesting that assertiveness and confidence, as ways of relating to others, become embodied through the development of strength and skill and through prevailing over opponents in competitive situations. Conversely, I. Young (1979) argues that the exclusion of women from sport has historically denied girls these kinds of formative experiences, with the result that their embodied senses of self were more likely to be awkward, fragile, and diffident.

Movement of Women Into Sports

Certainly the movement of women into many kinds of sports (though not so much into confrontational sports like football) has rendered this now less true as a description of women. However, arguably, even though there are today many women who achieve particular combinations of force and skill much more effectively than do many men, the persistence of "normal" differences in empowerment remains "one of the main ways in which the superiority of men becomes 'naturalized'" (Connell, 1983, p. 28). Moreover, the regular opportunities for the celebration of male superiority that are afforded by "Monday Night Football" or by "Hockey Night in Canada" may be especially important for men who feel threatened by contemporary changes in gender relations.

This comment leads us finally to the question of why men have been so defensive about the entry of women into sport.

EXCLUSION AND MEMBERSHIP: MALE HEGEMONY AND HEGEMONIC MASCULINITY

A male cliff diver explained, "This is a death-defying activity—the men are taking a great gamble to prove their courage. What would be the point if everyone saw that a woman could do the same?" (Bryson, 1983, p. 413). At one level, the refusal of Mexican cliff divers to compete in an Acapulco competition unless an American woman (who had qualified for the final in preliminary competitions) was forced to withdraw is self-explanatory. A proving ground for masculinity can only be preserved as such by the exclusion of women from the activity (see also I. Young, 1979). Yet the adamant, almost desperate quality of some men's reactions requires further exploration.

Erosion of Male Advantages

One starting point is to suggest that such reactions simply reproduce the Victorian concern with maximizing the differences between men and women; little has changed, in other words. The realities, of course, are that much has changed on the terrain of gender relations and that male dominance has been and is being challenged on a great many fronts. Dunning (1986) has proposed, in this respect, that male hegemony is strengthened to the extent that fighting skills and physical prowess are honoured in a society and that men have their own social institutions whereas women do not. Conversely, he argues, male advantages are eroded when society is pacified and when segregation of the sexes breaks down. If this analysis is astute, and I suggest that it is, it becomes easy to see why men who are threatened by these larger changes in gender relations talk loudly about the importance of all-male institutions and defend the importance of confrontation in "men's games."[2]

Such responses exemplify what Turner (1984) calls "patrism," an equivalent of the subjective racism that persists and is, in some quarters, sharpened as structures of legal segregation are broken down. Turner's argument is that the erosion of the legal and economic foundations of male hegemony has led to a defensive backlash among those men whose power in their own lives is directly threatened by the increasing legal and economic independence of women, as well as among those whose senses of themselves are threatened by assertive, subjectively independent women.

Erosion of Male Companionship in Sport

However, another aspect of the breakdown of segregation in sport invites fuller consideration. This is the significance of the erosion of sport as a site of specifically male companionship, which allows boys to be with boys and men with men and which allows men to initiate boys into traditions men have shared and enjoyed. The latter occurs in the conscious and institutionalized ways captured in Fine's (1987) account of the "specifically didactic roles" (p. 1) that some Little League coaches see for themselves. It occurs, of course, in the masculinizing practices of schools, discussed in the previous section. All such efforts, as masculinizing projects, would be scrambled by the presence of girls on boys' teams.

Yet initiation also occurs in more personal and warmly remembered ways, which are alluded to in Bryson's (1987a) analysis of the messages of a popular Australian commercial in which a father is taking his son to an important match. The father and son are depicted as doing something male together, and the boy, it is suggested, is especially delighted that his Dad is taking him, however briefly, into the world of men. That such a commercial resonates with the experiences of many men and boys is attested to by Oriard's (1984) discussion of what it meant to him to watch football with his father and by Inglis's (1977) discussions of fathers sharing sports talk with their sons and other men. Inglis suggests that what is happening in such exchanges is the sharing of men's emotional responses and judgements and the initiation of the boy into a male language and into male traditions. In these traditions, however, heroism and community are rendered concrete in ways that encourage male bonding and encourage the exclusion of women from the brotherhood of those who can understand (Oriard, 1984).

With respect to the bonding that can occur among male teammates, many have written lyrically about the comradeship and intimacy that can develop as men come to depend upon one another in a shared quest. Certainly, this kind of solidarity and companionship is a rare enough experience in modern life. Nesterenko, described in Terkel (1974), suggests that the intimacy he experienced on a successful team is not something he has been able to find elsewhere; men who have known this naturally treasure such memories and are uneasy about that which might alter or threaten the possibilities of such intimacy. What is really threatened by the entry of women into male preserves is opportunities for men to rehearse their ties as men and reaffirm their differences from women. For certainly women have forged strong bonds with one another in their own athletic quests, and men and women have known solidarity together when other struggles (e.g., labor strikes) have underlined their common interests rather than their differences.

Effects of Social Practices on Sport

It is important, in this respect, to recognize the effects on men (as well as women) of some of the social practices that surround sport, for these social practices as well as the physical practices described previously together constitute sport as a social institution. Professional athletes' accounts of the practice of "shooting beaver" and other similar antics in this all-male subculture (Bouton, 1971), as well as Dunning's (1986) more scholarly account of the misogynist and homophobic songs and jokes that are part of the tradition surrounding English rugby, serve as pointed reminders that much that is described as male comradeship has its darker side. It demeans and objectifies women, and it enforces and reinforces a certain standard of masculinity (i.e., aggressive, dominating, or "macho") among men.[3]

J. Thompson (1984) has pointed, here, to the role that humour can play in rehearsing in-group solidarity, in objectifying and demeaning "the other," and in deterring potential deviants or sympathizers. It would be difficult to deny that locker-room humour, and indeed the sexist humour that dominates many all-male environments, has served all of these functions. Certainly the accounts of Dunning (1986), Fine (1987), and others all suggest that sport as a male preserve remains a bastion of reaction, in which traditional masculinity is celebrated and other kinds of masculinity are disparaged and deterred. In such circumstances, Sabo (1985) suggests that we need to ask ourselves the following:

> Does the risk of ridicule lead some males to develop a more exploitative attitude toward dating, sex, and women? . . . Do male athletes learn to downplay love and relationships and how much they need and care about women? What sort of customs or rituals serve to put women down while solidifying male supremacist bonds? (p. 18)

There is evidence, indeed, that the power of such control mechanisms is even more pernicious among teenaged and preadolescent boys. Fine's (1987) description of the peer subculture that surrounds Little League underlines the extent to which learning to "present themselves to male peers as 'males'" (p. 110) means, for these preteen boys, learning to master the language of lust and learning how to pretend to as much sexual experience as is plausible. One outcome of such talk is to normalize a way of being male in which sexual desire is detached from tenderness for a person and indeed from interest in female company except for the purposes of sex. The effect is to establish a norm that equates masculinity with domination in male-female relationships. Finally, the effect also, as Fine's (1987) discussion of homophobic language makes clear, is to underline the taboos against homosexual attachments (see also Dunning, 1986).

We are reminded here of Craib's (1987) observation concerning the historical definition of masculinity as "not effeminate"; we need to consider the dynamics previously described in the light of P. Griffin's (in press) contention that homophobia is actively fanned in the single-sex subcultures that have surrounded sport and physical education. Homophobia serves to reinforce compulsory heterosexuality, at the very least; but Griffin also suggests that this idea operates as a constraint that keeps heterosexual people of both sexes within the boundaries of traditional masculinity and femininity.

Symbolic Interactionism

Fine's (1987) subsequent discussion of the preadolescent boy's need to demonstrate his own separation from the worlds of girls and of younger children is based in symbolic interactionism and in developmental psychology. Yet the need to stake a claim to adult gender identity does not in itself explain why this claim is to a gender identity that requires aggressive, dominant performances, especially if this version of masculinity is experienced by many men as awkward and inauthentic. As Turner's (1984) discussion of discourses of the body makes clear, we have to continually remind ourselves that even apparently "natural" processes like growing up are constituted for us in particular ways by the discourses of a patriarchal culture. The interactionist concept of "impression management" directs us to consider the social construction of behaviour at the interpersonal or small-group level. However, as Turner points out, the choice to present one's self in particular ways is almost inevitably a product of dominant discourses (even when the presentation flaunts or defiantly inverts them) about what constitutes a desirable self.

What is required is a recognition that the structures of gender relations we have referred to here are historically constructed structures of power that have empowered men over women. Therefore, specific masculinizing and feminizing practices need to be examined for the ways in which they contribute to reproducing these structures; these practices must not be depoliticized or naturalized, as the language of social psychology tends to do. Likewise, the history of specific masculinizing practices cannot be detached from the interests of men in the maintenance of male power. The specific character of hegemonic masculinity—competitive, confident, "able to dominate others . . . in situations of conflict" (Connell et al., 1982, p. 73)—is very much connected with the maintenance of male hegemony in the contemporary world.

CONCLUDING REMARKS

In contemporary Western culture, arguably, sport (and especially confrontational team games) ritualizes aggression and allows it to be linked with competitive achievement and, in turn, with masculinity. Following both Connell and Dunning, we can suggest that sport has become one of the most important sites of masculinizing practice in cultures (and within classes) in which other kinds of physical prowess have become devalued and in which direct aggression is officially illegitimate. Yet two points need to be noted.

First, the promotion of other sports ranging from racquet sports to running and swimming to wilderness sports and even skateboarding affords many new opportunities for the development of strength and skill—in other words, for empowerment. These opportunities are open, moreover, to people who do not typically shine in confrontational team games, to smaller men, and to women; this has broadened the recognized boundaries of masculinity (e.g., to include the boy whose claim to masculinity is asserted through achievement as a diver or a climber). Beyond this, the demonstrable achievements of women in such sports, indeed the presence of women in sport, have helped to weaken the popular association between sport and masculinity pointed to by Bryson.

At the same time, though, the continued place we accord to confrontational team games in our hierarchy of sports, and the continued acclaim we accord to the men who shine in them, mean that these games continue to offer important opportunities for masculinizing practices, in the politicized sense outlined in this chapter.

The major games, in other words, continue as institutions through which the reproduction of hegemonic masculinity, and through this, male hegemony, are actively pursued. To apply Dunning's (1986) framework, these games are typically institutions in which physical strength and fighting skills are celebrated, in which male solidarity (and especially solidarity among aggressive, dominating males) is also celebrated, and which therefore reinforce constraints on boys' experimenting with other ways of being male.

What are the implications of all of this for men? To begin with, it is necessary to affirm the value of sport and to celebrate the sense of confirmation and empowerment that is afforded by the embodiment of strength and skill in a perfectly executed dive, as well as the mutual understanding and teamwork that are experienced in a good team. These things are too widely known among men for us to deny them, even if we wished to. However, if we want to open a constructive dialogue with the many men for whom sport has been a formative (and positive) experience, it is important not to come across as "sport bashers."

At the same time, though, it is necessary to insist that these positive experiences are not for men alone and that sport not be used as a kind of initiation into a male tribe. This will make the kinds of empowering experiences that sport affords more readily available to women, at the same time that men will come to appreciate the companionship of women in task-oriented situations. Most importantly, though, "the mere entry of women into sport in greater numbers—even into masculinist sport—will begin to break down the masculinist meaning of sport" (I. Young, 1979, p. 51). And this is something that will benefit many (though not all) men, as well as women. A corollary of this, though, is that it is necessary to deconstruct the connection between empowerment and domination. We need to introduce boys and girls alike to the empowering experiences of skill and strength that are offered in many kinds of nonconfrontative sports, and we need to celebrate these more than we do fighting skills.

What are the prospects for such proposals and their likely effects? They probably are somewhat attractive to the many men who have experienced themselves as oppressed or limited by hegemonic masculinity or who have adapted themselves to it and worn it like an ''ill-fitting coat'' (Theroux, 1986, p. 309). Certainly the men's movement literature has articulated the gains that many men have hoped to realize from a loosening of the boundaries of legitimate male behaviour, which makes space for less aggressive and dominating ways of being male (see Carrigan et. al., 1985, for a critical analysis of this literature). Yet Carrigan also points out the need to recognize the connections between hegemonic masculinity and the maintenance of male hegemony and the need to understand that the erosion of the former will ultimately lead to substantial changes in the structures of gender relations—in other words, to substantial inroads on male privileges and power.

This indeed helps us to understand the effort put into the masculinizing practices described here and the value men have historically attached to teaching boys to be men and to the institutions where men could assume this didactic role. As Carrigan et al. (1985) suggest, breaking out of gender ''roles'' is much more than a matter of breaking with conventional thinking; it threatens interconnected structures of power that ultimately can affect men everywhere. This is why contemporary changes in gender relations are the object of continuing struggle among men, and why sanctions are so severe against those who ''let the side down'' by demonstrating different ways of being male.[4] Finally, this threat to men's power is why, following Craib, tensions between dominance and expressiveness and between independence and interdependence are likely to remain sources of profound internal conflict for many men in the years ahead. Androgyny is a chimerical solution, and changes in gender relations are likely to require painful readjustments for many of us.

Chapter 2

The Men's Cultural Centre: Sports and the Dynamic of Women's Oppression/Men's Repression

Bruce Kidd

Like many North American cities, Toronto has a strong feminist movement. During the most recent wave of activism, which began in the mid-1960s, women have mounted imaginative, well-organized campaigns for reproductive rights, publicly funded day care, and equal pay for work of equal value as well as against discriminatory hiring practices and sexist stereotyping in the media. These struggles are supported by a broad network of organizations, shelters, periodicals, bookstores, cultural groups, educational activities, and several archives. Feminist leaders have successfully linked their own efforts to other struggles in the workplace and community, especially those struggles for trade union rights and against racism. Yet these campaigns have been only partially successful in contesting and reducing women's historic disadvantage. The dominant, patriarchal institutions—the corporations, the state, and the mass media—have effectively contained women and marginalized their importance in mainstream discourse (Maroney & Luxton, 1987).

SPORT AS LEGITIMATION OF MALE POWER

An extremely fertile field for the reassertion and legitimation of male power and privilege has been sports. In fact, although its character is rarely admitted, the most successful cultural intervention in the realm of gender politics in Toronto during the 2 decades of second-wave feminism has been a men's project—a domed stadium. Ever since 1969, a group of male politicians, businessmen, sports writers, and media entrepreneurs have lobbied for a publicly financed covered stadium. Thwarted in the early 1970s, they were later successful and the new stadium opened in 1989. It already dominates the downtown skyline and the mass media, and it constitutes a massive subsidization and celebration of the interests of men.

I make no bones about linking the uphill battles of the Toronto women's movement to a new stadium. To be sure, both efforts have been influenced by a complex of social structures, institutions, and events, and in a fuller account, they could not be ignored. But the dynamic of gender—the subject of this book— has been paramount. I call the stadium the "men's cultural centre" (MCC). It was initiated by male politicians well known for their hostility to feminist causes, and it was developed by an almost exclusively male provincial crown corporation. At a time when women's crisis centers go underfunded, the developers obtained 25 acres of prime downtown public land and $85 million in public funds for the stadium. Its primary tenants will be the local franchises of the commercial baseball and Canadian football cartels, the Blue Jays and the Argonauts, which stage male team games for predominantly male audiences. The other major beneficiaries will be the public and private media corporations that sell male audiences to advertisers through their broadcast of male team sports (Jhally, 1984), the advertisers, and the businessmen who will stay in and entertain clients in the adjoining hotel.

No doubt the MCC is popular among women as well as men. It will be a great improvement over the existing stadium, increasing the pleasure derived from watching gifted athletes. But in many ways, the MCC will serve to buttress male power and privilege. It has directed public and private investment and consumption to largely male activities, preventing the alternative use of these resources in programs that would redress the disadvantagement of women. In the absence of comparable opportunities for female athletes, coaches, managers, and sports impressarios, the MCC will provide almost daily ideological justification for patriarchal power. Women as well as men are capable of difficult, dramatic, and pleasing feats of grace, agility, and teamwork, but we will never know it from this stadium. Women will be either rendered invisible ("symbolically annihilated"; Boutilier & SanGiovanni, 1983, p. 185-215) or reduced to handmaidens and sex objects (cheerleaders) along the sidelines. The effect is to reinforce the male claim to the most important positions in society and to a significantly larger share of the fruits of social labour. This effect is especially powerful because it is rarely acknowledged. If a city gave pride of place to a stadium where only Anglo-Saxons could play, there would be howls of protest, but in the matter of gender and sports, such favouritism is usually taken for granted. The only thing that might communicate this male orientation is appearance. Standing at the foot of a tall telecommunications tower, the development will be a giant Klaes Oldenberg–like sculpture of the male genitals.

Despite the suggestiveness of feminist scholarship, the question of gender and sports is widely considered only a "women's issue" and is reduced to a problem of distribution (i.e., females "lack" opportunities). The gendered nature of the activities themselves and the consequences for men are rarely examined. The purpose of this paper is to contribute to this long-overdue analysis. I will argue that in their origins and essential characteristics, sports must be considered a form of male practice through which different "masculinities" compete. I will also argue that by perpetuating the sexual division of labour, sports not only contribute to the ongoing disadvantage of women but severely limit men's opportunities for personal growth. Such an expedition is not without its terrors—it requires radical questioning of that which many of us have found joyously validating—but it is essential if we are to understand fully what it means to "be a man." I do not advocate the abolition of sports, for they can empower humans of both sexes in beneficial, exhilarating ways. But I contend that sports should be transformed, and I will suggest some initial steps.

DECONSTRUCTING THE "NATURALNESS" OF SPORTS

My starting point is the social history insight that sports as we know them today are not the natural, universal, and transhistorical physical activity forms they are commonly thought to be, played in roughly the same way by all peoples in all periods of human history; rather, sports comprise a family of different activities developed under the specific conditions of rapidly industrializing 19th-century Britain and spread to the rest of the world through emigration, emulation, and imperialism. Although modern sports are popularly equated with the athletic events of the ancient Olympic Games, for example, scholars now argue that the differences between the contests of antiquity and those of our own era significantly outweigh the similarities. We must seek to understand each of these competitive forms in its own terms (Elias, 1971; Guttman, 1978).

Few of us would recognize what we call sport in the athletics of classical Greece. By modern standards, these athletics were extremely violent. The combative events—the most popular contests—were conducted with little concern for fairness or safety. There were no weight categories to equalize size and strength, no rounds, and no ring. Bouts were essentially fights to the finish, which is not surprising when you consider that these competitions began as preparations for war. The modern Olympics are widely admired for their encouragement of participation for its own sake and personal growth through constant self-testing, but the ancients did not hold such ideals. Competitors prayed "Give me the wreath (of victory) or give me death!" because victory alone brought glory. Placings other than first were rarely recorded, because defeat brought undying shame. Although the Greeks had the technology to measure records in the running, jumping, and throwing events, they rarely did so; performance for itself—pursuing a personal best despite one's placing—was meaningless to them. In fact, champions tried to psyche their opponents into withdrawing so the champions could boast they had won without even having to compete. There were no team events because competitors did not want to share the glory of victory. No competitor would have congratulated an opponent for a fairly fought or outstanding triumph. Today's handshake would have seemed an act of cowardice to the ancient Greeks (Finlay & Pleket, 1976; D. Young, 1985). Nor were these fiercely competitive games common to all cultures living along the Mediterranean in this period. In fact, anthropologists have established that only warlike peoples have used their leisure for combative events (Sipes, 1973).

Contrary to widespread belief, the ancient Olympic Games were inextricably bound up with the prevailing system of power. To be sure, the Games stood above city-state rivalries, enabling all free Greeks to compete. The "Olympic truce" was one of their most ingenious accomplishments. But practically and symbolically, athletics heavily reinforced gender and class domination. The classical Greek citizen's wealth and culture largely depended upon the exploitation of women and slaves. Although the origins of this system of power are not fully understood, it is clear that many subordinates were kept in submission through the force of arms, with which the classical events were closely associated. Even when athletic training became specialized and lost its direct connection to military skill, the Games celebrated the subjection of women and slaves at the level of ideology by excluding them from eligibility and the glory of victory (Kidd, 1984).

SPORTS AS MALE PRACTICE

Armed with this insight about the social specificity of physical activity forms, we can begin to take a closer look at our own. Pierre de Coubertin did not revive the Olympics, as he liked to claim; he appropriated and recast the symbols of the ancient Games for a project of his own. He sought to combat the decadence and militarism of *fin de siècle* Europe by inculcating in young men the values he admired in English rugby and cricket (MacAloon, 1981). These activities had their beginnings in the rural folk games of the late Middle Ages. In the mid- to late 19th century, these activities were fashioned into the first modern sports (characterized by standard rules, a bureaucratic structure, the privileging of records, and the concept of fair play) by middle- and upper-class males in the increasingly elitist institutions of the public school, the university, and the private club (Dunning & Sheard, 1979). Innovators, organizers, and creative publicists like de Coubertin consciously regarded sports as educational, preparing boys and young men for careers in business, government, colonial administration, and the military by instilling physical and mental toughness, obedience to authority, and loyalty to the team (Mangan, 1981). When working-class males began to take up sports too, some groups refused to accommodate them; at the Royal Henley Regatta, for example, working-class oarsmen were excluded by definition until 1933 (Alison, 1980). But most groups eventually adopted the strategy of "rational recreation," in other words, incorporating working-class males as players and spectators under strict middle-class leadership as a means of fostering respect for the established order and reducing class tension (Bailey, 1978). As Richard

Gruneau (1983) has written, sports "mobilize middle-class bias" to this day (p. 134).*

Education and socialization through sports were consciously understood to be masculinizing. According to Thomas Hughes's influential *Tom Brown's Schooldays* (1867/1979), the romanticization of all-male Rugby School under Thomas Arnold, the most important thing to learn is what it takes to be a man. In the course of 6 years of rugby, cricket, cross-country running, and impromptu fistfighting, Hughes's young protagonist acquires courage, stamina, ingenuity, close friendships, and leadership, attributes traditionally associated with dominant class norms of masculinity. Hughes's best-seller inspired Coubertin to develop the ideology of the modern Olympics, and the book persuaded parents, schoolmasters, and youth leaders throughout the English-speaking world to encourage sports to combat effeminacy. When Theodore Roosevelt feared that his asthmatic son, Theodore Jr., was becoming too heavily influenced by his mother and sisters, the father persuaded his son to take up boxing as an antidote (Pringle, 1931; Silverman, 1973). Working-class men also imbued sports with notions of masculinity (Palmer, 1979). The most popular 19th-century games and contests—football, lacrosse, hockey, track and field, and boxing—were termed "manly sports." Although they have now lost the epithet, they continue to be encouraged for the same reason.

SPORTS AS MALE PRESERVES

The men who developed and promoted sports were careful to ensure that only males were masculinized in this way. These developers maintained sports as male preserves by actively discouraging females from participation. These men denied women adequate facilities and programs, ridiculed their attempts, and threatened them with the spectre of ill health and "race suicide." Male doctors and physical educators proposed that people have only a finite quantity of energy, which in the case of women is needed for their reproductive organs. If women consume this energy in vigorous athletic activity, went the argument, they not only undermine their own health but the future of the white race. Working-class men generally shared these prejudices and contributed to the exclusionary practices, which suggests that sports participation helped males strengthen and extend cross-class masculinist bonds. Economic and social conditions—long hours of domestic labour, differential and generally less adequate diets, and restrictive dress—also deterred many girls and women from sports participation (Atkinson, 1978; Lenskyj, 1986).

Editors' note: These ideas receive additional treatment in chapter 1.

Response to Feminism

These exclusions and the emphasis upon manliness in sports can also be considered a response to the rising voice of women. In 19th-century Canada and the United States, men introduced sports to public schoolboys and to the adolescent members of organizations such as the YMCA to overcome "the feminization of teaching" (Kett, 1977; D. MacLeod, 1986). The increased numbers of women teachers and their expanding feminine influence over boys' psychosocial development was a cause for manly concern. British sociologists Kevin Sheard and Eric 'Dunning (1973) have suggested a direct relationship between the boorish, sexist subculture of rugby—the public "moonings," songs of male sexual conquest of women, and exaggerated drinking—and first-wave feminism:

> The historical conjuncture represented by the simultaneous rise of rugby football and the suffragette movement within the upper and middle classes may have been of some significance with respect to the emergence of the specific pattern of socially tolerated taboo breaking. For women were increasingly becoming a threat to men, and men responded by developing rugby football as a male preserve in which they could bolster up their threatened masculinity and at the same time, mock, objectify, and vilify women, the principal source of that threat. (p. 12)

When women persisted, especially during the 1920s and 1970s, males continued to exclude women from their own games and contests, requiring women to play on a sex-segregated basis with inferior resources. Despite the available examples from agriculture, industry, and sports of women performing arduous "men's" tasks, many persisted in the belief that a distinct women's biology prevents them from competing in the male realm. (The argument assumes—falsely—that all males are the same in size, strength, and fitness. For most of the population, including trained athletes, those ranges overlap; Hubbard, Henifin, & Fried, 1982). Organizers have also tried to confine females to those sports believed to enhance middle- and upper-class concepts of femininity, such as swimming, tennis, and gymnastics, and to devise "girls' rules" to discourage the ambitious and aggressive play expected of boys and men.[1] Female athletes have also faced inordinate pressures to conform to the heterosexual expectations of most males (B. Kidd, 1983).

The Distributive Problem

One legacy of this pattern of development is the well-known distributive problem—the significant inequalities that continue to plague females seeking sporting opportunities and careers. In most countries, despite a decade of "progress," males still have access to more than twice the number of opportunities and public resources available for sport. The Olympic Games still hold more than twice as many events for men as for women. But the effect of sports is also relational—sports perpetuate the patriarchy by powerfully reinforcing the division of labour. By giving males exciting opportunities, preaching that the qualities males learn from sports are masculine, and preventing girls and women from learning in the same context, sports confirm the prejudice that males are a breed apart. By encouraging us to spend our most creative and rewarding moments as children and our favourite forms of recreation as adults in the company of other males, sports condition us to trust each other much more than women. By publicly celebrating the dramatic achievements of the best males in public stadia while marginalizing females as spectators, sports validate the male claim to the best jobs and the highest status and rewards. Sports contribute to the underdevelopment of the female majority of the population and the undervaluing of those traditionally "feminine" skills of nurturing and emotional maintenance, which are essential to human growth and survival.

COMPETING MASCULINITIES

Although men have created a sporting culture that sharply distinguishes between masculine and feminine, they also express different and frequently competing masculinities through sports. The preferences we express for different sports and positions within sports (e.g., individual vs. team, body contact vs. non–body contact, or games requiring spontaneous creativity vs. those relying upon set plays) are in part statements about what we value "in a man" and what sort of relations we want to encourage between men. When Charles Dickens championed boxing in *The Pickwick Papers* despite the 19th-century prohibition, he endorsed a method for men to settle their disputes that was more scientific, humane, and democratic than the duel (Marlow, 1982). The current debate about boxing—under radically different social conditions—is still about competing masculinities: Should we admire men who risk their most valuable and most distinctively human parts— their heads and their hands—to test themselves in a dramatic contest, or should we condemn them for stupidity? Hockey loyalties can be read in the same way. I know a number of Torontonians who cheer for the Montreal Canadiens because this team has never systematically practised the "beat-em-in-the-alley" tactics of the Toronto Maple Leafs. These fans value a particular masculinity—one that prefers skill and artistry to physical force and intimidation—more than geographical community.

There is little scope for the full expression of different masculinities in sports, however. As in every other sphere of Western culture, the broad range of actual masculinities is subordinated in public discourse and institutional expectation to a single dominant or hegemonic masculinity, which is highly competitive, tech-nological, and homophobic (Kinsman, 1987). Given the inordinate pressure to win, the emphasis upon measurable achievement as opposed to intrinsic satisfac-tion and aesthetic creativity, and the well-established dependence of the commercial sports upon male audiences, hegemonic masculinity in sports has been difficult to combat. Several years ago, Wayne Gretsky skated away from a fight in a nationally televised play-off game, clearly rejecting the dominant code of hockey masculinity (which emphasizes defending your honour by dropping your stick and gloves to fight) in favour of the intelligence and self-discipline of staying out of the penalty box. Although his action won him the admiration of hockey reformers, he was attacked as a ''wimp'' by most media commentators. More recently, he has begun to argue that fighting in hockey is a ''natural'' part of the game.

MEN'S FEARS

Social biologist Ken Dyer (1982) has shown that women's records in the measurable sports like track and field and swimming are now being broken significantly faster than men's records in the same events, and he has concluded that lack of opportunity—not biology—is the primary reason why female performances have always lagged behind. Projecting his findings into the future, he suggests that if opportunities for women can be equalized, in most sports the best females will be able to compete on a par with the best males. Imagine a woman winning the open 100 metres at the Olympics or playing in the National Hockey League!

Character Change of Sport

Performances once considered impossible are now commonplace in virtually every sport, but most men balk at Dyer's suggestion. Not only do they not believe it could happen, but the idea that it could frightens them. Men fear the changes in the character of sport that would come about if females played with men. ''You have to play softer with women,'' a softball official testified during an Ontario Human Rights Commission inquiry in explaining why he felt integrated competition, even in which the female players had made the team on ability, would reduce the satisfaction for males (Re Ontario Softball Association and Bannerman, 1978). But although this is unspoken, I believe men also fear the profound social and psychological changes that would result if women were understood to be fully competent in the special domain of men. For years, the Ontario Hockey Association (OHA) refused to allow females to play on any of its teams. In the most recent case, it refused to register 13-year-old Justine Blainey, even though she had made a team in a competitive tryout. The OHA went to court four times in an effort to stop her. In 1987 it lost, largely because of the equality provisions in the 1982 Canadian Charter of Rights and Freedoms (''Girl Wins,'' 1987). Was one 13-year-old female, or even 200 female players, going to topple the male hockey leadership and disrupt a 500,000-male strong, century-old organization? Hardly. There must be something deeper.

Disorientation of the Male Psyche

In part, what men fear is the disorientation of the male psyche. As Nancy Chodorow (1978) has argued, male children develop their identities positionally, by differentiating themselves from their mothers. Because the major tasks of child rearing have been performed by women, the primary interaction for young males has been with women, with the result that boys have great difficulty in identifying with their fathers. So, Chodorow says, in developing masculine identities, males are essentially learning to differentiate themselves from their mothers and from women in general. Males rehearse and strengthen this positional masculinity in activities that accentuate male-female differences and stigmatize those characteristics generally associated with women.

Although Chodorow does not discuss sports, it is clear that sports were developed for—and serve—that very purpose in the industrial capitalist societies with which we are most familiar. This was certainly my experience growing up in Toronto in the 1940s and 1950s. I played sports endlessly as a child. I simply gobbled up the rules, skills, strategies, and lore, none of which seemed to interest my mother, her friends, or girls of my own age. Certainly my peers and I rarely involved girls. I also learned to accept (rather than question) physical pain, to deny anxiety and anger, and to be aggressive in ways that were clearly valued as manly. I realize now that I gained an enormous sense of my own power when I could respond to challenges in this way and be emotionally tougher than my mother and younger sister. Yet this shows how shaky such positional identity can be, because when I put myself into the emotional state I remember from that period, I realize that I would have been devastated if a girl—no matter how gifted—had played for any of the teams I was so proud to make. Such a situation would have proclaimed to the world that I was "like a girl" and inadequate. At the deepest psychological levels, the blurring of sex roles undermines not only the male-privileging sexual division of labour but also the very process by which males raised within sexually segregated sports have gained personal validation and confidence. The vulnerability of positional identity also helps explain why so many athletes fear gay men: Because of the widespread but false perception that all gay men are effeminate (Kleinberg, 1987), gay men appear to betray "masculinity".

Loss of Nurturing

Males also fear the loss of traditional nurturing that might result if females were socialized through sports (and other predominantly male activities) to be as hard and unyielding as males. This helps explain why so many men are determined to keep sports a male sanctuary, why in the quintessentially masculine sport of boxing many jurisdictions still prohibit females from competing at all, even against other females. It also helps us understand the psychological weight of the pressures on female athletes to be what is considered feminine. To be sure, many females share these fears and support the status quo. As Dorothy Dinnerstein (1976) points out, males and females actively collaborate to maintain the existing gender arrangements—"nostalgia for the familiar is a feeling that has so far been mobilized in opposition to social change" (p. 229). But the price of such collaboration is extremely high.

MEN'S PROBLEM

The patriarchal nature of sports has harmed men, too. By encouraging and reinforcing a positional identity, sports have led us to limit our options as humans.

Inability to Express the Feminine

Sports have led us to deny feelings and to disparage—and therefore not to learn—interpersonal skills stereotypically associated with females. By teaching us a form of strength and assertiveness disconnected from emotional understanding and the skills of emotional maintenance, sports have encouraged us to close ourselves off from our own inner feelings and those of others. Through sports, men learn to cooperate with, care for, and love other men in a myriad of rewarding ways, but sports rarely teach men to get close to each other or to open up emotionally. On the contrary, the only way many of us express fondness for other men is by teasing or mock fighting (the private form of what has become a public form of tribute—the "roast"). Anything more openly affectionate would be suspect.

Inability to Value Intrinsic Reward

Chodorow and Dinnerstein argue that the development of positional identity has also contributed to the process by which males privilege abstract achievement, which in sport has meant victory and records. Because sports elevate external goals over intrinsic ones, sports have encouraged athletes to treat their bodies instrumentally, to undergo physical and psychological injury, and to inflict it upon others. The active repression of pain is an everyday part of the sports world ("No pain, no gain!" is a common slogan), but this ethic has ruined the careers of countless athletes and left many crippled for life. There are also psychological scars; the constant emphasis upon external goals leaves many unable to identify their own needs, let alone pursue them. At the same time, the sports culture labels as failures those who cannot make increasingly higher standards of performance (Butts, 1976).

Inability to Interact Appropriately With Other Men

Sports may well poison the athlete's dealings with other men. Connell (1983) has defined masculinity in terms of power and has suggested that sports instruct men in two aspects of power: the development of force ("the irresistible occupation of space"; p. 18) and the perfection of skill ("the ability to operate on the objects within that space, including other humans"; p. 18). The rules of football (all codes), basketball, boxing, hockey, and others for which territorial control is important almost literally conform to this definition, and I can't think of any sport where it doesn't fit.[2] Sports encourage athletes to treat each other as enemies, when in fact athletes are coplayers without whom the rewards of playing cannot be obtained. This is the other side of "that sweet spot in time," "walking tall," or the exhilaration of doing it right. Psychologists Tutko and Bruns say that "to be a champion, you have to be the meanest son-of-a-bitch in the valley" (1976). Such mental and physical competitiveness wins championships, but it also throws up enormous barriers to the development and maintenance of close relationships.

TOWARD MORE HUMANE SPORTING PRACTICES

There are no magic solutions to the situation I have described. It is deeply rooted in long-established patterns of child rearing and human interaction, and it is perpetuated by powerful economic and political interests. We cannot dismiss or abolish sports, nor should we want to. Potentially, sports can help all humans acquire self-mastery in pleasurable, health-strengthening, and popularly validated skills and rituals. Such opportunities are particularly important in societies in which work is increasingly automated and alienating. Sports can also provide highly accessible popular dramas in ways that strengthen community and confirm widely shared meanings. Hockey may be a puberty rite for male Canadians, but it is also a celebration of the creativity, energy, and élan of the human spirit in the depths of winter, the season of death.

The contradictions of modern sports can sometimes undermine the very privilege that they enshrine. In their claim to be democratic, sports organizations provide the arguments—and sometimes the playing surfaces—for the disadvantaged to demonstrate their rights to a better future. In the Olympic Games, for example, the universalist aspirations of the ruling International Olympic Committee (IOC) have paved the way for athletes from the poorest and smallest countries to compete, even when they have had little chance of winning medals. In turn, the overwhelming presence of Third World nations (there are now 164 national Olympic committees) has pressured the elitist, Europe-dominated IOC to support the international struggle against apartheid and racism and to begin a program of technical assistance to have-not countries.

Liberating sports from patriarchal (as well as class and First World) structures of domination will be a long and complex process. It will have to be undertaken in conjunction with similar efforts in other areas of everyday life. The outcome— how humans will pursue sports in a more egalitarian, less oppressive age—will largely depend upon the nature of those struggles because, as we have seen, forms of physical activity, including sport, are historically grounded. But that should not dissuade us.

Question Masculinist Bias

We can start by actively questioning the pervasive masculinist bias in the sports world. The language is rife with words and phrases that unconsciously reinforce the male preserve: *jock*, the popular metonym for athlete; *tomboy* to describe any bright, active girl who likes physical activity and is good at sports; and *suck* and *sissy* to condemn anyone who betrays fear or anxiety. These all remind us that sports were designed to harden males. We should question the use of these terms the way the civil rights movement did with *nigger* and *boy* and the women's movement has with *mankind* and *girl*; develop inclusive substitutes (such as *athlete* for *jock* and *young athlete* for *tomboy*); and then campaign to remove the offending terms from usage. It will also be necessary to change the practices as well. Although we will always admire physical courage, we do ourselves a disservice if we continue uncritically to condemn the expression of pain and uneasiness that is usually associated with being a "sissy."

Challenge Sexism and Homophobia

We should challenge the gross sexism and homophobia of that inner sanctum of patriarchy, the locker room. Allen Sack, who played on the 1966 Notre Dame championship football team, has said that in many ways football is a training ground for rape. In the game, players learn to control the field and dominate other players, and in the dressing room they endlessly fantasize and celebrate the male conquest of women (Burstyn, 1986). Gay bashing has also been encouraged and plotted in the locker room. It takes a different kind of courage to contest such explicit, omnipresent misogyny and homophobia. Much of what is said is often rich in humour. Yet it contributes to our own repression, as well as the denigration of others. If you contest locker-room talk, you'll get denial and anger—"it's just a joke, I'm not a pig!"—but you will also start a reconsideration.

Redefine the Rules and Values of Sports

We can also contribute by redefining the rules and values of sports to make them more inviting to everybody. Physical educators, coaches, and community groups of both sexes have amended rules to make games safer, more accessible, and more genuinely educative. In Canada, parents, players, teachers, and government leaders have contributed to the effort to eliminate the gratuitous violence of ice hockey. In my neighborhood, a community softball league has recently added a second first base (immediately adjacent to the original base, but on the other side of the foul line) and eliminated the necessity of tagging the runner at home, both of which reduce collisions between players. These changes often involve trade-offs (I was sorry to see the softballers discourage the slide) but they subtly reduce the premium on physical dominance. (When I was 9 years old, I was taught to throw a cross-body block at second, third, and home. "There's ten dollars on every bag," our coach would tell us, "and if you don't get it, he will.") These experiments, especially when they result from open discussion about the purpose of sports, should be encouraged. To opponents who appeal to tradition, we can point out that the rules of games have been continually changed for other reasons, so why not to make them more humane?

Make Sports More Than Contests

We should also struggle to change the way sports are regarded. Too frequently, they are characterized as battlefronts. Competitions are viewed as zero-sum contests, and athletes are expected to treat each other as enemies. Military metaphors abound: Players "throw the long bomb" and teams "whip," "punish," "roll over," and "savage" each other. This imagery is hardly coincidental: Throughout the century, sports have frequently been associated with military training. Instead, I suggest we consider sports glorious improvisations, dialectical play, or collective theatre; although competing athletes are cast as antagonists, they need each other if the discoveries and pleasures of the contest are to be enjoyed at all. As athletes, we should respect and care for each other as coplayers. The pregame friendship ritual of basketball rivals Isiah Thomas and Magic Johnson is a welcome example in this regard. As spectators, we should applaud the winner but not at the expense of other members of the company.

There are powerful incentives structuring games as contests, fueling the tremendous exhilaration of triumph. In North America, the mass media and governments have monopolized the interpretation of athletic performance, and the participant's voice has been distorted, if not silenced. But other cultural performers—painters, dancers, actors, filmmakers—and their audiences have begun to contest the corporate media's interpretation of their work, and athletes could well learn from their example. A sports culture that de-emphasized winning and emphasized an exploration of artistry and skill and the creative interaction of rival athletes would be much less repressive.

Support Feminists Working for Change

Finally, we should actively support those feminists struggling to combat sexism and inequality in sport, and we should admit to the privilege men enjoy in public projects like the domed stadium. We should not only support advocacy groups like the Canadian Association for the Advancement of Women and Sport (*and Sport* rather than *in Sport* was a conscious recognition that increasing opportunities will not be enough), but we should take the initiative in struggling with men. It is necessary to assure males who resist integration on the basis of ability that we are strong enough to survive an "invasion" of outstanding female athletes. Where the implementation of affirmative action programs will bring about cuts in existing male opportunities, we should strive to find additional resources and make more efficient use of the existing ones. The most difficult task will be persuading other men that gender-divided sports are not just a "women's problem" but in dialectical interaction harm us as well. Once there's a shared understanding of that, the critical redesign of sports can really begin.

CHESTER COLLEGE LIBRARY

Chapter 3

Masculinity, Sexuality, and the Development of Early Modern Sport[1]

Todd Crosset

Nineteenth-century physical educators and ideologues of early modern sport professed inherent connections between sport, morality, and manliness. This connection between manliness and sport was supported by quasi-scientific theories and was accepted as rationale for the first sporting clubs and physical education programs for young men in England and the United States. Despite turn-of-the-century social critics like Thorstein Veblen, who discounted this association (Veblen, 1953), the notion that sport was a manly activity retained credibility well into the 1950s.[2]

Since the late 1960s and the advent of the modern feminist movement, contemporary social theorists have made little use of the concept of manliness to explain the development of modern sport. Rather, manliness has been viewed primarily as an insignificant aspect of early modern sport. Sport historian J.A. Mangan (1981), for instance, describes the 19th-century notion of manliness in sport as a confused moral concept that embraced such "antithetical" notions as "success, aggression, and ruthlessness, yet victory within rules, courtesy in triumph, and compassion for the defeated" (Mangan, 1981, p. 135). This description reduces manliness to a mistaken notion and does not assign it a critical role in explaining 19th-century sport. Manliness is typically viewed as a front, a cover for nationalism or class cohesion. The portrayal of manliness as a confused excuse for male participation in 19th-century sport, however, misses the crux of its meaning.

A more plausible approach is to view the promotion of manliness in the 19th century as the primary ideological function and catalyst for the organization and growth of early modern sport. Sport, along with other social institutions of the mid-19th century, helped define male sexuality as distinct from female sexuality. The Victorian concept of manliness seen in conjunction with the expanding concern for sexuality during this period is critical to understanding the origins and meaning of modern sport.

Furthermore, by placing this concern for sexuality within the context of gender relations during the Victorian period, we can see that sport was part of a larger ideological battle. The 19th century was marked by drastic social transformations in the roles of men and women. Whereas an increase in power and roles for women occurred during the first half of the century, the second half of the century was characterized by a reactionary male bourgeois movement that emphasized male superiority and distinct sex spheres. Social institutions of the post–Civil War era, including sport, helped to promote these gender distinctions and separate gender roles.

The intent of this paper is threefold: first, to critically review the recent literature on the development of sport in Western society; second, to outline the context in which modern sport arose, describing not only the rapidly changing economic and political structures but also the growing discourse and concern for sexuality during the 19th century; and third, to investigate how this concern for sexuality was entrenched in the 19th-century justification of male sporting activities. It is argued that the discourse around sexuality was the primary medium within which competing concepts and ideologies about the "natural" positions of men and women in society battled, playing a new and integral part of mid-19th-century society. It is concluded that 19th-century sport gained meaning and support from the expanding discourse around sexuality, which in turn justified male dominance over women.

A CRITIQUE OF THE LITERATURE

This paper concentrates on the early forms of organized modern sport in England between 1820 and 1880 and in the United States between 1840 and 1890. The data used in this paper were found in secondary sources and therefore are not new. What is different is the framework within which the data are analyzed. This analysis takes gender politics to be one of the primary factors in shaping 19th- and 20th-century society. Similar types of analysis have been applied to various aspects of the Victorian period and have expanded or revised our conceptions of 19th-century society (Cott, 1984; Foucault, 1978; Lebsock, 1984; Ryan, 1975; Smith-Rosenberg, 1985).

Paradox of the Essence of Sport

The most popular theories of the development of sport depict sport as a reflection or a microcosm of society (Eitzen, 1984; Geertz, 1973; Gruneau, 1983; Guttmann,

1978). Theories of this sort support the notion that modern sport arose in conjunction with the transformation from an agrarian society to an urban-commercial-industrial society. The latter society is characterized by capitalism, specialization, secular actions, bureaucratization, class inequalities, rules and regulations, quantification, and a distinction between work and leisure. In Weberian terms, society had become rationalized; in Marxist terms, bourgeois. Via deduction, these theorists conclude that modern sport shares these characteristics. From this perspective, sport is a malleable, passive institution that takes on the characteristics of the society within which it exists.

Other theorists, however, claim sport only appears rationalized. Its essence, play, remains an irrational, nonquantifiable, voluntary, purposeless, and self-absorbing activity (Guttmann, 1978; Huizinga, 1950; Morgan, 1985). Unlike labor or other rational activities, sport and play cannot be fully explained or understood via simple application of Weberian or Marxist paradigms (MacAloon, 1987). The paradox that confronts these social-sport theorists, then, is this: How did a basically irrational activity become a major social institution in a rational era? Often this paradox is justified by excusing sport as a unique social institution. The following explanation by Allen Guttmann (1978) is typical:

> Paradox, yes. Contradiction, no. Sports are an alternative to and, simultaneously, a reflection of the modern age. They have their root in the dark soil of our instinctive lives, but the form they take is that dictated by modern society. Like the technological miracle of Apollo XI's voyage to the moon, they are the rationalization of the Romantic. (p. 89)

Such an explanation, however, seems wholly inadequate. Indeed, as Gruneau (1983) aptly notes, "human desires for fun, fantasy and excitement, or for personal mastery, drama or creative expression, are a shaky foundation" (p. 152) on which to build a causal explanation for the development of a major social institution. If the essence of sport, irrationality, is a part of human nature, it seems more logical that the growth of sport and play would slow during a period of increasing rationality. Obviously, this did not occur.

Social Function of Sport

One way to avoid this paradox is to examine the social functions attributed to sport. If 19th-century sport served a social function (real or perceived), sport may well have been viewed as a purposeful activity despite its irrational essence. A common response to this approach is that sport served to promote nationalism and/or class consciousness. It is clear that sport did serve these functions in the late 19th and early 20th centuries. It is wrongheaded, however, to suggest that these functions served as ideological catalysts for the development of sport. Western states expanded on existing sporting institutions to create international competitions that promoted nationalism (MacLeod, 1986). Class segregation within sport (the cult of amateurism) was less prominent in the mid-19th century than in the last quarter of that century. Indeed, it seems that early schoolboy sport was promoted as a means of blending the aristocracy with the bourgeoisie (Gillis, 1974; Gruneau, 1983; Hobsbawm, 1984). These popular avenues of exploration do not explain the growing popularity of sport in England prior to 1870 and in North America prior to 1880.

Feminist Analysis

Despite their attention to gender, feminist sport scholars have added little to our understanding of the development of men's sport in the 19th century. Feminist sport historians have concentrated on reclaiming the history of women in sport, which risks being lost (see Howell, 1982). The most critical historical works focus on the obstacles facing women's participation in sport (e.g., see Lenskyj, 1986). Feminist sociologists have tended to focus on the present conditions of women in sport. In general, feminist scholars view sport as an institution that reflects a male-dominated society. These kinds of analyses have drawn attention to the power of gender relations as an explanatory tool but reveal little toward understanding the origins of modern sport as a social institution.

Recently, some sociologists and historians have begun to apply a gender analysis to men in sport. Adelman (1986) notes in his history of sports in New York City that the concept of manliness was a major factor in the growth of modern sport. His analysis, however, is brief and fails to place this ideological function of sport in a broader social context. Similarly, Gary Alan Fine's ethnography of Little League baseball (1987) illustrates the extent to which male culture is learned via sports. Although Fine's work is a fine piece of qualitative research, he does not place his conclusions within an explanatory framework. As a result, his work is primarily descriptive. In contrast, sociologist Eric Dunning (Elias & Dunning, 1986) notes that manly rituals associated with sport are related to the power struggle between men and women. Unfortunately, he implies that women's power is increasing in a linear fashion. Such a notion does not take into account the historical ebb and flow of power dynamics between men and women (Messner, 1988; Millett, 1970).

What is needed is not so much an alternative to Weberian or Marxist explanations of the rise of modern sport as an integration of these explanations with a feminist analysis of gender and sexuality. But it is not enough to simply juxtapose social categories of gender, class, and race and apply them to sport. They must be woven together by an inductive analysis of sport, beginning with the most basic element of sport, the human body, and investigating its social meanings (Connell, 1987b). This investigation should not view sport merely as a receptor of these social meanings but as an institution whose members are actively involved in shaping and reshaping sport and society.

THE GREAT TRANSFORMATION AND THE SOCIAL DEFINITIONS OF SEXUALITY[3]

During the mid-19th century, Western society was marked by numerous and far-reaching social and economic changes, including the growth of urban industrial centers, an emerging industrial capitalist economy, and complementary social reforms (Polanyi, 1957). In addition, this social and economic order spawned political theories of liberalism that emphasized free will and individualism, thus legitimizing the ascendance of the bourgeoisie.

The rapidly changing Victorian society had a profound effect on the relations between men and women. Works by the feminist historians Lebsock (1984), Ryan (1975), and Smith-Rosenburg (1985) are especially illuminating because the social transformations of the late 19th century are viewed in light of the developments of the early 19th century. The same economic and social changes that helped to legitimize male bourgeois power increased the power of women, especially bourgeois women.

Transformation of the Family

One of the consequences of the urban industrial revolution was the transformation of the family unit. In England and the United States, the perpetuation of subsistence family farming was becoming less feasible because of the limited amount of land (Matthaei, 1982; Polanyi, 1957; Ryan, 1975). Children of subsistence farmers, who in another century would have worked for and been cared for by parents and the family economy, were dislocated, becoming the core of the increasing numbers of rural paupers. In the early 19th century, men and women alike were cast into the free labor pool and worked as wage laborers.[4] As a result, women's social roles were in flux. Women took on such roles as brewer, pioneer, merchant, mill worker, and religious leader as well as homemaker and fashionable urban lady. Nonetheless, Ryan (1975) notes that during this period "the female roles and images had not congealed into a cohesive and convincing new standard of womanhood" (p. 74). That is, these new positions for women were not supported by a commonly shared ideology.

Susan Lebsock's (1984) detailed study of the women of Petersburg, North Carolina, supports Ryan's thesis that women's roles expanded in the early 19th century. Lebsock also notes that women's economic independence and political influence increased during this time. In particular, women had strong influence over and power in religious institutions, charitable organizations, the reform movement, education, and midwifery. In addition, women's control of Petersburg's property deeds and the estates of deceased husbands increased (Lebsock, 1984). Smith-Rosenburg's (1985) and Ryan's (1975) works on the revival movement also illustrate a sphere in which women attained power and developed a uniquely female ideology. These female-centered groups were often characterized by community, piety, and celibacy. Smith-Rosenburg's (1985) research of homosocial relationships of Victorian women further documents an ideology held by women that was distinct from that of Victorian men. By the mid-19th century, a women's political movement arose to contest patriarchal assumptions, and this movement fought for women's right to divorce, to have an abortion, and to vote.

"But in the end," writes Smith-Rosenburg (1985), "both social disorder, and an open social structure which offered new freedoms to women and to youth, proved to be temporary" (p. 144). Scholars have begun to document the mechanisms through which men displaced women from positions of power in such areas as education, midwifery, charitable organizations, religious sects, and communities between 1870 and the turn of the century (Barker-Benfield, 1976; Cott, 1984; Ehrenreich & English, 1978; Lebsock, 1984; Ryan, 1975; Smith-Rosenberg, 1985). Although some institutions were still considered women's spheres, these institutions were generally directed by men. Women political activists toned down their demands, and by the turn of the century many women's organizations were transformed into private charitable institutions (Pleck, 1983).

Nature of Men and Women

Accompanying these changes in positions of power was a cohesive and convincing ideology about the nature and role of men and women.[5] Quasi-scientific justifications for the growth of the bourgeoisie and sharp distinctions between men's and women's spheres gained popularity during this period. In brief, women were thought to be by their nature physically and rationally inferior to men. This ideology was supported by a well-documented network of quasi-sciences and social institutions. Almost without fail, these experts and scientists related woman's inferiority and fragility to her genital organs (Barker-Benfield, 1976; Chesler, 1972; Ehrenreich & English, 1978; Foucault, 1978; Lebsock, 1984; Smith-Rosenburg, 1985). Accompanying this idea of female sexual inferiority was an ideology of male biological superiority that held strong well into the 20th century. Although this quasi-biological justification of the social order was challenged by feminists of that era, it became the dominant ideology. This ideology was grounded in the notion of sexuality.

Gender Politics

Until recently, gender or sexual politics were of little or no concern to historians of the Victorian period. Within the last decade, however, a few social theorists and social historians have discovered that the 19th century was marked by considerable interest in sexuality, sexual misconduct, and gender distinctions (Foucault, 1978; Weeks, 1985). These works challenge the commonly held notion that the 19th century was characterized by prudishness and a repulsion for sexual matters. Foucault documents that during this period, Western society was obsessed with sexuality and that discussion and concern for sexual matters actually increased. Foucault (1978) argues that this concern was promoted by the interrelations of three axes that constituted the 19th-century notion of sexuality. One axis was the sciences, which made sexuality their subject. Foucault (1978) writes:

> First there was medicine, via the nervous disorders, next psychiatry, when it set out to discover the etiology of mental illness, focusing its gaze first on "excess," then onanism, then frustration, then "frauds against procreation," but especially when it annexed the whole of sexual perversions as its own province. (p. 30)

The second axis was the system of power that regulated and policed the practice of sexuality. This system included the criminal justice system, which took punitive action against those who committed "crimes against nature"; social welfare policy, inspired by Malthusian economic theory, which made population and fertility rates its business; and educational institutions, whose primary concern was the continuous control of the sexuality of adolescents. From these institutions, Foucault (1978) writes, "radiated discourses aimed at sex, intensifying people's awareness of it as a context of danger and this in turn created a further incentive to talk about it" (p. 31). So powerful and numerous were these institutions that sexuality became a daily concern.

The third axis, Foucault argues, was the fact that individuals came to recognize themselves "as subjects of this sexuality." Where antiquity of ancestry was once the truth of one's being, by the late 19th century sexuality was the truth of one's being. Where bloodlines had justified the privileged position of the aristocracy, the nature of one's sex and the proper practice of sexuality legitimized male bourgeois power.

However, not all men attained power. Implicit in this ideology was the notion that successful men made themselves. It was believed that a man's natural energy could be squandered and that those in poverty brought their situations upon themselves. Poverty struck those who were lazy, perverse, or lacked virtue—those who lacked manliness. Manliness, therefore, became equated with success in the economic sphere.

Summarizing Sexuality in Victorian Society

In sum, women first gained and then lost economic and political power to men in the early stages of urban industrial growth. This loss of power was, in part, the result of a cohesive heterosexual male bourgeois ideology that defined men and women in terms of biology and sex. This ideology was promoted by a myriad of new scientific theories and social institutions that concerned themselves with sexuality and that justified the privileged position attained by the male bourgeoisie.

SEXUALITY AND THE DEVELOPMENT OF MODERN SPORT

Sport served as one of the social institutions of the late 19th century that played a critical role in socializing men to define themselves as biologically superior to women. Sport as we now know it originated during this period. Its primary institutional support was the public schools of England.

Athletics in Education

From 1850 to 1890, the playing of games became an obsession in England and the United States (Fletcher, 1984; Mrozek, 1983). In some schools athleticism took precedence over classical studies. The following report from a housemaster to the parent of a student illustrates the socially accepted importance of athletics as part of a young man's education: "I don't think too much attention need be given to the very bad report he has received from Mr. Roebuck, his classics master. He has played exceptionally hard and for the second year running we won the cock-house match'' (Mrozek, 1983, p. 96). Headmasters repeatedly defended this emphasis on athletics as necessary for the development of manly or muscular students. Similarly, Adelman (1986) notes that those involved in the early years of baseball in the United States also justified this child's game in terms of male development. An 1867 manual typical of the period states that baseball ''affords a field of development of the manly attributes of courage, nerve, pluck, and endurance'' (Adelman, 1986, p. 282).

Sport and sex were seen as polar opposite activities affecting the character of young men. Weak, intellectual boys were thought to suffer from perverse thoughts and actions. Strong, athletic boys were thought to be in control of their passions. One student of an English public school in the late 19th century exemplifies this line of thought, writing in his autobiography: ''I was sufficiently good at games to make intelligence and hard work pass as an eccentricity instead of being chastised as vice or personal nastiness'' (Gathorne-Hardy, 1977, p. 154). Often, bookish boys were accused of masturbation. If a boy did confess to this behavior or was caught masturbating, the remedy most often prescribed was physical exercise or hardy trips to the country.

Sport and Manly Energy

An explanation for why sport was thought to generate manliness can be found in the commonly held 19th-century theory of spermatic economy (Barker-Benfield, 1976; Mrozek, 1983).

> According to this theory, the human male possessed a limited quantity of sperm which could be invested in various enterprises, ranging from business through sport to copulation and procreation. In this context, the careful regulation of the body was the only path to conservation of energy. (Mrozek, 1983, p. 20)

Many believed that sport was an activity that regenerated the body and made for more efficient use of sperm.

Couched in this search for manly energy was the fear of exhaustion. If men had sexual relations with women or masturbated too often, they were likely to suffer from exhaustion. A man's productive powers were limited and could be depleted through excess sexual actions. Loss of too much sperm resulted in illness, physical weakness, and effeminate behavior (Barker-Benfield, 1976; Mrozek, 1983).

But it was not enough to avoid women and self-abuse (masturbation). Men were also thought to suffer ailments arising directly from inactivity (H. Green, 1986). One medical doctor wrote:

> The strong, the phlegmatic, the healthy, the well balanced temperments— those who live out-doors and work with muscle more than mind—are not tormented with sexual desire to the same degree or in the same way as the hysterical, the sensitive, the nervous—those who live in-doors and use the mind much and muscle very little. (Barker-Benfield, 1976, p. 25)

Hysterical, sensitive, and *nervous* usually refer to ailments of female sexuality. Without sport, then, boys became womanlike, delicate, and degenerate. Without sport, men could lose control over their own sexual desires, become susceptible to sexual excesses, and eventually suffer from sexual exhaustion. Bookish and weaker boys were commonly referred to as ''saps'' or ''wankers.'' Both expressions contain derogatory sexual overtones.

Conversely, sport was thought to regenerate the male body and thus make efficient use of male energy. The athletic male body became a symbol of masculine character, and physical vigor an indication of future successes in adult endeavors. In addition, athletic achievement and development of the body erased any question of a young man's sexual morals.

These functions attributed to sport in the 19th century still carried some legitimacy in the first quarter of the 20th century and influenced youth programs (MacLeod, 1986), political movements (particularly fascism; Hoberman, 1984), and education (Cohen, 1980). Dartmouth College President Hopkins summarizes the connections between male sexuality and sport (albeit with a guarded tongue) in this excerpt of a 1925 speech concerning the place of athletics in higher education:

> [The student is] susceptible to indirect and obscure impulses about which we know little, and that he responds variously to stimuli from within and without of whose origin we know nothing. It is not simply rhetoric when we discuss the function of the American college in terms of the development of manhood. . . . Neither in the remote past nor more recently have [students] been dehumanized as to appetites or passions, the control of which is the first step in developing true manhood and a step without which intellectual development is futile. . . . If the sole function of the college were to maintain a scholastic program, I should favor the elimination of athletics . . . [however] there seems to me to be a presumable connection . . . between athletics and many healthful features of college life today. (Hopkins, 1950, p. 171)

CONCLUSION

Only when gender analysis is applied to the development of sport can we begin to explain why sport bloomed in a society that was becoming increasingly rationalized. In a society concerned with sexuality and manliness, sport was a purposeful and rational activity. Just as accumulation of wealth served as a sign of salvation or a moral lifestyle during an earlier period, athletic prowess served to symbolize morality, rationality, and superiority in young men and was a measurable sign of clean living and future success.

Sport, in conjunction with psychiatry, family medicine, the criminal justice system, and a host of other social institutions, promoted a concern for sexuality. It functioned as an institution that along with other social institutions defined male sexuality as distinct from and superior to female sexuality. This definition was legitimized by quasi-scientific theories. Recent research indicates that these theories were part of an ideology that gained acceptance among the male bourgeoisie and was perpetuated by this group as it increasingly gained power in the second half of the 19th century. Male sexual superiority theories justified male power and legitimized a shift in gender relations. These same theories justified, in part, early modern sport. In turn, sport socialized its participants to accept the notion of male sexual superiority.

When early modern sport is seen as an institution that helped to define male sexuality, the contradiction of the rise of sport within an increasingly rational society is resolved. Mangan (1981) could not integrate sportsmanship's seemingly antitheoretical notions of victory at all costs with ideas about playing within the rules and respect for one's opponent. If, however, manhood is affirmed by superior achievement in sport, one's manliness is heightened by defeating an admirable and competent opponent. To defeat a "sap" proves little. Conversely, little is threatened by losing if all competitors are assumed to be manly men. Respect, then, was due any opponent, and in turn the honor was reciprocated. Thus the activity of sport as an affirmation of manliness was continually confirmed by one's opponents. In turn, the meaning of victory was heightened while the embarrassment of defeat dissolved. Seen in this light, the meaning of the Victorian expression "may the best man win" becomes clear.

For similar reasons, we can now understand the proliferation of rules and record keeping in 19th-century sport as more than a reflection of rational society. Because of the overriding concern for sexuality, men no doubt wondered if indeed they were more or less manly. Unrecorded informal sporting activities were unrelated, relativistic expressions of manhood. Through standardization of rules and the keeping of records of achievements over time, manliness became a standardized, meaningful, and seemingly knowable attribute.

The evidence presented here helps explain why sport as an institution grew in size and importance during the late 19th century. Although class, nationalism, and capitalism are important factors in the development of sport, any explanation of the rise of modern sport that neglects to take into account sexuality and gender is sorely lacking.

The argument developed here is not offered as an alternative to Weberian or Marxist explanations of the rise of modern sport. Rather, these explanations need to be integrated in order to fully understand modern sport and its origins (Connell, 1987b). The social meanings of the body, sexuality, and physicality in sport need to be blended with theories of social change and integrated with descriptions of race and class domination. This kind of perspective on sport will aid in gaining a more complete understanding of contemporary sport issues such as the exclusion of blacks and women from sport; the corresponding threat felt by the white male establishment from blacks' and women's athletic successes; the phenomenon of cheerleaders; the brutality and domination directed at effeminate boys; overt racism and nationalism associated with Olympic success; the heterosexual attractiveness associated with athletic men; and the corresponding projection of lesbianism toward female athletes.

Chapter 4

Baseball and the Reconstitution of American Masculinity, 1880-1920[1]

Michael S. Kimmel

All boys love baseball. If they don't they're not real boys.
—Zane Grey

Baseball is sport as American pastoral: More, perhaps, than any other sport, baseball evokes that nostalgic longing, those warm recollections of boyhood innocence, the balmy warmth of country air, the continuity of generations. More than this, baseball is a metaphor for America, "the very symbol, the outward and visible expression of the drive and push and rush and struggle of the raging, tearing, booming 19th century," as Mark Twain wrote in 1889 (cited in Barth, 1980, p. 182).

Baseball expresses the contradictions that lie at the heart of American culture. The ball park itself is a bucolic patch of green nestled in a burgeoning urban landscape. The relaxation of an afternoon spent languidly in the bleacher sun is a sharp counterpoint to the excruciating tension that hangs on every pitch. Carefully calculated strategies (like hit and run or the double steal) executed with drill-like precision contrast with the spontaneous enthusiasm of the great catch. The players' cold professionalism at the bargaining table is antithetical to their boyish exuberance on the field.

And baseball is about remaining a boy and becoming a man. Like other sports, baseball fuses work and play, transforming play into work and work into play, thus smoothing the transition from boyhood to manhood. Play as work generates adult responsibility and discipline; work as play allows one to enjoy the economic necessity of working. Some studies suggest that men who are successful as boyhood athletes become more successful in business than those who were not successful child athletes. Contemporary high-tech corporations have introduced team sports among managers on the premise that such teamwork will increase productivity.

But unlike other sports, baseball inspires a literary eloquence that is unmatched, perhaps because baseball is so delicately poised between boyhood and manhood. No other sport has produced a Roger Angell or a Donald Hall; interestingly, each explores the link between baseball and family memory. Angell (1982) writes that, for him, "going through baseball record books and picture books is like opening a family album stuffed with old letters, wedding invitations, tattered newspaper clippings, graduation programs, and curled up darkening snapshots" (p. 10), so that for writer and fan, baseball players "seem like members of our family, or like trusted friends" (p. 199). And Hall (1985) underscores how baseball "connects American males with each other, not only through bleacher friendships and neighbor loyalties, not only through barroom fights, but, most importantly, through generations" (p. 49). He continues:

> Baseball is fathers and sons. Football is brothers beating each other up in the backyard, violent and superficial. Baseball is the generations, looping backward forever with a million apparitions of sticks and balls, cricket and rounders, and the game the Iriquois played in Connecticut before the English came. Baseball is fathers and sons playing catch, lazy and murderous, wild and controlled, the profound archaic song of birth, growth, age, and death. This diamond encloses what we are. (D. Hall, 1985, p. 49, 30)

In this essay, I will examine one of the ways in which this diamond encloses what we are by looking at the historical links between baseball and masculinity in the United States. By focusing on the rise of baseball at the turn of the century, I will develop two themes. First, I will look at the ways in which the rise of organized participatory sports was offered as a corrective to a perceived erosion of traditional masculinity in the late 19th century. Second, I shall explore the rise of mass-level spectator sports as part of the shift in America from a culture of production to a culture of consumption. I will argue that baseball—as participatory and spectator sport—was one of the chief institutional vehicles by which masculinity was reconstituted and by which Americans accommodated themselves to shifting structural relations. By specifying the terms on which sports reconstituted American masculinity, I shall link participation and spectatorship and explore how baseball provided an institutional nexus by which turn-of-the-century men recreated a manhood that could be experienced as personally powerful while it simultaneously facilitated the emergence of a docile and disciplined labor force. The lyrical eloquence that baseball above other sports inspires derives, in part, from the sport's centrality in the effort to reconstitute American masculinity at the turn of the century.

FORCES[2]

The early 19th century provided a fertile environment for an expansive American manhood. Geographic expansion combined with rapid industrial and urban growth to fuel a virile optimism about social possibilities. The Jacksonian assault against "effete" European bankers and the frighteningly "primitive" Native American population grounded identity in a "securely achieved manhood" (Rogin, 1975, p. 162). But by midcentury, the male establishment began to waver as social and economic changes began to erode the foundations of traditional American masculinity. Westward expansion came to an abrupt end at the Pacific coast, and rapid industrialization radically altered men's relationships to their work. The independent artisan, the autonomous small farmer, and the small shopkeeper were everywhere disappearing. Before the Civil War, almost 9 of every 10 American men were farmers or self-employed businessmen; by 1870, that figure had dropped to 2 out of 3, and by 1910, less than 1 out of 3 American men were as economically autonomous. Increased mechanization and the routinization of labor accompanied rapid industrialization; individual workers were increasingly divorced from control over the labor process as well as dispossessed of ownership.

Simultaneously, social changes further eroded American men's identities. In the burgeoning cities, white men felt increasingly threatened by waves of immigrants. In 1870, for example, of the nearly 1 million people who lived in New York City, 4 out of every 9 were foreign-born (M.L. Adelman, 1986). And the rise of the women's movement in the late 19th century spelled the beginning of the end for men's monopoly over the ballot box, the college classroom, and the professional school. The appearance of the "new woman"—single, upwardly mobile, sexually active, professionally ambitious, and feminist—also seemed to exacerbate men's insecurity and malaise.

The Crisis of Masculinity

The crisis of masculinity in the late 19th century emerged from these structural and social changes, as "the familiar routes to manhood were either washed out or roadblocked" (M. Hartman, 1984, p. 12); men

> were jolted by changes in the economic and social order which made them perceive that their superior position in the gender order and their supposedly "natural" male roles and prerogatives were not somehow rooted in the human condition, that they were instead the result of a complex set of relationships subject to change and decay. (M. Hartman, 1984, p. 13)

The perceived crisis of masculinity was not a generic crisis, experienced by all men in similar ways. It was essentially a crisis of middle-class white masculinity, a crisis in the dominant paradigm of masculinity that was perceived as threatened by the simultaneous erosion of traditional structural foundations (e.g., economic autonomy and the frontier), new gains for women, and the tremendous infusion of nonwhite immigrants into the major industrial cities. It was a crisis of economic control, a struggle against larger units of capital that eroded work-place autonomy and new workers (immigrants and women), who were seen as displacing traditional American men. And it was also a political crisis, pitting the traditional small town and rural white middle-class masculinity against new contenders for political incorporation. It was a crisis, in this sense, of gender hegemony, of whether or not the traditional white middle-class version of masculinity would continue to prevail over both women and nonwhite men. And therefore, to understand how baseball articulated with these various dimensions of crisis in hegemonic masculinity, we will need to draw on analyses of the relations among various social classes, the relations between whites and nonwhites, and the relations between women and men.

Responses to the Crisis of Masculinity

Men's responses to the turn-of-the-century crisis of masculinity varied tremendously, especially given the simultaneity of the forces that seemed to be affecting middle-class white men. Some (comprising the antifeminist response) gave vent to an angry backlash against the forces that were perceived as threatening men, whereas others (comprising the profeminist response) embraced feminist principles as the grounds for a reconstitution of a new masculinity. A third response sought to revitalize masculinity, to return the vitality and strength that had been slowly draining from American men. This masculinist response was not as anti-female as it was pro-male, attacking the enervation of American manhood and developing those interpersonal and institutional mechanisms by which masculinity could be retrieved.[3] Often the masculinist response was articulated with an anti-modernist rejection of the city as evil den of corruption, where healthy country men were thought to be transformed into effete dandies and where hordes of unwashed immigrants threatened the racial purity of the nation. "Get your children into the country," one real estate advertisement for Wilmington, Delaware, urged potential buyers in 1905. "The cities murder children. The hot pavements, the dust, the noise, are fatal in many cases and harmful always. The history of successful men is nearly always the history of country boys" (cited in Jackson, 1985, p. 138). Surely the anti-urban sentiments that composed part of the masculinist response were also fueled by a nativist racism that saw the cities as the breeders of an immigrant threat.

The masculinist effort to stem the tide of feminization of American manhood included the development of the YMCA and the Boy Scouts, in which young boys could experience the remedial effects of the wilderness away from the feminizing clutches of mothers and teachers. If consumer society had "turned robust manly, self-reliant boyhood into a lot of flat chested cigarette smokers with shaky nerves and doubtful vitality," as Chief Scout Ernest Thompson Seton had it (D. MacLeod, 1983, p. 49), then the Boy Scouts could "counter the forces of feminization and maintain traditional manhood" (Hantover, 1980, p. 293).

The masculinist effort also included the Muscular Christianity Movement, in which, through texts like Thomas Hughes's *The Manliness of Christ* (1880) and Carl Case's *The Masculine in Religion* (1906), the image of Jesus was transformed from a beatific, delicate, soft-spoken champion of the poor into a muscle-bound he-man whose message encouraged the strong to dominate the weak. Jesus was no "dough-faced lick-spittle proposition," proclaimed itinerant evangelist Billy Sunday, but "the greatest scrapper who ever lived" (cited in McLoughlin, 1955, p. 179). A former professional baseball player turned country preacher, Sunday drew enormous crowds to his fiery sermons, in which he preached against institutionalized Protestantism. "Lord save us from off-handed, flabby cheeked, brittle boned, weak-kneed, thin-skinned, pliable, plastic, spineless, effeminate, ossified three-karat Christianity," Sunday preached (McLoughlin, 1955, p. 175). Masculinism also promoted a revived martial idealism and found a new hero in Theodore Roosevelt, because "the greatest danger that a long period of profound peace offers to a nation is that of [creating] effeminate tendencies in young men" (M. Thompson, 1898, p. 610).

And masculinism also found institutional expression in the sports craze that swept the nation in the last decade of the century. The first tennis court in the United States was built in Boston in 1876, and the first basketball court was built in 1891. The American Bowling Congress was founded in 1895 and the Amateur Athletic Union established in 1890. Sports offered a counter to the "prosy mediocrity of the latter-day industrial scheme of life," as economist/sociologist Thorstein Veblen (1899/1953, p. 208) wrote. Sports revitalized American manhood while they simultaneously "had taken the place of the frontier . . . as the outlet through which the pressure of urban populations was eased" (H. Green, 1986, p. 215).

Nowhere was this more evident than in the rapid rise of baseball, both as a participatory sport and as a spectator sport. Baseball became one of the central mechanisms by which masculinity was reconstituted at the turn of the century, as well as one of the vehicles by which the various classes, races, and ethnic groups that were thrown together into the urban melting pot accommodated themselves to industrial class society and developed the temperaments that facilitated the transition to a consumer culture.

PLAYING

In the late 19th century, America went "sports crazy" (Dubbert, 1979, p. 175). The nation had never been as preoccupied with physical health and exercise, and across the country Americans flocked to health spas, consumed enormous quantities of potions and elixirs (like the 63 imported and 42 domestic bottled waters advertised by one firm in 1900), lifted weights, listened to health reformers extoll the tonic virtues of country air and bland high-fiber diets, raced through urban parks on bicycles, and tried their hands at tennis, golf, boxing, cricket, and baseball (H. Green, 1986). The search for individual physical perfection indicated a hopelessness about the possibilities of social transformation and pointed to the intimately linked fears of the enervation of the culture and individual lethargy and failure of nerve.

Development of Body and Character Through Sport

Sports were heralded as character building, and health reformers promised that athletic activity would not only make young men physically healthier but would instill moral virtues as well. Sports were cast as a central element in the fight against feminization; sports made boys into men. In countless advice books that counseled concerned parents about proper methods of child rearing, sports were invariably linked with the acquisition of appropriate gender-role behavior for males. Sports were necessary, according to physician D.A. Sargent, to "counteract the enervating tendency of the times and to improve the health, strength, and vigor of our youth," because sports provided the best kind of "general exercise for the body, and develop courage, manliness, and self-control" (cited in Dubbert, 1979, p. 169). Sports aided youth in "the struggle for manliness," wrote G. Walter Fiske in *Boy Life and Self-Government* (cited in Mrozek, 1983, p. 207).

Manhood required proof, and sports provided a "place where manhood was earned" (M.L. Adelman, 1986, p. 286), not as "part of any ceremonial rite de passage but through the visible demonstration of achievement" (p. 286). Such demonstration was particularly important, because lurking beneath the fear of feminization was the fear of the effeminate—the fear of homosexuality—which had emerged in visible subcultures in urban centers. In England, for example, one newspaper championed athletics for substituting the "feats of man for the 'freak of the fop,' hardiness for effeminacy, and dexterity for luxurious indolence" (M.L. Adelman, 1986, p. 284).

Some were less sanguine about sports' curative values. Thorstein Veblen's blistering critique of the nascent consumer culture suggested that organized sports are an illusory panacea. For the individual man, athletics are no sign of virtue, because "the temperament which inclines men to [sports] is essentially a boyish temperament. The addiction to sports therefore in a peculiar degree marks an arrested development of the man's moral nature" (Veblen, 1899/1953, p. 200). And culturally, Veblen continued, sports may be an evolutionary throwback, as they "afford an exercise for dexterity and for the emulative ferocity and astuteness characteristic of predatory life" (p. 203).

Most commentators saw sports as the arena in which men could achieve physical manhood but also believed that organized sports would instill important moral values.[4] Here, especially, the masculinist response to the crisis of masculinity resonated with the anti-urban sentiments of those who feared modern industrial society. Sports could rescue American boys from the "haunts of dissipation" that seduced them in the cities—the taverns, gambling parlors, and brothels, according to the *Brooklyn Eagle* (cited in M.L. Adelman, 1986, p. 277). Youth needs recreation, the *New York Herald* claimed, and "if they can't get it healthily and morally, they will seek it unhealthily and immorally at night, in drink saloons or at the gambling tables, and from these dissipations to those of a lower depth, the gradation is easy" (cited in Adelman, 1986, p. 277).

The Link to Baseball

And what was true of sports in general was particularly true of baseball. Theodore Roosevelt listed baseball in his list of "the true sports for a manly race" (along with running, rowing, football, boxing, wrestling, shooting, riding, and mountain climbing). Just as horse racing had resulted in better horse breeding, health advocate Edward Marshall claimed in 1910, so baseball "resulted in improvement in man breeding" (cited in Spalding, 1911, p. 534). "No boy can grow to a perfectly normal manhood today without the benefits of at least a small amount of baseball experience and practice," wrote William McKeever in his popular advice manual, *Training the Boy* (McKeever, 1913, p. 91).

The values that baseball called into play were important to the man and central to the nation. The baseball player was "no thug trained to brutality like the prize fighter," noted baseball pioneer Albert G. Spalding, nor was he a "half-developed little creature like a jockey"; rather, he was an exemplar of distinctly "native" American virtues, which Spalding (1911, p. 4) alliteratively enumerated in *America's National Game*; "American Courage, Confidence, Combativeness; American Dash, Discipline, Determination; American Energy, Eagerness, Enthusiasm; American Pluck, Persistence, Performance; American Spirit, Sagacity, Success; American Vim, Vigor, Virility" (p. 4).

Such values were not only American but Christian, replacing the desiccated values of a dissolute life with the healthy vitality of American manhood. Moral reformer Henry Chadwick saw baseball as a "remedy for the many evils resulting from the immoral associations boys and young men of our cities are apt to become connected with" and therefore deserving "the endorsement of every clergyman in the country" (cited in M.L. Adelman, 1986, p. 173). McKeever (1913) added that "baseball may be conducted as a clean and uplifting game such as people of true moral refinement may patronize without doing any violence to conscience" (p. 101). Baseball was good for the bodies and the souls of men; it was imperative for the health and moral fiber of the body social. From pulpits and advice manuals, the virtues of baseball were sounded. As M.L. Adelman (1986) notes, baseball

> took manliness beyond a mere demonstration of physical prowess and linked it to virtues such as courage, fortitude, discipline, and so on. The argument concluded that if ball games called these virtues into play—as in fact they were critical to doing well at such sports—then ball playing was obviously one way of demonstrating manhood. (p. 106)

One central feature of the values that were instilled by playing baseball was that they appeared on the surface to stress autonomy and aggressive independence, but they simultaneously reinforced obedience, self-sacrifice, discipline, and a rigid hierarchy. This was equally true with other boys' liberation movements designed to counter the feminization of the culture. The Boy Scouts instilled a "quest for disciplined vitality" (H. Green, 1986, p. 261), in which scouts were taught, according to founder Lord Baden-Powell, to work hard, sacrifice, and be obedient to their fellow countrymen and the king. The results of this and other efforts were noted with glee by Octavia Hill, the celebrated English social reformer, in the 1880s:

> There is no organization which I have found influence so powerfully for good the boys in such a neighborhood. The cadets learn the duty and dignity of obedience; they get a sense of corporate life and of civic duty; they learn to honour the power of endurance and effort; and they come into contact with

manly and devoted officers. . . . These ideals are in marked contrast with the listless self-indulgence, the pert self-assertion, the selfishness and want of reverence which are so characteristic of the life in the low district. (cited in J. Hargreaves, 1986, p. 61)

For the boys learning to play baseball, these values were also underscored. Surely the team came first, and one always obeyed one's coaches and manager. What Veblen claimed about football is equally true about baseball:

The culture . . . gives a product of exotic ferocity and cunning. It is a rehabilitation of the early barbarian temperament, together with a suppression of those details of temperament which, as seen from the standpoint of the social and economic exigencies, are the redeeming features of the savage character.
    The physical vigour acquired in the training for athletic games—so far as the training may be said to have this effect—is of advantage both to the individual and to the collectivity, in that, other things being equal, it conduces to economic serviceability. (Veblen, 1899/1953, p. 204)

Sports reproduced those character traits required by industrial capitalism, and participation in sports by working-class youths was hailed as a mechanism of insuring obedience to authority and acceptance of hierarchy. If the masculinity on the baseball field was exuberant, fiercely competitive, and wildly aggressive, it was so only in a controlled and orderly arena, closely supervised by powerful adults. As such the masculinity reconstituted on the baseball field also facilitated a docility and obedience to authority that would serve the maintenance of the emerging industrial capitalist order.

WATCHING

Just as on the field, so in the stands: Baseball as a spectator sport facilitated an accommodation to industrial capitalism as a leisure-time diversion for the urban lower-middle and working classes. Ball parks were located in the city and admission fees were low, so that "attendance at baseball games was more broadly based than at other spectator sports" (M.L. Adelman, 1986, p. 149).

The Crafting of a National Pastime

Baseball did not spring to such popularity overnight, as restorer of both individual virility and national vitality; its emergence as the "national pastime" was deliberately crafted. In fact, in the early half of the 19th century, cricket was hailed for its capacity to instill manly virtues in its players. "Whoever started these boys to practice the game deserves great credit—it is manly, healthy, invigorating exercise and ought to be attended more or less at all schools," waxed the *New York Herald* (cited in M.L. Adelman, 1986, pp. 105-106). In 1868, the *Brooklyn Eagle* informed potential spectators of a cricket match that they were about to see a "manly game" (cited in M.L. Adelman, 1986, pp. 105-106). Baseball was regarded, in fact, as less than fully manly; one letter to the editor of a newspaper contended that

> You know very well that a man who makes a business of playing ball is not a man to be relied upon in a match where great interests are centered, or on which large amounts of money is pending. (cited in M.L. Adelman, 1986, p. 167)

By the late 19th century, the relationship between baseball and cricket had been reversed. The man who played cricket, Albert Spalding warned, regarded his match as a chance "to drink afternoon tea, flirt, gossip, smoke [and] take a whiskey and soda at the customary hour" (Spalding, 1911, p. 7).

How can we explain such a change? In part, the shift from cricket to baseball can be understood by the changing class and regional composition of baseball's players and observers. Whereas earlier in the century baseball had been the domain of upper-middle-class men, by the end of the century it was played almost exclusively by lower-middle-class men. Similarly, the rise of mass spectator sports— the erection of the urban stadium, the professionalization of teams and leagues, and the salaries of players—dramatically changed the class composition of the baseball fan. The values that were thought to be instilled by playing baseball were now thought to be instilled by watching baseball. And values of discipline, self-control, and sacrifice for the team and an acceptance of hierarchy were central to the accommodation of a rapidly developing working class to the new industrial order.

It was during this period of dramatic economic expansion in the late 19th century that baseball "conquered" America. In the first few decades following the Civil War, the baseball diamond was standardized, teams and leagues organized, rules refined, game schedules instituted, and grand tours undertaken by professional baseball teams (Barth, 1980). And though the earliest baseball teams, like the New York Knickerbockers, were made up of wealthy men, baseball was soon played by small-town lower-middle-class men and watched by their urban counterparts (Mrozek, 1983).

The urban baseball park was one of the new important locations for social life in the burgeoning late-19th-century city. Like the vaudeville theater, the department store, and the urban park, the stadium provided a world of abundance and fantasy, of excitement and diversion, all carefully circumscribed by the logic of urban capitalism. Here the pain and alienation of the urban industrial working life was soothed; the routine dull grayness of the urban landscape was broken up by these manicured patches of green. As Barth (1980) writes, the baseball park was a constructed imitation of a pastoral setting in the city, in which identification with one's professional team provided a feeling of community with anonymous neighbors; the ball park was a rural haven of shared sentiments in the midst of the alienating city.[5]

Baseball as Fantasy and Democracy

If masculinity had earlier been based on economic autonomy, geographic mobility, and success in a competitive hierarchy, baseball—among the other new social institutions of the turn of the century—allowed the reconstitution of those elements in a controlled and contained location. On the field, baseball promoted values essential to traditional masculinity: courage, initiative, self-control, competitive drive, physical fitness. In the stands, the geographic frontier of the midcentury was replaced by the outfield fences and by the mental frontiers between rival cities. (What we lose in reality we recreate in fantasy, as a Freudian axiom might have it.)

Baseball was fantasy and diversion. ''Men anxious to be distracted from their arduous daily routines provided a natural market for the product of the new industry'' (Barth, 1980, p. 151). And baseball was viewed by boosters as a potential safety valve, allowing the release of potential aggression in a healthy, socially acceptable way; it was a ''method of gaining momentary relief from the strain of an intolerable burden, and at the same time finding a harmless outlet for pent-up emotions'' which otherwise ''might discharge themselves in a dangerous way'' (Bruce, 1913, p. 106). For the fan, baseball was, Bruce noted, catharsis.

Like the frontier, the baseball park was also celebrated as democratic. The experience of spectatorship, baseball's boosters claimed, was a great social leveler:

> The spectator at a ball game is no longer a statesman, lawyer, broker, doctor, merchant, or artisan, but just plain every-day man, with a heart full of fraternity and good will to all his fellow men—except perhaps the umpire. The oftener he sits in grand stand or ''bleachers,'' the broader, kindlier, better man and citizen he must tend to become. (Bruce, 1913, p. 107)

''The genius of our institutions is democratic,'' Albert Spalding gushed. ''Baseball is a democratic game'' (Spalding, 1911, p. 6).

Such mythic egalitarianism, however, ignored the power relationships that made American democracy possible. For the experience of incorporation into community was based on exclusion: the exclusion of nonwhite men and the exclusion of women. The ball park was a ''haven in a heartless world'' for white lower-middle-class men, and the community and solidarity they found there, however based on exclusion, facilitated their accommodation to their positions in class society. Professional spectator sports maintained the ''rigid gender division and chauvinist masculine identity'' (J. Hargreaves, 1986, p. 43) as well as the strict separation between whites and nonwhites that provided some of the main cultural supports of class domination. While providing the illusion of equality and offering organized leisure-time distraction, as well as by shaping working-class masculinity as constituted by its superiority over women, baseball helped white working-class men accommodate themselves to the emergent order.

REPRODUCING

Baseball, as participatory sport and as spectator sport, served to reconstitute a masculinity whose social foundations had been steadily eroding; in so doing, baseball served to facilitate the reproduction of a society based upon gender, racial, and class hierarchies. For it was not just masculinity that was reconstituted through sports but a particular kind of masculinity—white and middle-class—that was elaborated. And part of the mechanisms of that elaboration was the use of white middle-class masculinity to maintain the social hierarchies between whites and nonwhites (including all ethnic immigrants to the cities), between upper classes and working classes, and between men and women.

These mechanisms were developed in the last 2 decades of the 19th century and the first 2 decades of the 20th century. In 1919, this world was shaken during the world series scandal that involved the infamous Chicago "Black Sox," who had apparently "fixed" the series. The scandal captivated American men, and a certain innocence was lost. Commercialism had "come to dominate the sporting quality of sports" (Filene, 1986, p. 139); heroes were venal and the pristine pastoral was exposed as corrupt, part of the emergent corporate order and not the alternative to it that people had imagined. But by then it was too late: The corporate order had triumphed and would face little organized opposition from a mobilized and unified working class. The reconstituted masculinity that was encouraged by baseball had replaced traditional definitions of masculinity and was fully accommodated to a new capitalist order. The geographic frontier where masculinity was demonstrated was replaced by the outfield fence; men's work-place autonomy and control were replaced, in part, by watching a solitary batter squaring off against an opposing pitcher. What had been lost in real experience could be reconstituted through fantasy.

The baseball diamond, as I have argued in this essay, became more than a verdant patch of pastoral nostalgia; it was a contested terrain. The contestants were invisible to both participant and spectator and quite separate from the game being played or watched. Baseball was a contest between class cultures, in which the hegemony of middle-class culture was reinforced and the emerging industrial urban working class was tamed by consumerism and disciplined by the American values promoted in the game. It was a contest between races, in which the exclusion of nonwhites and non-European immigrants from participation was reflected in the bleachers, as racial discrimination further assuaged the white working class. And it was a contest between women and men, in which newly mobile women were excluded from equal participation (and most often from spectatorship); the gender hierarchy was maintained by assuming that those traits that made for athletic excellence were also those traits that made for exemplary citizenship. The masculinity reconstituted on the ball field or in the bleachers was a masculinity that reinforced the unequal distribution of power based on class, race, and gender. In that sense, also, baseball was truly an American game. And if we continue, as I do, to love both playing and watching baseball, we will deepen an ambivalent love, which, like the love of family or country to which baseball is so intimately linked, binds us to a place of both comfort and cruelty.

Chapter 5

Rugby in the 19th-Century British Boarding-School System: A Feminist Psychoanalytic Perspective

Philip G. White
Anne B. Vagi

If one is to undertake a psychological or sociological study of masculinity in Western society, there is perhaps no more well-equipped laboratory than the sport arena. Here we commonly observe males exhibiting traditionally masculine qualities of physical power, strength, and violence within a milieu that rejects feminine values. The game of rugby provides a particularly appropriate area for the study of masculinity for a number of reasons. First, rugby is a mock-combat sport that developed from violent medieval folk games whose functions included the generation of a level of excitement and the opportunity to affirm masculine aggression in a sphere other than actual combat. Second, many other modern combat sports, such as the North American form of football, evolved directly from rugby and, as we will argue later, continue to function as vestigial enclaves of legitimized chauvinism. Third, in addition to the game itself, rugby has many cultural forms that combine the celebration of masculinity with the denigration of women and homosexuals.

AN EXPLANATION OF RUGBY

The game of rugby, both in its original folk forms and its more modern "civilized" forms, involves intense but legitimized violence. The object of the game is to carry the ball across the opponent's goal line in order to score a *try*. A combination of physical force and skill is invariably required to achieve this objective. Given the physical nature of the game, participation requires that the individual be willing to mete out and be the target of physical contact violent enough to cause physical injury. The qualities of physical toughness and courage are thus assets for rugby players and are highly valued within the rugby fraternity.

Most of the game's attendant cultural forms are enacted following the completion of the actual contest. Prefaced by and coinciding with the consumption of large quantities of beer occur a complex of rituals. Two prevalent components of these rituals will be described here. First, the singing of songs that reinforce masculinity by objectifying and vilifying women and homosexuals is central to tradition. Second, the male striptease is also an important component of rugby ritual. This performance may be enacted solo or en masse depending upon the accompanying song.

Interpretation From a Critical Perspective

Critical interpretations of the growth and development of the game and its attendant cultural forms have for the most part emerged from the conflict tradition within sociological theory. These interpretations, as discussed here, have much credibility but overlook the power of psychological interpretation. The purpose of this paper is to augment the sociological literature from a feminist psychoanalytic perspective that critically examines the mechanism by which boys developed ambivalences toward women through early immersion in a social world that demonstrated the privileges associated with being male and the lack of power associated with being female. We also examine the possible results of boys' isolation from their mothers on being sent to boarding schools during early childhood. We feel that this premature separation may have contributed to the development of both a hypermasculine sport such as rugby and the attendant antifemale rituals. We postulate that for boarding-school boys, the absence of feminine influence during a significant period of development had a detrimental effect on their subsequent relationships. In what follows, the traditional psychoanalytic view of masculine development is reinterpreted from a feminist perspective. Rather than assuming that gender roles are innately prescribed, an alternative position is taken emphasizing the importance of society and culture in producing and reproducing gender identity.

Interpretation From a Psychoanalytic Perspective

Psychoanalytic writers have focused on the Oedipal crisis, which occurs somewhere between the ages of 3 and 6, as the time when boys achieve some measure of psychological separation from their mothers in order to identify with their fathers and other males (Chodorow, 1978; Dinnerstein, 1976; Freud, 1940). The way in which this occurs is perceived differently by various writers, but the orthodox position holds that the young boy comes to perceive his father as a rival for the exclusive love of his mother. Because of the father's larger size and the power that he exerts in order to fulfill his role in patriarchal society, the son comes to realize that he cannot get rid of the father and have sole access to intimacy with the mother. The resolution of this crisis usually occurs when the boy transforms his rivalrous feelings toward his father into identification with him as a male who is fundamentally different from the boy's mother and other females. This allows the son to avoid the loser's position in the contest. Psychological differentiation between gender identities is reinforced by the influence of socially prescribed gender roles that associate maleness with privilege and femaleness with lack of power. This sense of maleness carries with it the sense that the mother, by virtue of her femaleness, is lacking in power (or even value) as a person and can therefore even become an object of derision. This is associated with considerable ambivalence, given that traditionally the mother and other women are virtually the sole source of emotional closeness and nurturance (Chodorow, 1978). If the mother is given up or lost as a love object, the young boy is emotionally cast adrift.

Our Interpretation

We suggest that the young boy's ambivalent feelings toward his mother are heightened by the experience of being separated from her in order to attend boarding school and that rugby and its rituals may have been developed as a vehicle for affirming his still-fragile masculinity. We contend that the ambivalence toward women that is begun in childhood continues into adulthood and is still prevalent in current society. This ambivalence, which may be heightened by the uncertainty about modern sex roles, is thought to perpetuate rugby practices in their present form. Men perceive a conflict between pressure to be masculine—independent, strong, unemotional—and demands placed upon them by women to be sensitive and emotionally responsive in relationships. We propose that rugby continues to serve a role in affirming men's senses of themselves as distinct from females.

A SOCIAL HISTORY OF THE DEVELOPMENT OF RUGBY

The origins of rugby football and other combat sports can be traced to a number of medieval folk games played in England as early as the 14th century (Dunning & Sheard, 1979). Although other writers have speculated about links between football games and earlier sport forms such as the Greek game *episkyros* (G. Green, 1953) and the Roman game *harpastium* (Titley & McWhirter, 1970), the evidence has been obscure. It is only in the literature and public records of medieval England that we find sufficient mention of football to have confidence in identifying the origins of the game here.

Rugby in the 1500s and 1600s

During the 16th and 17th centuries, a variety of ball games were played in peasant communities. Inflated animal bladders were used as balls, and trees and other natural objects were the boundaries and goals (K. Young, 1983). Going under names such as football, hurling, knappan, and camp ball, these games were delineated by rules that were oral and regionally specific (Dunning & Sheard, 1979). A central characteristic of these games, however, was the violence that created a mock battle between individuals or groups. As Dunning (1986) argues:

> The players engaged in the relatively free expression of emotion and exercised only a relatively loose form of self-control. In fact, such games were a kind of ritualized fighting in which groups were able to pit their strength against local rivals whilst, at the same time, generating, in a relatively pleasurable form, excitement akin to that aroused in battle. (p. 81)

The need to reproduce the excitement of real battle through mock battle is likely rooted in the cultural formations of the medieval period. First, violence and fighting were regular and open features of everyday life. Conflicts were commonly resolved by force because of the absence of effective state control over the use of force and the relatively high threshold of repugnance concerning physical violence during the medieval period. Second, the balance of power between the sexes was weighted in favour of males, who were better equipped physically to engage in such hostilities. Given the patriarchal nature of medieval society and the general lack of social control over the use of physical force, medieval folk games constituted a celebration and formalization of male aggression.

Rugby in the 1800s

A significant step in the direction of the institutionalization of football took place in the 19th-century British public schools (Dunning & Sheard, 1979). The game of rugby originally became popular at Rugby School in the early 19th century and then spread to other public schools in the 1840s and 1850s (Sheard & Dunning, 1973). Rugby enthusiasts then introduced the game into the elite universities of Oxford and Cambridge, perpetuating the game's exclusive character.

The role that football played in the public schools, to which the sons of the wealthy were sent to become both "men" and "gentlemen," has been the subject of some discussion in the literature (e.g., Dunning, 1986; Dunning & Sheard, 1979; Donnelly & Young, 1985; Sheard & Dunning, 1973; K. Young, 1983). These analyses provide explanations of the manner in which the sons of the middle and upper classes in England in the second half of the 19th century adopted and modified folk games for their own use.

These authors suggest that rugby and other physically interactive ball games have served several social functions. First, in the all-male milieu of the public schools, the competitive rough-and-tumble nature of these games facilitated the expression of canalized aggression not available in the otherwise sedentary life of the well-to-do class. Moreover, the game provided a sense of traditional masculinity, which was becoming more difficult to express in an increasingly urban-industrial society. As Sheard and Dunning (1973) observe:

> Under the urban-industrial conditions that were coming increasingly to prevail, it became more and more difficult for traditional upper and middle class norms of masculinity to find expression in the normal run of everyday life, and rugby football began to emerge . . . as one of the principal social enclaves where they could be legitimately expressed. (p. 6)

Men who began to perform white-collar jobs needed to find an outlet for their needs to have physical contact and competition with other men.

It has also been suggested that another factor contributing to the rapid growth in the popularity of rugby was the progress made by women during the second half of the 19th century in demanding a greater share of political and economic power. The coincidence of the growth of rugby as a manly game and the threat posed by suffragettes to male hegemony likely resulted in the game and its attendant cultural forms becoming, as Sheard and Dunning (1973) suggest, a male preserve:

> women . . . were increasingly becoming a threat to men, and men, we should like to suggest, responded among other ways by developing Rugby Football as a male preserve in which they could bolster up their threatened masculinity and, at the same time, mock, objectify and vilify women, the principal source of threat. (p. 8)

Similarly, Donnelly and Young (1985) have suggested that the particular forms of rugby players' responses during the late 19th century were influenced by the players' experiences in the all-male public schools. Expressions of machismo found among adult rugby players, these authors argue, are reflections of public school life:

> The drunkenness and vandalism represent a reaction to excessive controls, the singing of obscene songs—often to hymn tunes—becomes a parody of chapel hymn singing at school, and the vilification of homosexuals becomes an overt form of denial for heterosexual males who still apparently prefer an all-male setting based around a contact sport and communal bathing. The cultural forms permitted and encouraged the vilification of women during a time of apparent threat, and also allowed the re-creation of simple schoolday values such as comradeship and sportsmanship. (p. 22)

The connection between the growth of rugby and social context, as argued for by these studies, is persuasively made. At the individual level of analysis, however, it is unclear why the exclusively male milieu of the public schools generated an interest in a game that, while violent and masculine, included physical intimacy and emotional bonding. Moreover, little progress has been made to date in interpreting the psychological implications of isolating young boys in an all-male environment. It is to these issues that we now turn.

PSYCHOLOGICAL IMPLICATIONS
OF BOARDING-SCHOOL LIFE
FOR RUGBY AND ITS CULTURE

To our knowledge the extant literature contains no analysis of the relationship between the psychological impact of boarding-school life and the adoption of rugby by young boys and men as a chosen leisure activity and their surrounding the game with rituals that denigrate women and homosexuals. Although women may have been exerting their political presence in the adult world, it is certain that their role in the boarding-school society was minimal. At school the boys were isolated from their immediate family and, therefore, rigidly segregated from females in a thoroughly male-dominated culture from an early age (J. Hargreaves, 1986). Boys were commonly sent to boarding school at 8 years of age but occasionally as early as 3 or 4 (Gathorne-Hardy, 1977). In essence, they were taken away from whatever nurturant or loving relationships they had with their mothers or nannies and were plunged into a milieu bereft of affection or any benevolent feminine influence.

It is clear from the many accounts available to us (e.g., Gathorne-Hardy, 1977; Mangan, 1981) that life within these institutions was, by current standards at least, frequently brutish. Violence between schoolmasters and boys, and between the boys themselves, was common and expected. Beatings imparted on pupils by schoolmasters or the headmaster have become notorious for their severity. That such excesses were tolerated by parents is symptomatic of that age. During this time when interpersonal cruelty was commonplace, parents were frequently cruel to their children.

Relationships between the boys, especially between the larger, older boys and the smaller, younger boys, were no less violent. Fagging, a system that became formalized in the boarding schools, was effectively the expression of a power relationship in which big boys forced small boys to be their slaves, using physical force to exercise their power (Dunning & Sheard, 1979). Punishment for failing to complete a task or for doing it badly was meted out, usually with a beating (Lamb, 1959).

It is also apparent that sexual irregularities were also rife within the boarding schools. For example, in the 1840s and 1850s the Harrow School has been portrayed as a "jungle where lust and brute strength raged completely unrestrained" (Gathorne-Hardy, 1977, p. 80). We find evidence of schoolmasters at various times and places deriving sexual pleasure from their beatings of young boys, of schoolmasters forming homosexual relationships with young boys, of older boys engaging in sexual relationships with younger boys, and of boys seeking emotional and physical intimacy from each other.

Because these homosexual practices occurred in an enclave within a society in which men were expected to be heterosexual, it is to be expected that many boarding-school boys experienced feelings of guilt and confusion over their sexuality. There was a strong latent fear of women that was based largely on ignorance about the opposite sex. This fear may also have originated from the sense of abandonment by the mother that the young boys felt when they were sent away to school. A person who was perceived as withdrawing her caring so that one could go to reside in an emotionally bleak environment may understandably be imbued with a tremendous amount of power and even malevolence. It thus becomes plausible that a society in which boys formed their most intimate contacts with other boys, in which they became confused and guilty about their sexuality, and in which women (in their absence) were regarded with wonder and fear, fostered unbalanced sexual attitudes. It is likely that following their adolescent years spent in single-sex schools, these boys frequently experienced difficulty making adjustments to mixed society and to relationships with the opposite sex. These difficulties likely stemmed from fear that one could be abandoned by a woman, from an inability to accept women as genuine people, and from a tendency to polarize females either into goddesses or into objects for sexual gratification (Lambert, 1966).

It is interesting that in an environment in which there was such a paucity of contact between males and females, it was necessary for young men to aggressively express independence from women and "womanly" men such as homosexuals. *It is our hypothesis that the development of the physically intimate aspects of the sport, as well as the attendant antifemale rituals, was provoked not only by the threat of intrusion of women into the masculine domain as suggested by previous sociological speculation but also as a reaction to early loss of the nurturant and emotionally responsive mother.* To examine this supposition we should first refer to the developmental literature and then explore the possible unresolved psychological issues that rugby rituals did and continue to work through.

RUGBY RITUALS AS AN OUTGROWTH OF EARLY SOCIALIZATION

A large body of work documents the tremendous impact of a child's experience in the first several years of life on later ego development and identity (e.g., Bloom, 1964). Never again in human development do so many physical, emotional, and cognitive changes occur in such a short period of time. To successfully negotiate the challenges of infancy and early childhood, the relatively helpless youngster must form an intensely intimate bond with the mother figure. Through this first strong and passionate relationship the child develops a sense of self, first as merged with the mother and then as a separate being (Coopersmith, 1967; Dinnerstein, 1976; Sears, 1970). Ideally, this relationship also provides the child with the emotional supplies necessary to explore the environment and relate adaptively to others.

Change in the Family Structure

Historically, the mothering role has been performed by females. Feminist psychoanalytic interpretations of the production and reproduction of gender roles suggest, however, that these roles are defined by both innate and social factors (Chodorow, 1978). Certainly, an examination of the role of the family through time demonstrates that gender roles are, at least in part, historical products. In preindustrial history the household was the major productive unit of society. In this form of social organization, although the female performed the physiological function of childbirth and lactation, mothering did not dominate women's lives (Chodorow, 1978). Women held productive as well as childbearing responsibilities. The primacy of the family as an economic unit meant that the father was also physically present and, it is plausible to argue, had more connection with his children, even if primary caretaking was performed mostly by women.

With the development of capitalism, and subsequently industrialization, the family declined in importance as an economic unit. Household necessities such as food, cloth, and clothing that were once produced by women were now mass-produced in factories (Chodorow, 1978). This change in the dominant mode of production had significant repercussions for the role of the family and for the social organization of gender. As Chodorow (1978) points out, the rise of urban industrial capitalism brought about a public/domestic (i.e., male/female) dichotomy in social life. Motherhood increasingly became defined as women's destiny, bread-winning as men's. Primary caretaking of children increasingly became a task solely performed by women, because men were actually physically removed from the home, often for up to 12 hours a day, 6 days a week. Participation in the labour force sharply reduced men's participation in family life. Through this process, then, the nurturant role of women became emphasized simultaneously with the eclipse of their economic role. In other words, the transformation of the dominant mode of production to capitalism resulted in the sexual division of labour as we know it today.

A result of men's physical and emotional distance from family life and their uninvolvement in child care is the burden on mothers in developing their sons' masculine identities. With the mother as primary caretaker, a boy must learn the masculine gender role in the relative absence of a masculine role model. Within a patriarchal society, however, masculinity is idealized. In this social milieu, Chodorow (1978) argues that for a boy:

> dependence on his mother, attachment to her, and identification with her represent that which is not masculine. . . . A boy rejects those qualities he takes to be feminine within himself, and rejects and devalues women and whatever he considers to be feminine in the social world. (p. 181)

The Intimacy Conflict

Although boys reject the "softness," closeness, and nurturance they associate with femininity, there is a simultaneous need for closeness and intimacy (Messner, 1987c). The need to maintain a separateness from affective relations and yet to retain the opportunity to seek closeness with others is resolved, it is argued, by psychological and cultural/ideological mechanisms (Horney, 1932).

Dinnerstein (1976), for example, suggests that resolution of the competing desires for female emotional sustenance and identification with men comes through gaining control over women and therefore one's own sense of vulnerability. This sense of control may be achieved by rejecting women, by denying them equal status in relationships, or by otherwise downplaying the role women take in meeting men's emotional needs. This solution eases the apparent conflict between the wish for ongoing access to intimacy and the wish to participate in masculine power-oriented activities.

The conflict between simultaneous longing for and rejection of emotional intimacy with the mother can be heightened if the young boy is separated from his parents, as in being sent to boarding school. In this situation, the child can be deprived of both the opportunity to distance himself from his mother and the perception that he has achieved some measure of independence from her, because this separation is forced upon him. He thus has to cope with both a perceived rejection by his nurturant caretaker and a relatively powerless relationship with his father and the older male students and instructors in the school. Bowlby (1969) speaks of the young child's distressed reaction to parental loss, and many subsequent writers have examined the link between loss of a significant relationship and childhood depression. The young boy is also deprived in the boarding-school environment of the emotional comforting and support that may help him cope with his loss. In a patriarchal society in which only women attend to boys' and men's emotional needs, a boy separated from his mother may be truly bereft.

We propose that in Victorian England, boys in boarding school developed intense and intimate relationships with each other, in part to forge their newfound masculinity and in order to compensate for the loss of nurturance from the primary parent. Rugby and its associated social practices served both to institutionalize these relationships and provide a context within which boys could act out ambivalent feelings toward the females who abandoned them. For example, the rough-and-tumble nature of the game may have substituted, at least in part, for the physical nurturance normally provided by the mother. The cultural forms involving the denigration of women that came to be associated with the game are also likely based, in part, on the early loss of the mother figure through segregation from her or the perceived need to give up feminine ties. In the socializing after the game, all players from the two opposing teams traditionally united in a hall or another area that was insulated from the presence of women to engage in heavy drinking, accompanied by the singing of songs to denigrate and vilify women and homosexuals. Songs peculiar to the nascent rugby subculture clearly express simultaneous aggression and desire for female sustenance. The best example we have encountered is a song whose chorus is "bite the nipple off, suck that tit," which expresses exquisitely the concurrent rage and need for the lost mother.

Rugby Songs and Rituals

The songs about homosexuals are also highly ambiguous and may have served either to legitimate the erotic feelings that these young men did, in fact, often develop toward each other or to mock homosexuality and, as such, validate heterosexual masculinity. Take, for example, the popular lyrics,

For we're all queers together,
Excuse us while we go upstairs,
For we're all queers together,
That's why we go 'round in pairs.

It is unclear whether the homosexual feelings and behaviours that were acted out in the boarding schools were reflections of a truly high rate of homosexuality in this population or whether they became a legitimized means of obtaining power and intimacy that could not be obtained through relationships with women. We suspect that the latter explanation is more plausible. It may be that in an all-male society, "women," or homosexuals, must be created so that the heterosexual males can obtain emotional caretaking from and/or power over supposedly inferior others. The Victorian boarding-school culture may have been similar to modern-day prisons for men, where situational homosexuality is widespread.

The tradition of singing songs in general may have formalized the link between all rugby players. Gathorne-Hardy (1977) comments on the role of song in strengthening solidarity among public school boys. Given the precariousness of individual relationships to family members and others, rugby players may have developed the tradition of song as an identifiable and easily recalled symbol of their enduring membership in a group. More recently, Messner (1987c) has argued that games and sports provide young men with the opportunity to connect with others in a context that maintains clear boundaries.

Postgame socializing also involved ritualized stripping. An example is the players' linking arms in a circle and singing the "Zulu Warrior" song while a young man in the middle takes off his clothes. It would be difficult to think of another context in which exhibition and celebration of the male body by other males can be accomplished outside of an overtly homoerotic situation. We argue that the intense physical contact in the game of rugby developed as a way to provide physical intimacy between the players, who originally were denied access to such contact from parental figures. Postgame consumption of alcohol subsequently lowered inhibitions and permitted even more explicit cohesion and bonding among males to the exclusion and rejection of females, who had previously been either unreliable in satisfying players' needs or unable to compete with pressure to "become a man." Some of the songs and nude activities allowed homoerotic expression in a macho and socially acceptable context.

The rituals of the rugby subculture also continue to meet the psychological needs of the young men who presently participate in it, although more for some than for others. It is interesting to note that most avid participants in the singing of antifemale songs and the ritualized nudity tend currently to be young men on university teams. These 18- to 22-year-old men are at an age at which they are moving out of adolescence and are struggling with the consolidation of adult identity. Some of the major developmental tasks they must contend with at this time include separating from parents, establishing sexual identity, and developing the ability to establish and maintain an adult love relationship. It is not unusual for late adolescents to experience conflicts concerning their dependencies on their parents. These adolescents may act rebellious or mildly antisocial in order to prove to themselves that they are indeed independent and/or to express anger at rules and restrictions that are placed on them. The drinking after rugby games, the deviance of many of the songs, and the ritualized stripping can allow players to act in a deviant and rebellious way while still remaining within the parameters of acceptable rugby behaviour.

Sexual identity and relationships also tend to be preoccupations of late-adolescent men. Pressures to become sexually experienced and skilled can create significant anxiety, especially when legitimate fears about relationships cannot be expressed. There appears among men to be a bravado regarding sex that masks a real vulnerability about whether they can in fact live up to women's expectations. Rugby rituals address these concerns about independence and sexuality in a concrete and socially acceptable way. Many of the songs are about sexually insatiable women and include lyrics reassuring young men that their concerns about sexual prowess are not unique. The "Engineer's Song," for example, tells how an engineer built a mechanical penis for his wife, who could "never be satisfied." In sum, the denigration of women and homosexuals also reduces their power and makes them appear less threatening on a personal level.

CONCLUSIONS

In summary, we offer a feminist psychoanalytic interpretation of the development of rugby and its attendant cultural forms. This approach is significant for a number of reasons. First, there has been sociological theorizing about the functions of rugby for men, but there has been virtually no examination of the psychological origins of the game and its rituals. The feminist psychoanalytic perspective lends itself to use in this study because rugby was developed by boys and men who experienced a critical separation from both mothers and women in general at a significant developmental stage. Females figure prominently in their virtual exclusion from the game of rugby and in their inclusion as objects of vilification in rugby songs. Feminist theory, therefore, provides some illumination of how this group of men's attitudes toward women were and continue to be shaped. We believe that feminist psychoanalytic theories can be as significant when applied to men as to women.

Second, we address the importance of the historical context that underlies our psychoanalytic interpretation. The extant historical and sociological writings on rugby provided an excellent platform for our arguments. The structure of the British boarding schools and their peculiar cultures furnished a unique milieu which, as we argue, likely had a cardinal impact on the psychological development of those given to their charge. The adoption and refinement of folk football by the young students living in these schools were congruent with the needs that likely developed from the types and consequences of the interpersonal relationships to which they were limited.

Third, and more speculatively, we feel that our analysis has some bearing on the contemporary functions not only of rugby but also of other sport forms that promulgate sexism and homophobia. The values that came to be imbued in the game of rugby as a consequence of its origins in the all-male boarding-school system have been, in our view, reproduced over time and are still normative within, as Sheard and Dunning (1973) would coin it, this "male enclave."

Proportionately few rugby players today have been separated from their mothers to attend boarding school, but the form of the game as well as the attendant rituals have been for the most part preserved. A comparison between the social and psychological forces of the present with those of Victorian England suggests that the relevant issues that perpetuate these practices are still salient. For example, whereas during the Industrial Revolution women were only beginning to make their economic and political presence felt, contemporary men must contend on an increasingly regular basis with competent women who can compete with them and potentially threaten them in academic, vocational, and social contexts. Contemporary women in general are less dependent on their partners for financial support than in the past and can thus make more demands on men for emotional responsiveness, shared household and parenting duties, and other previously feminine characteristics. The transition for men from adhering to traditionally masculine characteristics of autonomy, power over women, and emotional independence to meeting current demands for sensitivity, shared interpersonal responsibility, and the treatment of women as equals is novel. These changes represent an unprecedented loss in power in gender relationships. Moreover, the process of resocialization into new roles is hindered by an absence of appropriate models. The stress that these conflicting pressures can create may be relieved by retreating to the historically established masculine domain of rugby or to other sports that have come to act similarly as male enclaves. These sports may now provide a forum, perhaps even more than previously, for men to reaffirm their masculinity in an unambiguously male arena.

PART II

$\female$ $\male$

Contemporary Research

Feminist analyses of sport have expanded our understanding of various issues that are already familiar to sport sociologists (such as competition, aggression, violence, health, and injuries). In addition, feminist perspectives have raised issues and research questions that are not so familiar: the implications of sport for gender socialization; sport and sexuality; sport and the devaluation of women in male culture; and the conflicts and possibilities of "cross-sex sport." And, as the articles in this section demonstrate, when feminist perspectives on sport are extended to examine boys' and men's experiences in sport, myriad new and exciting research questions are raised.

In the first article, through an examination of a case study of an Australian "iron man," R.W. Connell illustrates some of the contradictory aspects of hegemonic masculinity. Though the iron man publicly symbolizes all that is valued in hegemonic masculinity—the highly skilled and powerful body, the supposedly virile heterosexuality, and the commercial success—his life and relationships are revealed to be both oppressive to women and extremely limiting to the man himself. In the next article, Michael Messner contrasts the meaning and experiences

79

of athletic careers for men from lower status (blue-collar, poor, and/or minority) backgrounds with those of men from higher status (middle-class, mostly white) backgrounds. Messner's findings—that there are similarities and important differences—underline Connell's point that social institutions such as sport must be examined in terms of how they structure relations between various masculinities, as well as between women and men. Along these same lines, Richard Majors argues in his article that racism makes living up to hegemonic conceptions of masculinity problematic for young black males, who find in sport a place to express a uniquely "cool pose."

The next two articles examine gender relations in specific athletic contexts. First, Don Sabo and Joe Panepinto examine the experiences of U.S. football players who labor under authoritarian coaches. The hierarchical relationship between coach and player is viewed within the context of social reproduction theory. The authors explore the extent to which young football players conform to or deviate from hegemonic models of masculinity, with a special focus on the social-psychological or ideological mechanisms that generate male bonding and compliance with patriarchal authority. Next, Alan Klein's case study of a southern California bodybuilding subculture raises fascinating issues concerning masculinity and the body. In the bodybuilding subculture, "gender narcissism" creates a context in which hustling and homophobia coexist, thus blurring the distinction—commonly so important in athletic contexts—between homosexual and heterosexual identity.

Next, Brian Pronger utilizes a phenomenological analysis to argue that because sport is essentially an institution in which heterosexual masculinity is constructed and naturalized, gay male athletes within this institution develop ironic sensibilities about themselves, their bodies, and sporting activity itself. Interestingly, Pronger's argument about gay men and sport raises some questions that are similar to those raised by Richard Majors's article on black athletes. Marginalized and subordinated men (gay or black) may find in sport an arena in which they can express a uniquely ironic or expressive masculinity that is, in some ways, resistant to the heterosexist or racist domination that these men face. Yet in adopting as their expressive vehicles many of the aspects of hegemonic masculinity as it is defined in sport, these men continue contributing to the subordination of women as well as further limiting their own relationships and personal development.

The final two articles in this section examine athletic contexts in which traditional conceptions of gender are being altered or challenged. First, Laurel Davis examines the recent phenomenon of men moving into cheerleading, an activity traditionally considered "feminine." Rather than constituting a breakdown of gendered boundaries in sport, Davis argues, male cheerleaders actively work to construct masculine identities in cheerleading. Thus, the hegemonic meaning of masculinity is reconstituted, but not essentially undermined. Finally, Ellen Staurowsky finds in her examination of women coaching male athletes that the presence of a female coach of boys' teams calls into question many patriarchal assumptions about sport and coaching itself. Her report of the discrimination and resistance that women coaches encounter from parents, teachers, and athletic administrators exposes the intricate ties between gender expectations and the perpetuation of male privilege and leadership in sport. These articles suggest that we cannot wish away (or play away) sexism, heterosexism, racism, and class inequalities without an expanded theory and practice of liberation, an issue that is taken up in Part III.

Chapter 6

An Iron Man: The Body and Some Contradictions of Hegemonic Masculinity[1]

R.W. Connell

It is a basic proposition of current research and political work on masculinity that masculine character is socially constructed, not inherited with the Y chromosome (Carrigan et al., 1985). A good deal of writing—unfortunately not so much actual research—has explored the processes through which masculinity is socially constructed. The main problem with this literature is that it has accepted (a) a unitary model of what masculinity is (the idea of the "male sex role") and (b) a more or less smooth and consensual idea of how character is constructed (through "socialization").

Both assumptions must now be rejected. It is clear that there are different kinds of masculine character within society that stand in complex relations of dominance over and subordination to each other (Connell, 1987b). What in earlier views of the problem passed for the "male sex role" is best seen as *hegemonic masculinity*, the culturally idealized form of masculine character (in a given historical setting), which may not be the usual form of masculinity at all. It is also clear that masculinities are constructed through processes that are often discontinuous or contradictory (and often experienced as such), for which the model of a "socializing agency" will not work. This has been most clearly seen in psychoanalytically influenced thinking about the formation of masculinity (Craib, 1987).

But though these points have now been clearly registered in theory, there is a conspicuous shortage of research that explores these dynamics and arrives at some practical grip on the current dialectic concerning masculinity.

In this paper I hope to add to the empirical material on hegemonic masculinity by means of a case study of a champion sportsman. The study is based on a tape-recorded life-history interview, one of a set obtained by Norm Radican, Pip Martin, and the author in an Australian study of contemporary changes in masculinity. The case raises interesting questions about the interplay between the body and social process in the construction of masculinity. The case suggests some lines of thought about sport and its commercialization as a phenomenon of gender and class relations.

I hope also to illustrate the usefulness of the life-history method for studying these social processes. There has been a recent revival of interest in life-history research, but it tends to be presented as merely the subjective side of social science (e.g., Plummer, 1983). I would argue that life-history research gives us a great deal more than this. Properly handled, the theorized life history can be a powerful tool for the study of social structures and their dynamics as they impinge on (and are reconstituted in) personal life.

BEING A CHAMPION

Steve Donoghue is an "iron man." This deliberately pretentious phrase is a technical term in surf sports. The iron-man race at surf carnivals is an event involving a combination of swimming, running, and surf-craft riding. Both short and long forms of the race exist; the long races may take 4-1/2 hours to complete. In surf sports, this event occupies a position analogous to a combination of the marathon and the pentathlon in track and field. A champion of the iron-man event holds a great deal of prestige. Steve is one of a very small group of athletes who trade the national championships among themselves.

Steve, who is in his early 20s, lives in a beachfront flat with his girlfriend. He gets up at 4:30 every morning to start his training, which takes 4 to 5 hours a day. When it is done he has the rest of the day to himself, because he has no job. More exactly, his job is to be an iron man and to market himself as a sports personality.

The training schedule is rigorous and, at his level of performance, essential—as Steve explains in a fascinating passage of the interview.

A   The main thing . . . is the discipline and motivations side of it. [If] you can't put the 5 hours in every day, it doesn't matter how old you are—you're not going to win. You've got to have the talent, you've got to have the technique and the ability and everything—and the training is what counts really. Your natural ability only takes you so far, about 60 to 70% of the way, and the rest is where the training comes in, and you've got to be able to. If you are 28 or 30 you have still got to have the time to train. [If you] haven't got business problems, or kids through marriage,

or whatever, well, then you'll be right . . . Just as long as you keep
loving it, you can keep backing up and wanting to train and really feeling
keen the whole time, you've got no troubles.

Where does the love come from?
I don't know. I love the beach. And I love the sun and everything to
do with the water. The waves, the water. I love the idea—I've always
loved this, even when I was at school—of being able to make a living
out of sport. I have loved the idea of not having to work, like a strict
9 to 5 set job, you know, like other people, being indoors . . . Five hours
a day is still a lot but it is something which I enjoy that people are not
telling me what to do. And there's not a set wage, if I go well I can
really make a lot of money out of it. I just like that. I like everything
to do with it really. I like the people I get involved with.

This lyrical picture of pleasure and success in the sun and water is characteristic
of Steve's self-presentation in the interview. Though there is ideology here, much
of the feeling and tone is genuine enough; Steve has realized a schoolboy dream.
It comes as something of a shock, then, to find that he also talks of his regime
this way:

B   You're up at 4:30 to go training and that goes most of the day. And you
are too tired to go out anyway and you've got to get your rest. It is a
pretty disciplined sort of life. It's like being in jail.

This sudden douche of cold water comes in the middle of a discussion about
girl friends. Steve notes that "a lot of the guys don't have girl friends." It is
just too hard to combine with training: "The girl wants to go out with you all
the time and, you know, party here and there." This affects the athlete's performance. So Steve's coach "doesn't like it, tries to put it down, tries to stop anything
serious." (The coach has a financial interest in his athlete's performance, although
Steve does not mention this.)
Steve has a girl friend, who drifted in and out during the interview. And that
seems to be her status in Steve's life, too. She is given a clear message about
what really counts for him:

C   Yes, I've got a girl friend. I think there is no problem as long as you
don't have to go out all the time, [as long as] they understand that, and
you've got to take training first, and competition first. That's your living,
that's your life. That's what I enjoy the most. It is hard, though . . .
It's good if you have a girl friend that is involved with sport, involved
with the same sort of interest that you've got. Not iron man or like that!
But the same sort of, doing the training here and there so it can work
out. Well, when you're doing some training, well, they'll do something
else. And if you have someone who is completely different, which I have
had girl friends in the past like that, it doesn't seem to work. You might

start off all right, but you end up splitting up, because you fight all the time. It gets on their nerves when you are training all the time, you won't go out here and there. It's just ratshit.

What would be the attraction for the "girls" in Steve's life (the slightly childish language is also characteristic) in having a lifestyle not far removed from that of an armchair? In the first place, this is par for the course in the Australian surfing subculture, which is male supremacist to a marked degree (Pearson, 1982). If a "girl" stands up for her own interests, Steve disposes of her and acquires another. As he notes complacently elsewhere in the interview, he has "never had trouble" with sexual relationships. And in conventional terms, he is a real catch. He is handsome, healthy, easygoing, sexually experienced, famous, and on the verge of becoming rich.

Steve's "job" of being an iron man nets him around $100,000 a year in prizes, sponsorships, and endorsements. This is a phenomenal income for a young man with no inherited property who is recently out of high school. Asked where he would see himself in 5 years' time, he replies simply, "A millionaire." His aim is to have $1 million by the time he retires, at about 30. At present he is expanding his sponsorship deals with several large companies, is buying into surf businesses, and has just signed up with a multinational marketing company:

D   I just want to keep winning, keep winning, and keep rolling the money. So when I do get off I've got something to show for what I've done.

Fame is accepted with the same combination of pleasure and complacency as the cash and the sex. He wanted fame, and now he enjoys it. But there is a problem:

E   Well, you can go out at night and you've got to set an example for yourself. You can't go stupid like other people can. Like Joe Blow can get away with drunk-driving charges and no one will know. If it was me it would be on the front page. Things may be not even that serious. Because if I was just mucking around down the street—it's hard really, people think "He's got to do this" and they set you in a certain way . . . behave in your own limits, you can't go wild or anything. If I go out at night I can't get in a fight. That can happen because people think they can . . . say smart comments, and you can hear them, and they try and big-note themselves with friends. And I've had fights before where people have, I have just snapped. But that's only happened once or twice, that's not bad really, considering some of the situations I've had.

This is very much a problem about masculinity. Steve, the exemplar of masculine toughness, finds his own exemplary status prevents him from doing exactly what his peer group defines as thoroughly masculine behaviour: going wild, showing off, drunk driving, getting into fights, defending his own prestige. It is also clear in this passage how social the whole business is—the smart-aleck banter among friends, the social pressure that "sets you in a certain way." Here we have a vivid glimpse of the production of an exemplary masculinity as a *collective practice*. It is an accomplishment not of Steve as an individual (throughout this passage he is kicking against the pricks), but of the whole social network in which Steve finds himself enmeshed.

SOFT PATH, HARD GOAL

How did he get to be an exemplar of masculinity? Steve's own account of his childhood and adolescence portrays a simple progression from active child to schoolboy hero to adult champion. He seems to swim endlessly through a warm bath of admiration from family, teachers, and friends. His grandfather was a sporting hero in his generation, and Steve pictures himself as growing up effortlessly in the same mould.

Without denying the reality of this euphoric picture, we may question what it means. Steve's childhood was not a conventional idyll: His parents separated when he was young, and he has few memories of the family together. His clearest childhood memory of his father is a game of hide-and-seek on the day of the weekly visit, when his father vanished and could not be found for 45 minutes. At the least, this is a memory of anxiety. It is hardly overinterpreting to suggest that this remains a haunting memory, because the "lost father" was and is a major emotional issue for Steve.

His mother ran the show, and she figures as the main adult in Steve's narrative of growing up. She moved with her children to another city, paid Steve's school fees (at a private school—the family was wealthy), encouraged and organized his swimming, and paid for his travel to championship meetings. He sees her as having the same qualities as him—"intelligent and strong like I am"—and unwilling to be pushed around. There is some identification here, and she remains an emotional presence for him. Asked near the end of the interview his views on violence, he says the only scene he can imagine that would provoke him to murder would be "if someone killed my mother." The girl friend does not figure. (Nor does the conventional idea that a man looks for a partner like his mother make any sense in this case.)

Yet Steve also records, without apparent emotion, that she moved to another city after the children had left the nest; the loss does not seem to be devastating. Indeed, he is now pleased to be reestablishing contact with his father, who is taking an interest in his son's career and helping him negotiate sponsorship deals. Steve has not lacked figures to model himself on: grandfather, father, mother, and even mother's lover, who turns out to be another champion, if not quite of the top rank. Of the four figures it is the most remote figure, the grandfather, with whom Steve prefers to identify. There is a slightly eerie sense of "the double" here:

F I myself got most of my talent and who I am, sporting-ability-wise, from my Mum's dad. He was a sporting freak . . . good at all different sports. That's where I was lucky to get it. He was a lot like me when he was

younger, I've seen a lot of photos. There was one photo in particular
when he had just joined the army, in his uniform. It scared the shit out
of me because it was my hair on the—it was exactly—I just freaked out.
"No this can't be right," it was amazing.

The emphasis on the remote grandfather is interesting, because everything else
points to Steve's having been inserted into his career by a close network of family,
friends, and school. He remembers anxiety about moving up to high school—
fear of being physically beaten up by the big boys—but soon formed a group
of friends and stuck with them right through school. Physically big as a child,
he did well in school sporting events and particularly well in swimming. By age
13 he was far enough advanced in formal competition that he gave up football
in order to specialize in swimming—a decision that signals the shift from sport
as pleasure to sport as a kind of career.

Sport was a career path that elicited a lot of communal support. Steve was the
school swimming champion, and his prowess won the district competition for
his school. He was "a bit of a hero" and a leader among his peers, and he was
treated with indulgence by his teachers. As we have noticed, his mother supported
this effort for all she was worth: No doubt parents derive considerable pleasure
from having a sporting hero for a child. Steve's regime as a teenager involved
swimming in the morning, school in the day, then more swimming at night. He
didn't much want to study, and he completed high school mainly because his
friends were still there. When he left school, the study part simply dropped out
of his day and the swimming part went on.

At this point Steve was handed over to a new network, and the transition has
been complete—Steve hardly sees the once close-knit group of high school friends
any more. Asked what makes someone decide to take up the iron-man event,
Steve describes a social practice rather than a choice:

> **G**   There is no decision really. It's just that you've got to be round the beach
> for starters. And you have got to be involved with the surf club, so that
> narrows it right down. You've got to have a love of the water. You've
> got to have a swimming background, pretty well. And you've got to be
> disciplined and dedicated enough to put the time and work in.

The surf club is a key part of the new network. Steve joined it as a teenager
and was thus absorbed into a slightly older peer group, a group of young adult
men absorbed in a cult of physical masculinity. The surf club in Australia is a
high-profile voluntary organization with a public service rationale—it organizes
beach lifesaving services—but also with a strong sporting and social flavour. Its
networks merge into competitive sport on one side and consumer capitalism
(especially advertising and sporting goods retailing) on the other. In both directions, Steve was brought into contact with "older guys" and absorbed some of
their sexual, commercial, and technical know-how. His first coital experience
was organized at the surf club and witnessed by his friends there, when he was
about 17:

H   I remember the first time I had sex with a girl; I was at a toga party down at S. Surf Club and I was round the rocks and that—pretty funny, yes—all the guys came round and watched. . . . She was older than me, she must have been over 20 I'd say, and she just dragged me round there. I just thought "oh here we go." . . . I was really drunk anyway and I was sort of laughing. "Where are we going?" . . . I had all the boys following me so I had to put on a good show.

Did they watch?
Yes.

Did that bother you?
No, I was laughing. I ran back and I was the hero.

As his career became focussed and he began to earn big money, Steve's peer group once again narrowed and stabilized. "My friends are the guys I train with." The replay is almost conscious: "All the training you do, and all the time you put in, you are around them nearly as much as you are at school." With his authoritarian trainer in the role of a schoolmaster, the continuity is striking, though the setting is now different. The peer group travels around the country to the big events, and the classroom furnishings are black leather-upholstered couches, expensive video systems, and live-in girl friends.

THE BODY AND THE SELF

Masculinity is not inherent in the male body; it is a definition given socially to certain characteristics. Masculinity requires, of course, some somatic compliance, to use Freud's phrase from another context. If the body is very much at odds with the social definition, there is trouble, as in the situations of transvestites and transsexuals. In Steve's case, the somatic compliance was being tall and strong as a child.

He remembers this with pleasure, and the key to the memory is the social meaning of being big. Steve's bodily attributes were appropriated in quite specific social practices. One was the rough-and-tumble atmosphere of an all-boys school, where Steve's group depended on him:

I   We all stuck together; it was really good. I was sort of—I was always bigger than the rest of the guys, I sort of looked after them.

The element of nurturance here is very interesting. The other practice was competitive sport organized by adults. Steve's size meant that he won competitive events early on, consistently enough to define him as a champion in the making. His body was certainly given this definition before adolescence, because at 13 he was making the career decision to specialize in swimming.

In Steve's pseudotechnical discussion of the components of success, quoted in Extract A, he acknowledges both elements. He calls the somatic compliance "natural ability," and he theorizes it as inherited from his grandfather (Extract F). He also acknowledges the highly specific social practice that appropriates the body (training, feeling keen, not having business problems) and turns it into an engine of competitive success.

To call this discussion pseudotechnical is to say that Steve's representation of this process is highly ideological. (I would guess he is quoting his coach, whose relation to sporting ideology is discussed in the next section.) This is not to deny Steve's precise knowledge of his body and its capacities. All top-level sports performers do have this knowledge. Indeed, it is common among adolescent boys engaged in sport, whatever their level of skill. Teenage football (soccer) players "develop an accurate and detailed knowledge of their own bodies' capacities, and their exact suitability for different positions in the team" (Connell, 1983, p. 19). Steve Donoghue is quite eloquent about the particular kind of skill that is involved in top-level performance in his sport. It is far from being pure brawn.

J   I can spread my energy over a 4-hour race to not die, to not have to start up slowly. I can start at a pace and finish at a pace every time. When I swam, I used to do 200 metres, which is four 50-metre laps. I can start off, and any 50 is pretty well to the tenth of a second the same time each lap, and I wouldn't even be looking at a watch . . . It's mental. You've got to be fit to do it, but there are so many guys that are fit and not many are able to do that . . . I'm just lucky naturally. But also distance-wise I can measure the distance out without having to think about it and say "Right this pace you are going, you will be able to keep going to the end and you will have no energy left at the end— you will have done the best race you can do over that distance." And I've just done that all the time.

What Steve calls "being lucky naturally" is in fact a skill developed by 10 years of hard practise.

There is more to this than a technical knowledge of skills and capacities. Steve's whole person has become caught up in practices that centre on his body and its performances. Asked "Where would you like to be as Steve? Nothing to do with business or money, just you," he fumbles and then starts to grapple with this nexus:

K   I haven't even thought about it. I might be just the way I am, but I don't, I never look to the future. Everything is—not day to day—but season to season. I am more interested in winning and racing than anything, and that takes up my whole time, all the preparation and the time I put in. Last winter I was up at T. [surf resort]; we were training 5 hours a day, and the only thing I was thinking about was getting through that day and getting to the next day. Having to make my body, too much energy and not enough rest, to be functional at as good a rate for the next day's training session. That is all I would be thinking about.

In effect, the body becomes the focus of the self in quite a radical way. Social life is drastically curtailed to suit the logic of peak bodily performance. As Steve remarked (Extract B), "It's like being in jail." Even more strikingly for a fit young heterosexual, sexual life is monitored and constricted because of its effect on performance. The kind of regime Steve sustained at school, and sustains now, leaves little room or energy for interests outside his sport. Even his casual peer group life is centred on others in the sport. Despite coming from a bourgeois background, he had little interest in schoolwork, seems to have no cultural interests beyond popular music, and cannot sustain a relationship with a woman who has interests outside of sport (Extract C).

The picture, then, is of a psychological focus on the body together with a severely constricted social world and an impoverished cultural world. This is confirmed by a series of questions, asked at the end of the interview, about Steve's views on current issues. They are conventional to the point of banality:

L *Feminists?*

I don't like the ones that dress up in men's clothes and that sort of stuff, but I just think I don't mind women doing that sort of stuff. I'm the sort of guy that opens the car door for a girl all the time.

Gay men?

I've got no gay friends—I don't think I have. I'm not into television and hairdressing and anything like that. . . . As long as they keep to themselves and away from me I'm happy. I'm against them really. I can't see the reason why they are—I can't understand it—but a lot of people say they are born that way so I don't know. I'm [with a laugh] not into bashing them or anything like that.

Politics?

Nothing to do with it whatsoever. . . . The last vote they had here I didn't even know it was on that day. [Voting is compulsory in Australia.] I was down the beach in the surf.

In this bleached, featureless world centred on the care and maintenance of his body, punctuated by races, it is not surprising that Steve's only tangible goal (Extract D) is to collect dollars: "Keep winning, keep winning, and keep rolling the money." He has in view no use for the money except being able to live in comfort, so his only way of defining a purpose is to pick an arbitrary figure. The $1 million is "just a goal, just something that I might aim for"; he is almost apologetic about its arbitrariness. The business of winning has consumed his life. With everything in life subordinated to bodily performance as the means of success, there is nothing very tangible that the success is for; so a goal has to be invented within the mechanism of races and dollars to give Steve the impression that his effort is leading to something worthwhile.

This cycle could, of course, be disrupted, and the most likely disruptions are an injury (Steve has had some); a pregnancy (Steve could easily afford an abortion but the girl friend of the day might insist on marriage and in that case would have a lot of social pressure behind her); or the emergence of a new champion who overshadows Steve and thus undermines his worth to sponsors. The last will certainly happen in time, but Steve has specialized in an event in which champions are good for a relatively long period. He has carefully researched this point and has concluded that an iron man does not peak until "around 30 or close to . . . so in that way I've got at least 5 years left."

WANTING TO WIN: THE IDEOLOGY OF COMMERCIAL SPORT

Steve's attempts to make sense of his experience—his daily life is a highly unusual one for a young man—draw heavily on the ideological complex that has developed around the intersection of competitive sport and the commercial mass media. This nexus gives him his livelihood, so it is, not surprisingly, his first port of call for interpretations.

Very much in the foreground is the business of winning. The classic Olympic ethic of valuing the participation rather than the victory—always contradictory in competitive sports—is ignored and with it amateurism. Steve has always seen sport as a way of earning a living (Extract A). To do that he has to win, keep winning (Extract D), and be focussed on winning all the time (Extracts C and K).

The basis for this is "natural talent" and being "lucky" in one's capacities (Extract A and J). This is media talk: It is the language in which a champion projects modesty in a television or newspaper interview after a big victory. The talent has to be developed, and Steve claims to have added to what nature gave him. It is again characteristic of media constructions of championship that this claim is a moral one. Steve acquires ideological virtue by his rigorous training regime; this is what he insists makes a champion.

Steve does not talk much about his coach in the interview, but the coach's presence is clear. Leading coaches often function as organic intellectuals (Gramsci's [1971] phrase) of commercial sport, articulating a meaning for, and a public defence of, the practices in which the whole industry is engaged. Coaches are likely to be a good deal older than the youthful champions, and to a considerable extent their successes as coaches depend more on their skills as ideologists—persuading their charges to stick to the training regime and psyching them up for big events—than on their technical knowledge. An index of this is the spectacular failure of the government-funded Australian Institute of Sport, over the last few years, to make its more technocratic approach to sport training the dominant one.

Steve gives an interesting glimpse of his coach's ideological tactics:

M When I compete for a big race I get myself worked up. My coach has always said he used tactics like hating people—well, not hate—but, I suppose hate the opposition through things they have said about me. And he uses that to get me riled up to win, thinks I always get better when I am angry. And he has used that, he has even put that in [media] articles and stuff.

Clearly, Steve's coach is trying to articulate masculinity and sporting performance through aggression. It is a common tactic in body-contact sports like football.

I have the impression that this is not a very appropriate device for Steve. He is not an aggressive character. The tone in which he discusses his sport is euphoric, not mean; he talks more about loving the water than wanting to do down enemies. He is certainly competitive, but that is a settled practice, a feature of the organization of his life, rather than an outgrowth of hostility. When Steve talks about the psychological side of competition, he inflects it in a rather different way. He talks of 'mental toughness' and his ability to 'control the pain' and to 'make my body believe that I am not hurting as much as I am.'

Again this is borrowed language: Steve got these terms from sport psychologists who tested him and explained to him their ideas about why he won. But it is probably closer to the particular version of masculinity that Steve has constructed for himself around the lonely business of long-distance sporting performance. This is an inward-turned competitiveness, focussed on the self.

The commercialization of sport gives Steve one other way of seeing himself.

N The thing with sponsors is that they are after an individual. The people I am sponsored with, except the beer company, it's just me. It's no one else to do with the surf, or anything like that. So obviously they were after what I had done, and also my personality, my looks.

You haven't ever felt like a body being marketed?
No not really. I'm an individual. It's funny, like even with board riding there might be a bloke who is not as good as the other guy but his personality, and just the way his charisma—he'll get a bigger amount of sponsorship than the other guy. It's just an individuality.

The irony of this, given what we have already seen of the impoverished social and cultural life Steve leads, hardly needs underlining. A "personality," in media terms, is simply someone who has publicity; it is a question of recognizability, not of content. So even Steve's claim to individuality is a standard package constructed for him by his employers.

REFLECTIONS

Steve lives an exemplary version of hegemonic masculinity. To live it does not mean to understand it. Steve has great trouble giving an account of masculinity when directly asked to explain his remark that "men should be men":

O I don't know, I really don't know. I just meant that as—I think just being strong and not—I was talking about gays, I think. I don't know. I don't even know why I said it really, just came out.

What do you think it means to be a man, for you?
Not be a gay; I don't know. I've done interviews on that sort of stuff
before, people said, "You're scared of spiders and all that sort of stuff?"
Yes I am; I have got fears like any other people. I am scared of heights.
So I don't think any of that has got anything to do with being a man.

The best he can do, with a lot of beating about the bush, is "be strong" and "not be a gay." Other respondents in our study, less exemplary than Steve, have much more complex and fluent answers to this question.

The exclusion of homosexual desire from the definition of masculinity is, of course, a key feature of modern hegemonic masculinity (Carrigan et al., 1985), and it makes sense for Steve to grasp at this straw, especially because his life has long been substantially homosocial (i.e., an all-boys' school, a masculinized surf club and peer group, and a masculinized sport). His consciousness of this is tellingly shown by his specific (and quite unnecessary) exclusion of iron-man events as possible sports for his girl friends (Extract C). It is a familiar point that there is a lot of homosexual affect floating around in such milieux. Steve simply blanks this out (Extract L).

To say that a particular form of masculinity is hegemonic means that it is culturally exalted and that its exaltation stabilizes a structure of dominance and oppression in the gender order as a whole. To be culturally exalted, the pattern of masculinity must have exemplars who are celebrated as heroes. Steve certainly enacts in his own life some of the main patterns of contemporary hegemonic masculinity: the subordination of women, the marginalization of gay men, and the connecting of masculinity to toughness and competitiveness. He has also been celebrated as a hero for much of his life, in school and in adult sport. He is being deliberately constructed now as a media exemplar of masculinity by the advertisers who are sponsoring him.

It is here that the contradictions poke out. Being an exemplar of masculinity actually forbids Steve to do many things that his peer group and culture define as masculine (Extract E). Steve experiences this prohibition as a very tangible pressure. Similarly, sustaining the training regime that yields the bodily supremacy, giving him his status as a champion, is incompatible with the kind of sexual and social life that is expected by affluent young men (Extract C). In this case Steve's coach articulates the prohibition, and Steve manoeuvres around it as best he can.

At a deeper level, the articulation of self and body that sustains Steve's performance is contradictory. We have noticed the focussing of both his social and his psychological life on the body and the inward-turned competitiveness that seems related to his particular sport. There is a definite narcissism here, a point that has often enough been observed about athletes. This is a problem within the dominant cultural construction of masculinity as outward turned and denying the subjective.

Even more of a problem, the narcissism is necessarily unstable, unable to rest in self-admiration or indulgence (which would destroy the performance). In Steve's construction of competition (see Extracts A, G, J, and K and his remarks about controlling pain), the decisive triumph is over oneself and specifically over one's body. The magnificent machine of Steve's physique has meaning only when subordinated to the will to win. And that, as we have already seen, is a curiously hollow construction in Steve's psychological makeup. The will to win does not arise from personal "drive" (a familiar word in sport talk that Steve, tellingly, does not use at all). It is given to him by the social structure of sporting competition. It is his meaning, as a champion.

So we are returned to the social structures in which masculinities are produced. Indeed, we are led to see masculinity as an aspect of social structure, not just a form of personal character. As an aspect of gender relations, here meshed with consumer capitalism, hegemonic masculinity appropriates Steve's body and gives it a social definition. But it does this in ways that are full of contradiction, visible even behind the euphoria of Steve's tale of pleasure and success.

The long-term effect is hard to judge, but the short-term effect is clear. Steve gets his pleasure and success at the cost of his adulthood. I have remarked on oddly childish turns of phrase and thought and on the psychological continuity of Steve's life since the beginning of high school. He is, of course, young, but most other men his age are facing the problems of earning livelihood, constructing long-term relationships, building households, making hard choices, and facing social issues. Steve has been taken in hand by the institutions of competitive sport and commerce and protected from common issues and problems. Though Steve cannot see it, for he has little experience of the world, his employers genuinely do not want an individual. They want someone to occupy a spot constructed by the social organisation of masculinity and the needs of commerce: a handsome, happy, nicely spoken, beach-sport hero who will make no difficulties about advertising their products. (Steve is, for example, sponsored by a beer company, which not everyone would see as a responsible move by a sporting champion.) At the moment he neatly fits the spot, and as long as he keeps up his winning status and his image, the money will keep rolling in and Steve will be preserved in his extended adolescence. One wonders what resources he will find for handling adulthood when the winning stops.

Chapter 7

Masculinities and Athletic Careers: Bonding and Status Differences[1]

Michael A. Messner

The growth of women's studies and feminist gender studies has in recent years led to the emergence of a new men's studies (Brod, 1987; Kimmel, 1987b). But just as feminist perspectives on women have been justifiably criticized for falsely universalizing the lives and issues of white, middle-class U.S. women (Baca Zinn et al., 1986; Hooks, 1984), so, too, men's studies has tended to focus on the lives of relatively privileged men. As Brod (1983/1984) points out in an insightful critique of the middle-class basis and bias of the men's movement, if men's studies is to be relevant to minority and working-class men, less emphasis must be placed on personal lifestyle transformations and more on developing a structural critique of social institutions. Although some institutional analysis has begun in men's studies, very little critical scrutiny has been focused on that very masculine institution—organized sports (Messner, 1985a; Sabo, 1985; Sabo & Runfola, 1980). Not only is the institution of sport an ideal place to study men and masculinity, careful analysis of sport would make it impossible to ignore the realities of race and class differences.

In the early 1970s, H. Edwards (1971, 1973) debunked the myth that the predominance of blacks in sports to which they have access signaled an end to institutionalized racism. It is now widely accepted in sport sociology that social institutions such as the media, education, the economy, and (a more recent and controversial addition to the list) the black family itself all serve to systematically channel disproportionately large numbers of young black men into football, basketball, boxing, and baseball, where they are subsequently "stacked" into low-prestige and high-risk positions, exploited for their skills, and, finally, when their bodies are used up, excreted from organized athletics at a young age with no transferable skills with which to compete in the labor market (H. Edwards, 1984; Eitzen & Purdy, 1986; Eitzen & Yetman, 1977).

Although there are racial differences in involvement in sport, it seems that class, age, and education differences are more significant. Rudman's (1986) initial analysis revealed profound differences between whites' and blacks' orientations to sports. Blacks were found to be more likely than whites to view sports favorably, to incorporate sports into their daily lives, and to be affected by the outcome of sporting events. However, when age, education, and social class were factored into the analysis, Rudman found that race did not explain whites' and blacks' different orientations. Blacks' affinity to sports is best explained by their tendencies to be clustered disproportionately in lower income groups.

The 1980s ushered in what Wellman (1986) calls a "new political linguistics of race" (p. 43), which emphasizes cultural rather than structural causes (and solutions) to the problems faced by black communities. The advocates of the cultural perspective believe that the high value placed on sports by black communities has led to the development of unrealistic hopes in millions of black youths. These advocates appeal to family and community to bolster other choices based upon a more rational assessment of "reality." Visible black role models in many other professions now exist, they say, and there is ample evidence to prove that sports careers are, at best, bad gambles.

Critics of the cultural perspective have condemned it as conservative and victim blaming. But it can also be seen as a response to the image of black athletes as little more than unreflexive dupes of an all-powerful system that ignores the importance of agency. Gruneau (1983) has argued that sport must be examined within a theory that views human beings as active subjects who operate within historically constituted structural constraints. Gruneau's reflexive theory rejects the simplistic views of sport as either a realm of absolute oppression or an arena of absolute freedom and spontaneity. Instead, he argues, it is necessary to construct an understanding of how and why participants themselves actively make choices and construct and define meaning and a sense of identity within the institutions in which they find themselves.

None of these perspectives considers the ways that gender shapes men's definitions of meaning and choices. Within the sociology of sport, gender as a process that interacts with race and class is usually ignored or taken for granted—except when women athletes are studied. Sociologists who attempt to come to grips with the experiences of black men in general, in organized sport in particular, have almost exclusively focused their analytic attention on the variable *black* while uncritically taking *men* as a given. Hare and Hare (1984), for example, view masculinity as a biologically determined tendency to act as a provider and protector that is thwarted for black men by socioeconomic and racist obstacles. Staples (1982) does view masculinity largely as a socially produced script, but he accepts this script as a given, preferring to focus on black men's blocked access to male role fulfillment. These perspectives on masculinity fail to show how the male role itself, as it interacts with a constricted structure of opportunity, can contribute to locking black men into destructive relationships and lifestyles (Franklin, 1984a; Majors, 1986).

This chapter will examine the relationships among male identity, race, and social class by listening to the voices of former athletes. I will first briefly describe my research. Then I will discuss the similarities and differences in the choices and experiences of men from different racial and social class backgrounds. Together, these choices and experiences help to construct what Connell (1987b) calls "the gender order." Organized sport, it will be suggested, is a practice through which men's separation from and power over women is embodied and naturalized while hegemonic (white, heterosexual, professional-class) masculinity is clearly differentiated from marginalized and subordinated masculinities.

DESCRIPTION OF RESEARCH

Between 1983 and 1985, I conducted 30 open-ended in-depth interviews with male former athletes. My purpose was to add a critical understanding of male gender identity to Levinson's (1978) conception of the "individual lifecourse"—specifically, to discover how masculinity develops and changes as a man interacts with the socially constructed world of organized sports. Though the sample was not randomly selected, an effort was made to see that the sample reflected a range of difference in terms of social class background, race, age, and levels of success in athletic careers. Most of the men I interviewed had played the (U.S.) major sports: football, basketball, baseball, and track. At the time of the interview, each had been retired from playing organized sports for at least 5 years. Their ages ranged from 21 to 48, with the median age 33. Fourteen were black, 14 were white, and 2 were hispanic. Fifteen of the 16 black and hispanic men had come from poor or working-class families, whereas the majority (9 of 14) of the white men had come from middle-class or professional families. Twelve had played organized sports through high school, 11 through college; 7 had been professional athletes. All had at some time in their lives based their identities largely on their roles as athletes and could therefore be said to have had athletic careers.

MASCULINE IDENTITY AND ORGANIZED SPORT

Earlier studies of masculinity and sport argued that sport socializes boys to be men (Lever, 1976; Schafer, 1975). Through sport, boys learn cultural values and behaviors such as competition, toughness, and winning at all costs, which are culturally valued aspects of masculinity. Although offering important insights, these early studies of masculinity and sport suffered from the limiting assumptions of a sex role theory that seems to assume that boys come to their first athletic experiences as blank slates onto which the values of masculinity are imprinted. This perspective oversimplifies a complex reality. In fact, a young boy brings an already-gendered identity to his first sports experience, an identity that is struggling to work through the developmental task of individuation (Chodorow, 1978; Gilligan, 1982). Yet, as Benjamin (1988) has argued, individuation is accomplished, paradoxically, only through relationships with other people in the social world. So, though the major task of masculinity is the development of a positional identity that clarifies the boundaries between self and other, this separation must be accomplished through some form of connection with others. For the men in my study, the rule-bound structure of organized sports became a context in which they struggled to construct masculine positional identities.

All of the men in this study described the emotional salience of their earliest experiences in sports in terms of relationships with other males. It was not winning and victories that seemed important at first; it was something fun to do with fathers, older brothers or uncles, and eventually with same-aged peers. As a man from a white middle-class family said, "The most important thing was just being out there with the rest of the guys—being friends." A 32-year-old man from a poor chicano family, whose mother had died when he was 9 years old, put it more succinctly:

> What I think sports did for me is it brought me into kind of an instant family. By being on a Little League team, or even just playing with kids in the neighborhood, it brought what I really wanted, which was some kind of closeness.

Though sports participation may have initially promised "some kind of closeness," by the ages of 9 or 10, the less skilled boys were already becoming alienated from—or weeded out of—the highly competitive and hierarchical system of organized sports. Those who did experience some early successes received recognition from adult males (especially fathers and older brothers) and held higher status among peers. As a result, these boys began to pour more and more of their energies into athletic participation. It was only after they learned that they would get recognition from other people for being good athletes—indeed, that this attention was contingent upon being a winner—that performance and winning (the dominant values of organized sports) became extremely important. For some, this created pressures that served to lessen or eliminate the fun of athletic participation (Messner, 1987a, 1987b).

Although feminist psychoanalytic and developmental theories of masculinity are helpful in explaining boys' early attractions to and motivations in organized sports, the imperatives of core gender identity do not fully determine the contours and directions of the life course. As Rubin (1985) and Levinson (1978) have pointed out, an understanding of the lives of men must take into account the process-like nature of male identity as it unfolds through interaction between the internal (psychological ambivalences) and the external (social, historical, and institutional) contexts.

To examine the impact of the social contexts, I divided my sample into two comparison groups. The first group comprised 10 men from higher status backgrounds, primarily white, middle-class, and professional families. The second group comprised 20 men from lower status backgrounds, primarily minority, poor, and working-class families. Although my data offered evidence for the similarity of experiences and motivations of men from poor backgrounds, independent of race, I also found anecdotal evidence of a racial dynamic that operates independently of social class. However, my sample was not large enough to separate race and class, so I have combined them to make two status groups.

In discussing these two groups, I will focus mainly on the high school years. During this crucial period, the athletic role may become a master status for a young man, who is beginning to make assessments and choices about his future. It is here that many young men make major commitments to—or begin to back away from—athletic careers.

Men From Higher Status Backgrounds

The boyhood dream of one day becoming a professional athlete—a dream shared by nearly all the men interviewed in this study—is rarely realized. The sports world is extremely hierarchical. The pyramid of sports careers narrows very rapidly as one climbs from high school, to college, to professional levels of competition (H. Edwards, 1984; Harris & Eitzen, 1978; Hill & Lowe, 1978). In fact, the chances of attaining professional status in sports are approximately 4/100,000 for a white man, 2/100,000 for a black man, and 3/1,000,000 for a hispanic man in the United States (Leonard & Reyman, 1988). For many young athletes, their dreams end early when coaches inform them that they are not big enough, strong enough, fast enough, or skilled enough to compete at the higher levels.

Decision to Forgo a Sports Career.   Six of the higher status men I interviewed did not wait for coaches to weed them out. They made conscious decisions in high school or in college to shift their attentions elsewhere, usually toward educational and career goals. Their decisions not to pursue athletic careers appeared to them, in retrospect, to be rational decisions based on the growing knowledge of how very slim were their chances for success in the sports world. For instance, a 28-year-old white graduate student said:

> By junior high I started to realize that I was a good player—maybe even one of the best in my community—but I realized that there were all these people all over the country and how few will get to play pro sports. By high school, I still dreamed of being a pro—I was a serious athlete, I played hard—but I knew it wasn't heading anywhere. I wasn't going to play pro ball.

A 32-year-old white athletic director at a small private college had been a successful college baseball player. Despite considerable attention from professional scouts, he had decided to forgo a shot at a baseball career and enter graduate school to pursue a teaching credential. As he said:

> At the time I think I saw baseball as pissing in the wind, really. I was married; I was 22 years old with a kid. I didn't want to spend 4 or 5 years in the minors with a family. And I could see I wasn't a superstar, so it wasn't really worth it. So I went to grad school. I thought that would be better for me.

Perhaps most striking was the story of a high school student-body president and top-notch student who was also "Mr. Everything" in sports. He was named captain of his basketball, baseball, and football teams and achieved all-league honors in each sport. This young white man from a middle-class family received attention from the press and praise from his community and peers for his athletic accomplishments, as well as several offers of athletic scholarships from universities. But by the time he completed high school, he had already decided to quit playing organized sports. As he said:

> I think in my own mind I kind of downgraded the stardom thing. I thought that was small potatoes. And sure, that's nice in high school and all that, but on a broad scale, I didn't think it amounted to all that much. So I decided that my goal's to be a dentist, as soon as I can.

In this man's sophomore year of college, the basketball coach nearly persuaded him to go out for the team, but eventually he decided against it:

> I thought, so what if I can spend 2 years playing basketball? I'm not going to be a basketball player forever, and I might jeopardize my chances of getting into dental school if I play.

He finished college in 3 years, completed dental school, and now, in his mid-30s, is again the epitome of the successful American man: a professional with a family, a home, and a membership in the local country club.

How and why do so many successful male athletes from higher status backgrounds come to view sports careers as "pissing in the wind" or as "small potatoes"? How and why do they make these early assessments and choices to shift away from sports and toward educational and professional goals? The white, middle-class institutional context, with its emphasis on education and income, makes it clear to them that choices exist and that the pursuit of an athletic career is not a particularly good choice to make. Where the young male once found sports to be a convenient institution within which to construct masculine status, the postadolescent and young adult male from a higher status background simply transfers these same strivings and to other institutional contexts: education and careers.

Importance of Sport.   For the higher status men who had chosen to shift away from athletic careers, sports remained important on two levels. First, having been a successful high school or college athlete enhances one's adult status among other men in the community, but only as a badge of masculinity that is added to the former athlete's professional status. In fact, several men in professions chose to be interviewed in their offices, where they publicly displayed the trophies and plaques that attested to their earlier athletic accomplishments. Their high school and college athletic careers may have appeared to them as small potatoes, but many successful men speak of their earlier status as athletes as having "opened doors" for them in their present professions and in community affairs. Similarly, Farr's (1988) research on "good old boys' sociability groups" shows how sport, as part of the glue of masculine culture, continues to facilitate "dominance bonding'' among privileged men long after active sports careers end. The college-educated, career-successful men in Farr's study rarely express overtly sexist, racist, or classist attitudes; in fact, in their relationships with women, they ''often engage in expressive intimacies'' and ''make fun of exaggerated machismo'' (p. 276). But though they outwardly conform more to what Pleck (1982) calls ''the modern male role,'' their informal relationships within their sociability groups, in effect, affirm their own gender and class status by constructing and clarifying the boundaries between themselves and women and lower status men. This dominance bonding is based largely upon ritual forms of sociability (e.g., camaraderie and competition), ''the superiority of which was first affirmed in the exclusionary play activities of young boys in groups'' (Farr, 1988, p. 265).

In addition to contributing to dominance bonding among higher status adult men, sport remains salient in terms of the ideology of gender relations. Most men continued to watch, talk about, and identify with sports long after their own disengagement from athletic careers. Sport as a mediated spectacle provides an important context in which traditional conceptions of masculine superiority, conceptions recently contested by women, are shored up. As a 32-year-old white professional-class man said of a feared professional football player:

A woman can do the same job as I can do—maybe even be my boss. But I'll be *damned* if she can go out on the football field and take a hit from Ronnie Lott.

Violent sports as spectacle provide linkages among men in the project of the domination of women while at the same time helping to construct and clarify differences among various masculinities. The previous statement is a clear identification with Ronnie Lott as a man, and the basis of the identification is the violent male body. As Connell (1987b) argues, sport is an important organizing institution for the embodiment of masculinity. Here, men's power over women becomes naturalized and linked to the social distribution of violence. Sport, as a practice, suppresses natural (sex) similarities, constructs differences, and then, largely through the media, weaves a structure of symbol and interpretation around these differences, which naturalizes them (J. Hargreaves, 1986). It is also significant that the man who made the statement about Ronnie Lott was quite aware that he (and perhaps 99% of the rest of the U.S. male population) was probably as incapable as most women of taking a ''hit'' from someone like Lott and living to tell of it. For middle-class men, the tough guys of the culture industry—the Rambos, the Ronnie Lotts who are fearsome ''hitters,'' who ''play hurt''—are the heroes who prove that ''we men'' are superior to women. At the same time, these heroes play the role of the primitive other, against whom higher status men define themselves as modern and civilized.

Sport, then, is important from boyhood through adulthood for men from higher status backgrounds. But it is significant that by adolescence and early adulthood, most of these young men have concluded that sports careers are not for them. Their middle-class cultural environment encourages them to decide to shift their masculine strivings in more ''rational'' directions: education and nonsports careers. Yet their previous sports participation continues to be very important to them in terms of constructing and validating their status within privileged male peer groups and within their chosen professional careers. And organized sport, as a public spectacle, is a crucial locus around which ideologies of male superiority over women, as well as higher status men's superiority over lower status men, are constructed and naturalized.

Men From Lower Status Backgrounds

For the lower status young men in this study, success in sports wasn't an added proof of masculinity; success was often their only hope of achieving public masculine status. A 34-year-old black bus driver who had been a star athlete in three sports in high school had neither the grades nor the money to attend college, so he accepted an offer from the U.S. Marine Corps to play on their baseball team. He ended up in Vietnam, where a grenade blew four fingers off his pitching hand. In retrospect, he believed that his youthful focus on sports stardom and his concomitant lack of effort in academics made sense:

> You can go anywhere with athletics—you don't have to have brains. I mean, I didn't feel like I was gonna go out there and be a computer expert, or something that was gonna make a lot of money. The only thing I could do and live comfortably would be to play sports. Just to get a contract—doesn't matter if you play second or third team in the pros, you're gonna make big bucks. That's all I wanted, a confirmed livelihood at the end of my ventures, and the only way I could do it would be through sports. So I tried. It failed, but that's what I tried.

Similar, and even more tragic, is the story of a 34-year-old black man who is now serving a life term in prison. After a knee injury at the age of 20 abruptly ended what had appeared to be a certain road to professional football fame and fortune, he decided that he "could still be rich and famous" by robbing a bank. During his high school and college years, he said, he was nearly illiterate:

> I'd hardly ever go to classes and they'd give me Cs. My coaches taught some of the classes. And I felt, "So what? They *owe* me that! I'm an *athlete*! I thought that was what I was born to do—to play sports—and everybody understood that.

Reasons for Pursuing Sport.   Are lower status boys and young men simply duped into putting all their eggs into one basket? My research suggested that there was more than "hope for the future" motivating these men. There were also immediate psychological reasons why they chose to pursue athletic careers. By the high school years, class and ethnic inequalities had become glaringly obvious, especially for those who attended socioeconomically heterogeneous schools. Cars, nice clothes, and other signs of status were often unavailable to these young men, and this contributed to a situation in which sports took on an expanded importance for them in terms of constructing masculine identities and status. A white, 36-year-old man from a poor, single-parent family, who later played professional baseball, had been acutely aware of his low-class status in his high school:

I had one pair of jeans, and I wore them every day. I was always afraid of what people thought of me—that this guy doesn't have anything, that he's wearing the same Levis all the time, he's having to work in the cafeteria for his lunch. What's going on? I think that's what made me so shy. . . . But boy, when I got into sports, I let it all hang out [laughs] and maybe that's why I became so good, because I was frustrated, and when I got into that element, they gave me my uniform in football, basketball, and baseball, and I didn't have to worry about how I looked, because then it was *me* who was coming out, and not my clothes or whatever. And I think that was the drive.

Similarly, a 41-year-old black man who had a 10-year professional football career described his insecurities as one of the few poor blacks in a mostly white, middle-class school and his belief that sports was the one arena in which he could be judged solely on his merit:

I came from a very poor family, and I was very sensitive about that in those days. When people would say things like ''Look at him—he has dirty pants on,'' I'd think about it for a week. [But] I'd put my pants on and I'd go out on the football field with the intention that I'm gonna do a job. And if that calls on me to hurt you, I'm gonna do it. It's as simple as that. I demand respect just like everybody else.

''Respect'' was what I heard over and over when talking with the men from lower status backgrounds, especially black men. I interpret this type of respect to be a crystallization of the masculine quest for recognition through public achievement, unfolding within a system of structured constraints due to class and race inequities. The institutional context of education (sometimes with the collusion of teachers and coaches) and the constricted structure of opportunity in the economy made the pursuit of athletic careers appear to be the most rational choice to these young men.

The same is not true of young lower status women. Dunkle (1985) points out that from junior high school through adulthood, young black men are far more likely to place high value on sports than are young black women, who are more likely to value academic achievement. There appears to be a gender dynamic operating in adolescent male peer groups that contributes to their valuing sports more highly than education.

Franklin (1986) has argued that many of the normative values of the black male peer group (e.g., little respect for nonaggressive solutions to disputes, contempt for nonmaterial culture) contribute to the constriction of black men's views of desirable social positions, especially through education. In my study, a 42-year-old black man who did succeed in beating the odds by using his athletic scholarship to get a college degree and eventually become a successful professional said:

By junior high, you either got identified as an athlete, a thug, or a bookworm. It's very important to be seen as somebody who's capable in some area. And you *don't* want to be identified as a bookworm. I was very good with books, but I was kind of covert about it. I was a closet bookworm. But with sports, I was *somebody*, so I worked very hard at it.

For most young men from lower status backgrounds, the poor quality of their schools, the attitudes of teachers and coaches, as well as the anti-education environment within their own male peer groups made it extremely unlikely that they would be able to succeed as students. Sports, therefore, became the arena in which they attempted to "show their stuff." For these lower status men, as Baca Zinn (1982) and Majors (1986) argue in their respective studies of chicano men and black men, when institutional resources that signify masculine status and control are absent, physical presence, personal style, and expressiveness take on increased importance. What Majors (1986) calls "cool pose" is black men's expressive, often aggressive, assertion of masculinity. This self-assertion often takes place within a context in which the young man is quite aware of existing social inequities. As the black bus driver, referred to previously, said of his high school years:

> See, the rich people use their money to do what they want to do. I use my ability. If you wanted to be around me, if you wanted to learn something about sports, I'd teach you. But you're gonna take me to lunch. You're gonna let me use your car. See what I'm saying? In high school I'd go where I wanted to go. I didn't have to be educated. I was well respected. I'd go somewhere, and they'd say, "Hey, that's Mitch Harris[2], yeah, that's a bad son of a bitch!"

Majors (1986) argues that although "cool pose" represents a creative survival technique within a hostile environment, the most likely long-term effect of this masculine posturing is educational and occupational dead ends. As a result, we can conclude, lower status men's personal and peer group responses to a constricted structure of opportunity—responses that are rooted, in part, in the developmental insecurities and ambivalences of masculinity—serve to lock many of these young men into limiting activities like sports.

SUMMARY AND CONCLUSIONS

This research has suggested that within a social context that is stratified by social class and by race, the choice to pursue or not to pursue an athletic career is explicable as an individual's rational assessment of the available means to achieve a respected masculine identity. For nearly all of the men from lower status backgrounds, the status and respect that they received through sports were temporary; the status and respect did not translate into upward mobility. Nonetheless, a strategy of discouraging young black boys and men from involvement in sports is probably doomed to fail, because it ignores the continued existence of structural constraints. Despite the increased number of black role models in nonsports professions, employment opportunities for young black males actually deteriorated in the 1980s (Wilson & Neckerman, 1986), and nonathletic opportunities in higher education also declined. Although blacks constitute 14% of the college-aged (18 to 24 years) U.S. population, as a proportion of students in 4-year colleges and universities, blacks have dropped to 8%. In contrast, by 1985, black men constituted 49% of all college basketball players and 61% of basketball players in institutions that grant athletic scholarships (Berghorn, Yetman, & Hanna, 1988). For young black men, then, organized sports appear to be more likely to get them to college than their own efforts in nonathletic activities.

But it would be a mistake to conclude that we simply need to breed socioeconomic conditions that make it possible for poor and minority men to mimic the "rational choices" of white middle-class men. If we are to build an appropriate understanding of the lives of all men, we must critically analyze white middle-class masculinity, rather than uncritically take it as a normative standard. To fail to do this would be to ignore the ways in which organized sports serve to construct and legitimate gender differences and inequalities among men and women.

Feminist scholars have demonstrated that organized sports give men from all backgrounds a means of status enhancement that is not available to young women. Sport thus serves the interests of all men in helping to construct and legitimize their control of public life and their domination of women (Bryson, 1987a; Hall, 1987a; Theberge, 1987). Yet concrete studies suggest that men's experiences within sports are not all of a piece. As Brian Pronger's research suggests (in chapter 11 of this volume), gay men often approach sports differently than straight men do—with a sense of irony. And my research suggests that although sports are important for men from both higher and lower status backgrounds, there are crucial differences. In fact, it appears that the meaning that most men give to their athletic strivings has more to do with competing for status among men than it has to do with proving superiority over women. How can we explain this seeming contradiction between the feminist claim that sports link all men in the domination of women and the research findings that different groups of men relate to sports in very different ways?

The answer to this question lies in developing a means of conceptualizing the interrelationships between varying forms of domination and subordination. Marxist scholars of sport often falsely collapse everything into a class analysis; radical feminists often see gender domination as universally fundamental. Concrete examinations of sport, though, reveal complex and multilayered systems of inequality: Race, class, gender, sexual preference, and age dynamics are all salient features of the athletic context. In examining this reality, Connell's (1987b) concept of the gender order is useful. The gender order is a dynamic process that is constantly in a state of play. Moving beyond static sex role theory and reductionist concepts of patriarchy that view men as an undifferentiated group that oppresses women, Connell argues that at any given historical moment, there are competing masculinities—some hegemonic, some marginalized, some stigmatized. Hegemonic masculinity (that definition of masculinity that is culturally ascendant) is constructed in relation to various subordinated masculinities as well as in relation to femininities. Thus, the project of male domination of women may tie all men together, but men share very unequally in the fruits of this domination.

These are key insights in examining the contemporary meaning of sport. Utilizing the concept of the gender order, we can begin to conceptualize how hierarchies of race, class, age, and sexual preference among men help to construct and legitimize men's overall power and privilege over women. We can alo see how, for some black, working-class, or gay men, the false promise of sharing in the fruits of hegemonic masculinity often ties them into their marginalized and subordinate statuses within hierarchies of intermale dominance. For instance, as Richard Majors argues in the next chapter of this volume, black men's development of "cool pose" within sports can be interpreted as an example of creative resistance to one form of social domination (racism), yet it also demonstrates the limits of an agency that adopts other forms of social domination (masculinity) as its vehicle.

Indeed, as Connell's analysis of an Australian iron man (Chapter 6) has already demonstrated, the commercially successful, publicly acclaimed athlete may embody all that is valued in present cultural conceptions of hegemonic masculinity—physical strength, commercial success, and supposed heterosexual virility. Yet higher status men, although they admire the public image of the successful athlete, may also look down on him as a narrow, even atavistic, example of masculinity. For these higher status men, their earlier sports successes are often status enhancing and serve to link them with other men in ways that continue to exclude women. And these men's decisions not to pursue athletic careers are equally important signs of their status vis-à-vis other men. Future examinations of the contemporary meaning and importance of sport to men might take as a fruitful point of departure the idea that athletic participation and sport as public spectacle serve to provide linkages among men in the project of the domination of women while at the same time helping to construct and clarify differences among various masculinities.

Chapter 8

Cool Pose: Black Masculinity and Sports[1]

Richard Majors

Sport, as a social institution, emerged in the 19th and 20th centuries in response to a shifting constellation of class and gender dynamics. Not only did sport make a crucial contribution to the ideological naturalization of men's superiority over women, popular belief held that working-class men and men of color could not possibly compete successfully with "gentlemen." Thus, as a homosocial environment within which white upper- and middle-class males sharpened their competitive skills, sport became an important institution in which the superiority of hegemonic masculinity was supported and reproduced, while women and other (subordinated) men were marginalized (Connell, 1987b).

Interestingly, since World War II—and especially in the last 15 years—athletic roles within major organized sports in the United States have come to be dominated by black men. The dynamics of this historic shift—and the extent to which the contemporary dominance of certain sports by black males is more a sign of continued racism than a sign of progress—have been examined elsewhere (H. Edwards, 1973, 1984; Tygiel, 1983). The goal of this chapter is to illustrate how contemporary black males often utilize sports as one means of masculine self-expression within an otherwise limited structure of opportunity. After a brief discussion of contemporary black men and masculinity, this chapter will show how what the author calls "cool pose" (i.e., a set of expressive lifestyle behaviors)

Carrington

is often developed and used by black men as a response to the limits that institutionalized racism places on their other opportunities for self-expression. This chapter will argue that sport has become a major institutional context for the expression of cool pose, and that although self-expression through athletics does offer a small number of black males an escape from the limits imposed by poverty and racism, for the majority, sport is a form of self-expression that ultimately can lock them into their low-status positions in society.

BLACK MEN AND MASCULINITY

Despite the recent proliferation of men's studies programs and the resultant publications based on this growing academic interest in masculinity (Brod, 1987; Kimmel, 1987b), research on how ethnicity, race, and socioeconomic status affects the development of masculinity remains limited. In particular, black males are either rendered invisible or are viewed as helpless victims of a racist system. With a few exceptions (e.g., Cazenave, 1984; Franklin, 1984a; Majors, 1986, 1987), there has been a noteworthy dearth of literature on black men's actual responses (i.e., survival strategies, coping mechanisms, and forms of resistance) to a limited structure of opportunity. The problems facing black males today are so serious, and their consequences so grave, it is tempting to view these men primarily as victims. In fact, Stewart and Scott (1978) have argued that there is a contemporary "institutional decimation of black males," which these authors describe as the "coordinated operation of various institutions in American society which systematically remove black males from the civilian population" (p. 85). Indeed, recent research has shown that young black males are experiencing unprecedented setbacks in their struggles for economic and educational equality in the United States, a nation that holds equal opportunity as one of its founding principles (Gibbs, 1988; Larson, 1988). Black men are among the predominant victims of an entire range of socioeconomic, health, and stress-related problems. These problems include, but are not limited to, higher rates of heart disease, hypertension, infant mortality, mental disorders, psychiatric hospitalization, homocide, unemployment, suspension from school, imprisonment, and morbidity and low life expectancy (Bulhan, 1985; Cordes, 1985; Gite, 1985; Heckler, 1985).

   Black males have responded in various ways to this constricted structure of opportunity. What is of interest here is how black males' relationships to dominant definitions of masculinity have figured into their responses to institutionalized racism. Many black males have accepted the definitions, standards, and norms of dominant social definitions of masculinity (being the breadwinner, having strength, and dominating women). However, American society has prevented black males from achieving many aspects of this masculinity by restricting their access to education, jobs, and institutional power. In other words, the dominant goals of hegemonic masculinity have been sold to black males, but access to the legitimate means to achieve those goals has been largely denied black males (Staples, 1982). As a consequence of these conditions, many black males have become *men manqué*; because of the many frustrations resulting from a lack of opportunities in society, many black males have become obsessed with proving manliness to themselves and to others.[2] Lacking legitimate institutional means, black males will often go to great lengths to prove their manhood in interpersonal spheres of life (e.g., fighting, the emotional and physical domination of women, and involvement in risk-taking activities; Majors, 1986; Staples, 1982).

COOL POSE AS AN EXPRESSION OF BLACK MASCULINITY

Institutional racism and a constricted structure of opportunity do not cause all black males to exhibit antisocial behaviors, nor do these problems succeed in erasing black men's expressions of creativity. In fact, black men often cope with their frustration, embitterment, alienation, and social impotence by channeling their creative energies into the construction of unique, expressive, and conspicuous styles of demeanor, speech, gesture, clothing, hairstyle, walk, stance, and handshake. For the black male, these expressive behaviors, which are a particular manifestation of what the author has elsewhere described as cool pose (Majors, 1986, 1987), offset an externally imposed invisibility, and provide a means to show the dominant culture (and the black male's peers) that the black male is strong and proud and can survive, regardless of what may have been done to harm or limit him. In other words, the expressive lifestyle is a "survival strategy that makes oneself interesting and attractive to others . . . through [the process of] making oneself an interesting object, through the cultivation of an aura . . . that elicits rewarding responses from others" (Rainwater, 1966, p. 214).

Although black people have been forced into conciliatory and often demeaning positions in American culture, there is nothing conciliatory about the expressive lifestyle. It is adaptation rather than submission. In that sense, then, cool pose is an attempt to carve out an alternative path to achieve the goals of dominant masculinity. Due to structural limitations, a black man may be impotent in the intellectual, political, and corporate world, but he can nevertheless display a potent personal style from the pulpit, in entertainment, and in athletic competition, with a verve that borders on the spectacular. Through the virtuosity of a performance, he tips the socially imbalanced scales in his favor and sends the subliminal message: "See me, touch me, hear me, but, white man, you can't copy me!" The expressive lifestyle invigorates the demeaning life of black men in white America. It is a dynamic vitality that transforms the mundane into the sublime and makes the routine spectacular.

BLACK MALE EXPRESSION AND SPORT

Sport has become one of the major stages upon which black males express their creativity. For example, in football, Butch Johnson and Billy "Whiteshoes" Johnson were two well-known athletes who exhibited expressive lifestyle behaviors on the playing field. Both men were known for their fancy dances and "spikes" in the end zone after a touchdown. To further accentuate themselves (i.e., to be "cool"), these athletes wore wristbands and hung towels from their pants. In basketball, Julius "Dr. J" Erving, Darryl Dawkins, Michael Jordan, and other black players have been known for their expressiveness as well as their considerable skills. Erving may best symbolize the emergence of this expressive style among black basketball players. On the court, Erving was known for his very creative, graceful, and agile performance. His style of play was exemplified by his famous "ceiling-climbing, high-flying, gravity-defying" dunks, for which he would often start his take-off at the foul line.

Cool pose in sport can sometimes be interpreted as cultural resistance to racism. The fists-raised demonstration on the victory stand in the 1968 Olympics was not the only characteristic of Tommie Smith's and John Carlos's protests against racism in the United States—these athletes also ran while wearing black socks and sunglasses. Similarly, Muhammed Ali's expressive style—his boasting, his poetry, his dancing, his ritualistic "hair combing" while holding a mirror after his bouts—can be interpreted not simply as personal vanity but as one athlete's defiant expression of resistance to a society that uses black males as its warriors—both as pugilists in the ring and as soldiers in Vietnam. Because black (and hispanic) men showed up disproportionately as drafted combat soldiers, and then as casualities in Vietnam (Staples, 1982), it is not surprising that many U.S. blacks identified with the style and substance of Ali's performances. Meanwhile, many whites in the media, the government, and the public were profoundly threatened by it.

Expressive behaviors are not, of course, restricted merely to professional athletes. College, high school, and playground athletes also mimic, develop, and use expressive styles. As Wolf (1972) has noted of young black males,

> The school yard is the only place they can feel true pride in what they do, where they can move free of inhibitions, and where they can, by being spectacular, rise for the moment against the drabness and anonymity of their lives. . . . When you jump in the air, fake a shot, all without coming back down, you have proven your worth in incontestable fashion . . . thus, when a player develops extraordinary "school yard" moves . . . [they] become his measure as a man." (p. 170)

Black males' appropriation of sports as an arena of self-expression is an example of human agency operating within structural constraints. Faced with a lack of resources, facilities, services, goods, information, and jobs, black males who live in poor black communities have taken a previously white-dominated activity and constructed it as an arena in which they find accessible recreation, entertainment, stimulation, and opportunities for self-expression and creativity. Sports play an important and—in some limited ways—a positive role in many black males' lives. However, as we shall see, there is a downside to the relationship between black males and sports.

BLACK MALES AND ORGANIZED SPORTS

The sports establishment does not operate as an apolitical, asocial enterprise, but as part of the larger society. As such, sports are not an alternative to "real life," but a reflection of the racist economic and social system that supports them (W. Morgan, 1983). As Messner demonstrated in the previous chapter, this reflection is often distorted in such a way that, for the individual, sport often appears to be one of the few arenas that provides true equal opportunity. This distortion of reality draws young black males into athletic careers in disproportionately high numbers, and this distortion ultimately guarantees that the vast majority of black males will find sports to be a professional dead end (H. Edwards, 1984).

Despite its apparent equality and integration, sport remains an extension of the dominant racist economic system, which serves to exploit those who are already professional or college athletes and to mislead those who are merely aspiring athletes. In fact, even the apparent integration at the player level is misleading (H. Edwards, 1982; Yetman & Eitzen, 1972). As evidenced by recent statements made by prominent white men in professional sports concerning how blacks supposedly "lack the necessities" to be field managers, racism lives on within organized sports. Indeed, black managers, coaches, and front-office personnel are exceedingly rare, with most sports organizations owned, operated, and managed exclusively by whites. Furthermore, there is racial segregation in sport by playing position (Curtis & Loy, 1978; Eitzen & Tessendorf, 1978), as any devotee of football is especially aware after the media attention Doug Williams received for being the first black quarterback to start in the Superbowl. Black males also find themselves represented in disproportionately high numbers as athletes in sports to which they have had access, such as basketball, football, baseball, boxing and track. Meanwhile, blacks are underrepresented in sports to which they have not had access, such as golf, auto racing, swimming, hockey, and soccer. As H. Edwards (1984) writes,

> Patterns of black opportunities in American sport are consistent with those in society at large, and for the same reason—deeply rooted traditions of racial discrimination. I contend that racial discrimination in both sport and society is responsible for the disproportionately high presence of extremely talented black athletes in certain sports on the one hand and the utter exclusion of blacks from most American sport and from decision-making and authority positions in virtually all sports on the other. (p. 9)

Despite the large number of black males who participate in sports, less than 6% of all the athletic scholarships given in the United States go to blacks. Just as damaging is the fact that an estimated 25 to 35% of high school black athletes do not even qualify for scholarships because of academic deficiencies. Of those black athletes who ultimately do receive athletic scholarships, as many as 65 to 75% may not ever graduate from college (H. Edwards, 1984; Spivey & Jones,

1975; Talbert, 1976). Among the approximately 25 to 35% of the black athletes who do graduate from college, about 75% of them graduate with either physical education degrees or with degrees in majors that are especially created for athletes. As one might suspect, such "jock degrees" are often not acceptable in the job market, given the growing emphasis on the need for math, science, engineering, and computer training in today's high-tech market. In the final analysis, because such a small percentage of these college athletes will be drafted by a pro team, and those who actually play will find that the average professional career is short, many once-aspiring black athletes will find themselves back out on the streets with academic degrees that may not help them survive—much less succeed—in the "real world."

SUMMARY AND CONCLUSION

It has been argued here that cool pose (expressive lifestyle behaviors) as expressed by black males in sports may be interpreted as a means of countering social oppression and racism and of expressing creativity. Moreover, the demonstration of cool pose in sports enables black males to accentuate or display themselves (i.e., "Here I am, world; watch me, see me, hear me, I'm alive"), obtain gratification, release pent-up aggression, gain prestige and recognition, exercise power and control, and express pride, dignity, and respect for themselves and for their race. However, the emphasis on athletics and on cool pose among black males is often self-defeating, because it comes at the expense of educational advancement and other intellectually oriented activities that are integral aspects of the dominant forms of masculine power and success today.

Furthermore, although cool pose is an example of creative agency in response to one form of social domination (institutionalized racism), cool pose also illustrates the limits of an agency that adopts another form of social domination (hegemonic masculinity) as its vehicle. Because hegemonic masculinity is ultimately about men's domination of women (and some men's domination of other men), black men's adoption of cool pose as a response to institutionalized racism is often self-defeating. This response ultimately does not put black males in positions to live and work in more egalitarian ways with women, nor does it directly challenge male hierarchies. Cool pose demonstrates black males' potential to transcend oppressive conditions to express themselves as men. In rejecting the false promise of patriarchal privilege, black males might move from individual transcendence to social transformation. A critical examination of black males' relationship to sports is an important requisite of this movement.

Chapter 9

Football Ritual and the Social Reproduction of Masculinity[1]

Donald F. Sabo
Joe Panepinto

This chapter focuses on the relationship between the football coach and his players in order to understand how football ritual contributes to the social reproduction of masculinity. The masculinity-validating dimensions of football ritual have always been one of the game's prominent cultural features (Kimmel, 1987b; Messner, 1988). Football's historical prominence in sport media and folk culture has sustained a hegemonic model of masculinity that prioritizes competitiveness, asceticism, success (winning), aggression, violence, superiority to women, and respect for and compliance with male authority. The ability to persuasively initiate and legitimate this model of masculinity has, in part, allowed men who inhabit positions of power and wealth to "reproduce the social relationships that generate their dominance" (Carrigan, Connell, & Lee, 1987, p. 92). Therefore, in addition to reinforcing sex inequality, football's reproduction of hegemonic masculinity has also helped maintain class inequality by masking and legitimating the processes that advantage some groups of males and marginalize or disadvantage others.

Football ritual is seen here as a locus of interaction between structural, cultural, and psychological processes that engenders players and prepares them for life within the "sex-gender system." The sex-gender system refers to a "set of social relations which has a material base and in which there are hierarchical relations between men and solidarity among them, which enables them in turn to dominate women" (Hartman, 1979; p. 223). Hence, the sex-gender system has two major, interdependent structural dimensions. The first is sex inequality, which allows for male domination of women. The second is the intermale dominance hierarchy, which fosters solidarity among males, conformity to hegemonic models of masculinity, and acceptance of status inequality among male groups.

The coach-player relationship is the epicenter of football ritual. Much previous research on coaches has explored the value orientations of coaches, their personality traits, and the coach role (Gould & Martens, 1979; Sage, 1974). More recent work focuses on the gender of coaches; Fine's (1987) and Chambliss's (1988) respective studies of Little League baseball coaches and elite swimming coaches offer valuable, detailed analyses of the men's athletic experiences. What is missing from these studies, however, is a theoretical framework that facilitates a critical feminist analysis of the coach-player relationship, that is, one that contextualizes this relationship within the larger sex-gender system.

In this study, we used a "bottom-up" perspective to analyze the coach-player relationship. We modeled our approach after Effron (1971), whose literary analysis of Cervantes's epic novel was done through the eyes of Sancho Panza rather than Don Quixote. Likewise, we sought to explicate coach-player relations by interviewing players, not coaches. Our discussions with former football players were also guided from the outset by a feminist-informed anthropological framework that assumed that football ritual resembles primitive male initiation rites in fundamental ways.

THEORY: FOOTBALL AS MALE INITIATION RITE

Ritual is organized action. La Fountaine (1985) asserts that ritual derives from social structure, and through the allocation of roles and the shaping of individual identity, ritual occasions "mobilize this structure in action" (p. 11). Lukes (1975) emphasizes that ritual is "rule governed activity of a symbolic character which draws the attention of its participants to objects of thought and feeling which they hold to be of special significance" (p. 291). Hence ritual can be seen as a dynamic process that at once reproduces the structure and cultural ethos of a community and, at the same time, enables the community to enmesh itself in its own identity. "We engage in rituals," Leach (1976) says, "in order to transmit messages to ourselves" (p. 45).

A ritual can be described as patriarchal when it contains elements of gender socialization that promote and express institutionalized patterns of both sex segregation and male dominance. The most thorough anthropological treatment of patriarchal ritual is found in studies of male initiation rites (Benedict, 1959; Godelier, 1986; Herdt, 1982b; Moore, 1986). Through these rites F. Young (1965) states, boys "learn the definition of the male situation maintained by the adult males" (p. 30). Masculinity rites in male-dominated societies contain several common elements:

• **Man-Boy Relationships**. Masculinity rites entail ongoing interaction between two key groups: older men, or "officiants," and younger men, or "initiates." Officiants are socially visible occupants of midlevel statuses who define and orchestrate rituals that recruit and motivate selected initiates to engage in appropriate behaviors, beliefs, and values. Officiants are not the architects of ritual; rather, they attend to its social construction in light of a larger, long-standing cultural blueprint.

• **Conformity and Control.** Officiants use a variety of methods to induce conformity to the rules and requirements of ritual. In order to control their tribal charges, officiants may instruct, pressure, console, chide, implore, threaten, punish, or trick to achieve compliance and conformity from initiates.

• **Social Isolation.** Male initiates are socially isolated from family and other tribal groups, especially girls and women. Whereas the virtues of men and masculinity are extolled, women and femininity are ignored or denigrated. Among the Sambia of New Guinea, for example, boys are told by adults that female spirits wish to kill and eat them. Such threats frighten boys who, in turn, turn to officiants for guidance and protection (Herdt, 1982a). Hence, tribal teachings about gender distill from and are amplified by structured sex segregation.

• **Deference to Male Authority.** The initiation process at once introduces boys to the wider male status hierarchy and acclimates them to male authority. The relationship between officiant and initiate conveys information about hierarchical rank and authority. Knowledge or special skills are usually taught according to some hierarchical scheme, and initiates are encouraged to pass from one stage or level to another, moving ever closer to the achievements of elder, higher status males.

• **Pain.** Initiation rites are filled with the infliction of pain on initiates. For example, Zuni boys from New Mexico are flogged with yucca whips, Nandi boys from East Africa face ingenious tortures linked to circumcision, and in some North American tribes torture is self-inflicted (Benedict, 1959). Courage and ability to endure pain not only set initiates apart from uninitiated boys and from women, these qualities place initiates above these other groups as well. Sex inequality and the intermale dominance hierarchy are thus reproduced.

Football ritual contains the above elements of primitive male initiation rites (Sabo, 1987). First, football is a social theater with an all-male, intergenerational cast. The older-coach/younger-player relationship develops over many years and, at least in part, is defined as a testing ground for adult manhood. Second, though the individual styles of coaches may vary from authoritarian to facilitative, they exert a great deal of control over their players and insist on conformity (Coakley, 1986). Third, football ritual unfolds in sex-segregated contexts such as the locker room and playing field. Coaches and players most often train, travel, eat, and recreate in all-male settings. If women are present, they are usually in subservient positions vis-à-vis men (i.e., cheerleaders, stewardesses, fans, and mothers who clean uniforms and serve meals at banquets). Fourth, football is also hierarchically structured. The most obvious status difference is between coach and players, but additional rankings exist between head coach and assistant coaches, first-team and second-team players, and stars and average players. Authority is concentrated almost totally in the coach, and players are expected to obey the rules. And finally, football ritual is filled with pain. As one former professional stated, ''From the moment training camp opens until the season is long over, [players] do not have a day that is free of some degree of injury and pain" (Mix, 1987, p. 55).

In summary, we drew from the anthropological literature in order to identify the ideal typical elements of primitive male initiation rites in male-dominated societies. This was done for two reasons. Theoretically, it enabled us to understand the coach-player (officiant-initiate) relationship within the contexts of football ritual and the larger sex-gender system. Methodologically, the resulting ideal type helped us decide what directions to explore in the interviews.

METHOD

We conducted 25 in-depth, semistructured interviews with a convenient sample of former football players. Seventeen had played through high school and college, though six did not complete their degrees. One had professional experience, and seven were strictly high school players. All but one of the men were white and came from either working-class or middle-class backgrounds. There were 20 face-to-face interviews and 5 telephone interviews. Following the ideal/typical contours of primitive male initiation rites detailed above, interviews generally focused on

- the coach-player relationship,
- conformity,
- social isolation,
- male authority, and
- pain.

In contrast to traditional approaches to interviewing, we assumed that interaction between social scientist and interviewee was intersubjective in character rather than occurring between an objective, unbiased, or detached observer-interviewer and the object of scientific scrutiny (Eichler, 1989). Both interviewers are former intercollegiate football players themselves. This fact was immediately communicated with our subjects, and furthermore, disclosures about our own experiences on the gridiron were part of the interview.

RESULTS

The interviews revealed many similarities between the coach-player relationship and the officiant-initiate relationship within primitive masculinity rites.

Coach-Player Relationships

The football coach fulfilled many of the requirements of the officiant role. Coaches and players spent many hours together learning football lore, rehearsing complex maneuvers, developing physical skills, and performing in games before the community. Most interviewees stated that football was the most important aspect of their lives. Relationships with coaches, therefore, were primary, and players perceived them this way. Some remembered coaches with deep affection and admiration. A former high school player said, "He was like a god to me, like he was 8 feet tall." Another explained, "My father died when I was young and Coach Johnson, I think, became kind of a father to me. I loved and admired him." Most players had mixed feelings toward coaches. They used descriptive terms ranging from "good man," "incredible guy," and "a real leader" to "a crazy man," "a real prick," and "mean son of a bitch."

He wasn't exactly a god, but we sometimes thought of him that way. . . . As a freshman and sophomore, I'd have done anything for him. Anything! By my junior year, though, I thought he was much too inflexible.

Over the years you learn that coaches are out for themselves, especially at the college level. You're their meal ticket, their glory ride. They're the boss, you're the employee.

Regardless of sentiment or circumstances, all players agreed that coaches exerted an important influence on their "growing up."

Conformity and Control

Coaches exerted a great deal of influence over their athletes' lives. In addition to teaching the basic rules of the game itself, coaches imposed training rules such as curfews, exercise regimens, dietary and dating restrictions, study programs, and sometimes clothing regulations. They not only taught boys how to train, tackle, and block, but also to dress and act like football players and gentlemen on and off the field.

Conformity and control were secured in several ways. Often coaches, particularly coaches with winning reputations, exercised astounding amounts of personal control over the athletes simply through what Crosset (1986) calls the "promise of grandeur." As one player put it, "The formula was 'follow my orders and win games.'" Although during the interviews some players expressed anger at coaches' pressures or demands to conform, others saw this as a necessary part of the game and life. Indeed, as one stated, "We wanted to conform. He taught us that you have to learn to work with a team if you're going to succeed at anything." Others felt that coaches helped them stay out of trouble, cut back on drug use, and take school more seriously.

Some coaches manipulated in-group/out-group tensions to insure conformity. One player offered, "We had been losing for so long that we would do anything he asked us to do because he made us believe we would win. . . . He acted like our best friend—turned us against other groups and the administration so that we would never look at him as the source of our problem." Another offered, "One of his favorite sayings was '90% of the people you meet are going to be assholes. You, gentlemen, are the 10%.'"

Ridicule was another tactic used to induce conformity. Athletes would be "chewed out" during practices, on the sidelines at games, or during team reviews of game films. Ridicule was often tinged by homophobia and misogyny. One coach hung a bra in a player's locker to signify that player wasn't tough enough. In order to inflame aggression or compliance, coaches called players "pussies" or "limp wrists" and told them "go home and play with your sisters" or "start wearing silk panties." These messages affirm asymmetric and opposed categories of gender (i.e., masculine vs. feminine).

Most coaches capitalized on the developmental urges of their preadolescent and adolescent charges to forge autonomous, individuated identities distinct from adult prescriptions. Coaches defined the challenges and struggles of the game in highly individualistic or self-fulfilling terms. Boys were encouraged to "excel," "stick it out," or "go the distance" for themselves, to perceive football as a test of personal resolve, toughness, and allegiance to peers. As one former college player observed,

> When I started out in grade school, the game was just fun. Later in high school it became a big quest to prove myself. I never was quite sure what I was proving (I'm still not), but I worked like crazy and did almost everything the coach said.

Conformity was thus cloaked by rugged individualism but, in effect, independence striving became accommodation. As Mailer (1968) observed, "There are negative rites of passage as well. Men learn in a negative rite to give up the best things they were born with, and forever."

Social Isolation

One form of social isolation is sex segregation. As Fine's (1987) study of Little League baseball players shows, a "distinctive maleness" is engendered by homosocial leisure settings. Football coaches arranged for and enforced homosociality in many ways. Practices were closed to cheerleaders and inquiring moms. Boys were often told to avoid too much contact with or attachment to girls; deeper involvement was said to promote distraction, siphon energy, and erode team loyalty. Two married college players said their coach exhorted them to avoid sexual relations with their wives for 3 days before games; it was argued that sex would dull their competitive edge.

Players who developed more committed relationships with women reported being chided by coaches and teammates. The message was that being "pussy-whipped" is no asset to individual athletic excellence and team success. Indeed, the demands placed on many college players made pursuing or maintaining serious relationships unfeasible.

> We were figuring it out one night before an away-game at Boston College. During the season, we went to classes 5 days a week, we had 3-hour practices 5 days a week followed by team meals. Friday night was psych-up time and Saturday was game day. Sunday we reviewed game films for 3 hours and had a team meeting, not to mention that we were sore as hell and couldn't move worth a damn. The only time we could chase girls was Saturday nights

after home games, and, even then, the coaches said they'd prowl the bars to catch somebody drinking or breaking curfew. The only thing we had time for was going to class, playing ball, and jerking off.

As is the case with primitive masculinity rites, the structured exclusion of women tended to exaggerate masculine traits and abilities and devalue feminine ones. One former college and professional player suggested,

Football is a macho game, the ultimate expression of macho in America. You look at yourself as the ultimate physical male and so look at other genders differently . . . if they can't compete with me, they can't be on the same level as me.

As Bryson (1983) argues, there are two ways sport ritual leads to male dominance and the "inferiorization" of females: first, by linking maleness to highly valued and visible skills, and second, by linking maleness with the positively sanctioned use of aggression/force/violence. Football does both.

Deference to Male Authority

Primitive ritual fixes and affirms boundaries and involves ideas about hierarchical order. So, too, the coach-player interaction helped develop a "hierarchical aware-ness" in players or what Chodorow (1978) would label "positional identity." How did this awareness take root?

Coaches occupy the highest status position within the social organization of the team. The coach-officiant also links players to the larger community and sex-gender hierarchy. High school coaches, for example, are fixed in a complex web of school boards, principals, parents, and community leaders (Sage, 1987b). Boys learn about the structure and workings of both the sex and male-dominance hier-archies through observations of their coaches' interactions with the wider com-munity. Players recognized that coaches were answerable to powers who reside outside the ritualized contours of the game (e.g., high school or college coaches defer to administrative and booster club leaders; professional coaches cater to ownership or local governmental officials). As one player described it,

I was a guard so, when we won, my line coach was happy. When we lost, he'd catch hell from Coach Parker [the head coach] who would have to answer to the principal. . . . Our school also had a long winning streak and a reputation in the city and state to uphold.

Coaches also taught boys useful lessons in how to comport themselves with school officials, the media, government, and important fans. One college player recalled how "we were taught how to speak to journalists, what to say about our opponents and teammates." Another stated,

Football helped me overcome shyness, helped me handle myself with im-portant people. In high school I once met the bishop who presented our team with an award. I had to make a speech.

Like their primitive counterparts, coach-officiants used social isolation to enhance their control and authority. Consider this example detailed by an interviewee. Upon their arrival to campus, players were instructed to drag their mattresses over to the un-iced hockey rink and place them along the boards. Sixty players slept on the floor of the rink without electricity or alarm clocks. Each morning, the players were collectively awakened by the snapping on of the house lights and the voice of the head coach coming across the public address system. One player recalled,

> The physical things he made us do did not bother me as much as the mental part. I can't walk into the rink to this day without thinking about it. . . . He knew what he was doing, he wanted to establish who was the boss.

Players often described their coaches as military officers. The coaches were said to be tough, like drill sergeants who whipped people into shape. Some coaches seemed to demand complete obedience. Most of the interviewees expressed some disbelief at their own tendencies to obey orders blindly and follow lockstep along any path laid out by their coaches:

> I still like the guy but I can't believe what I did. It was like a form of blind obedience. . . . I just thought that these were the steps we have to take and the system is probably right. . . . He was shaping my mind and I knew it. At first when I heard him call himself El Supremo, I thought he was only kidding. Now, looking back on it, I think that maybe he really believed it.

In summary, the coach-player relationship was a vehicle for boys to learn about and adjust to life within the intermale dominance hierarchy of football and hierarchical organization in general. Some players wholeheartedly accepted the coach's authority as legitimate whereas others secretly defied or resented it. Both groups, however, adapted to and at least outwardly conformed to the coach's authority.

Infliction of Pain

Coaches orchestrated and rationalized a variety of pain-inducing experiences. Physical pain was inflicted by injury, playing while hurt, excessive conditioning, contact drills, and fighting. Five interviewees reported being punched or slapped by coaches, though this was not normal practice. Emotional pain was inflicted by verbal criticism, public ridicule for errors or inadequacies, and humiliation by benching or demoting players.

Interviewees enthusiastically shared stories of coaching techniques that "drove us to the limits." Coaches assured players that pain is an inevitable part of the game, and interviewees seemed to have bought the axiom "jock, stock, and knee brace." Athletes reported participating in many pain-inducing activities that were organized (i.e., ritualized) by coaches as part of the training regimen or as a form of punishment.

> He'd make us run wind sprints until half the team dropped.

At preseason camp, to sort out who was meanest, he'd stick two guys in the pit and whoever got out first was better. It wasn't really football, because guys would just punch and scratch the hell out of each other until somebody managed to crawl out.

If we had a poor practice, we'd run the tires until somebody puked or dry heaved, or he'd have us beat the shit out of each other in tackling drills or something like that.

Coaches also taught players to inflict pain on their teammates and opponents. In order to prepare boys to play the game, coaches necessarily teach players to physically "punish the other guy." Despite the inherent "logic" of such training tactics within the game, the net result is that players (much like ancient gladiators) are ritualistically accomplices in one another's physical brutalization.

Players talked about learning to play with pain as one of football's greatest lessons. A former Big East player capsulized his coach's rationale as, "If you can get through this, you can get through anything." Some expressed disbelief that they were able to get through their ordeals at all.

Physically, few coaches could get away with what he did to us. I'm surprised that the trainer didn't do anything about it. Our bodies were completely abused.

We all worshipped the ground he walked on, but he was also a huge prick. He beat the shit out of us and we loved him for it. It sounds weird now, but that's the way it was.

Coaches de-emphasized the degree of physical suffering and probability of serious injury. Players were taught to deny pain. Coaches encouraged boys to "toughen up," to "learn to take your knocks," and "to sacrifice your body." Boys were expected to "run until you puke" and "push until it aches." Permanent injury and debilitation sometimes resulted. Coaches' responses to players' pains and injuries varied between mild empathy to studied indifference. A high school player recalled,

It was during a scrimmage and I heard Joe's nose pop from 10 feet away. The blood was shooting right out of his face. Coach Benson came over, took one look at him, yelled for the trainer, and said so everybody could hear, "OK, he's done. Get a warm body in here."

Many interviewees suspected that there may have been other agendas beneath the painful training practices. For example, one player felt that the physical abuse served to psychologically condition players to accept the coach's authority. The player mused that "the more exhausted people are, the more accepting." Another observed that there was a point where the infliction of pain became an end in itself. On his college team, painful episodes became so ritualized that their importance overshadowed the stated purpose for practice—improved performance. As one former college player reflected, "It was counterproductive to the real goal of playing; the punishment for losing interfered with our ability to remedy our losing ways.''

Pain infliction facilitates the domination of the mind through the body (Scarry, 1985). In primitive masculinity rites, pain infliction is the central element that bonds initiates together, induces a psychological change in them, and distinguishes them from women and male underlings. In football ritual, we suggest, pain appears to cement hierarchical distinctions between males, fuse the players' allegiance to one another, set men apart from and above women, and solidify the coach's authority within the intermale dominance hierarchy (Sabo, 1986).

FOOTBALL AS MASCULINITY RITUAL

Officiants of primitive masculinity rites are, in part, the social-psychological managers of boys' gender identity development. Officiants arrange for significant actors within the community to engage one another in ways that convey gender expectations and prepare boys for adult life. So, too, did coaches interpret the meaning of the game for the player-initiates: a "manly" enterprise, "preparation for life," "more than just a game," "a sport that requires great sacrifice," or "a game you'll grow to love."

Many of the meanings that coaches reportedly attached to football revolved around hegemonically masculine themes: distinctions between boys and men, physical size and strength, avoidance of feminine activities and values, toughness, aggressiveness, violence, and emotional self-control. Sometimes the coach's masculine counsels were overt: "Football is the closest thing to war you boys will ever experience. It's your chance to find out what manhood is really all about." More often than not, however, the processes of gender learning were covert or expressed mainly through the structured interplay of power and role relations between coach and players, players and women, or among teammates themselves. Indeed, interviewees were often at a loss for words when asked how their coaches had helped shape their identities as men. This oddity or contradiction may be partially explained by La Fountaine's (1985) observation that, despite the significance of certain meanings or values for the community, they are "rarely recognized by the participants for whom ritual has its own purpose" (p. 12).

In contrast to this reticence about gender, all interviewees espoused the view that football helps make for success in later life. They saw football as "training for life" and held that both good and bad experiences with coaches were "necessary lessons" for success. Indeed, the coach's emphasis on hard work and competition was repeatedly cited as the most valuable lesson of the football experience. As one 37-year-old sales representative put it, "Football taught me how to define goals and work my ass off to achieve them. There are no free rides in this life." A law student explained,

> In spite of what he did, he taught us benefits we'll carry for the rest of our lives. [We] have to learn to be competitive, because it is a competitive world. You have to be a real tough bastard to get to your goal.

In summary, we discovered that the coach-player relationship simultaneously served as a training ground for hegemonic masculinity and a fountainhead of achievement ideology. Indeed, the masculine strivings of players were inextricably tied to their mobility aspirations. Despite their relative successes or failures in life, players came away from football with an abiding belief in the American Dream ideology (i.e., hard work and personal sacrifice lead to economic success). Football's messages about manliness, male dominance, and women's place in the world were ultimately filtered through the men's perceived relations to the class system. In the final analysis, it was impossible to discern where "homo patriarchus" ended and "homo economicus" began.

SUMMARY

Much Marxist-inspired analysis of sport attempts to show how sport ideology and athletic socialization transmit status or class position. Such efforts are consistent with general reproduction theory, which explains "how societal institutions perpetuate (or reproduce) the social relationships and attitudes needed to sustain the existing relations of production in a capitalist society" (J. MacLeod, 1987, p. 9). For social reproduction theorists like Bourdieu (1977, 1978) or Althusser (1971), however, the theoretical attention paid to social class relations has dwarfed the analysis of gender and sex inequality. In contrast, previous feminist analyses of men have categorically treated them as an undifferentiated monolith, the collective dominators of women. Men's myriad relations to one another within the intermale dominance system, and how and why their relationships to women vary throughout the class system, remain underresearched and unexplicated.

This study shows that the football coach-player relationship can be understood as a nexus of patriarchal ritual that reproduces hegemonic forms of masculinity as well as competitive behavior and achievement ideologies that are more closely tied to class inequality. Football is a type of male interaction that perpetuates male privilege through dominance bonding (Farr, 1988). In-depth interviews helped us to discern "the extent to which, and in what ways, sport is involved in the mediation of ideas and beliefs, some of which become linked to the interests of classes and dominant groups, and others of which are concealed" (J.A. Hargreaves, 1982, p. 15). Our research shows that it is the patriarchal aspects of football ritual that have been concealed.

The interviews also demonstrate that gender dynamics represent only one aspect of the coach-player relationship. At this stage of its development in the American political economy, football ritual appears to be just as much a source of achievement ideology as it is gender initiation. The emphasis on meritocratic ideologies is particularly evident in corporate advertising and mass media portrayals of the game. Indeed, the cultural efficacy of the football player and coach as living symbols of manliness may be waning while other models for masculinity are ascendant. As a former Baltimore Colt from the 1960s era put it, "When we played men were really men not like these bums today with their briefcases and goddamn stock portfolios" (Donovan, 1987). In truth, pro-football players have joined labor, which is now a third-class power in America; big biceps make as little sense in the picket line as in the corporate boardroom. NCAA Division I coaches, like their professional counterparts, are becoming fixtures in upper level management, and coaches are increasingly identified more with winning and fiscal outcomes than with shaping the manly destinies of young subordinates.

The lessons born of boys' manly struggles with coaches, teammates, and opponents, therefore, are simultaneously linked to the reproduction of larger systems of both gender and class relations. The football coach is not simply a man doing a job. Although it is true that, increasingly, aspects of the coach's role are defined by the occupational structure of the postindustrial capitalist order, he is also a man among men, a cultural figurehead, an agent of social reproduction within a homosocial world who introduces boys to the ever-changing sex-gender system and its hegemonic model of masculinity.*

Editors' note: This chapter has focused on relationships between male coaches and male football players. In chapter 13, Ellen Staurowsky examines emerging relationships between female coaches and male athletes. Reflection on these two chapters prompts interesting theoretical questions. Will women's influence in athletic ritual significantly alter the processes of gender identity development? Will the gender-political outcomes be liberative within a feminist political context, or will the potentially liberating impacts of feminine values and practices be muted, distorted, or even co-opted by pre-existing structural and cultural constraints?

Chapter 10

Little Big Man: Hustling, Gender Narcissism, and Bodybuilding Subculture

Alan M. Klein

The following case study examines the social and psychological dimensions of masculinity within the sport subculture of southern California bodybuilding. There, one can find a variety of behaviors and conventions that exaggerate, yet reflect, American notions of masculinity. Within bodybuilding there is a very troubling yet prevalent practice known as "hustling." Hustling is the selling of sex to gay men and is the behavioral conflux for a variety of male traits: hypermasculinity, homophobia*, and narcissism. I argue that hustling

- supports the comic-book notion of masculinity so prevalent in bodybuilding,
- fulfills some bodybuilders' needs for admiration,
- is for many a temporary response to an economic crisis in the competitive bodybuilder's pursuit of success, and
- is crisis causing for those involved who must maintain heterosexual self-perceptions while engaging in homosexual practices.

---

*Editors' note: Pat Griffin and James Genasci provide a detailed definition and discussion of homophobia in chapter 17.

Borrowing from Matza (1969) and Reiss (1971), I show how hustling is carried out and how its practitioners juggle self-identity.

Riding on the coattails of the health movement, cultural fears of aging, and an increased cultural receptivity to mass spectacle, bodybuilding has experienced unprecedented growth in the past decade (Klein, n.d.; Lasch, 1979). Some of that growth is due to the resurgence of an atavistic notion of masculinity (e.g., films such as *Rambo* and *The Terminator* and New Wave fashion and hairstyles) that has articulated what bodybuilders have always accepted as a standard for men. Comic-book masculinity depicts men one-dimensionally as stoic, brave to a fault, always in control, aggressive, competitive, and above all well built.[1] No form of sport or popular culture seeks to replicate the trappings of this notion of masculinity more than bodybuilding.

The chapter begins with a description of the setting in which the research was conducted. Next, some social and psychological aspects of the bodybuilding subculture are discussed. Special attention is given to exploring links between men's emotional insecurities and what I call "gender narcissism." Analytic focus then shifts to consideration of the ties between hustling, homophobia, and the gender identity of male bodybuilders.

THE SETTING

This study is based on anthropological fieldwork carried out between 1979 and 1985 at one of southern California's foremost gyms (here given the fictitious name of Olympic Gym). A few blocks from Muscle Beach and among some of the world's elite gyms is Olympic Gym, home to many world-class bodybuilders. The proximity of these facilities to each other and the pull of Hollywood's media industry exaggerate many of the flamboyant qualities of bodybuilding subculture.

Despite a membership of over 1,500, the real bodybuilding community at Olympic Gym consists of a core of only about 150 devotees, who follow the lifestyle of bodybuilding more or less full-time. This means working out seriously enough to develop the physique of a bodybuilder and having the gym become the center of one's life. One's social relations, economic opportunities, and psychological balance revolve around the gym, much as the church or street corner functions for the religious observant or the urban social group (Aschenbrenner, 1975; Kaiser, 1979).

The core community, however, is constantly in flux. Few bodybuilders wind up staying at Olympic Gym longer than 5 years. The women, who now comprise about 30% of the population, are substantially different from the men in their social relations, goal orientations, and backgrounds (Klein, 1985b) and are not properly part of this study. At Olympic Gym, most range in age between 19 and 25. Racial composition is increasingly mixed, and race relations are good overall. Because the gym is so well-known, it draws its members from all over the world, lending Olympic Gym a cosmopolitan air unlikely for a gym.

For all the change in Olympic Gym, there is a definite social structure, one that reflects its position in the bodybuilding hierarchy (Klein, 1985a). Six increasingly larger strata can be distinguished and ranked in terms of status. From top down, these are

- owners and managers,
- professional bodybuilders,
- amateur bodybuilders,
- gym rats,
- members at large, and
- pilgrims and onlookers.

Southern California bodybuilders have, over decades, evolved a subculture replete with its own shared terminology, behavior, and values. As with all sub-cultures, there is a cultural and social distance necessary to forge a collective identity—a separation that often comes from being considered marginal or deviant by the larger society. Southern California bodybuilding has had a difficult rela-tionship with the wider society. These days, however, under the guise of superior fitness and cultural popularity, bodybuilders relate to the outside world through a veneer of arrogance, a superiority that continues to veil a deep-seated inferiority. This institutional insecurity is rooted in popular suspicions held about bodybuilders.

BODYBUILDING AND ITS PSYCHOLOGICAL UNDERPINNINGS

Five years of interviewing clearly documented that a major reason many male bodybuilders gravitate to the sport is low self-esteem, which for many triggered a need to compensate by building their physiques. The physique, it could be ar-gued, is a mask or wall between low self-esteem and a potentially threatening outside world. If done within the supportive environment of the subculture of bodybuilding, the process of building oneself up can boost self-confidence. This is often projected as arrogance, so characteristic in subjects' comments about out-siders (e.g., referring to them as "pencilnecks") or their public posturing.

The "Neurotic Element"

Traits such as shortness or stuttering are seen by bodybuilders as afflictions, and insecurities about these traits continue to pull people into bodybuilding decades after the first Charles Atlas ads appeared in comic books and men's magazines. Hence, unlike most sports that use positive impulses to recruit devotees, body-building has always recruited on the basis of what sport psychologist Butts (1976) termed the "neurotic element."

I don't know. I guess I wanted some size. I was, you know, real skinny.

Yeah, I guess there's an element of insecurity in me that will always make me unsatisfied with my build. I think it's true of most of the guys around

here. You don't think that he [pointing] walks like that [exaggerating his mus-
culature] because he's secure, do you?

We couldn't read. We had dyslexia, and the other kids picked on us. So we
got real good at sports and always backed each other up.

The needs of bodybuilders for acknowledgment and admiration are much greater
than for the public at large (Thirer & Wright, 1985). As a subculture, bodybuilding
institutionalizes many of its participants' concerns, objectifying neuroses so that
participants may partially overcome them. This is done by promoting a shared
worldview in which securing size is equated with psychological enhancement.
Yet for some, the needs for admiration and acknowledgment continue to go unmet.

Hypermasculinity and Bodybuilding Subculture

The feelings of insecurity of many bodybuilders are often masked by veneers
of power. The institution of bodybuilding not only makes a fetish of the look
of power but also fosters identification with and reliance upon figures of power
(Klein, 1985b). The claim here is that the institutionalized narcissism of bodybuilding, hypermasculinity, and homophobia is in part a reaction against feelings
of powerlessness. This view is also shared by Adorno (1950), who in interpreting the authoritarian personality associated it with hypermasculinity: overly
muscled bodies, boastfulness, swaggering independence, and worship of power.
Joseph Pleck (1982) goes so far as to claim bodybuilding is "perhaps the archetypal
expression of male identity insecurity," a view shared by Sprague (1982), who
in testing a sample of men and women at Olympic Gym found a high degree of
insecurity.

GENDER NARCISSISM: THE LINK BETWEEN
HUSTLING AND PSYCHOLOGICAL NEED

The feelings of powerlessness and low self-worth that bodybuilders work to overcome are manifested in a craving for admiration. But in bodybuilding terms, admiration is dependent on building a powerful-looking physique and finding people
to acknowledge it. The latter hinges upon *mirroring*, a psychoanalytic term for
having one's ideal sense of self reflected back to oneself through relations with
others.

Narcissism as discussed by Kohut (1971) and Kernberg (1975) deals not simply
with the excessive self-love so popularly associated with narcissism, but with a
deep sense of self-loathing, the origins of which are hotly debated in psychoanalytic
circles. The continuum of narcissism runs from essential (as in healthy ego
development) to pathological (as in expressionless, socially anomic individuals).
For bodybuilders, mirroring is critical to enhancing self-esteem, hence narcissistic
mirroring becomes a functional phenomenon (Klein, 1987).

Mirroring occurs in two ways: direct and indirect. Direct mirroring occurs
through having one's ideal self (the way one would like to be seen) directly

reflected back to him or her through another person. The compliment or other expression of acknowledgment is an example of this. Indirect mirroring can also occur through one's association with a figure or lifestyle. Here, an ideal sense of self (via an external source) is identified and mirrored back through one's ability to emulate the lifestyle of the hero or role model. Arnold Schwarzenegger, for instance, is a hero to many young bodybuilders. When the bodybuilder takes on the lifestyle of the hero, the hero becomes accessible; hence Schwarzenegger can become an extension of the self without any personal contact. Through the body-builder's association with other like-minded questers, a community is formed, and the bodybuilder builds a bridge between his or her psychological needs and the outside world.

Admiration of a bodybuilder's physique declines as one moves away from the subculture. There continues, however, a grudging admiration of the physique, depending on the gender viewing it. In a 1981 street-corner sample of women in a northwestern city, 94% of the women queried (n = 105) ranked photos of bodybuilders as *extremely repulsive* (or a 5 on a scale of 1 to 5, with 1 being *extremely attractive* and 5 being *extremely repulsive*). The same photos shown to men (n = 120) netted only a 49% *extremely repulsive* rating (Klein, n.d.). In short, men were somewhat more drawn to the idea of the male form vis-à-vis themselves than women were.

The non-erotic appreciation of one's own gender, I call gender narcissism. According to this, each sex views its members in two ways: (a) as distinct from the viewer, and hence subject to comparison with the viewer, and (b) as extensions of the viewer. Men and women can see other members of their sexes in comparative terms using criteria to separate one person from another, as when one man views another relatively as more or less attractive or successful. In this sense other men are considered distinct, and all forms of competition as well as more subtle invidious comparisons are prevalent.

However, we also view others as extensions of ourselves.[2] For example, I see one person is powerful, handsome, and highly intelligent, but as a man (or woman) he or she excels relative to me (or as I might do under somewhat different conditions). This dynamic is manifested in such things as compliments or role modeling. Gender narcissism is appropriate here because one has an ideal sense of self reflected back to oneself by behaving or looking like the role model. In this way, gender narcissism is a continuum connecting one person with another.

For men, who in our society have relatively few forms of bonding available to them, the mirroring forthcoming through gender narcissism is potentially very therapeutic. However, homophobia, another element in the masculine complex, short-circuits this potential. The fear of being thought of as gay, or the fear of homosexuality in general, works to curb the expression of gender narcissism and fuels hypermasculinity as well.

For these men, insecurity is incompletely handled by the formal structures of their subculture. Additional admiration is often sought after. Because, as I will argue, hustling of gays constitutes one source of admiration for bodybuilders, the fear of being perceived as homosexual triggers an intensified homophobia as a defense.

Homophobia, then, acts as both a precondition and a consequence of a weakness in the male identity complex. Homophobia is part of most male socialization and results from the inability to establish a more substantive male bonding. As a consequence, the potential benefits that result from gender narcissism are either prevented or truncated.

HOMOPHOBIA

The fear of homosexuality (i.e., homophobia) functions in the socialization of males to establish a standard for permissible and prohibited behavior and values.[3] Working to limit possible behavioral responses in men, Lehne (1976) points to athletes as the only male exception to many homophobic prohibitions: "Only athletes and women are allowed to touch and hug each other in our culture. Athletes are only allowed this because presumably their masculinity is beyond doubt" (p. 124).

This athletic exception turns on a fundamental contradiction, however, one brought out in the autobiography of Dave Kopay, a 10-year veteran of the National Football League (NFL) who emerged from the closet and onto the front pages of many major daily newspapers when he suddenly acknowledged being gay.

> David Kopay's story raises the question not how could he emerge from his super masculine society as a homosexual, but how could any man come through it as purely heterosexual after spending so much time idealizing and worshipping the male body, while denigrating and ridiculing the female. (Kopay & Young, 1977, p. 117)

Kopay's termination from the NFL was as extreme as the excessive and vindictive news coverage. American male anxieties had been hit at the core. Pro-football players especially, it was thought, don't become gay, because they are the gatekeepers of masculinity.

Other examples that juxtapose exaggerated masculinity and homosexuality can be found in the widespread locker-room banter that often centers on homosexuality. Often what begins as a joke evokes very serious and menacing responses. Ironically, then, rather than reducing anxiety (as it is supposed to), joking about homophobia also works to generate anxiety around homosexuality. The practice of hustling is the activity that most brings together these disparate elements into a particularly thorny set of sociological and psychological issues for those who engage in it.

HUSTLING AND BODYBUILDING

The selling of implicit or explicit sex by a bodybuilder to someone gay is called by bodybuilders "hustling," and it appears to be widespread among southern California's most competitive bodybuilders.[4] Hustlers do not consider themselves gay, however. They claim heterosexuality as their sexual preference and hence must find a way to justify what they see as homosexual practices with heterosexual identities (Reiss, 1971). The few hustlers who are gay are seen as gay rather than as hustlers, even though they all engage in the same exchanges.

Hustling was very difficult to learn about directly through interviewing, and for years hustlers did not talk openly to me about it. Because it was so taboo, there were many unanswered questions pertaining to its frequency and forms of rationalization.[5]

Actually, hustling can cover a range of behaviors from popping out of a cake nude at gay parties, to nude photography or pornography, to explicit sex with another man. "You do what your conscience lets you do," as one man put it. All hustling is paid for, however, and all hustling is with gay men.

Incidence of Hustling

Hustling is widely condemned, yet judging by interview and observation, quite common. Estimates from a wide variety of Olympic Gym's core community claim that anywhere from 50 to 80% have at one time hustled or do so now. Even if that estimate were halved, the lower estimate (25%) would still be significant enough to warrant considering the practice widespread. The stigma attached to hustling is so great that only six hustlers granted me formal interviews on the subject. Six others admitted to hustling but limited their comments. Still others could be observed engaged in transactions (e.g., setting up dates and negotiating with potential clients). Despite the formal disapproval and discomfort associated with hustling, it seems to be increasing, prompting one well-placed member in the gym to comment:

> When I first came here I wasn't aware of half of the situation, even though I had a few people hit on me. Before, people had to prove to me that they were gay, now you gotta prove to me that you're straight. Yes, if anything hustling's increased.

A set of 12 out of 80 or 90 men is small, but this small number of hustlers willing to admit to the practice underscores the sensitivity of the matter.

Hustling As an Economic Strategy

Both the money involved and the extensiveness of the network make hustling the bulwark of bodybuilding's underground economy. As such hustling enables competitors, particularly amateurs, to subsidize their training and lifestyles until they either succeed in turning professional or drop out of competition. In the 12 cases of hustlers for whom I was able to document shifts in status from amateur to professional, all but one quit hustling. In short, hustling is an important economic strategy in an environment where access to resources is very limited.

Were one to work for a living, training would have to fit into the few pockets open before or after work. Given the modest educational background of most men in my sample, finding employment that allows that much freedom yet pays enough for training is not likely.[6]

It's not that I'm trying to make it [hustling] okay for me. This is a constant conflict in myself, because I don't have to be one. But, I trained for the Mr. America for 8 hours a day—8 hours of some sort of training. I couldn't do that working 12 hours a day in some shipyard. I simply couldn't do it.

Segments of the gay community have been bankrolling aspiring bodybuilders in southern California for decades. Gay patrons can be found on the margins of the subculture as well as in positions of importance (e.g., entrepreneurs, contest promoters, gym owners, judges, competitors, and gym members).

Hustling As a Psychological Strategy

The need for admiration that many bodybuilders have may be only partially satisfied within the institutional and cultural confines of the subculture. It seems that quite a few crave additional acknowledgment, and for them a natural bridge exists between them and segments of the gay community. Whether these bodybuilders exploit that bridge or not is another matter. This potential source of psychological gratification gains impetus from the difficulty most bodybuilders have succeeding in the southern California bodybuilding scene. Competition for titles is keen, getting into the magazines is very difficult, and the caliber of bodybuilders is world-class. Informants often languished in obscurity in Los Angeles after having been highly successful elsewhere. In gay circles, one can more easily receive admiration or even become a minor celebrity.

Drifting Into Hustling

Matza's (1964, 1969) and Davis's (1971) notion of drifting into deviant identity was also evident in some of the people I interviewed. Drift allows one to account for the time and psychological processes needed to alter one's thinking and take on a new identity.

The high risk in going to Los Angeles to compete is coupled with the youthfulness and naiveté of many of the men making the trek. Their economic vulnerabilities quickly become apparent to any veteran bodybuilder as well as to the gays on the fringes of the community. Many veterans (gay and straight) offer these new arrivals tips on survival, some offering places to stay and jobs. This is commonly done in the spirit of camaraderie. Some veterans, however, are looking to "hit on" (make sexual advances to) these youthful questers.

I knew a gay guy back in New York. One gay guy, and I liked him. I respected him. When I came out here I had guys hitting on me, and I didn't even know it. I had a guy hand me a card that said he was a photographer. He said, "If you wanna make some bucks, give me a call." I said, "Geez, thanks. That's great! Here's a guy doin' me a favor, wants to take photos of me." I didn't have any [photos] in my portfolio. That's great. Boy did I learn. It was my ass he wanted.

When such offers turn into powerful sexual pressures, the pressures may overwhelm a young bodybuilder, forcing him into an act of hustling. Davis (1971) discusses the same psychological pressures among young prostitutes as they slip into an identity premised on moral trespass.

Once involved, hustlers move into a network of gays who seek out bodybuilders. Hustlers begin to place and answer ads (some explicitly for sex, others for "escort service") in the larger gay newspapers. Most, however, stay within the very personal network of the gym subculture or the larger network of gays from Palm Springs to San Francisco. Typically, this means a "repeat business" of calling to make arrangements or waiting to be called. Some hustlers establish large clienteles, which they guard against other hustlers, and very well-known hustlers can command as much as $500 a visit. A few hustlers have parlayed hustling into lucrative gay-porno film careers. New arrivals to the scene are lured in more easily through accounts of the many famous bodybuilders who hustled in the past.

HUSTLING AS PERSONAL CONFLICT

Every hustler interviewed reported some conflict in terms of the juxtaposition of hustling and heterosexual identity. Reiss's (1971) study of street delinquents as hustlers pointed to a set of behaviors to which hustlers adhered to avoid such conflict and social stigmatization. The norms that bodybuilders use to separate themselves from homosexuals appear not to work as well.

It is ironic that so many strands of the American male psyche are brought together in hustling: needing to be seen as virile and sexually desirable, male bonding, disdain for effeminacy, competition, and aggression. One hustler stated it quite eloquently:

It's kinda sad. We put ourselves in a bad social position. I know people who hire us for posing, but there's more expected than that. It puts bodybuilding in a shitty position—to be laughed at. Who's gonna help bodybuilders? A bunch of homosexuals, that's who. We're everything the U.S. is supposed to stand for: strength, determination, everything to be admired. But it's not the girls that like us, it's the fags!

The potential crisis inherent in hustling must be weighed against the needs it meets. The ease with which money is made is one compelling factor, but there is also psychological reinforcement at work that both considers the hustler's myriad needs and causes him a great deal of anxiety.

Juggling one's self-concept and rationalizing how others feel about it make hustling difficult to handle. Many simply deny it. One top professional pointed to the hustler's avoidance behaviors as an index that makes hustlers easy to spot; he noted that hustlers often won't look him in the eye as a result of a public stand he took on hustling. Sometimes, he pointed out, the hustler is so conflicted as to develop nervous twitches.

At times, the strain of acting straight while hustling reaches crisis proportions. In the years spent studying the gym, there were three reported suicide attempts as well as a greater number of bodybuilders who in response to their conflicts repudiated the subculture altogether. Some joined religious groups, perhaps in an effort to quell inner turmoil.

The promoters and officials of the sport who dominate bodybuilding ideology seek to conceal or downplay the institution of hustling. They see this practice as threatening their vested interests. These people have, on more than a few occasions, threatened to censor bodybuilders, cutting them off from their mail order ads in magazines and thereby wiping out their businesses if the bodybuilders are too open about hustling. At Olympic Gym hustling is officially repudiated, though there is a tacit understanding that hustling is imperative for survival.

Psychological Coping and Hustling

In order to facilitate these opposing moralities (hustling and heterosexuality) and reduce anxiety, bodybuilders make use of *compartmentalization* as a defense. Hustlers compartmentalize by separating their hustling from their straight life, prompting one young hustler to claim:

> Hey, it's tougher for gay guys to hustle cuz they gotta be into it. But me, I can get it on with anybody. It's like I'm two different people.

Because the gym is an intimate universe, however, the separation so important to identity management is always in jeopardy, hinging on the first angry outburst by another bodybuilder. Walking into the gym, a hustler hopes that others won't confront him with barbs or wisecracks, which can become the source of serious confrontations.

The time and emotional commitment hustling demands can create a host of problems for a serious heterosexual relationship. The women involved not only have to accept infidelity from their partners but the homosexual nature of the infidelity as well. From the men's perspective, mixing the two can prove too complicated and, as this hustler phrased it, too morally problematic.

> On any given time I can go out with a woman. But it's not very satisfying, like a regular kind of relationship. Women demand time, and I'm too involved in bodybuilding. . . . I miss her [pointing to pictures of an ex-mate that are all around his apartment]. I lived with that girl for a year and a half. But it's not that good. Several [women] know what I'm doing. Some can handle it, but some can't and that's another reason. I couldn't lie, that's why I'm not living with anybody.

In one instance a hustler, confessing to the woman he had been involved with about his "California" activities, got her to come out to Los Angeles. She seemed to understand, yet whenever they argued, she would seize on his hustling past. Driving by his apartment, she would scream (much to his chagrin), "Charlie! You're a goddamn faggot!" Other hustlers, however, make the transition back to their heterosexual relations more easily.

Sexual activity among competitive bodybuilders is an area of life that must be carefully parceled out. The rigors of dieting, of training, and more importantly of excessive steroid use severely curb the capacity and will for sex. Trying to juggle homosexual and heterosexual contacts exacerbates this situation. One hustler (who was also gay) who was close to two other hustlers and their female mates pointed out some problems:

I used to hear these guys going on about their girls. The girls did this and that, and how great they were sexually. But, I knew their girls real well, and they'd talk about how these guys would only go down on them [perform oral sex to bring them to climax] in order to get them off, ya know? But they, the guys, couldn't get it up. They couldn't get hard-ons no matter what. The girls were always goin' on about being horny.

Coping by Compartmentalizing

Compartmentalizing also makes use of the ideology of heterosexuality. Here, the hustler clings to a self-description of being heterosexual while abstaining from heterosexuality. It was not uncommon for men who had not had heterosexual relationships for 2 or 3 years to refer to themselves as straight by invoking their past: pointing to pictures of ex-mates or excessively referring to ex-mates as if they were momentarily coming back.

Psychological and/or social distance is another dimension of compartmentalization. Reiss (1971) and Humphreys (1970) point out that the hustler's need to deny the possibility of being emotionally dependent or involved in any way with the other party is critical. Kirkham's (1971) study of homosexuality in prisons also shows that for most inmates who maintained heterosexual identity despite homosexual activity, two conditions must be met. First, the participants must believe that they only engage in the act because they lack the opportunity for heterosexual contact. Second, they must be emotionally distant from the act. To ensure this distance, they often punctuate their sex acts with violence or macho toughness.

Like Reiss's "peer-queer" relations, hustlers at the gym restrict their practices to oral sex with the hustler being fellated. However, there are accounts in the gym of hustlers resorting to a wider series of behaviors than reported in Reiss's work. Nude dancing at parties as well as sex acts beyond the norm are occasionally reported. Generally, the hustler sets up the rules, but if the gay male is particularly assertive or powerfully connected in the bodybuilding community, this may be altered. The result is a good deal of jockeying for control in the relationship.

Despite the symbiosis, this relationship is rooted in negativity. This in itself is sufficient to create an adaptive distance. Among themselves, each side denigrates the other. Hustlers prefer to see themselves as exploiting gays for quick money. For the gays, being able to buy hustlers equals control over men who seemingly denigrate gays. Each side also winds up feeling stigmatized by the relationship. For gay men the stigma comes from having to buy sex when they ought to be desirable enough to have it offered to them. They, in turn, project their self-loathing onto bodybuilders, who they see as brutish and vulgar. Because the bodybuilder often tries to establish the ground rules, gays tend to see bodybuilders as overly aggressive, whereas bodybuilders, having to deal with their homophobia, view gays as the source of their corruption. This, of course, exacerbates their homophobia. In short, resentment abounds as each party is reluctantly fused to the other through the vagaries of the market and the pull of the id.

As viewed by two gay bodybuilders who were knowledgeable of the southern California hustling scene, characterizing of gays as loathsome predators is the fabrication of the hustler who must protect himself from doubts about his sexuality:

> Truth is that there are a lot of gays around bodybuilding who are kind, giving people. We didn't want a thing to do with most of the young hustlers, but they'd hang around us. It got so bad that we'd hear them coming up the stairs and go, "Oh, no, don't answer the door." They'd even paw us, literally, and try to do other things that they thought we'd like, you know, just to get our attention.

Homophobic reactions are sometimes violent (Dundes, 1985). Gays at Olympic Gym recount tales of the contradictory feelings that hustlers sometimes have toward them:

> I remember Stan G. He'd grab gays who came into the gym to watch bodybuilders. He'd grab them and say, "Okay fag. I want you out." Well, I saw him in the Village in New York, and he said he didn't really feel that way, but felt like he was expected to do it.

Symbiotic Relationship of Hustling and Homophobia

Hustling and homophobia are mutually dependent and are instrumental in maintaining the hustler's heterosexual identity. Engaging in homosexual behavior works to perpetuate homophobia, and homophobia as an escape valve thrives on this form of homosexual prostitution:

> I'll tell you, being involved in it [hustling] reaffirmed my whole thing with straightness. I remember in San Francisco, I was involved in all this, and you start seeing these people as leeches and vicious. That's okay for some people, but that's not the way I wanna go.

Hustling may intensify heterosexual identification by giving concrete focus to homophobia. Emotionally removed from the homosexual relationship by keeping it at the level of exchange, the hustler distinguishes himself from the gay male who would do it for lust or love. The hustler sees gays as men who have seduced him into homosexual acts, and this resentment convinces him, despite all evidence to the contrary, that he remains heterosexual. Additionally, however, the needs he has for esteem and for being physically appreciated—needs met primarily by men—can be realized as he affirms his heterosexuality. Hustling is in the novel position of both resolving and creating crises in self-esteem and self-definition. The tenacity of hustling behavior, despite condemnation from every side, is evident in the following:

> You don't think about it while you're doin' it [hustling]. It's after you stop that it gets really heavy. You don't know how hard it is to stop hustling.

CONCLUSION

From a social-psychological vantage point, hustling in bodybuilding was shown to be frought with difficulties. Compartmentalization, in various forms, was seen as the primary mechanism by which bodybuilding hustlers tried to maintain their heterosexuality.

Our society's excessively rigid notions of masculinity find an intensified expression in bodybuilding and in hustling in particular. While fostering behavior and values that underscore virility and macho posturing, the bodybuilding subculture simultaneously creates new problems stemming from some of those same sources. One important result, though it is beyond the strict scope of this study, is the potential damage to males and society caused by this restrictive mind-set. Because culturally derived male traits of homophobia, hypermasculinity, and gender narcissism all exist in a dialectical relationship with female traits, what we see in our examination of men is misogyny, the reification of maleness, and a disdain for the effeminate. Bodybuilding's exaggeration of form can be interpreted as a cultural reaffirmation of cartoon masculinity, the reduction of sex to caricatures (e.g., Rambo or Barbie and Ken dolls).

Chapter 11

Gay Jocks:
A Phenomenology
of Gay Men in Athletics[1]

Brian Pronger

Imagine walking into the crowded reception area of a major athletic facility at an international swimming competition. You have spent the last year training intensively, expecting that today you are going to swim faster than ever before. The foyer is packed with athletes, all of whom are at their peak of physical fitness, ready to race. The place is exciting.

On the deck just before the race the energy is amazing. So much power and speed in one place is awe inspiring. Everywhere you turn there are men stretching and shaking the tension out of their powerful muscles—lithe bodies being tuned for the last time before the final event. You, too, are ready to fly into action at the sound of the gun. Bang! In less than a minute the race is over. You swam your personal best—victory.

The last event in the meet is the relays, in some ways the most exciting part of any meet. Team spirit is at its height, and these guys are ready to tear up the water.

As each swimmer flings himself into the pool there is a burst of energy, lane after lane. These are men pushing themselves to the limit; every fibre of every body feels itself to be the consummation of power and masculinity. The race is over. The mood is ecstatic.

Relief. You, with your teammates, hit the showers with the hundred or so other swimmers. Everyone is exhausted and delirious from the racing. This time in the showers, overwhelming with steam and muscle, marks the end of an athletic experience. These powerful men know what it means to be men and athletes.

You exchange an ironic glance and a knowing smile with the blond swimmer from Thunder Bay next to you. The two of you, in the midst of this concentrated masculinity, also know a great deal about what it means to be athletes and men. As gay men, you and your friend from Thunder Bay have experienced many things in common with the other men at the competition, most of whom are probably straight. Other experiences, however, have been and will be different. The following is an exploration of some of those unique differences.[2]

This paper uses a phenomenological perspective to shed light on those experiences that gay men have in athletics that are unlike those of nongay men. It is essential to remember that many of the experiences of men who are not gay are also open to gay men. I will argue that the experience of being gay is a matter of context, that is, of understanding oneself in the light of socially constructed sexual and gender categories. These are contexts through which one can pass through different periods of life, from day to day and from moment to moment. This fluidity of context can predispose some men to a special way of interpreting the world that is ironic. This ironic point of view can shape the experiences that gay men have in athletics.

HISTORICAL AND THEORETICAL INTRODUCTION

The first problem faced in any investigation of gay men is defining about whom we are speaking. When we discuss the anthropology or sociology of women, it is fairly clear to whom we refer. However, when we talk about gay men, we are presented with a moving target. Definitions of sexuality have changed over the years (Foucault, 1978; Katz, 1983; J. Marshall, 1981; Plummer, 1981; Weeks, 1986). Michel Foucault and Jeffrey Weeks have suggested that the heterosexual and homosexual categories are not ahistorical and unchanging; they depend upon complex historical circumstances. The homosexual category emerged in the 18th and 19th centuries, and its creation was related to the development of capitalism and the triumph of the positive sciences (Weeks, 1981). Before that time there were no homosexuals, only homosexual acts. Foucault and Weeks argue that the creation of sexual categories such as *heterosexual, homosexual, pedophile*, and *transvestite* comprise a form of social control (Foucault, 1978; Weeks, 1981). Through confinement of legitimate sexuality to heterosexuality and the family, and through the marginalization of other machinations of sexual expression, the social behaviour of individuals has, by and large, been controlled in the service of social order and economic productivity.

Most recent research on homosexuality has focussed on the social historical forces that have shaped and conceptualized the lives of contemporary men and women. The concern has been with the creation of sexual categories (Plummer, 1981). This phenomenological investigation, as a study of the way in which athletic experience emerges for gay men, is concerned not so much with the categories themselves as with the ways that individuals interact with historically constructed sexual categories in athletic settings.[3] In conjunction with my study of gay men in athletics, I conducted indepth interviews with 30 gay-identified men and two heterosexually identified national coaches. There was no attempt to obtain a statistically valid sample; such an approach is impossible in the study of gay men, because the meaning of being gay is highly subjective and therefore ambiguous.

Contemporary gay men, like anyone else, find themselves in a world of meaning, a world that has changed over time under the influence of a multitude of historical and cultural circumstances. The anthropologist Clifford Geertz (1973) said that "man is an animal suspended in webs of significance he himself has spun" (p. 5). Culture, Geertz says, is such a web, and the study of it is a search for meaning. As gay men approach an athletic experience, they may confront athletic culture and find meaning in it through a special gay sensibility has developed out of a unique web of significance drawn from the experience of being gay in a straight world. As we shall see, the world of athletics is a gymnasium of heterosexual masculinity. The unique experience that gay men can have of athletics involves the special meaning they find in masculinity.

POWER, MASCULINITY, AND ATHLETICS

In their review of the sociological literature on masculinity, Carrigan, et al. (1985) write, "One of the central facts about masculinity, is that men in general are advantaged by the subordination of women" (p. 590). One of the techniques for the subordination of women by men is a complex semiotic of masculine and feminine behaviours that communicate power. As Foucault (1976) has explained, power is

- a multiplicity of force relations,
- a process that transforms, strengthens, or reverses those relations,
- the support that those force relations find in one another, and
- the strategies that these relations employ.

In patriarchal society, men have power over women; the practice of masculine behaviour by men and feminine behaviour by women is the semiotic instrument of this power.

A common understanding of the difference between masculinity and femininity can be seen if we look at the dictionary; a number of important themes emerge. Power is the distinguishing feature of masculinity, whereas lack of power is the distinguishing feature of femininity. The *Oxford English Dictionary* (OED) defines *masculine* as "having the appropriate excellences of the male sex; manly, virile, vigorous, powerful." Interestingly, whereas *masculine* is defined in terms of "excellences," the OED offers a depreciative use of *feminine*, which is "womanish, effeminate." In this depreciative use, the powerlessness that is associated with femininity is borne out. The OED defines *effeminate* as "to make unmanly; to enervate. To grow weak, languish."

One form of masculine behaviour is the development and display of physical strength, an important phenomenon in the world of athletics. The masculine development and display of physical strength by men, in conjunction with its lack in women, embody Foucault's conception of power. Power, as a multiplicity of force relations, can be seen in the dominant and subordinate positions of men and women, respectively. As a process that transforms, strengthens, or reverses those relations, the masculine development of physical strength certainly fortifies the power relations between men and women. The complementarity of masculinity and femininity, of strength and weakness, functions as a system of support that the force relations between men and women find in one another. The actual development and display of physical strength is one of the many strategies that these force relations employ (see Foucault, 1978, pp. 92-93). Masculinity, then, is a strategy for the power relations between men and women; it is a strategy that serves the interests of patriarchal heterosexuality. Athletics, as a sign of masculinity in men, can be an instrument of those power relations.

GAY MEN AND MASCULINITY

Given the patriarchal heterosexual significance of masculinity, it can have a special meaning for gay men. In their personal lives, many urban gay men do not benefit significantly from the hegemony that masculinity is meant to afford men; some live their lives in virtual isolation from women. Others experience their relations with women as ones of equality. Women are sensitive to the difference between men who may see them as potential lovers, sexual partners, or victims of rape and those men who have no sexual interest in women and pursue them as friends on an equal basis. All the gay men I interviewed told me their relationships with women are very good; the men feel themselves to be on equal terms with women, and women seem to trust these men more than they do other men. A rower told me:

> My involvement with women is extremely important. I would guess that a lot of my closest friendships are with women, and it's a very central thing to what I am doing, doing things with women and being close to women, very important. I would guess it would be a very even split between women

friends and men friends. . . . I don't notice anything unequal any more so than with my men friends.

This ease of social intercourse makes possible personal relations with women that are not patriarchal. The patriarchal signification of the masculine/feminine spectrum of behaviors, therefore, has little meaning to gay men in their personal lives. I am not suggesting that gay men are immune to patriarchal advantage. In a patriarchal society, certain things are automatically accorded men, such as privileged professional and financial advantage over women in economic life. But here I am describing the personal experiences that gay men have with women. In gay men's personal interactions with women, masculine patriarchal semiotics are generally inappropriate and insignificant.

Although gay men are not actively involved in hegemonic relations with women, these men are not unaware of the use of the masculine/feminine spectrum of behaviours. Because gay men grow up in a predominantly heterosexual world, they have learned the standard language of masculinity. In coming out, which is a process of becoming gay-identified in some public contexts, one becomes resolved that one is not part of the mainstream of society and that, in some way, one fits the socially constructed category of the homosexual or gay man. In this often-long process, we reinterpret the predominantly heterosexual world in which we find ourselves.

One of those reinterpretations, I propose, is of the meaning of masculine and feminine behaviour. Gay men can come to see that the power relations for which the semiotics of masculinity and femininity constitute a strategy have little to do with their lives. The meaning of masculinity, consequently, begins to change. Although masculinity is often the object of sexual desire for gay men, its role in their lives is ironic. Said one of my interviewees:

For gay men, masculinity has this kind of double edge to it; on the one side it's something they find erotically attractive to them in some ways, but on the other side it's the area which they are least able in some ways to perform correctly. For me to be masculine in my real life [like many gay men, he has developed muscles so that he can pretend to be masculine while pursuing sex] is a very difficult feat—it's something I'd have to work at constructing.

Like this man, many gay men may consciously employ masculine behaviours, yet I have also noticed that other gay men, shortly after coming out, start to show more effeminate mannerisms.[4] As one man told me, "Gay men are aware of more flexibility in these things than others." Indeed, for many gay men, masculinity and femininity cease to be experienced as what one *is*, and they become, quite consciously, ways in which one *acts*.

GAY MEN AND EFFEMINACY

Early theories of homosexuality were concerned with its aetiology (J. Marshall, 1981). Homosexuality was categorized by 19th-century medicine as a psychosocial disorder. The source of this disorder was in what was then considered to be the biological formation of gender. It was thought that homosexuality was a symptom of gender confusion. Many gay theoreticians maintain that the old conception of homosexuals as effeminate is simply fallacious. Gay men, theoreticians claim, are just as masculine as heterosexual men (Levine, 1979). Any sense of incongruity, therefore, between homosexuality and athletic participation would be a misunderstanding of the true case of homosexuality. Such a reading ignores both the intrinsically heterosexual meaning of masculinity (as a semiotic instrument for the subordination of women) and the historical influences that have shaped homosexuality. My research suggests that this meaning and history cannot be so easily dismissed. Gay men are aware of the popular effeminate image of homosexuality. This image is important as a point of reference for the sense of identity and behaviour of many gay men. Furthermore, there are gay men who intentionally employ effeminate behaviour. Effeminate behaviour in men is clearly seen to signify homosexuality, and gay men who want to call attention to their sexuality can do so by behaving effeminately. Said Quentin Crisp (1968), "Blind with mascara and dumb with lipstick, I paraded the streets of Pimlico. . . . My function in life . . . was to render what was already clear, blindingly conspicuous" (p. 114).

Gay men can employ masculine and feminine behaviours at will, depending on the social context and what they are trying to express. Most gay men have had the experience of "butching it up" when trying to hide their homosexuality. Likewise, many know what it means to "let your hair down" and "camp it up" among friends. This variability in the use of masculine and feminine behaviours indicates an important dimension to the experience of being gay, which is the experience of fluidity.

THE FLUIDITY OF BEING GAY AND PASSING AS STRAIGHT

Whereas Foucault and others have argued that the homosexual category has come to define the entire person (1978), I suggest that gay men experience substantial fluidity in the application of the category to themselves. Gay men contextualize their experiences. They apply culturally received categories of homosexuality at different times and under different circumstances. In a comment that was similar to those of many of the men I interviewed, one said:

Basically, my day-to-day life is quite straight, except for lunch, the informal social occasions when I can let loose with a gay reference. Socially, maybe 2 or 3 times a week, it's getting together for dinner or going to a bar, just me and my lover; we don't live together yet. There are gay times in the week and not gay times of the week. There is a fluidity to being gay.

By the implementation of gay sensibilities (which I will describe shortly), in reference to the historically constructed category of the homosexual, gay men can create gay cultural contexts not only in gay-community settings but also in nongay settings, such as mainstream athletics. Gay culture is not limited to life in the more or less formal institutions of the gay community such as bars, sports clubs, political groups, and churches. Gay culture (keeping in mind that culture is a "web of significance") is the world in which gay people meet—socially, intellectually, artistically, emotionally, politically, sexually, spiritually, and athletically. Gay culture can be expressed wherever there are gay people.

Gay men pass in and out of gay contexts, moment to moment, day to day, and through different periods of their lives. Gay contexts are created not only by the presence of gay men but also by their decisions to interpret a situation as gay. Consequently, it is possible for a gay man to go to a gymnasium, be completely involved in the athleticism of his workout, and experience that time as being simply athletic, devoid of any gay significance as far as he is concerned. Another day, he may go to the same gymnasium and find the same men there doing much the same exercises as they were previously; this time, however, he sees the experience as a gay experience. That is, he may find the situation sexy; he may find it ironic (as I will explain shortly); he may decide that he is with only other gay men and experience a sense of gay fraternity. The gay context depends on the man's interpretation. Self-concept also depends upon personal interpretation. A man who is a runner may enter the Boston Marathon, an event that he considers to be very important to himself athletically. His concerns are whether he will finish, what his time might be, or how painful the experience will be. Here, his concept of himself is overwhelmingly that of a runner. The same man could enter the same marathon another year, and having decided to wear a singlet with a large pink triangle emblazoned with the word *gay*, he sees himself as a gay runner and his participation in this race as an expression of his pride in being gay.

The fluidity of homosexuality is enhanced by the fact that gay men can and often do pass as straight men. In a society that assumes that everyone is heterosexual, it is relatively easy for homosexual men to "pass." This ability is a distinguishing feature of the homosexual minority; people of colour cannot easily pass as white, and women have a difficult time passing as men. Passing is particularly important in mainstream athletic culture where heterosexuality is expected (Kidd, 1987; Kopay & Young, 1977). Certainly, it is usually necessary for gay men to pass as straight in the potentially sexual situations of men's locker rooms and showers.

Afraid of losing their positions on teams, as a result of the compulsory heterosexuality of sport, many gay athletes find it necessary to hide their homosexuality by passing as straight. I interviewed an international competitive rower who said it was essential to seem to be heterosexual:

> You did everything you could to hang on to your seat, to make the crew, that you would never jeopardize—you wouldn't even tell the coach you had a cold. You could be *crippled* and you'd hide it from the coach, because if there's any perceived weakness, they'll put somebody else in the boat. So to hint that I was gay was to kiss rowing goodbye.

THE IRONIC GAY SENSIBILITY

The experiences of fluidity and passing can dispose gay men to a special way of understanding the world. This can lead one to a special knowledge that is uniquely gay. Schutz (in Zaner and Enggelhardt, 1974) argues that a phenomeno-logical account of knowledge reveals that it is basically social. This, he says, leads to the notion of the "social distribution of knowledge," which is demon-strated in the different knowledge that men and women have in our society. I argue that just as gender in sexist society affords people special knowledge that emerges from their positions in society, so too sexual orientation, in a society that is divided along those lines, privileges people with characteristic knowledge. Gay irony is a unique way of knowing that has its origins in the social construc-tion of heterosexist society. The ways that gay men think are very much the results of having to deal with homophobia. To avoid suffering in potentially homopho-bic settings like athletic teams and locker rooms, gay men learn to pass as straight. Passing predisposes gay men to a sense of irony.

From an early age, gay men are aware of this important irony—they seem to be heterosexual when in fact they are not. Most social relations are organized around heterosexuality. For boys, the social side of sports is heterosexual. One's teammates form a "boys-wanting-girls club." When a young male athlete socializes with his teammates, inside or outside the locker room, talk is often about sex with girls and the problems of dating. Bars, clubs, or athletic dances held to mark the end of a sporting season or a school victory are always hetero-sexual functions. In their early years, most young gay people follow this social pattern.

A gay man may follow these patterns, but because he is not really part of the heterosexual action, the budding gay man is aware of himself as an outsider, an observer. The position of the observer is an ironic stance (Muecke, 1982). A young homosexual person can be aware of himself as an outsider without having understood himself as homosexual. In fact, this sense of being an outsider may lead to one's self-identification as homosexual. During this time the foundation for a young gay person's sense of irony develops. In his position as an observer, the young gay man, probably unconsciously, masters some of the basic skills of the ironist. As he grows older he becomes increasingly aware of himself as the observer who seems to be part of the action. Although he may never define his world as ironic, the gay man may, nevertheless, employ irony unwittingly. (One need not analyze and define the formal structure of a way of thinking or being in order to use that structure in day-to-day-life.) Growing up in a world in which heterosexuality is taken for granted, then, gay people may be introduced to the rudiments of irony. By developing this sense and seeing his world as ironic, the gay man can manipulate the socially constructed incompatibility of the appearance and the reality of his sexuality.

Wayne Booth (1974) says that fundamental to irony is its invitation to reconstruct something deeper than what is apparent on the surface. While inviting one to see deeper than the superficial appearance and thereby understand what is actually meant, irony preserves the appearance. The total truth includes both appearance and reality. This technique for understanding reality while maintaining a cosmetic appearance is very useful to gay men while passing as straight. It is a technique that many of us learn to use at very young ages simply in order to survive. Because gay men feel at home with irony, even when "the closet" is not an issue, they continue to interpret their worlds ironically. Because irony brings with it a sense of superiority, a sense of looking at the world from a higher place (Muecke, 1982), each gay ironic experience is a sublime reaffirmation of a gay worldview.

Gay irony is a way of thinking, communicating, and being that emerges out of the experience of being gay in a society in which people tend to believe that everyone is straight. It is a sensibility that is essentially fluid both through the lives of individuals and throughout society. The phenomenon of being gay is a matter of context; so too is the invocation of gay irony. Not all homosexual people see themselves as "gay," and not all gay people use irony. Being gay and the use of irony are conceptual dispositions and techniques that people use to think about themselves and interpret their worlds. Irony is a form of interpretation, a way of understanding that develops out of the experience of individuals' interactions with sexual and gender categories. Gay irony, therefore, is best understood as a tendency to interpret experience ironically rather than a consistent standpoint shared by all gay men.

THE IRONIC EXPERIENCE
OF GAY MEN IN ATHLETICS

In our society, which places great importance on sex and restricts "legitimate" sexuality to heterosexuality and the family (Foucault, 1978), the assumption is that virtually everyone is heterosexual. This is almost universally the case in athletics, where, for example, men and women's locker rooms are always segregated. The assumption is that the heterosexual desires of men and women may be stimulated if male and female athletes were to see each other naked. The fact that men may find it sexually stimulating to be in a locker room full of other naked male athletes is either ignored or sublimated through aggressive, homophobic, and sexist humor.

The popular images of the athlete and the gay man are virtually antithetical. The history of homosexuality has constructed a less than positive and healthy conception of the homosexual man, whereas the popular image of the athlete is quintessentially healthy and positive. Many writers have suggested that athletics and healthy heterosexual masculinity are popularly equated: Bob Connell, David Kopay, and Don Sabo, to name only a few. Certainly, the popular image of the athlete as a healthy model citizen is unlike the judicial, medical, and religious models that have categorized the homosexual man as a criminal, pathological, degenerate sinner (J. Marshall, 1981; Weeks, 1981). Being both athletic and gay presents a seeming contradiction, one of which many gay athletes are aware. Many of the gay athletes to whom I spoke said that when they were younger, they thought it was impossible to be both athletic and gay. This juxtaposition of the popular models of athletics and homosexuality, of appearance and reality, in the lives of gay athletes is a significant contribution to the ironic experience of gay men in athletics.

Anagnorisis

Gay men subtly communicate their shared worldview by using irony. This subtlety has important implications for gay men; it allows them to remain undiscovered by the uninitiated, thereby affording them some protection from the expressions of homophobia that frequently accompany detection. Especially important in gay irony is *anagnorisis*, which is the observer's recognition of the ironist as an ironist with a deeper intent than that which is immediately apparent on the surface. Anagnorisis occurs when the interpreter of the irony realizes the irony in the situation. In anagnorisis, the gay ironist not only reveals meanings that have been concealed by appearances, he also reveals himself. Eye contact is the way gay men usually recognize each other in nongay settings. One manifestation of this eye contact can be a subtle, knowing look, which can be the clue for mutual anagnorisis. One man told me about being in a university weight room and watching an athlete to whom he was attracted lifting a weight. To most observers, the scenario would appear to be quite straight. A man whom he didn't know was standing nearby and watching the same athlete. Moving from the athlete to each other, their admiring eyes met, and with no more obvious gesture than a slight pause in their gazes, they became aware of their secret fraternity. In their sententious exchange of glances, having as novelist John Fowles said, "the undeclared knowledge of a shared imagination," their worlds touched. They uttered not a word.

Acting Versus Being

As a result of coming out in some contexts, gay men become more consciously aware of passing in others; gay men can start to see others' uses of masculinity as a technique for passing. This insight can bring them to a heightened awareness of their uses of masculinity as an ironic form. Rather than thinking of themselves as being masculine, gay men can come to think of themselves as acting masculine. In the 1970s, the disco group "The Village People" epitomized this masculine (and I think intensely ironic) act. Their outfits were ironic caricatures of masculinity: construction worker, policeman, Indian, and a hypermasculine-looking man with a mustache (a style known as the "clone"). One of their hit songs had the lyrics, "Macho, macho, man; I wanna be a macho man." The clue to their irony lies in the fact that they don't say they are macho men; rather, they "wanna be" macho men. That is, they look like macho men when in fact they are not. The macho look, especially that of the clone, became very popular in gay ghettos across North America and parts of Europe. The deep and sometimes subliminal irony of the gay masculine clone style[5] may best be appreciated in the light of Wallace Stevens (1977): "The final belief is to believe in a fiction, which you know to be a fiction, there being nothing else. The exquisite truth is to know that it is a fiction and that you believe in it willingly" (p. 163).

Two Ironies of Muscular Bodies

The attraction that many gay men have for masculine men presents a uniquely gay male interpretation of masculinity. Athletic, muscular bodies are masculine bodies. The popularity of muscles among gay men is evidenced by the predominance of muscular iconography in gay liberation magazines, erotica, and soft-core and hard-core pornography. Over the last 15 years or so, there has been a substantial migration of gay men to gymnasiums, so much so that some major cities have gymnasiums where the majority of members are gay men. The development of muscular bodies by gay men presents two important ironies. In the *Leviathan* (1651/1968), Hobbes says that "Forme is Power, because being a promise of Good, it recommendeth men to the favour of women and strangers" (p. 151). The well-defined muscular body is a sign of strength, an indication of the power that has historically been given to men. The armour of Roman centurions was an exaggerated sculpture of a muscular male torso. The intention, no doubt, was to create the appearance of considerable strength, which would inhibit those who wished to usurp the officer's power. The truly masculine man with his muscular body asserts his authority over women and inhibits other men; his muscular appearance is meant to deter other men. This signification of muscular bodies is commonly understood. A gay man with a muscular body, however, has little intention of asserting his authority over women and may well have every intention of attracting other men. The significance that gay men give to the athletic body is ironic in that the masculine appearance that normally is meant to inhibit men emerges as an invitation to men.

The second irony of gay muscular bodies involves a dualism of mind and body. The muscled athletic male body is an expression of a powerful masculine mental disposition. John Hoberman (1984) points out that many prominent fascist leaders have exploited the athletic body (not necessarily their own bodies; i.e., they surround themselves with athletes) to express their power. Idi Amin, 6 feet and 4 inches, who before ascending to power in Uganda was the Ugandan heavyweight boxing champion, used his considerable athletic build to dramatize his political power (Hoberman, 1984). Someone who has developed a powerful body is perceived as also having the mental resolve to mobilize his body into masculine action. By masculine action, I mean seizing patriarchal opportunities as they are presented and inhibiting other men. Some muscular gay men can be effeminate; here we have the irony of an effeminate mind in a masculine body. One man I interviewed did weight lifting exclusively as a masculine sexual lure. Pinpointing the fluidity, superficiality, and therefore irony of this masculinity, he said he used it

> as a tool to pick up men. I think I tend to exempt myself from, well, as I think a lot of gay people do, from the standard divisions [of] male and female, masculine and feminine. That we can make up our own rules and borrow from one and the other equally, according to what you find palatable or useful or stimulating or interesting.

This gay ironic play with masculinity is highlighted in radical drag. A man with bulging biceps and thunderous thighs wearing a slinky dress and a tiara is, through the juxtaposition of a masculine body and feminine clothes, expressing the overt irony of seeming to be "masculine" when he is also "feminine."

CONCLUSION

In conclusion, because being gay is a fluid experience and because gay men are in the unique position of being able to pass as straight in a society that assumes that everyone is heterosexual, some gay men have developed a special way of interpreting the world that is based on the manipulation of appearance and reality (i.e., the ironic gay sensibility). This is a view of the world that many gay men can apply at will and with which they feel very comfortable. It is an instrument of understanding that plays on the subtleties of life and reveals meanings that are particularly close to the unique experiences of gay men.

The semiotics of masculinity and femininity reveal an intricate spectrum of behaviours for the communication of power in the service of patriarchal heterosexual relations. Although gay men do not benefit significantly in their personal lives from the hegemony that masculinity is meant to afford men, gay men do employ masculine behaviour. The meaning that gay men find in masculinity is distinctive in its sexual and ironic signification.

The gay experience of athletics is a matter of context. Entering into an athletic situation, a gay man can be an athlete whose world is dominated by purely athletic experience: pain, sweat, exertion, the joy of movement. He can be an earnest gay person running a race as a representative of gay pride. He can be a national swim team member covertly communicating with his gay teammates through ironic innuendo. He can be a solitary gay person working out in a crowded university weight room, privately savoring the ironic fact that he is in the midst of a macho temple that for him is almost exploding with sexuality.

At the beginning of this chapter, you were invited to imagine yourself as a swimmer at an international competition. You may remember that after the meet, in the showers, you exchanged an ironic glance and a knowing smile with a friend from Thunder Bay. As gay athletes, your worlds met. In those glances and smiles were distilled personal and cultural histories of homosexuality, masculinity, femininity, sex, and irony.

Chapter 12

Male Cheerleaders and the Naturalization of Gender

Laurel R. Davis

Cheerleading, when it emerged in the late 1800s, was an exclusively male activity. When females entered the cheerleading world during World War I, they were seen as treading on male territory, the territory of sport, and as being in danger of becoming masculinized (Gonzales, 1956; Hatton & Hatton, 1978; Morton, 1952). In the 1940s and 1950s, cheerleading came to be dominated by females as males dropped out of the activity in large numbers (Manfredi, 1983), and by 1970, cheerleading was considered a naturally feminine activity. In the late 1970s, males began to reenter cheerleading at the collegiate level.

This research was initiated to explore gendered meanings in contemporary mixed-sex cheerleading. The focus of this paper is on male cheerleaders as they negotiate gendered meanings in the feminine preserve of cheerleading.[1] My findings illustrate that male cheerleaders work to construct masculine images in modern cheerleading and that a sexual division of labor emerges from their efforts. In the end, cheerleading works to naturalize masculine and feminine ideals, maintaining the images of the cheerleader as naturally female, the spectator as naturally male, and the existing sexual division of labor as naturally the only way to perform. Historical variations of gendered meanings in cheerleading along with the modern male cheerleader's conscious work to construct traditionally gendered meanings are evidence that these meanings are socially constructed.

Data for this study come from field observations of junior high school, high school, and collegiate cheerleaders; analyses of manuals, guidebooks, and the popular literature on cheerleading; and 22 in-depth unstructured interviews. The subjects interviewed included 10 collegiate cheerleaders, 6 collegiate basketball players, and 6 spectators. Each of these three groups consisted of equal numbers of women and men. Two of the cheerleaders and four of the basketball players were black, and the rest of the subjects were white. Only the spectators deviated from the traditionally conceived college age. Six of the cheerleaders had previously cheered for both women's and men's sport, two for just women's sport, and two for just men's sport at the collegiate level. Each of these subgroups consisted of equal numbers of women and men.

CHEERLEADING AS A FEMININE PRESERVE

Cheerleading is perceived as a naturally feminine activity. Among other things, female cheerleaders are stereotyped as good looking, sexy, supportive, bouncy, and bubbly. It is assumed that young girls idolize and want to be cheerleaders. As a female cheerleader put it, "It's just the girl thing to do." A male cheerleader stated, "Basically, when you think of cheerleading, you think of girls." Cheerleading is often viewed as the female place in sport, as this male cheerleader was aware:

> I never thought about a guy becoming a cheerleader. It just didn't click with, like, growing up in sports and stuff like that. Like, the guys were the ones that were playing sports and the girls were the one cheering for them.

Female Cheerleaders and the Feminine Image

An important part of the feminine image of cheerleading is the notion of the female cheerleader as petite and attractive. It appears that the selection of only petite females for cheerleading squads serves two purposes: to enable male cheerleaders to perform difficult lifting maneuvers with ease and to ensure that female cheerleaders fit dominant standards of beauty. The aesthetic importance of size is illustrated by the fact that pom-pom girls, who are not lifted by males, are often required to be small; one spectator called fat cheerleaders "a distraction." Proper height, weight, skin color, hair color and texture, facial features, makeup use, and dress are viewed as crucial in the selection and presentation of female cheerleaders. A spectator who had some experience selecting cheerleaders felt that "cheerleading should be based on beauty first and athletic qualities second."

Many of my subjects perceived sport spectators as mostly male. As one male athlete put it, "I would say that the majority of the people there would be male." A male spectator stated that cheerleading "gives dirty old men something to look at with binoculars." The spectators are seen as interested in only females as aesthetic objects, and therefore female cheerleaders, rather than the males, are presented as central in sex-mixed cheerleading. As this male cheerleader observed,

> They get a lot more attention than we do . . . because they're girls. . . . And they'd take pictures of the girls constantly, and all. They don't want guys in them.

There is a common public view that males cannot help looking at the female cheerleaders because they are so attractive, as this male spectator's comments indicate:

> The way they pick them it's kind of hard not to notice sometimes. . . . Any red-blooded American male is going to be hard pressed not to notice them when they go past you.

One way that males look at female cheerleaders is as sex objects. As one male athlete said, the female cheerleader stands for "a sexy woman that's out there, that doesn't mind flaunting her body."

Cheerleaders symbolize dominant ideals about how females should look and act in our society. For example, female cheerleaders are seen as representing an ideal female body. In addition, cheerleading sends messages about what are appropriate activities for females or for females in sport. The female cheerleader represents support for males, especially the male athletes. As Lenskyj (1986) points out, "The presence of attractive, admiring women validates the display of masculinity and machismo on the playing fields" (p. 101). The place for women in sport is seen as on the sidelines engaged in activities that should not be taken too seriously by the sport community.

Male Cheerleaders and the Feminine Image

Because cheerleading represents a space for defining proper ways of being female, male cheerleaders symbolically take on some of this meaning. Almost all of my subjects mentioned a stereotype of male cheerleaders as feminine. All the male cheerleaders stated that they once held this stereotype, and that at some point in their lives they never would have considered participating:

> I thought of cheerleading as being something sissy, at that time. I've heard people who said, "Wow, you know, I don't think that's too masculine."

Related to this feminine stereotype was the notion that male cheerleaders are subathletes who lack either the drive or ability to compete in a traditional sport. Subjects also expressed the notion that male cheerleaders are homosexual. As one male cheerleader recalled, "I thought cheerleading was gay." The prevailing logic was that male cheerleaders are considered feminine because they are involved in an activity defined as feminine, and feminine males are defined as gay. The comment by this female cheerleader was typical:

> The females represent something that a cheerleader should be . . . just that it's a feminine thing to do. And when guys try to do it, they're just, that's why they're seen as fags, or whatever.

It was primarily males who were perceived as negatively judging and stereo-typing male cheerleaders. Cheerleaders reported that male spectators sometimes yelled derogatory names at male cheerleaders during games. Here, a male athlete admitted some of his feelings:

> I look at [the female cheerleaders] all of the time. . . . I'm just appreciating beauty. . . . But, a guy? Man, I don't want him sitting on my face, man! "I don't mind you cheerleading, but, you know, I would prefer girls."

Some male newspaper columnists were also considered to have negative attitudes toward male cheerleaders, as this female cheerleader observed:

> [The writers] are saying that male cheerleaders are totally ruining the image of what a cheerleader should be, and they shouldn't be out there clapping their hands, and they look like fags.

Some male subjects even received negative reactions from their own fathers when they first started cheering. As this male cheerleader explains, "My Dad's not too into it . . . he just thinks that sports are what guys should be doing and girls should be cheering."

MALE CHEERLEADERS AND THE CONSTRUCTION OF A MASCULINE IMAGE

Traditional female cheerleading activities include dancing to music, motions (arm and leg movements that are timed with a cheer), tumbling, and stunts such as lifting, pyramids, and partner and group posing. Male cheerleaders avoided cer-tain behaviors perceived to be feminine in order to construct images that they felt were appropriate for men and useful in combating the stereotypes. Dancing, for example, was considered a female movement and was not done. As one male cheerleader said, female cheerleaders "do a lot more dancing than we do. We just kind of hang out and watch them and just goof around." Male cheerleaders also performed motions with a different style and less often than female cheer-leaders. Often during a cheer or dance routine, the males stood flat-footed behind the females doing occasional stiff arm movements that were coordinated with their female partners' much more active movements. Sometimes the men did no arm movements at all, but clapped or used megaphones to back up the female cheer-leaders vocally. A female cheerleader observed,

> It doesn't seem like the guys like to do motions very much. . . . It seems like that's when they're overstepping the women's bounds and what they're supposed to be doing.

Masculinity Through Tumbling and Stunts

The male cheerleaders seemed to value two activities far more than any others: tumbling and stunts. For inexperienced males, tumbling quickly became central to what they defined as their roles in cheerleading. Stunting was also clearly essential. As one male cheerleader stated, "The only thing I liked about cheerleading when I came here . . . was the stunting." On most sex-mixed cheerleading squads, males generally perform the base roles during the stunts; males lift, hold, and catch female cheerleaders.

In stunts, the males demonstrate something that is seen as crucial to being defined as athletes and as men—physical strength. As one female cheerleader commented, "I think that they like to get out there and show how strong they are as far as partner stunts and tumbling." A male athlete directly tied this demonstration of strength to masculinity:

> If a guy can hold up two girls, then another guy can hold up four girls. See, that's like a challenge for the other guy . . . that brought in the masculine part of [cheerleading].

Possession of a muscular physique was viewed as essential by these male cheerleaders, because it too was seen as representing strength.

Control was yet another aspect of stunting that male cheerleaders valued and that further defined them as masculine. A male cheerleader referred to this control when he commented, "When you can do a stunt, you know you're in command . . . and you have your partner. Your partner trusts you." Control was directly tied to notions of masculinity by this female cheerleader who said, "It seems like they're proving that they're not [feminine]. . . . They're lifting the girls, they're in control."

The male cheerleader's efforts to maintain a masculine image were not apologetic in nature. He saw himself as acting in a manner that was consistent with all men at all times. The only problem, according to the male cheerleaders, was to get the public to understand that male cheerleaders do masculine things.

The overall result of the male cheerleader's image work was a gendered differentiation of cheerleading activities that is perceived as natural. As one male cheerleader commented in regard to males and females in cheerleading, "Without them even trying, they're going to have different purposes." Here, a male athlete described his version of the division of labor:

> I think what a female is there [for], really, [is] to show her flexibility and her beauty . . . the all-American girl, you know, with the smile and everything. And I think the guy's supposed to smile, but he's supposed to show that masculinity out there, like, you know, he'd throw her up, he'd catch her, you know. He's always stiff, you know, and doing pushups to how many points scored. . . . It's always that masculinity and femininity.

The Division of Labor

When viewed from one extreme, the males can be seen as secondary cheerleaders who assist the females. Evidence of this outlook was expressed by a male cheerleader when he said:

> [Male cheerleaders] are more of a support . . . to the female cheerleaders.

To me, it's almost like the guy cheerleaders are there almost to make the female cheerleaders look good.

As one female athlete stated, male cheerleaders bring ''a lot more things into cheerleading,'' but ''girls can cheer by themselves.''

Although no one declared that males could not do what females do in cheerleading, almost all of my subjects regularly declared that females were incapable of doing what male cheerleaders do, especially feats that involve strength. A female athlete commented:

And now that cheerleading has become basically a sport itself, you're getting to where you're doing a lot more physical activity, which, some of it is too hard for women to do, as in, you know, physical labor.

My subjects generally felt that female cheerleaders are too small to perform feats requiring strength and that it would be quite humorous to see women, especially larger, masculine-like women, performing the strength roles in cheerleading. As this male athlete stated:

Man, I'd have to see that! . . . That doesn't sound likely, I don't think. To get real large women, and they'd throw the girls up? . . . I mean, that almost starts to turn into a comedy.

THE NATURALIZATION OF GENDER IN CONTEMPORARY CHEERLEADING

Recent work by scholars from such varied traditions as feminist literary criticism, semiotics, postmodernism, cultural studies, and French feminism focuses on socially constructed practices that are held to be natural. Connell (1987b) asserts, ''To interpret social relations as natural is, fundamentally, to suppress their historicity'' (p. 246). The emerging method of deconstruction, therefore, is being used to identify and analyze the social and cultural origins of human beliefs.

Deconstruction of Body Practices

A particularly fruitful set of activities to deconstruct comprise body practices, because these are often seen as rooted in some universal state of biology. Some body practices that are defined as natural are central to the maintenance of patriarchal gender relations, because these practices are constructed to portray males as physically superior to females and therefore imply that males are generally superior to females (e.g., B. Brown & Adams, 1979; Haraway, 1983; Wittig, 1982). Sport is a body practice that has often served as a male preserve, reinforcing notions of a natural superiority of males (Birrell & Cole, 1986; J.A. Hargreaves,

1986; Willis, 1982). One current project of feminist scholars of sport is to deconstruct sport practices and lay bare underlying gender ideology.

Deconstruction of the
Feminine Image of Cheerleading

The data from this study suggest that several basic interpretations of the presence of males in cheerleading allow for the perpetuation of the public image of cheerleading as an essentially female role. One interpretation is the "old-fashioned view," with which male cheerleaders are labeled as feminine and gay and are understood to be less than men or men who do not count as real men. Second, male cheerleaders are seen as secondary cheerleaders who assist the female cheerleaders. The males' facilitating the presentation of the female cheerleaders maintains and actually reinforces the traditional image of the female cheerleader. In addition, the secondary role of male cheerleaders may reduce the intensity of public reaction to the male cheerleader's role of support for male athletes, because male cheerleaders are seen as supporting female cheerleaders, who support the crowd, who support the male athletes. In other words, the male cheerleader's support of other men is indirect, hence negative reactions to the homosocial supporting role may be softened. Third, males are seen as doing an equally important kind of cheerleading as females, but it is also seen as a different kind of cheerleading (i.e., the sexual division of labor in cheerleading). People who take this perspective often imply that male cheerleaders are just like any other athlete and are more athletic than female cheerleaders.

None of these three interpretations seriously challenges traditional gender ideology. Cheerleading continues to be seen as a natural activity for females, when in reality cheerleading helps to construct what is perceived as natural.

Not only are cheerleaders seen as female, but spectators are seen as naturally male. The assumption that the male audience is voyeuristically fixated on the female cheerleaders helps to structure the performances and presentation of cheerleaders. For example, by using the concept of the "male view" we can see how our mediated view of female cheerleaders is sexualized because the male view of a cameraman often helps to frame female cheerleaders as erotic objects (Berger, Blomberg, Fox, Dibb, & Hollis, 1985; Kaplan, 1983; Mulvey, 1985). This type of camera work objectifies and sexualizes females, and it is based on and reinforces the notion of male voyeurism as natural and heterosexuality as universal for all men.

Deconstruction of the Image
of Physical Attractiveness

Another aspect of gendered behavior that cheerleading helps to construct as natural is the prevailing image of what constitutes physical attractiveness. Most of my subjects discussed appearance as central to cheerleading, but none of them seriously questioned the standards of appearance or noticed the often-implicit racism in the standards. The subjects assumed that the standards were universal and trans-historically appealing.

Deconstruction of the Sexual Division of Labor

The sexual division of labor that I have discussed throughout this paper was seen by my subjects as the commonsense way to do things. I came to understand cheerleading as a space where the demonstration of strength is the central aspect of what males do. Female cheerleaders, on the other hand, were seen as unable to perform activities that require strength. Cheerleading, in this sense, is similar to Haug's (1987) description of gymnastics: "The display of strength is to male gymnastics what the concealment of strength is to its female equivalent" (p. 177). Strength, then, comes to be seen as a naturally male possession. Left unquestioned are how all-female squads manage to perform so many stunts that involve strength and why only physically small females are selected for cheerleading squads. The possibilities of selecting larger women as cheerleaders, the demonstration of strength by women cheerleaders, strength training for women cheerleaders rather than just for the males, or males being lifted by others (males or females) are perceived to be both unaesthetic and unnatural.

I argue, as have others (Birrell & Cole, 1986; J.A. Hargreaves, 1986; Willis, 1982), that the most central aspect of defining masculinity is physical strength. Sport is a social practice that males have traditionally reserved for the demonstration of strength and hence masculinity. As Birrell and Cole (1986) write, "Men need sport to be men" (p. 17). Cheerleading, through its sexual division of labor, has become a space to demonstrate men's supposed superiorities in strength and physical prowess and, by implication, male superiority in general.

CONCLUSION

The male cheerleader has entered a world that reinforces traditional images of femininity, and because of this, he risks being labeled feminine or gay. In response, male cheerleaders work to present an image that they feel fits dominant cultural ideals of what is male appropriate. The most crucial activity for males in cheerleading is stunts, with which the demonstration of strength is interpreted as proof of masculinity. A result of the male cheerleader's image work is the construction of a sexual division of labor in cheerleading that appears to be natural. This division of labor reinforces traditional gender beliefs, including notions of men's natural physical superiority. The traditional image of the female cheerleader as an ideal symbol of femininity remains intact. In addition, both the actual performances and mediated presentations of female cheerleaders continue to be structured in ways that cater to spectators who are assumed to be voyeuristically oriented males who mainly perceive the female cheerleader as a sex object. This practice continues to construct the spectator as naturally male and heterosexual.

Any feminist transformative potential that could have been enhanced when males reentered cheerleading in recent times has seemingly been lost by the construction of a sexual division of labor. The male cheerleader has become increasingly accepted because the image he has constructed and continues to construct does not challenge traditional gender notions or power relations, but rather reinforces them. Cheerleading, as a feminine preserve, remains to be seriously challenged.

Chapter 13

Women Coaching Male Athletes[1]

Ellen J. Staurowsky

The contention that Euro-American sport is a representative system of cultural hegemony has been proposed by M.A. Hall (1985) and J.A. Hargreaves (1982). Sustained by an obvious patriarchal structure, sport emphasizes those instrumental qualities (i.e., dominance, aggressiveness, competitiveness, and risk taking) traditionally valued as important in male development. Oglesby (1984) points out that expressive qualities of submissiveness, naturalness, improvisation, and dependency, often associated with female development, are thought not to have a place within this system. Through a higher valuation of male qualities, sport systems create and reinforce a gender link between sport and masculinity.

The underrepresentation of women in coaching and leadership positions speaks to the strength of the connection between sport and gender. There is an underlying assumption that links sport expertise with masculinity and leadership with male superiority. This assumption has permitted the notion that coaching male athletes is the exclusive responsibility of male coaches. In this context, male coaches are perceived to function as the embodiment of the masculine athletic ideal, and the role of coach, it is held, requires that manly qualities be imparted to the next generation. Further, this context effectively perpetuates a belief that the feminine in sport, and symbolically the feminine in males, are secondary or nonexistent. For those participants who are gendered female, there is an automatic devaluation of experience, of achievement, and of self.

In recent years, sport as a male enterprise has received critical analysis from researchers, disaffected male athletes, and sport feminists. Male dominance, as exemplified by a traditional sport model, which of necessity viewed women as interlopers, has been contested on several fronts. Clearly, the emergence of females coaching male athletes is one example of a challenge to the male sport system.

The purpose of this research was twofold: to describe the experiences and issues of female coaches who lead and teach male athletes and to examine the impact these coaches have on males within the sport patriarchy.

METHODOLOGY

Potential subjects were defined as female coaches of traditional male sport teams at the high school level. The teams these women coached include baseball, basketball, football, lacrosse, and soccer. It was recognized that females also coach males in many individual sports. Because individual sport teams had the potential to operate as coeducational units, these coaches were automatically eliminated from the pool in order to strictly focus on the relationship between female coaches and all-male teams.

The identification of subjects was difficult, because no central source listed these coaches. Through use of the *Clell Wade Coaches Directory for 1987-1988*, announcements to colleagues requesting referrals, and journal and article citations, I determined 10 women in the northeast region of the United States to be viable subjects for this study. They resided in Maine, Massachusetts, New York, New Jersey, Pennsylvania, West Virginia, and the District of Columbia.[2]

Subjects were first notified by letters informing them of the project and requesting that they agree to be interviewed. Additionally, general background information was obtained through a written, self-report, biographical survey. Items on the survey included education, sport-playing experience, coaching experience, and coaching success.

Eight of the 10 available subjects were interviewed in person, and 2 were interviewed by phone. Each interview lasted approximately 1 hour.

An intensive interview technique was used. The data-collection method was structured within a feminist-oriented framework, and several assumptions were made about the format and design of the interview. First, the interview would contain a degree of subjectivity and value for the subject and for the interviewer due to the importance and significance of the subject's role as coach. Second, the interview process would be a source of validation for these coaches, all of whom work in isolation, having no other female coach with whom to interact. And finally, the interview protocol, although containing structured questions, would be influenced by the subject to allow for the subject to respond freely to open-ended questions and for the interviewer to follow the subject's lead.

RESULTS

The females interviewed in this study presented personal histories and stories that were widely divergent in certain respects and strikingly similar in others. The survey and interview material revealed parallel experiences and views across situations. The findings generated by this study will be presented in the following four subsections:

- The issues and concerns of females coaching male athletes
- Professional relationships with male coaches and officials
- Attitudes of parents
- Responses of male athletes

Issues and Concerns
of Females Coaching Male Athletes

The women who tread upon the patriarchal turf of coaching all-male teams identified a number of common concerns and experiences. They were met with varying degrees of resistance, and as the interviews progressed, the intricate gender issues these women faced began to become more articulated and observable. These issues ranged from sexist wisecracks from male coaches, to problems associated with establishing authority with players and fellow coaches, to outright sex discrimination in the professional realm.

Characteristically, these pioneer coaches entered this uncharted territory with strong and confident wills, forgiving hearts, resilient natures, and more than a modicum of humor. In all, they were certain of their purposes and were successful in steering courses to guide themselves, their teams, and their colleagues in this new enterprise.

They worked diligently to be perceived as just other competent coaches in the universe of coaches, but there were times when they appeared unsure of the gender issue in themselves and awkward and frustrated in the situations they encountered. Though they initially expressed frustration about the issue of gender, the coaches resisted describing anything that seemed unfair or suspect.

Later in the interviews, through faltering half-completed sentences and whispered comments about hurtful moments, these females voiced problems with which they struggled daily. As each subject explored the material of her own experience, it became clear that an already difficult job was further complicated by vestiges of her own upbringing. In situations that subjects hesitated to mention, references were made to the exacting price the sport environment required of female coaches and their teams in exchange for disturbing the status quo.

Though they acknowledged that the climate warmed toward them over time, the coaches harbored concerns, almost unspoken, that both they and their teams were targets of veiled sexism. They cited glances and gestures from other teams, verbal references to the disgrace of losing to a woman, and the implication that their teams were tainted by the presence of women leaders. Attempting to verbalize her concern, one coach explained, ''Other male coaches were saying to their teams, 'Guys, you've got to beat that team because you can't lose to a woman.' [This] makes me concerned for my men [and theirs].'' Another coach, in trying to account for scores being run up on occasion, observed:

I don't know if the other coach was gung-ho . . . or wanted to prepare his guys or . . . wanted to beat a woman. I can't say. I know there were instances

where their first string played an awful lot when the score was [lopsided]. . . .
Ok, I was a little hurt but my guys were demoralized.

Most of the coaches balked at drawing unequivocal conclusions about sexist actions directed at them or their teams. Their concerns were often expressed in the form of queries such as this: ''There were times when I wondered what the other coaches' motivations were. Was there a sexist twist to it?''

Some reported that their teams were penalized because of the association with a female leader. One coach recalled being greeted by a chorus of snickers, titters, and catcalls when preparing to play another team. During warm-up she noticed an exchange of words between the two teams that left her players visibly upset. The content became apparent when her winning team, on their way back to the bus, heard members of the losing team call out, ''Dykes, lesbians, and your coach is too.''

This type of attack was often present in more subliminal fashion, and it was the root of worrisome questions for both players and coaches. Because they occupied roles typically held by ''strong'' male figures, several coaches wondered if their presence was harmful to the boys. Their concerns about the absence of a strong male figure were further confounded by an awareness that many of their players came from single-parent families in which the mother was the prominent figure.

In contrast to the majority of coaches who hesitated to directly address sexism, one coach was certain she had experienced discrimination on the basis of sex. The subject, Wanda Oates, the first woman to be appointed the head coach of a high school football program at F.W. Ballou High School in Washington, DC, was asked by the school district to resign her position before she assumed her responsibilities. The case went into a collective bargaining stage due to the irregularities in the school district's treatment of her situation. Ms. Oates regarded her treatment as sexist and argued that the school district as well as her male colleagues in the department were opposed to her serving as the head football coach because of her gender. She was very certain of two things: that she could have turned the football program around at Ballou High School and that her gender, not her competence, was the primary consideration in the battle over the football-coaching position she sought.[3]

Professional Relationships With Male Coaches and Officials

Developing relationships with other coaches and officials was another complication for these females. There was a period in the first season when every new situation presented a social dilemma. At contests, the female coaches were mistaken as well-wishers, relatives, athletic trainers, managers, statisticians, reporters, or potential dating companions despite having teams in tow, carrying clipboards and whistles, and wearing clothing with *coaching staff* emblazoned on it.

Male coaches and officials often seemed unable to recognize female authority in the male sport realm. Difficulty in establishing one's authority can have serious limiting consequences for a coach trying to do a job. Consider the basketball coach who reported that when she stood in the coaches' box, an official said, "Lady, sit down and shut up." When she approached the official at halftime, he indicated he wasn't aware of who she was. The unspoken questions in this example were, who else would have been standing in the coaches' box, and why couldn't the official figure that out?

Similar confusion and awkwardness surfaced during a long string of first experiences: the first coaches meeting, the first convention, the first time a woman spoke at a meeting. Several coaches commented that, prior to their emergence on the scene, coaches meetings were held in bars. Others said that their male colleagues referred to cleaning up their language and being more selective in their choice of topics for discussion in deference to a woman being present. As one female coach said, "Some people don't want me there. It's all the boys off to camp, and what's she doing there?"

The coaches who persisted with their teams experienced gradual reductions in tension between themselves and their male colleagues. As visible evidence of their expertise emerged, the women coaches reported greater feelings of acceptance. The male-female issue, however, never fully disappeared. Encounters with male coaches unable to cope with losing to a woman happened with regularity. The women observed that less secure coaches, "the little petty tyrants, the guy who is not doing so well," tended to be obnoxious. That adjustment problems endured is evident in one coach's exasperation:

> I'm trying so hard to be competent. That is where my mind is at. And yet other people are seeing this little person obviously not male. And sometimes there is an initial barrier. "You're a girl." And I say, "Yes, but I'm trying to be a coach first."

Attitudes of Parents

The receptions women coaches received from parents, particularly fathers, were similar to the receptions from male coaches. There was general acceptance, although a visible and vocal minority caused trouble. Resistance was evident. Several coaches encountered athletes whose fathers discouraged their children from playing for a woman because it might be bad for them.

One father dealt with his concern for the coach's ability by delivering a handwritten commentary on lineups, strategy suggestions, and other information meant to be useful to the coach at the end of each practice. Another father expressed concern when a female coach cursed while talking to players at halftime. The father felt "that was unseemly behavior for a woman." The father was not concerned about the word per se or his son's exposure to it but the gender of the person who uttered it.

The women coaches felt that the potential for greater resistance was somewhat mitigated by the presence of other women, mostly mothers. One coach stated, "I think the fathers knew that the other women would not tolerate them taking shots at me because I was a woman."

Responses of Male Athletes

Compared to male coaches and parents, the male athletes displayed the least amount of resistance to and generated the most amount of respect for these women coaches. Each coach and team dealt with issues surrounding the coach's gender. Some of these included her competence, her authority and control, her style, and communication.

In describing her first year as head coach of a male team, one coach remarked, "The boys didn't know what to think. It was kind of a novelty. Some thought it was going to be so easy." Another coach reported that her boys did not pay attention when she was instructing. When she offered advice or corrections, she occasionally heard a boy mumble, "I'd like to see you get out here and do it better." As seasons progressed, however, these problems dissipated.

Although doubts about competence affected most coaches, one had a very different experience. Because she had received a superior rating on a standard test that qualified coaches in that school district, she said, "The boys knew right away that I could do the job."

These coaches consistently reported a prevalent male perception that women coaches were not as tough as men coaches. Would she be tough enough? seemed to be a question that emerged as part of a script that the coaches felt the boys were obligated to enact. One coach was called before an athletic board, comprised of staff and students, to defend her decision to dismiss two players from her team. She recalled, "I survived the test. That's when the message got through. 'She really means it.' " Coaches who had built bases of power and control early and who demonstrated that they would act to preserve these bases seemed to be tested less. Indeed, most interviewees experienced greater senses of urgency about quickly establishing authority and control with male teams than they had with coaching female teams in the past.

All the women coaches reported that emphases on team and individual communication were important elements in their coaching styles. The male athletes were unaccustomed to being asked about their insights and feelings regarding their performances or that of the team. One coach explained that she planned time at the end of each game and practice. After an initial adjustment phase "the guys really looked forward to our little chats. They'd get upset if we missed one."

In addition to open communication, the women coaches favored fair and firm treatment of their athletes. The coaches reported that the boys noticed a difference between humiliating and denigrating treatment used by many prominent male coaches in their schools and the practices of the women coaches. Several female coaches who had been with programs for more than 1 year observed that it was not uncommon for some of the best athletes in the school to leave a primary sport to play on their teams, thus expressing their preference for a less violent and authoritarian form of treatment.

Finally, and perhaps stereotypically, the coaches reported that the male athletes seemed to be most aware of the presence of a female in the areas of demeanor, personal conduct, and appearance. Prior to the interview, one coach asked her team if they had any thoughts they would like her to convey in the interview. They said:

Tell her [the interviewer] for us that we think you're a detail freak. We think that's probably female. Our helmets have to be clean. We have to remember our mouth guards. We have to be thoughtful to bystanders. We have to make sure the nets are up a certain way. We figure that's female.

Another coach said, "A woman's touch seemed to bring some class to these guys. I feel a little maternal instinct with these guys."

CONCLUSION

The exploratory nature of this study precludes drawing unequivocal conclusions about women coaches or the males with whom they interact in the sport establishment. However, the findings do help extend thinking about gender issues in sport.

The phenomenon of women coaching boys, although perceived by some to represent a lapse of responsibility on the part of the gatekeepers of the sport patriarchy, provides a unique view of the fundamental assumptions upon which standards in sport are based. Women's presence raises profound questions about male supremacy and directly challenges the patriarchal notion that maleness is the key prerequisite for coaching and for leadership.

Clearly, male teams coached by women serve as testing grounds for gender expectations in sport. The active process of working together for both coaches and players provided a reality check for their own stereotypical gender expectations. Contrary to traditional understanding, the evidence suggested that women coaches are competent and tough enough to coach males. At the same time, the boys did not reject women coaches out of hand, and they demonstrated little difficulty in accepting women as leaders.

The significance of the "women-coaching-males" phenomenon is that it threatens the sport patriarchy and represents a means of transforming the sport status quo. Through deflection, denial, and outright rejection, the sport patriarchy in this country and internationally has effectively promoted a segregationist view of sport. At its core, this segregated reality preserves sport as an all-male domain while reducing the female element to an appendage that Oglesby (1988) describes as "sport-for-women."*

The enforced segregation of men and women in sport has been damaging. An idealized system thought to promote the values of honesty, fair play, positive relationship building, and loyalty has produced more than its seemly share of corruption, violent behavior, and disregard for the rights of others. The traditional male sport system, to which males and females are subjected in equal measure, is not as healthy as surface impressions imply.

---

*Editor's note. See Oglesby's discussion in the epilogue of this book.

To clarify this assertion, the patriarchy, by intent or accident, has purposely weakened its own leadership structure through the differential use of gender as a criterion for promotion and inclusion. The traditional sport establishment has never realized its capabilities, because the best women leaders, to be counted among the best leaders, have largely been ignored.

As a concept, comprising insulation and sanctity, the all-male sport domain is outmoded (Staurowsky, 1987). Oglesby (1988) has recently called for a transformation beyond the abstractions of sport as manhood maker and of sport-for-women. Instead she favors the development of a reconstructed feminist view of sport that would better serve the developmental needs of people. Women coaching male athletes might well be one example of that kind of transformation.

Female coaches, by their presence and work with the traditional future heirs to leadership positions in sport (i.e., adolescent males), are in positions to lay claim to a slim piece of prime real estate in the sport hierarchy. Within this context, sport has the potential to become a place where the limitations posed by a dichotomous worldview based on gender can be explored and understood. Female coaches can make profound contributions in this regard by serving as agents for change within the sport system.

That task, however, is considerable and not easily achieved. The self-protection mechanisms within the patriarchy specifically punish those who threaten its structure and cultural imperatives. The lessons to be learned from the emergence of female coaches in all-male sport domains could be lost.

Women who coach male teams are challenging the stereotype of coach as father figure, male protector, and male authority. For the first time there is an emerging feminine counterpart in the form of the coach as mother figure, female protector, and female authority.

The issue here, however, is not to establish coaching counterparts. The challenge is for females and males in sport to work with conviction toward conceptualization of coaching and sport as human enterprises, inclusive of that which is valuably male and female. This study, therefore, points to a need to further articulate a transcendent view of sport that ventures beyond conventional gender consciousness and coaching practices.

PART III

Challenges, Changes, and Alternatives

As we saw in Part I, feminist scholars have begun to rethink sport as an institutional element within the larger political economy and culture in which ideologies of male superiority and structures of male domination are constructed and naturalized. Concrete studies are now uncovering, as we saw in Part II, some of the processes through which males—as athletes and as spectators—bond together in sporting practices that help to construct hegemonic masculinity, while continuing to marginalize and subordinate women, men of color, and gay men. Yet, as several contributors have already revealed, the power of hegemonic masculinity is never total, is often fraught with internal contradictions, and can thus be challenged.

Critical feminist perspectives do more than highlight and analyze these contradictions and historical developments. One purpose of critical feminist theory is to facilitate understanding of the conditions that sustain and constrain us, an understanding that enables us to envision possibilities for changing society for the better. In substance, aim, and process, critical feminist theory implies a commitment to a moral vision and a liberating social goal. In our critical labor to unravel and understand the oppressive dimensions of sport (i.e., class, race, gender, and physical oppression), we endeavor to transform sport and, through it, ourselves and the wider society. We are practitioners of what some feminists call "personal politics" or what Jurgen Habermas calls "emancipatory science."

The articles in this section move toward both a more inclusive theory and recommendations for humane change in sport and society. The first two articles in this section invite us to identify and examine developing avenues of resistance and change in sport. First, Lois Bryson argues that several Australian sports have especially served to reinforce male hegemony and reduce women and other marginalized groups to inferior status. She argues that "sport is not a monolithic institution" and that both structured male dominance and its concomitant ideologies can be challenged. She offers concrete suggestions for challenging the prevailing ideologies and eroding the structural bases of the athletic status quo. Next, Susan Birrell takes on the crucial task of building a theoretical conceptualization of gender and race in sport. She argues that we must move beyond reductionism and develop more inclusive views of sport, power, and inequality by blending feminist cultural studies with critical theories of race relations. She suggests that rather than superimposing hierarchical theories on oppressed peoples from our privileged positions as scholars, we instead develop theory starting from the standpoint of oppressed peoples, especially women of color. New forms of activism and research might follow from listening seriously to what Birrell calls "critical autobiography."

The next two articles offer descriptions and analyses of concrete practices that have been created to challenge masculine hegemony in physical education. First, Barbara Humberstone advocates "sensitive and careful integration" by teachers to break down the sex segregation so common to conventional physical education. Humberstone's analysis of a British outdoor-adventure centre shows that despite the fact that the activity was consciously constructed to offer an alternative to sex-segregated and competitive sport, some gender differences stubbornly persist (partly due to some male teachers). Yet, she observes, many boys found in the experience a context in which they rethought narrow conceptions of masculinity and learned to see females in a new light. In the following article, Pat Griffin and James Genasci criticize the compulsory heterosexuality of conventional physical education and offer concrete suggestions for confronting and breaking down homophobia among physical educators and sport researchers.

The final article by Ann Hall offers an overview of the development of feminist sport sociology. Hall summarizes the various theoretical strains within sport sociology from the 1960s to the present. We are reminded of the philosopher Leibnitz's insight that "the present is saturated with the past and pregnant with the future." Hall's analysis illustrates how far scholars have come in theorizing gender and sport and suggests new directions for research and sociological practice. Although she endorses the emergent spate of feminist studies of men, masculinities, and sport, her critique of men's studies illustrates some of the potential pitfalls in this approach.

Chapter 14

Challenges to Male Hegemony in Sport

Lois Bryson

People tend to accept without question that men are far better at sport than women because men are stronger, faster, and tougher. If it were not important to be skillful, strong, fast, and, in particular, tough, this misconception would not matter. But sporting prowess is positively valued and is a basis through which social and economic power are distributed. To be better at sport (by implication even for those men who do not participate in athletics) is symbolically translatable into being better or more capable in other areas of life. Through a dialectical process, women, who are culturally defined and perceived as incapable of equaling men at sport, are rendered inferior and, by inference, less capable in many areas of life.

The dialectical element of the ideological processes underpinning contemporary sport is of crucial importance. These processes construct a form of dominant masculinity and in doing so define what is not approved. Each cultural message about sport is a dual one, celebrating the dominant at the same time as inferiorizing the "other." This dominant form of masculinity has been usefully called hegemonic masculinity (Carrigan, Connell, & Lee, 1985), and the message it conveys renders inferior not only femininity in all its forms but also nonhegemonic forms of masculinity. The inferiorising of the "other" is most frequently implicit, though it is also explicitly and graphically conveyed when, for example, coaches, supporters, and commentators chastise their team for playing like girls or poofters.

Sport's very physical nature gives it special significance because of the fundamental link between social power and physical force. Sport is a major arena in which physical force and toughness are woven into hegemonic masculinity and the resultant ideology transmitted. The celebration of "real men" as strong and tough underscores the fact that men are in positions (have the right?) to dominate.

Radical feminists such as Susan Brownmiller (1975), Andrea Dworkin (1981), and Mary Daly (1978) see coercion as the major source of male dominance over women, and although other theorists propose rather more compounded causation, physical coercion is universally recognised as an irreducible dimension of power.

Thus sport is an ideal medium for conveying messages of gender domination. Not only is sport associated with physical power and an important, admired social activity, but it is also something to which we are exposed daily and from very young ages. Sport is an immediate mass reality, and with increasing commercialization and media exposure, the ever-present nature of this reality is likely to be magnified.

DEFINING THE TARGET

Given the wide range of activities encompassed by the term *sport*, it is necessary to specify just which sports I consider central to the processes of the reproduction of male dominance. What are the flag carriers of hegemonic masculinity? We are certainly not equally exposed to all sports, and the type of exposure varies as well. Australia has close historical links with Britain and shares the same sporting heritage. Key sports include codes of football (e.g., soccer) (the actual code varies between states) and men's cricket. These are sports that quintessentially promote hegemonic masculinity and are sports to which a majority of people are regularly exposed. A recent national survey showed that a total of 81% of males over 16 years of age expressed interest in football and 73% in cricket. The figures for females were lower though still substantial—61% and 59% respectively (Brian Sweeney and Associates, 1986).

Historically, these are the sites on which notions of modern sport and sports performance in Australia were fashioned; hence, taking account of collective memory, exposure to these sports has been greatest. Historically, their message was strengthened by their early association (particularly in the case of men's cricket) with the development of a sense of nationhood, which was fostered by success in international matches, particularly against Britain (W. Mandle, 1976). The crowds at major international cricket matches are renowned for their ritualistic celebration of male dominance, partly through "cricket larrikinism," an aspect of which is harrassment of women spectators (Cashman, 1984). The history of cricket illustrates very clearly that Aborigines are also excluded by hegemonic masculinity. The first Australian cricket team to make an international tour to Britain was an all-Aboriginal team in 1868; the first non-Aboriginal team toured 10 years later. Although the Aboriginal tour was a resounding success, it has been all but totally overlooked in written and unwritten history of the game.

Most Australians, though more men than women, follow local football teams and generally keep abreast of reported national cricket events. Because football and cricket are team games, this not only provides an effective environment for cementing gender solidarity but also an environment that provides for players a network of people who have great potential for reinforcing the values embedded in the enterprise.[1]

In Australia, virtually all boys are introduced to cricket and the relevant code of football from a young age. Most houses have yards, and so family and neighbourhood peers are important. These are also the basic sports pursued at school. Virtually all little boys are taught to kick, throw, and bat. Fewer are taught to play tennis or golf or to sail, surf, or ski. Where such sports are taught, they will almost invariably be taught in addition to the basics of football and cricket. Although football and cricket play key roles, most sports, with the possible exceptions of specially constructed nonsexist sports such as korfball* and those explicitly considered women's sports, have been co-opted to a greater or lesser degree to contribute to the construction of hegemonic masculinity. The net effect is that women collude with male hegemony and largely accept the biological explanations offered for their "inferior" performances, even when there is no face validity for such explanations, as with darts and billiards.

In all sorts of ways, then, and every day, the major sports to which we are exposed construct and reconstruct male dominance through a complex of ideological processes that link maleness with valued skills and the exercise of sanctioned and highly valued strength, power, and aggressiveness. Thus, sport plays a crucial part in the construction and maintenance of people, in the development of "gender as personality" (Connell, 1987b). Only through understanding this personality construction and the way it leads to a perpetuation of male dominance can any challenge to male hegemony be proposed. Although such counterproposals are the ultimate goal of this discussion, it is first necessary to look at sport's contribution to hegemonic masculinity and the way sport contextualizes and shapes male personality development. Four facets will be explored: inferiorizing the other, connecting masculinity with violence, constituting personal power, and the strategic positioning of sport in gender development.

INFERIORIZING THE OTHER

Although hegemonic masculinity inferiorizes some men as well as women, women form the major target group for exclusion. Thus, throughout this paper I shall be mainly concerned with women as "the other." It is not by chance that men who do not measure up to hegemonic masculine criteria are likely to be redefined in feminine terms, as, for example, sissies or fairies.

The message of male superiority embedded in sport takes a great deal of its power from the fact that performance is routinely understood in terms of biology, which in turn is accepted as immutable. Paul Willis has pointed out that an ideology that claims to be based on biological differences is exceptionally powerful, because it claims a naturalness that denies challenge (Willis, 1982). Of course, it is clearly inaccurate to see biology as immutable (Birke & Vines, 1987), and certainly the

---

Editors' note: Korfball is a competitive, coeducational team sport that was developed in the Netherlands during the early 20th century. Teams are equally divided by gender, and cross-sex interaction is extensive and vigorous. The International Korfball Federation now consists of more than 15 national associations. For information and scholarly analysis of gender issues in korfball, contact Dr. Bart Crum, Free University, Amsterdam, Netherlands.

use to which physical capacity can be put is malleable, as even the most cursory glance at the evolution of world sporting records demonstrates (Dwyer & Dyer, 1984). However, as Anthony Giddens (1979) notes, ideology consists precisely in the "capacity of dominant groups. . . . to make their own sectional interests appear to others [and one might add to their own group] as universal." He points to such a capability of persuasion as "one type of resource involved in domination" (p. 6).

The appearance of universalism is also a characteristic of the criteria used to assess successful performance. Scores, distances, times, heights, and weights are recorded and compared, and this lends an apparently factual validity to claims to superiority. Even when women participate separately, there is an implicit male standard against which they are judged at least in relation to strength, speed, and power. When it comes to gracefulness, rhythm, and beauty, as in gymnastics or ice dancing, women's talents may be recognised, but these attributes are not accorded the preeminent status of those attributes thought of as male. This smuggled-in hierarchical system of valued attributes very neatly exposes the ideo- logical nature of the biological justification of male superiority. There can be no biological basis for admiring more highly those performance criteria thought of as masculine.

Where women's performances do challenge the myths of male superiority (as with long-distance ocean swimming, where women hold most of the world records), these performances are largely ignored (Dyer, 1982). Where recognition is given, the mode of celebration is often a thinly veiled celebration of woman as sex object, which effectively removes women from competition. This clearly occurred at the 1988 winter Olympics in the publicity given to the winning perfor- mance of Katerina Witt in ice dancing.

The importance of the maintenance of the myth of male superiority through the inferiorisation of women was most graphically illustrated in the now oft-quoted case of the 1978 Acapulco cliff-diving championships. One of the male competi- tors, complaining about having to compete against finalist Barbara Mayer Winters, stated, "This is a death defying activity—men are taking a great gamble to prove their courage. What would be the point if everyone saw that a woman could do the same?" The potential challenge to male hegemony was headed off when the organizers disqualified Winters before the final dive, claiming this was for her protection (J. Kaplan, 1979). This is not an isolated case; it is possible to make a very long list of similar examples (Bryson, 1983; Dyer, 1982; M. A. Hall & Richardson, 1982). Indeed, the process of inferiorisation of women as the other— and if this fails, their exclusion—is quite fundamental to contemporary sport.

CONNECTING MASCULINITY AND VIOLENCE

When we consider sport, masculinity, and personality formation, there is no need initially to search for complex sociological or psychoanalytic interpretations of what is going on. There is clear historical evidence that sport was often promoted with an explicit goal of enhancing masculinity as well as, though somewhat less explicitly, providing a means to control the working class. Though the origins of sport lie deep in history, the origins of modern sport are much more recent and generally located in 19th-century Britain. Those who promoted "muscular Christianity" (Baron de Coubertin was spurred by this doctrine to establish the modern Olympics) were concerned with promoting sport for men because of its effects on male identity, solidarity, and the exercise of power.

Sport and Social Control of the Working Class

In their analysis of the development of rugby, Dunning and Sheard (1979) point to the way in which in the working-class areas in the north of England, Rugby League was "a means of expressing the tough and aggressive norms of masculinity" (p. 221). In Yorkshire between 1890 and 1893, there were 71 deaths and 121 broken legs recorded from the sport, as well as numerous minor injuries. This violence, Dunning and Sheard suggest, was gradually brought under control by middle-class administrators, for a number of reasons. First, it was difficult to keep the game going with so many injuries, and second, the sport was professional and investments had to be protected. Finally, the middle class feared that sports-related violence might encourage the working class to be violent in other circumstances. Thus, administrators recognised a need to civilize the game but "without 'emasculating' Rugby to such an extent that it could no longer serve as a vehicle for celebrating the 'manliness' norms of players and spectators" (Dunning & Sheard, 1979, p. 222).

Australian culture generally has been very strongly shaped by its working-class elements via its links with Britain. John Hargreaves (1986) in tracing the role sport has played in class politics in Britain stresses its powerful effect on "the reproduction of sexual divisions" (p. 79), seeing working-class males taking sport into their lives to compensate for "changes in occupational structure and in work organization" (p. 79) and partly in response to the threat posed by the suffrage movement. Because of the centrality of sport to working-class men's lives, along with "the pub, music hall, and the popular press" (p. 79) sport became a primary source within working-class culture "for the construction of male chauvinist identities" (p. 79). Hargreaves observes, "Women's almost total exclusion, in all but the most passive and subordinate capacity as helpers and spectators, from a valued, deeply meaningful part of working-class men's lives, signalled their inferiority" (p. 79).

Aggression in Rugby

These developments resonated in Australia. The Rugby League code, which Dunning and Sheard (1979) write about, became the dominant football code in New South Wales, and Australia developed its own code—Australian rules football. This had its origins in the state of Victoria, and the early games were unruly and often violent affairs. Umpires were particularly at risk, and a system of protection was gradually developed, for example, through the institution of separate dressing rooms. Although the codification of football attempted progressively to contain the more dangerous direct aggression of both players and crowds, aggression, force, and power remained featured ingredients of the game. As one Australian rules founding player claimed in 1870, "Football is essentially a rough game all the world over, and . . . not suitable for . . . poodles and milksops" (Grow, 1986, p. 25). Such a claim would be totally at home in an Australian Sunday sports report today.

These notions of toughness were (and still are) supplemented with notions about self-reliance, independence, and character development, principles promoted by the muscular Christianity movement in the mid-19th century. In his analysis of press coverage and the development of Australian football, Grow (1986) suggests that the view that "participants would develop manliness, leadership skills, gracious acceptance of defeat" (p. 34) underpinned much of the influential press reportage from the 1860s. In the Australian colonies as well as in England, the "well-worn Wellingtonian adage that the battle of Waterloo was won on the playing fields of Eton was argued with conviction" (D.W. Brown, 1987, p. 177). Thus can we trace the incorporation of controlled violence into a positively sanctioned male activity.

Different Emphasis on Male and Female Sport

The explicit maleness of the movement is highlighted once again by what was being constructed for girls. Sport was being promoted as an activity for girls to promote good health. In the early days of the Ladies' College in Melbourne, which opened in 1875 and was the first school to offer a secondary education to girls that was academically equivalent to that offered to the boys of wealthy families, some recognition was given to health and physical development. However, this was not in order to fit the young ladies for the key roles of empire, for winning battles, for leadership, or for "pluck—downright bull-dog pluck" (D.W. Brown, 1987, p. 178). Physical culture was merely offered as an optional extra, though some of the girls themselves soon recognised the advantages of boys' games for fun, enjoyment, and excitement, and a suggestion was made by one of the girls that a football club be established (Crawford, 1984). They felt constrained by adult attitudes, and one student complained that they were expected to give up their interests in sporting activities at the age of 12 while boys "had all the luck—they could play football and cricket for at least half a lifetime" (Crawford, 1984, p. 68).

Today boys are still taught in a quite straightforward way that sport is a significant part of manliness. The achievement of basic skills of ball throwing, kicking, and batting is a project to which boys are introduced at a young age by proud committed fathers and often mothers as well. Girls are introduced to the same skills but in a negative manner—as something that they cannot do well. The skill development projects into which girls drift, such as skipping, hopscotch, and hula hoops, are not considered junior forms of highly valued adult skills but the activities of childhood.

CONSTITUTING PERSONAL POWER

Because toughness is explicitly built into the male sporting enterprise, at the same time as boys are taught various skills, they are taught the needs to be tough and bear pain. From the age of about 7 years, boys in Sydney can be seen practicing a strange rite of running at and into each other, an activity that tends to leave half on the ground, with many crying in pain. Any bemused, anxious, or ignorant observer will be told this is "learning to tackle" (for rugby). Despite its minority status as an official sport, boxing is an activity that most boys are introduced to and practice within their peer group. Boys learn to defend themselves and others. Girls receive no such explicit training in the basics of physical attack or defense; thus is the message conveyed that females are not powerful and indeed are in need of protection—male protection. A Canadian woman who teaches women self-defense recently pointed out that the first thing she has to teach most women who come to her class is how to make a fist (*Toronto Star*, January 6, 1982, p. 1).

Through sport, males who subscribe to the hegemonic rules maintain a monopoly over force and aggression and are rewarded with the right to first-class citizenship. Even when women do enter the sporting arena, they avoid contact sports and are positively discouraged from demonstrating aggressive behaviour and physical strength. Women weight lifters and shot-putters routinely have their sexuality questioned. Here the messages are clear. Women are not strong, and if they are, there is a presumption of masculinity. Direct tactics are still utilized to ensure that women do not stray too far from an approved definition of what sports are suitable for women. In 1984, the premier of New South Wales banned a bout of kick boxing that had been planned between women contestants by invoking a clause relating to "the preservation of good manners and decorum" from the Theatre and Balls Act of 1908 (*The Age*, September 14, 1984, p. 5).

THE STRATEGIC POSITION OF SPORT IN MALE GENDER DEVELOPMENT

The direct training in power and forcefulness that boys receive has profound effects. Connell (1987a) points to the way in which preoccupation with force and skill becomes embedded in the body, which is then translated "into muscle tensions, posture, the feel and texture of the body." In this way power "becomes naturalized . . . [and] important in allowing a belief in the superiority of men . . . to be sustained by men who in other respects have little power" (p. 85).

Socialization and psychoanalytic theories have long told us that gender formation for boys is more problematic than it is for girls. Boys need to break their early identification with their mothers, yet, since the industrial revolution and the separation of work and home, there are not many men around on a day-to-day basis on whom boys can model behaviour. The distancing of males from females can thus be understood to be an urgent and emphasized reaction based on some uncertainty and even anxiety about the development of a masculine personality.

The history of the British male's enthusiastic embracing of sport in the 19th century makes sense against an understanding of a threat to earlier ways of establishing masculine identity. Today, research suggests that despite (or because of) the absence of a day-to-day figure from whom masculine behaviour can be modeled, boys actually learn their gender behaviours earlier than girls. Also, feminine characteristics in boys (the sissy) are more frowned upon than are masculine characteristics in girls (the tomboy; Oakley, 1981).

This psychosocial explanation of the processes involved in personality development also helps to account for the fact that many men learn too well and exhibit aggressive and violent behaviours that extend beyond socially approved bounds. In contemporary society, it is men who fill the goals, assault women and men, and generally commit acts of violence. The ideological significance of this male monopoly of violence is underscored by the fact that this state of affairs is publicly unacknowledged.

Theorists such as Dorothy Dinnerstein (1976) and Nancy Chodorow (1978) provide insight into the psychodynamics of the gendering of personality. They emphasize child care, and the fact that women invariably are responsible for child care, as the pivotal element in gender power relations. Were men to participate in child care equally, Chodorow suggests, such a violent distancing and other personality differences would be avoided. Although this explanation suffers from seeing women's oppression as emanating from social practices rather than from men's practices, a point to which I'll return, it does highlight child care as a critical site for any challenge to male domination.

Psychoanalytic theory helps us understand why sport is so enthusiastically taken up as part of the project of male personality development. This theory helps explain the ritualistic element in much dominant sport, which in turn helps us understand the effectiveness of the learning. Major sporting fixtures are likely to have all-male casts and to be staged in a ritualistic manner with women acting in an adulatory manner that highlights the "heroism" of the male performances. The effectiveness of ritual can be seen as largely due to its frequency and the setting in which people are confronted by "objects of thought and feeling which they hold to be of special significance" (Lukes, 1975, p. 291).

CHALLENGING THE HEGEMONY

The analysis so far has shown the way sport contextualizes and shapes male development in a fashion that oppresses women as well as men whose interests are not served by hegemonic masculinity. For anyone interested in creating greater equality, a conclusion that begs to be drawn is this: Have nothing to do with "such a self-indulgent festival of masculinity" (Graydon, 1983, p. 8). Although such a reaction may be entirely understandable (and my own erstwhile position), it is not strategically defensible. Sport is far too important a social institution to abandon to those who currently benefit disproportionately from it. Masculine claims to superiority are enormously effective, resulting in the usurpation of not only social and psychological benefits, but vast material ones as well. The men who have control over virtually all sport, including women's sport, have far better access to facilities and reap infinitely greater economic rewards from their involvement directly in sport and in the infrastructure that surrounds sport.

Clarify Equality

To discuss a challenge to this position, we must start by being clear about what sort of equality we are seeking. This in turn raises a question addressed by the editors at the outset of this volume—just who are we and what are our goals? As a feminist one might merely claim a half share for women in everything regardless of any assessment of its desirability. Such a position has a face simplicity; wresting away currently held advantages would not prove an easy exercise, but sketching out the agenda is easy. When we look to the situation of excluded men, however, the flaws in a simple redistributive approach become very evident. The fact is that the dominant ideology within sport is incompatible with genuine equality. Hegemonic masculinity by its very nature revolves around domination and construction of the other as inferior.

In considering our vision of a just society, we must ask this: Do we want women and excluded men to share equally in all things including acts of violence, the waging of wars, and the maintenance of class relationships? In promoting dominant sport as it is constituted today, we are inevitably giving tacit support to its negative as well as its positive features: its competitiveness, aggressiveness, hierarchy, domination, conflict, and discrimination. In terms of political approaches, the dilemma is the classic one between a liberal approach and a more radical one. A liberal approach takes the general framework of society as quite acceptable, apart from a few blemishes (which for feminists include gender inequality). The liberal approach accepts that these blemishes can be overcome with a little effort and in the fullness of time as part of industrial society's inevitable "progress." This, however, is a doubtful assumption. As Susan Birrell and Diana Richter (1987) point out, the liberal change brought about in the United States under Title IX "to remedy women's exclusion from sport has merely resulted in incorporation and has failed to accomplish the far-reaching changes in sport some feminists had advocated" (p. 396).

A more radical approach locates the fundamental problems in the social structure. There is concern that achieving gender equality should not be at the expense of perpetuating other major forms of inequality, such as race and class inequality. This is the stance taken in this chapter. In a really egalitarian society, there is no place for the highly competitive, capitalistic, manipulative sports that divert excessive resources to the already-privileged few, diminish losers and noncompetitors, and subject participants themselves to such pressures that winning is likely to take precedence over health and other personal and social interests.

It is beyond the scope of this chapter to do more than simply assert that the capitalist system is not consistent with a truly just society. Radical change is certainly necessary to secure humane changes, although at the level of practical politics, liberal solutions will need to be pursued in the short run as well. Changing the system is a long-term project. We need to be clear about our objectives but pursue changes where opportunities present themselves (i.e., pursue changes that move things in the right direction, no matter how slightly). Alliances will be strategically formed and at times with unexpected groups. The affirmative action programs within the public service in Australia have been the result of an unlikely alliance between male public servants with a managerialist focus and feminists (Bryson, 1987b).

Three Sites for Challenge

There are three interlocking sites on which the challenge to sport must be mounted:

- the specific site of sport itself,
- the points at which sport intersects other institutions, and
- the personal level.

Looking first to sport itself, it is clear that despite its strongly masculine flavour, sport is not a monolithic institution. As with other sites of social life, the hegemonic position has been continually contested. Of course, ignoring or incorporating challenges and expunging them from history are standard tactics for maintaining the status quo. The areas of overt challenge have gradually been extended, and women have expanded the range of their general physical as well as sporting activities. Myths about female anatomy have been officially dispelled, though their effects linger. Gains in acceptable women's dress have been fundamentally important, and today dress presents fewer restrictions, though the high-heel shoe (the modern-day equivalent of the old Chinese practice of footbinding, which so horrified Westerners) remains a sexual symbol and one that clearly limits a woman's physical competence.

In Australian sport, bicycling and tennis were encroached on at the end of last century, and few areas now remain free from at least some form of challenge. A recent landmark was the inclusion of the women's marathon in the 1984 Olympics. Women are also demanding greater control and fairer access to the financial rewards of sport. These challenges to the construction of women by the dominant ideology as inferior are vital for women's sense of their own power as well as necessary to alter men's perceptions.

Participation in sport itself remains problematic, though. The processes that disadvantage women and groups of marginalised men are often submerged and can be maintained in spite of women's participation. Where sporting activity is defined and judged according to the dominant values and on male terms, women's participation can in fact enhance hegemonic masculinity and reinforce women's inferior status, via processes that trivialise women's achievements.* If we are

---

Editors' note: Many women weight lifters, for example, endorse training goals and athletic values that are consistent with traditionally masculine principles and practices (e.g., develop greater physical power, be highly competitive, adopt a "no pain, no gain" approach). Yet, if women are successful, they are derided for not being as strong, as big, or as muscled as male weight lifters, or for being too much like men, too masculine. Women professional golfers in the United States fall prey to similar no-win dynamics. They are either faulted for not being quite as strong and hard-hitting as male pros or accused of acting like men or being lesbian. Bryson's point here is that in either case, the end result is the same: Women are devalued, and traditional sexist athletic values and domain gender assumptions are maintained.

to make our challenge to the hegemonic position effective, we need ultimately to capture and change the current definitions. We need to expand the qualities admired as skilful and important to include rhythm, grace, and other facets of sporting activity; to de-emphasize competition and a fanatical approach to sport; and to broaden participation and promote the understanding that if a thing is worth doing, it is also worth doing badly. Of course, the increasing commercialization of sport presents strong countervailing forces to such an enterprise.

Even though commercialization needs to be treated cautiously in terms of our long-term goals for a just society, commercialization may also offer opportunities. One perennial judgement about women's sports is that they are intrinsically less interesting than men's, a view clearly based on dominant views of sport. Norman May, one of Australia's best known sports commentators and a member of a recent federal inquiry into women, sport, and the media (Working Group on Women in Sport, 1985), has pointed to the way sporting events are not intrinsically interesting at all, but are made interesting. To illustrate his point he cites the America's Cup (which turned yachting into a popular media event over a brief period of its history) and the television hype that has been given in Australia to snooker and lawn bowls; these three sports are hardly intrinsically spectacular.

In tackling sport as part of a total picture of male domination, action must be directed to many fronts, to all sites at which sport intersects with other institutions. To see the challenge as restricted to the site of sport per se is to treat sport as an integrated and unified institution; this itself plays into the hands of dominant interests. Only within ideology has sport a unity. Where paid employment is involved, sport should be treated as an industrial issue. This opens up the relevant equal opportunity framework and the possibility of legal challenges. Access to clubs and facilities, control of sporting associations, or challenges to unfair rules might appropriately be tackled under antidiscrimination legislation. Elements of discriminatory advertising or reporting fall within the regulatory system of the media, educational discrimination within the general educational framework, and so on. Women need to gain decision-making power over resources allocated for sport and must not only demand a half share wherever the resources are dispersed but must demand that their share be spent how they wish—child-care facilities might be preferred to a new international car-racing circuit. Such action represents a liberal approach but has the advantage of empowering women and fostering genuine structural change.

Because sport cannot be divorced from other institutions of society, projects of a separatist kind cannot at present and by themselves be effective in bringing about significant change. Nonetheless, establishing countersporting activities such as women's and gay games is important because these activities advance the redefining process by acting as demonstration projects that allow the development of alternative forms (see Birrell & Richter, 1987); such activities also facilitate the development of solidarity among members of excluded groups, which in turn opens up possibilities for consciousness raising and political action. These activities are also fun and of personal benefit to participants. Such separatist strategies will only affect male hegemony if large enough numbers can be won over to the alternatives to significantly alter the support that dominant sport receives.

These alternative forms of sport can also provide a basis for the personal projects of reconstruction that are necessary if gender equality is to be made a reality. The personal is indeed an important political site. Although those attracted to alternative sports may well be those least in need of such reconstruction, all women and men, to greater or lesser degrees, are constructed in relation to the dominant ideology. In particular we need to heed Connell's (1987a) point that "conventional masculinity is to an extent, hegemonic masculinity in bad faith" (p. 215). Connell (1987) points to the way men "can enjoy patriarchal power, but accept it as if it were given to them by an external force, by nature or convention or even by women themselves" (p. 215). Gender relations should rather be seen, he suggests, as a "collective project in oppression" (p. 215). This highlights the need not only for social structural change but also for individual projects of reconstruction. Structural change can readily be subverted to serve dominant interests if the problem is seen as society's rather than as men's. People do have some choice over their behaviour. Similar logic applies to racial inequality and to the situations of the disabled. Although structural change is important, ultimately there is a dimension of oppressive social relationships that must be tackled directly at the personal level. This casts doubt on the faith placed in changes such as shared child care, as Chodorow and Dinnerstein both propose. Though clearly such sharing has benefits and is a necessary condition for equality, it is not likely to prove sufficient.

CONCLUSION

I have been able to provide only the barest outline of key elements of challenge to male hegemony in sport. As with all programs for change, there are no magic solutions that can be applied. However, the fact that books like this are being produced and, hopefully, widely read is a further step in the process. I hope that those who read these chapters will more clearly recognize the need for change and be better armed for the challenge to the status quo.

Chapter 15

Women of Color, Critical Autobiography, and Sport[1]

Susan Birrell

In recent years, as feminist scholars in sport studies have turned attention to the cultural meanings of the exclusion of women from sport, these scholars have moved the field toward increasingly comprehensive theories of sport as a gendered cultural form (Birrell, 1988a). Earlier research traditions grounded in liberal feminist theories were replaced by radical and socialist feminist approaches. Most recently, feminist scholars at the most critical edge of socialist feminism have advocated blending materialist-based analyses of gender relations with cultural studies theories to provide a "feminist cultural studies" (Cole & Birrell, 1986).

The most effective blending would highlight not only class relations and gender relations, but racial relations as well. The strong materialist base of both cultural studies and socialist feminism ensures attention to class relations, and socialist feminism ensures a focus on gender relations, but neither theory as presently conceptualized provides adequate theoretical attention to the issue of racial relations.

The neglect of race is a serious criticism leveled at scholars in all fields, not just those in sport. Many feminists have acknowledged this problem, and the most engaging debates in feminist circles currently focus on the issue of "theorizing difference" (Barrett, 1987; Martin & Mohanty, 1986). Unfortunately, sport studies scholars remain largely oblivious to these debates. We have become increasingly aware of sport as an institutional site for the reproduction of relations of privilege and oppression, of dominance and subordination, structured along gender, race, and class lines. But we have yet to launch any sort of sophisticated analysis of racial relations in sport. We continue to treat race as a variable rather than a relationship of power, and we have confined our attention almost exclusively to Black male athletes.

This tendency obscures and reduces diversity in sport in four ways. First, it equates *race* with Black, obscuring other racial groups such as Chicanos, Asian Americans, Jews, and Native Americans. Second, very little mention is made of the interrelationships between race, sport, and sexuality, or between sport and masculinity. Third, class is completely obscured through our practice of reading *race* as *race/class* and letting the analysis go at that. Finally, and of most immediate concern here, *Black athlete* usually means *Black male athlete*, an equation that obliterates gender. One can count on one hand the number of published analyses that specifically focus on women athletes of color (T.S. Green, Oglesby, Alexander, & Franke, 1981; Houzer, 1974). Some unpublished descriptive work on Black women athletes is available (Abney, 1988; Alexander, 1978; Barclay, 1979; Murphy, 1980), and we may find race as a variable in some of our research traditions (Greendorfer & Ewing, 1981), but no profound analyses have yet been begun. Even less material is available concerning Native American women (Oxendine, 1988), Asian American women, Chicanas, and members of other Hispanic groups.

The writing that does explore race and sport is generally superficial. It includes well-intentioned but theoretically limited critiques of sport as a racist institution (H. Edwards, 1969; Hoch, 1972); personal accounts of the exploitation of Black athletes (Wolf, 1972); a glut of tediously repetitive studies on stacking; and quantitative studies that reduce race to a variable. A more profound approach is to conceive of race as a culturally produced marker of a particular relationship of power; to see racial identity as contested; and to ask how racial relations are produced and reproduced through sport.

The purpose of this paper is to suggest strategies for broadening our theoretical frameworks and theorizing difference within the field of gender relations and sport. To that end I advocate exploring and delineating connections among theories of racial relations, the writings of women of color, cultural studies, and postmodernist discourse theories. Racial relations theory, for example, offers a well-developed theoretical framework that can provide important insight into the dynamics of racial relations and sport (Birrell, 1988a; Centre for Contemporary Cultural Studies, 1982; Mirande, 1985; Omi & Winant, 1986). However, as enlightening as that tradition is, gender relations are completely obscured within it. This ignorance is difficult to understand among scholars whose work is focused on inequality and oppression, who explicitly advocate political change through their research, and who are clearly aware of the double exploitations of class and race. To explore the connections and interactions among relations of race, class, and gender, we must supplement racial relations theory and feminist cultural studies with the writings of women of color, read through postmodernist discourse theory. We must explore the challenge that the writings of women of color pose to mainstream scholarship, racial relations theory, feminist theory, and cultural studies.

Racial relations scholarship, produced almost exclusively by men, has alienated many women of color (Garcia, 1986; Orozco, 1986; B. Smith, 1983) who find that they are neither the subjects of racial relations theory nor the intended audience of such tracts. Perhaps as a result, few women of color are attempting to join that tradition and produce explicit theories of racial relations.[2] Nor are they comfortable with most feminist theory, which, while focusing on gender, too often obscures race. The goal of women of color is to remain true to their identities as women of color; that is, they do not attempt to disengage either their sex or their color from their selves for purposes of analysis. By acknowledging the inextricability of gender and race, their writing attempts to accomplish a simultaneous analysis of these forces.

However, their work is often difficult for traditionally trained social scientists to appreciate, for it deliberately departs from the paradigms and practices of mainstream theoretical discourses. The language women of color use, the styles they invoke, and the terms of their analyses result in a discourse that must be approached on its own terms if we are to benefit from the insights these women provide. Although the analysis that follows does not explicitly mention sport, I contend that any analysis of sport, gender, and racial relations must begin with an appreciation of the issues and concerns as they are understood and articulated by the women themselves.

THE CHALLENGE OF WOMEN OF COLOR[3]

Distinctive feminist movements within the Black community and the Chicano community began in the early 1970s (Mirande & Enriquez, 1979; B. Smith, 1983) and grew out of experiences in the civil rights movements of the 1960s. Women of color became increasingly conscious of racism in the women's movement and sexism in the Black or Chicano movement. Within the Chicano movement, for example, Chicanas committed to an analysis of their particular concerns were ridiculed as *agabachadas* ("Anglocized") and *antiraza* (anti-Hispanic) by their Chicano brothers, a treatment that created two factions among politically committed Chicanas: loyalists and *feministas* (Mirande & Enriquez, 1979). Cherrie Moraga's essay "A Long Line of Vendidas" (1983) is testimony to the continuing struggle against sexism within the Chicano community. Likewise, Black women who explored their own feminist concerns were accused of disloyalty to the Black movement, a strategy detailed by Smith (1983), who takes it to task for "divert[ing] Black women from our own freedom" (p. xxv).

White feminists were seen as equally ignorant and unsupportive of the concerns of women of color. White feminists were harshly criticized for setting political agendas filled with their own middle-class issues and producing theories that were abstract, inaccessible, and based on only White experiences. Moreover, women of color were skeptical of forming both practical and theoretical alliances with White women if those alliances required them to sever relations with men because women of color felt acutely the need to bond with men to oppose White skin privilege. This tension between women of color and both White women and men of color spilled over from the liberation movements of the 1960s into the academic liberation movements of the early 1970s.

The Critique of Theory

The anger of women of color about their treatment within dominant theoretical traditions has produced a critical, often deconstructive, analysis of particular theories and the practice of theorizing itself. Although women of color clearly have complaints about theory produced by White men in the academic mainstream and by men of color, it is with White feminists that feminists of color engage in the most critical and energetic debates over theory.

The critique of theory begins with the "local" complaint about the absence of women of color from theory. What White feminists have chosen to theorize and the contents of those theories often make no sense in terms of the racial experiences of women of color. A common method in this critique is the measuring of theory against personal experience, a process inevitably resulting in theory being judged inadequate because "it doesn't speak to my experience" or "I can't find myself in that theory." As Hooks (1984) sees it,

> much feminist theory emerges from privileged women who live at the center, whose perspectives on reality rarely include knowledge and awareness of the lives of women and men who live in the margin. As a consequence, feminist theory lacks wholeness, lacks the broad analysis that could encompass a variety of human experiences. . . . (p. x)

She adds, "White women who dominate feminist discourse today rarely question whether or not their perspective on women's reality is true to the lived experiences of women as a collective group" (p. 3).

Women of color are particularly dissatisfied with liberal feminist theory and the programs for change grounded in it. For example, the much-applauded movement of women into the work force and the subsequent celebration of the superwoman who is wife, mother, and career woman are laughable to women of color, whose worst moments in history include their double exploitation as breeders and laborers under slavery (A. Davis, 1981; Carby, 1982). But their antipathy for radical feminism is equally strong. Some see the radical feminist posture of separatism as politically divisive because it "makes an ideology out of distance and the exclusion of the 'other' " (B. Smith, 1983, p. 1). Lourde's "Open Letter to Mary Daly" (1984), in which she criticizes Daly's obscuring of the experiences of women of color, is a classic example.

Critiques of the practice of theorizing itself focus on a number of interrelated problems.[4] Hooks's (1984) definition of theory as "the guiding set of beliefs and principles that become the basis for action" (p. 30) expresses a primary orientation of women of color. Many disdain theory as an elitist exercise that has no use in the "real" world. They feel the need to tie their writing to the community. Thus following Lourde's (1984) explicit call for the transformation of anger into revolutionary energy, many women of color continue to value analyses grounded in emotion to the dispassionate theorizing they associate with Western academics. Women of color fear that under the auspices of White feminists, feminism and feminist theory are losing their critical and radical edge. And these women strongly resist the tendencies in theory to abstract, to generalize, and to reword experience, fearing that their concerns and experiences will be overlooked, devalued, or actively subverted. They do not trust White middle-class academics, both women and men, who act as custodians and guardians of theory. It has not escaped the attention of women of color that those of us who have the most to say about theorizing difference say it in the most inaccessible way, to privileged audiences who need specialized schooling to render the discourse comprehensible.

In her excellent essay "The Race for Theory," Christian (1987) makes a particularly convincing argument about the way theory—in this case literary theories of poststructuralism and deconstruction—strips the meaning of experience from a text and silences the very people who text was meant to empower.

> The race for theory, with its linguistic jargon, its emphasis on quoting its prophets, its tendency towards "Biblical" exegesis . . . its preoccupations with mechanical analyses of language . . . its gross generalizations about culture, has silenced many of us to the extent that some of us feel we can no longer discuss our own literature. (p. 53)

Moreover, the race for theory has distracted people of color from their own goal: "Many of my peers who had previously been concentrating on . . . the reclamation and discussion of past and present third world literatures, were diverted into continually discussing the new literary theory" (Christian, 1987, p. 57). And they must do so in a language "which mystifies rather than clarifies our condition" (p. 55). As a result, women of color often view theory as one more colonizing experience that renders them invisible or attempts to assimilate them within White culture—or White theory, the "unity through incorporation" (Martin & Mohanty, 1986, p. 193) that Pratt (1984) warns against. Quite correctly, women of color resist such epistemological colonization.

Christian (1987) also voices a complaint about theory's tendency toward prescription:

> I, for one, am tired of being asked to produce a black feminist literary theory. I consider it presumptuous of me to invent a theory of how we *ought* to read. Instead I think we need to read the works of our writers in our various ways and remain open to the intricacies of the intersection of language, class, race, and gender in the literature. (p. 53)

Telling people how to read their own experience is, to Christian, an act of textual colonization. Clearly, women of color are struggling with the issue: How can the theoretically dispossessed repossess theory without being possessed by it? Rather than join the discourse as it has historically been constructed, they have chosen to engage in deconstructive work and to formulate their own conceptions of what should count as theory. These conceptions are founded on identity politics and standpoint epistemology.

Theorizing Difference: Identity Politics

B. Smith (1983) marks the self-conscious beginning of Black feminism in 1973 with the formation of the Combahee River Collective. The collective's "Black

Feminist Statement'' (1981), issued in 1977, was a manifesto of members' consciousness as Black women within racist, sexist, classist, and heterosexist society. A central theme in the statement was ''identity politics,'' a concept that has become a political rallying point not just for Black women but for any group marginalized or oppressed by dominant cultural groups and practices. Identity politics criticized the arrogance of racist feminism and sexist racial movements and provided the necessary rationale for a new form of cultural struggle based on an affirmation of racial pride and identity:

> Focusing upon our own oppression is embodied in the concept of identity politics. We believe that the most profound and potentially the most radical politics come directly out of our own identity, as opposed to working to end somebody else's oppression. (Combahee River Collective, 1981, p. 212)

In effect, they stated quite clearly that political commitment begins at home.

Identity politics issued a clear challenge to feminists to build theories that reflect the diversity of women's realities; to move beyond the totalizing concept of women—invariably White, middle-class, and heterosexual; and to begin to conceptualize difference within feminist theories. The response from both White feminists and feminists of color has been a close examination of the assumptions, strengths, and limitations of discourses grounded in identity politics.

As presently conceptualized, identity politics assumes that membership in a particular oppressed group provides the necessary and sufficient grounds for consciousness. This position accepts without reflection the realities of particular oppressed groups (i.e., it assumes that Blacks or Chicanos or Whites are biologically real groups rather than collective identities forged out of particular relations between vested interest groups and the ''others'' they seek to exploit). The problematization of race has not yet been addressed within the discourse on identity politics. Thus, identity politics is based on an appeal to essentialism in that it contains the assumption that consciousness of oppression is an automatic result of bearing an identity of oppression.

Conceptualizing identity as fixed and essential leads to the conclusion that differences between women are insurmountable. Thus, although positions based on identity politics may create necessary political solidarities within groups by drawing attention to the totalizing discourses in feminist theories, that stance reproduces White women and women of color as ''naturally'' oppositional groups (Martin & Mohanty, 1986).

In her essay ''Identity: Skin, Blood, Heart,'' Pratt (1984) questions ''the all-too-common conflation of experience, identity and political perspective'' (Martin & Mohanty, 1986, p. 192). Writing from a White feminist's perspective, Pratt uses the concept of home to explore the conflicting feelings evoked by the need to be grounded in the familiar (identity politics) and the commitment to move beyond the boundaries of privilege. As C. Kaplan (1987) summarizes it: ''We must leave home . . . since our homes are often sites of racism, sexism, and other damaging practices'' (p. 194). Pratt's text

> unsettles not only any notion of feminism as an all-encompassing home but also the assumption that there are discrete, coherent, and absolutely separate

identities—homes within feminism, so to speak—based on absolute divisions between various sexual, racial, or ethnic identities. (Martin & Mohanty, 1986, p. 192)

In doing so, Pratt creates "a dynamic feminist theory of location and positionality" (C. Kaplan, 1987, p. 194).
Bulkin (1984) also examines the impact of identity politics and warns that

if narrowly conceived . . . "focusing on our own oppression" can have drawbacks, hampering our attempts to understand issues that are necessarily complex and often intertwined. It can, for example, result in what [Jan Claussen] . . . has called "hunkering down in one's own oppression," refusing to look beyond one's identity as an oppressed person and, in some instances, wearing that identity as a mantle of virtue. (1984, p. 99)

And Hooks (1984) argues that identity politics, intended to unify members of a marginalized group, also provides a rationale for dominant discourses to continue exclusionary practices: "Slogans like 'organize around your own oppression' provided the excuse many privileged women needed to ignore the differences between their social status and the status of the masses of women" (p. 6).

The danger is that unrestrained identity politics might become mired in a self-interest that forecloses any thoughtful discussion of complex racial issues. Thus we retreat to a position of "natural" authority legitimated through our particular identity—oppression privilege (Bulkin, 1984)—and we avoid struggling with difficult issues that confront us. And oppression privilege can become what Bulkin (1984) has called horizontal violence, as we engage in a sort of destructive "one-downmanship," ranking oppressions, taking doctrinaire stances on the unquestionable authority of our national identities, not daring to leave the comforts of home.

Bulkin's essay "Hard Ground" (1984) begins to work through the very difficult task of acknowledging the complex dynamics among different forms of oppression. She urges us to resist "the danger of leveling oppressions, of failing to recognize the specificity of each" (p. 107) and to acknowledge the particularity of oppressive circumstances: "The degree of oppressiveness *depends* on the form that a given oppression takes at different times, in different locations, for different individuals" (p. 111). Thus, where the Combahee River Collective and others have talked about a "simultaneity of oppressions," Bulkin insists on confronting the complexity of interacting oppressions and dealing with particularities that specific circumstances produce. In other words, it is not a question of whether it is harder to be a woman, a Black, or a Jew—or even a Black Jewish woman—but of what particular set of oppressive relations is most dangerous at a particular time and place.

Hooks (1984) argues that rather than focus exclusively on the narrow confines of one particular experience of oppression, "Women must learn to accept responsibility for fighting oppressions that may not directly affect us as individuals" (p. 6). Moreover, we must acknowledge that no one is purely oppressed, just as no one lives a life of pure privilege: Privilege, oppression, and domination are all relative terms. They are, as Kaplan (1987) argues, issues of "positionality."

Theorizing Difference: Standpoint Epistemology

As a basis for theory and analysis, identity politics must be supplemented with a position that recognizes the achievement of consciousness as an intervening process between identity, experience, and theory. Consciousness then becomes the grounding for a standpoint epistemology, a position articulated in Marxist theory and adopted by some feminists, most notably Hartsock (1983). The standpoint argument is that those who have been systematically excluded from or only marginally involved in the cultural discourse—the oppressed—stand in a truer relation to social reality than do dominant groups. Having no stake in reproducing dominant repressive cultural forms, and thus free of the illusion that such forms are natural and good, they render a more complete analysis. These positions are consistent with W.E.B. Du Bois's notion of the double consciousness of Blacks in cultures dominated by Whites and what Sandoval has called "oppositional consciousness" (cited in C. Kaplan, 1987, p. 187). In all these conceptualizations, identity and consciousness exist in a dialectical relationship.

Hooks (1984) offers the most explicit statement of standpoint epistemology as it relates to race:

> Living as we did—on the edge—we developed a particular way of seeing reality. We looked both from the outside in and from the inside out. We focused our attention on the center as well as the margin. We understood both. This sense of wholeness, impressed upon our consciousness by the structure of our daily lives, provided us an oppositional world view—a mode of seeing unknown to most of our oppressors, that sustained us. (p. ix)

Central to Hooks's argument is the notion of marginality, a theme present in much of the writing of women of color and evident in the titles of some works, including Hooks's subtitle "From Margin to Center," Lourde's *Sister Outsider*, and Anzaldua's *Borderlands/La Frontera*. Looking on from the margins, from the borderlands, women of color are positioned to voice a critique of dominant forms of theory and an alternative grounded in a standpoint epistemology.

Home Truths and Critical Autobiography

The common theme joining these critiques of dominant theory was a recognition of dominant discourse as an act of intellectual colonization. This analysis can be linked to culturalist theories in the racial relations literature and to cultural feminist positions. Resistance to dominant notions of theory and the ensuing contest over theory are evidence that the acts of writing and theorizing are intended to lead to cultural survival. Thus, although the work these women produce to understand themselves as subjects of theory is not recognized within the dominant discourse as theory, their writing, they argue, fulfills the purpose of theory while ignoring—or transcending—traditional forms. Thus, women of color do not write to produce explicit theories of their oppressions and experiences: They write to textualize those experiences. They are writing, as Christian (1987) says, to save their lives: Writing is an act of recovery, of survival, of resistance, of revolution.

They are writing themselves out of a tradition of enforced silence and absence, and they intend for their writings to be read as theory. Christian (1987) clearly articulates this position:

> People of color have always theorized—but in forms quite different from the Western form of abstract logic. And I am inclined to say that our theorizing (and I intentionally use the verb rather than the noun) is often in narrative forms, in the stories we create, in riddles and proverbs, in the play with language since dynamic rather than fixed ideas seem more to our liking. . . . The women I grew up around continuously speculated about the nature of life through pithy language that unmasked the power relations of their world. . . . My folk, in other words, have always been a race for theory— though more in the form of the hieroglyph, a written figure which is both sensual and abstract, both beautiful and communicative. (p. 52)

One clear strategy is to recover and celebrate one's cultural heritage by producing autobiographical texts that preserve the authenticity of cultural experience. Thus, in less than a decade, a literary tradition has emerged from women of color[5] that might appropriately be labeled "critical autobiography," for what these writers have in common is an epistemological grounding in the authenticity of individual experience placed in tension with dominant structures of racial and gender relations. In critical autobiography, theory is understood to be implicit in the text, and the individual whose experience is the crucible for theory is read as representational: She is both the subject of the text and the theorizer of the experience. Such a stance reflects the belief that women of color learn about oppression firsthand, through their lives, whereas White women read about oppression in their theory books. B. Smith (1983) says, "I learned about Black feminism from the women in my family" (p. xxii), whereas Hooks (1984) observes, "[It is] just another indication of the privileged living conditions of middle and upper class white women that they would need a theory to inform them that they were 'oppressed' " (p. 10). Women of color believe they learn their theory in their lives, so they write their lives as theory. Their accounts are "home truths" (B. Smith, 1983).

To avoid being judged as merely "archival" (JanMohamed & Lloyd, 1987) or as counterrevolutionary—a potential Marxist critique—the critical autobiography must not dwell in romantic culturalism but move on to render a critical analysis of the tensions between identity, experience, and consciousness. For example, the meaning of color within Chicano culture is explored in both Moraga's "La Guera" and Anzaldua's "La Prieta" (in Moraga & Anzaldua, 1983). Individually, Moraga and Anzaldua recount their own experiences as light-skinned or dark-skinned Chicanas; taken together, their narratives are particularly stunning. Moraga's essay in particular reveals the internal struggle between the value her family put on being fair skinned ("everything about my upbringing . . . attempted to bleach me of what color I did have," p. 28) and her growing consciousness of the cultural betrayal this embodies. In other essays, Anzaldua (1987) uses language as a metaphor to explore the difficult status of the *mestiza* who must dwell on the borderlands.

Ultimately, however, critical autobiography must be judged not on its ability to recover personal pain but on the extent to which it moves beyond the personal to the representational. C. Kaplan (1987) and Martin and Mohanty (1986) praise Pratt's essay for the way she has brought a critical analysis to the evaluation of her own experiences. Pratt deconstructs the assumption that experience provides insight in and of itself. It must be theorized first, if by theorizing we mean placed in critical dialogue with particular conditions of oppression. As Martin and Mohanty (1986) note, "In Pratt's narrative, personal history acquires a materiality in the constant rewriting of herself in relation to shifting interpersonal and political contexts. This rewriting is an interpretive act which is itself embedded in social and political practice" (p. 210). Thus Pratt

> succeeds in carefully taking apart the bases of her own privilege by resituating herself again and again in the social, by constantly referring to the materiality of the situation in which she finds herself. The form of the personal historical narrative forces her to reanchor herself repeatedly in each of the positions from which she speaks, even as she works to expose the illusory coherence of those positions. (Martin & Mohanty, 1986, p. 194)

In so doing, Pratt has avoided "two traps, the purely experiential and the theoretical oversight of personal and collective histories" (Martin & Mohanty, 1986, p. 210).

As they work to reconstitute theory, through critical autobiography and other practices, feminists of color have much in common with materialist and culturalist positions in racial relations and with feminist theories that emanate from radical, materialist, or feminist cultural studies positions. These include the equation of theory with meaning, grounding theory in everyday life experiences, and privileging "insider" information as authentic. Criticisms of this position include the essentialist assumptions of identity politics and the belief that identity politics and oppression consciousness form an epistemological basis for theoretical authority; the uncritical acceptance of the authority of experience; the tendency for autobiographical authority to become merely individualistic or ideosyncratic accounts; and a confusion of the relationship among theory, text, experience, and subject, so that experience is often taken *as* theory.

The authority of experience in particular requires further examination, for it underlies the epistemological positions taken by racial relations theories, some radical or cultural feminists, and the writing of women of color. Hooks (1984) warns that experience is often not critically examined:

> All too often the slogan "the personal is political" became a means of encouraging women to think that the experience of discrimination, exploitation, or oppression automatically corresponded with an understanding of the ideological and institutional apparatus shaping one's social status. As a consequence, many women who had not fully examined their situation never developed a sophisticated understanding of their political reality and its relationship to that of women as a collective group. They were encouraged to focus on giving voice to personal experience. (p. 24)

To Hooks (1984), "Personal experiences are important to feminist movement [sic] but they cannot take the place of theory" (p. 30). In the same vein, JanMohamed and Lloyd (1987) argue that "archival work" (i.e., uncritical autobiography) cannot take the place of theory:

> Archival work is essential to the critical articulation of minority discourse. At the same time, if this archival work is not to be relegated by the force of dominant culture to the mere margined repetition of exotic ethnicity, theoretical reflection cannot be dispensed with. (p. 8)

The complaint that theory is inadequate because "it doesn't speak to my experience" assumes that experience offers direct entrée to reality and that one must collect such experiences to form an accurate picture of reality or theory. But experience is not *pure*, and it is not *owned*: It is always mediated, set within a context of cultural conditions, and subject to preferred readings already in place. To accept experience as unproblematic not only falls into an essentialist position but also denies the political nature of all discourses, even those invented by the self as autobiography. Moreover, such a stance, as elaborated by Stanley and Wise (1983), eventually regresses to a point of total relativism—every woman her own theorist—because every woman experiences the world uniquely, and only she can speak authoritatively to that experience.

To avoid such exercises in theoretical anarchy, we must examine how certain commonalities of experience or ideologies of experience structure individual lives. Thus we must reascend from personal accounts to the level of critical autobiography and the commonality and generality informed by an explicit theory of structural relations such as cultural studies and discourse theory.

Minority Discourses and the Comforts of Home

Sport, as we understand it, is absent from the writings of women of color, so it is not immediately evident how such an extensive review of their writing can help us develop a better analysis of racial relations and sport. One response is that we need to investigate absence as a real phenomenon and ask how the absence of sport provides insight into particular cultures. Even more important, if we are to understand gender and racial relations in sport, particularly as they relate to women of color, we cannot remain in our old theoretical homes, for we have seen how that approach has limited us. Instead we need to increase our awareness of issues in the lives of women of color as they themselves articulate these issues.

An excellent starting point is to reread the themes that dominate their discourses. Women of color write about identity and the tension between their individual lives and their developing cultural consciousness; they explore the tie between identity and home, both literal and symbolic; they lament their forced exit from the land, their deterritorialization through the diaspora and the lost Aztlan (the Mexican lost homeland); they express pain and anger over their deculturation, alienation, marginalization, and deracination; they search for home—to return, to recover, to represent themselves in a literature of home. It is a discourse of separation, positionality, and cultural struggle against colonization in all its forms—geographic, economic, linguistic, textual, academic. It is what Deleuze and Guattari (1986) call a "minority discourse."[6]

Coming out of the modern literary movements of poststructuralism, postmodernism, and deconstruction, discourse theory focuses on the analysis of a text—broadly understood to include lived experiences and cultural forms such as sport. In critical response to its literary precursors that assign the text ontological status, discourse theory recognizes a text as a historically produced, politically expedient re-presentation of particular cultural relations. The analysis of the text explicates the ways in which cultural forms are inscribed with particular preferred meanings and circulated to a public in order to obtain its consent to a "natural order" of things.

Particularly pertinent to the topic at hand is the analysis of "minority" discourse, by which Deleuze and Guattari (1986) do not intend to refer to qualities that inhere in the literary works of the "masters." To Deleuze and Guattari (1986), "Minor no longer designates specific literatures but the revolutionary conditions for every literature within the heart of what is called great (or established) literature" (p. 17). As C. Kaplan (1987) points out, "The issue is positionality" (p. 189), and JanMohamed and Lloyd (1987) add,

> "Becoming minor" is not a question of essence (as the stereotypes of minorities in dominant ideology would want us to believe), but a question of position—a subject-position that can only be defined, in the final analysis, in "political" terms, that is, in terms of the effects of economic exploitation, political disfranchisement, social manipulation, and ideological domination on the cultural formation of minority subjects and discourses. It is one of the central tasks of the theory of minority discourse to define that subject-position and explore the strengths and weaknesses, the affirmations and negations that inhere in it. (p. 11)

What discourse theory provides, then, is a method by which to reread minority texts "as indications and figurations of values radically opposed to those of the dominant culture" (JanMohamed & Lloyd, 1987, p. 10) and to recognize both the material conditions of textual production and the hegemonic tastes that relegate certain literatures to the margins of dominant discourses. For example, in her excellent article "Deterritorializations," C. Kaplan (1987) uses the insights of minority discourse theory to reread several texts by women of color[7] and to carefully explicate the themes of home and exile.

Discourse theory provides fresh methods of analysis, but it has not escaped critical scrutiny, particularly from feminists (Christian, 1987; Hartsock, 1987) who fear that this method for exploring the imperialism of cultural hegemony is itself guilty of exercising a certain hegemonic privilege within academia. Moreover, regardless of its critique of the politics of cultural production, the move by discourse theory to reduce all phenomena to the level of discourse and to problematize the subject of that discourse is at best apolitical and at worst counterrevolutionary. When one focuses on minority discourse, one is comfortably distanced from the flesh-and-blood realities of racial oppression.

Concerned about the disengagement that follows from its epistemological stance, Hartsock (1987) argues that "post-modernism represents a dangerous approach for any marginalized group to adopt" (p. 191). She questions its "intellectual moves":

> Somehow it seems highly suspicious that it is at this moment in history, when so many groups are engaged in "nationalisms" which involve redefinitions of the marginalized Others, that doubt arises in the academy about the nature of the "subject," about the possibilities for a general theory which can describe the world, about historical "progress." Why is it, exactly at the moment when so many of us who have been silenced begin to demand the right to name ourselves, to act as subjects rather than objects of history, that just then the concept of subjecthood becomes "problematic"? Just when we are forming our own theories about the world, uncertainty emerges about whether the world can be adequately theorized? Just when we are talking about the changes we want, ideas of progress and the possibility of "meaningfully" organizing human society becomes suspect? And why is it only now that critiques are made of the will to power inherent in the effort to create history? (p. 196)

Hartsock (1987) proposes remedies that include the reaffirmation of subjectivity—"we need to engage in the historical and political and theoretical process of constituting ourselves as subjects as well as objects of history" (p. 204)—and the reestablishment of "an epistemological base that indicates that knowledge is possible—not just conversation or a discourse on how it is that power relations work" (p. 205).

These critiques raise serious questions about the political stance and thus the theoretical worth of discourse theory as it is presently constituted. Minority discourse theory responds to Hartsock's first suggestion by privileging the subjectivity of the author, but those who practice this theory must be careful not to embrace too tightly its problematic epistemology. Perhaps discourse theory can be transformed through a blending with the more politically motivated cultural studies approach, which follows the Marxist tradition of valuing theory as an instrument for change rather than just interpretation.

Cultural studies and discourse theory are most clearly linked through their attention to the analysis of the cultural. Their focuses on cultural forms as cultural productions subjected to contesting forces attempting to reproduce dominant relations or to resist cultural annihilation instruct us to discover the dynamics of these struggles over meaning, to recognize ideologies as vested and differentiated, and to explore the making and remaking of hegemonic consent. The challenge is to bring a both politically and theoretically strong tradition to bear on the analysis of racial relations, class relations, and gender relations in sport and, in so doing, to reformulate and empower the theory itself.

The Absence of Sport

Sociologists need to seriously address the absence of sport from the writings of radical women of color. Black women, for example, do not critique the inordinate importance sport holds in the lives of their brothers, nor do they appear to be aware of the increasing visibility and potential exploitation of Black women in big-time college athletic programs. Yet an analysis of the way that sport works to produce ideologies of gender within Black communities might present a challenge to current theories drawn primarily from observations of dominant White middle-class notions of gender relations. Dominant readings of masculinity within the Black community and the part that sport may play in the production and reproduction of ideology need to be addressed against the historical backdrop of gender relations. The meanings attached to masculinity were transformed from their African roots through the conditions of slavery in the United States (A. Davis, 1981; Hooks, 1981). Sojourner Truth's famous question, "Ain't I a woman?" reminds us in a powerful way that femininity, like masculinity, is a totalizing concept that requires deconstruction into constituent femininities and masculinities (Brod, 1987) produced within particular communities.

Further insight into the complexities of gender relations and sport could be gained by expanding our observations to include Chicano culture. The analysis might begin with an examination of *machismo* and *hembrismo*, the cultural stereotypes of the swaggering male and the passive female that have been soundly criticized by Chicano scholars (e.g., Mirande & Enriquez, 1979). We might explore how sport, or its absence, figures into the reproduction of these ideologies. The topic is particularly provocative given United States cultural assumptions about the necessary connection between masculinity and sport. We surely have much to learn about the interaction of these gendered, racial stereotypes and the construction of ideologies of gender relations in sport.

Following the thematic lead of Chicana writers, we should explore the ways in which mainstream U.S. sport works to reproduce marginality and thus participates in the making and remaking of the individual as "alien." Perhaps Chicanas are not writing about sport because they perceive it to be a cultural form invested with an aura of otherness: For them, U.S. sport is too mainstream, too alienating, too colonizing. It is anathema to their cultural struggle.

The single most provocative work on racial relations and sport takes up these themes. Though largely ignored by sport studies, C.L.R. James's *Beyond a Boundary* (1963) is a remarkable commentary on positionality as James attempts to reconcile his growing cultural consciousness as a West Indian with his infatuation for the decidedly British cultural forms of cricket and the plays of Thackeray. In his personal journey toward increasingly radical and Marxist sensibilities, James produces his own analysis of the complex relationships between identity, consciousness, and home. It is a model of analysis our field would do well to emulate.

TOWARD A CRITICAL THEORY
OF RACIAL RELATIONS

The task facing those who seek to produce a more theoretically sophisticated analysis of racial relations and sport is a delicate one with both theoretical and political dimensions. The long-term goal must be to produce critical theories of racial relations sensitive to the complexities of class and gender relations as well.

As an analytical approach, cultural studies offers a bright promise. It has a general framework for understanding relations of dominance and subordination, an insistence on analyzing the particular conditions of those relations, and an array of conceptual tools to advance the analysis. However, cultural studies needs to be decentered from class relations and broadened to take into account gender and racial relations. In the search for a theoretical approach that takes into account both the intersections and the relatively autonomous spheres of gender relations, class relations, and race relations, feminist cultural studies offers one theoretical expansion, and the writings of women of color provide another. Critical autobiographies can be read within the tradition of discourse theory in which the new emphasis on minority discourse provides a critical framework for examining the subjectivity of marginalized groups.

Thus, the tradition of feminist cultural studies and critical autobiography can be connected. However, we must attend to a significant issue as we explore the nature of those connections: Is the study of racial relations—and its application to sport—to be added to, blended with, comprehended within, or integrated into established or developing theories? Or should it remain a separate theoretical enterprise? What are the epistemological bases and political implications of such choices? We must be careful to find a way to connect these discourses so that we can preserve their separate insights and produce an even more powerful, critical, and radical way of theorizing about the connections between race, class, and gender. At this time it seems wisest to take a lesson from the resistance of women of color to such assimilative tasks, regardless of how sensitively those tasks are conducted. We must work to familiarize ourselves with theories that use racial relations as their point of privileged access rather than risk colonizing the experiences of people of color within our current theories. As Haraway (1985) and others would urge, we need to work not toward unity and synthesis but toward affinity—always sensitive to the complex of subordinate and dominant relations, but, for now, privileging the most overlooked example of those relations. The new insights produced through such connections will enrich our analyses of cultural relations as they interact with sport.

Chapter 16

Warriors or Wimps? Creating Alternative Forms of Physical Education

Barbara Humberstone

Male hegemony is produced and perpetuated through the particular images of masculinity constituted by dominant forms of sport prevailing in our society. Sport and physical education (PE) are significant domains in which these dominant forms

---

Editor's note: Our developmental editor at Human Kinetics Publishers reacted strongly to this chapter. We wanted to share some of her comments with our readers. She wrote in her initial review: "This chapter sure brought back memories! Modified rules in P.E. classes for coeducational sports made me angry even in high school. In basketball the boys couldn't shoot without a girl having touched the ball, and in volleyball boys couldn't spike and the ball had to be hit by a girl once per side. I also played interscholastic volleyball. A new gymnasium was built my freshman year. Practice for boys' basketball would begin just about the time we volleyball players would be preparing for district playoffs. There was no question, however, that the boys, just beginning their season and more than likely just conditioning, would have the new, big gym and we girls would be relegated to the small gym (often called the 'girls' gym') with its low ceilings and short end lines. If we wanted the better facilities we had to practice at 6:00 a.m. or come back to school after 6:00 p.m. when the boys were done. It was infuriating."

of masculinity are reproduced, but they may also be sites of contestation. In this chapter, the author summarizes a study that explored whether a particular physical education curriculum can transform rather than reinforce male hegemonic models.

A growing body of literature concerned with theoretical issues in feminist analyses of sport has attempted to understand how sport contributes to the production and reproduction of patriarchal gender relations and social structures[1]. For example, the different ways in which gender is interpreted through Canadian university PE programmes, where PE is studied as an academic discipline, are shown to reinforce stereotypical views of differences in men's and women's performances and participation while marginalizing cultural explanations (Dewar, 1987b). Sherlock (1987) demonstrates the powerful effect of macho ideology in the training of physical educators in Britain. For the most part, however, the focus has been on women's experiences in and of sport and on ways that women and girls make sense of and interpret these experiences. Unless we also attempt to understand the ways in which boys and men are shaped and constrained by (or enabled to challenge) dominant masculinities in and through sport, we cannot hope to sensitize both women and men to the possibilities of challenging and subverting structured male power. As Jeff Hearn (1987) points out, ''It is not possible to simply *understand* 'women' and 'women's oppression' in an un-dialectical way, that is, without reference to and without an understanding of those who, and those structures which, oppress women'' (p. 44).

Critical historical analyses of sport have highlighted the ways in which sport has historically legitimated and supported the reproduction of patriarchal gender relations in society. Phillips (1980) and Mangan (1987) have identified strong links between traditional sport, the constitution of acceptable masculinities, and imperial ideology. The cult of masculinity, celebrated through traditional sport, has provided for a blind acceptance of the ''virtues'' of warring. This is no more vividly demonstrated than by the Australian sociologist Carroll's (1986) fascination with the ''grace'' of violence and denigration of the wimps who do not share his view. ''It is the warrior drive and the warrior ethos that are resurrected in modern team football'' (p. 93). He is adamant that women should not be permitted into this virtuous brotherhood. Sport, then, is a central agency through which gender identities and relations are constituted and tested. Gender acts as a powerful cultural and ideological force that subtly moulds both individual perceptions and group process. In sport, gender both reflects and frames the realities that are observed. Through these are mediated narrow and distorted perspectives of what constitutes appropriate and valued forms of physical activities, perpetuating stereotypical assumptions that reinforce appropriate and expected (yet different) behaviours for women and men. The complex web of interconnections between cultural values, gender identity development, and gender stereotypes surrounding sport is mediated through the PE curriculum. Girls and boys may accept, reject, or accommodate to the cultural and ideological messages within the curriculum.[2] It remains to be seen whether physical educational experiences can be constructed in ways that convey messages counter to the macho, warrior ethos.

PHYSICAL EDUCATION AND THE MAINTENANCE OF MALE HEGEMONY

The curriculum area of PE has only recently become an issue of interest for interpretative research and critical feminist or socialist analyses[3]. Analysts suggest that two main cultural and structural factors that reflect and maintain male hegemony are writings on PE teachers and sex segregation. Most research teaching has basically reified the stereotypically masculine images of PE and PE teaching. Pupils and teachers are frequently observed to display various characteristics of toughness, aggressiveness, and competitive zeal (Whitehead & Hendry, 1976). In a discussion of the strategies that teachers adopt in order to maintain classroom control, Cohen and Manion (1981) implicitly link physical education with a mode of domination that encourages physical and verbal attacks and diminishes pupil self-esteem and confidence.

PE has been identified as a subject in which teachers sometimes use such activities as changing and showering to humiliate pupils and deprive them of their self-esteem. Such uncritical acceptance of these pedagogical descriptions highlights the paucity of detailed analyses of alternative forms of PE teaching, the symbolic nature of traditional PE, and the myths that surround it.

Sex segregation traditionally found in school PE is also frequently seen outside of class. Delamont (1980) observed that segregative patterns in the playground stemmed from the fact that boys monopolized the main activity space to play football and excluded those girls who wished to participate. Assumptions that equate sport with masculine competence help justify and make sense of this pattern of exclusion and inclusion. The mythological place in British culture occupied by football, like many other traditional team games, symbolizes sexual divisiveness and the emphasis upon male domination that is associated with machismo.

Traditional sex segregation in British PE lessons does little to create greater understanding between the sexes. It augments attitudes that announce and celebrate the stereotypical polarities of masculinity and femininity in sport; cooperation and the recognition of similarities between the sexes is stifled. Undoubtedly, without sensitive and careful integration, neither girls nor boys can fully realize their own potentials, nor those of the other sex. However, merely mixing boys and girls together for PE without creating a change in teaching approach may only serve to exacerbate misconceptions and mistrust between the sexes and further reinforce masculine hegemony. And yet, it appears obvious that underlying assumptions about gender cannot be exposed and understood without challenging cultural images of sport. A number of studies of mixed PE classes in schools have demonstrated that challenging gender stereotypes is no easy task (Abigail, 1985; Duncan, 1985; M. Evans, 1985; P. Griffin, 1983; Lopez, 1985). Many studies evidence the creation of hostility between the sexes. Boys exhibited egotistic behaviours and aggressive confidence in themselves, whereas girls were disinclined to assert themselves. Certainly, it is not only separatist feminists who maintain

that girls need space away from boys so as to facilitate a more successful development of girls' skills and confidences in PE (Scraton, 1987). Nevertheless, no matter
how much girls gain within all-girl supportive environments, male hegemonic
models still predominate, and male oppression and violence (subtle and overt)
are inescapable unless both women and men attempt to understand and provide
alternatives. In addition, substantial evidence now identifies problems many boys
experience in all-male environments. These problems are associated with the
considerable pressures placed upon boys to conform to nonemotional, uncaring
masculine stereotypes (Askew & Ross, 1988).

DEVELOPING ALTERNATIVE CONTEXTS
FOR PHYSICAL EDUCATION

This chapter reports on the experiences and reactions of male pupils to a
coeducational curriculum that, although not designed to help them recognize the
traditional gender assumptions associated with physical activity, did enable pupils
to challenge many of these assumptions. As a participant observer in a large,
British outdoor-adventure center at Shotmoor,[4] I utilized an ethnographic approach
to explore the participants' experiences and perceptions (Hammersley, 1983;
D. Silverman, 1985). This method allows a researcher to examine both individual
perception and decision making as well as to identify contextual and ideological
constraints. The main focus of data analyses was on how gender-related attitudes
and beliefs were created, maintained, or challenged within the context of the physical activities at the centre.

The outdoor-adventure centre provided a variety of physical activities, water-
and land-based in summer and land-based, frequently under cover, in winter.
The study was undertaken during the winter, and groups of school pupils between
the ages of 10 and 16 years attended the regular programme for 1 week with
their school teachers (both male and female from mixed-sex schools), who
frequently but not always were physical educators.

The programme aimed to provide an introduction to a variety of risk-taking
activities that included climbing on an artificial wall, abseiling,[5] skiing on a dry
slope, track cycling, and a confidence course. The philosophies that most of the
predominantly male Shotmoor teachers espoused were those associated with a
"progressive" ideology more readily found in primary schools.[6] These teachers
saw it their responsibility to empower pupils to realise their true potentials. The
activities were seen merely as vehicles to achieve this end.

Shotmoor provides an alternative context for experiencing gender relations in
several ways. First, boys and girls share the physical activities together, usually
having equally limited experiences of them. Differences in physical appearances
are reduced because girls and boys wear similar uniforms. Second, teachers, girls,
and boys share similar privileges. School teachers frequently participate along-
side their pupils, and Shotmoor teachers encourage use of their first names. Third,

elements of danger mediated by the teacher create shared experiences of responsibility and independence for boys and girls through which they become more sensitive to and conscious of each other's emotions and capabilities.

One visiting school PE teacher (Mr. Ball) described his pupils' experiences at the institute in the following way:

> They [the pupils] all have new experiences with a new activity, and it's not necessarily competitive, so they are learning new skills together, which tends to bind them together. Even your fat Jo Bloggs can go round the cycle track, and the good footballer will encourage him. Often the good lads won't do the free abseil but the little girls manage to climb up the walls. It's learning socially as well as learning a new activity. . . . It's often not only the good footballers who choose to come but also those who are on the periphery of sport.

Mr. Ball's comment illustrates the differences between physical education in the context of the institute and physical education in the typical school. He identifies these differences in terms of the curriculum content, the ways in which the learning experience was made available to pupils, and the ways in which pupils evaluated themselves and each other. In particular, he points to the nature of the interaction between pupils. Furthermore, he suggests that in this particular teaching context, those pupils conventionally considered to be physically more able both acknowledged and supported rather than denigrated those pupils generally viewed as physically less able.

BOYS' EXPERIENCES AT SHOTMOOR

Adventure education at the institute also helped both girls and boys challenge conventional notions of physical ability and cultural concepts of gender. Many boys experienced apprehension during the activities, and they found that teachers did not denigrate them but encouraged them to overcome their fears and give support to other anxious pupils. In many of the classes, some girls frequently outshone most of the boys. This surprised the boys, who were not used to girls participating with them in physical activities and certainly did not expect girls to be as physically competent. As one amazed boy said, "We're supposed to be the stronger sex!" These kinds of experiences and insights contrast markedly with boys' standard perceptions of the traditional, sex-segregated British school PE curriculum of soccer, rugby, and cricket, which boys generally consider proper sport only for themselves.

Perceptions of Sport's Masculinity

The differences between the two forms of curriculum and the contradictory messages that are conveyed through them about gender and physicality emerge in the following short extract of an interview with Dave, a white, working-class, 13-1/2-year-old boy, who was interviewed at the end of his week's stay at Shotmoor. He was a keen and very able athlete and had been selected to play soccer for the city youth team. In his account, we see the ways in which traditional sport is perceived as exclusively masculine and how it attributes lower status to girls and their abilities. Dave, however, does show a certain sensitivity to, and appreciation of, the position and inexperience of girls.

Dave: It's unusual to see girls playing football or cricket or rugby, 'cause it's all physical games, isn't it?

BH: But you think it's different here; is it—or not?

Dave: All the activities I done are like this—it's equal, absolutely equal, 'cause they've never done it before. So we're all on the same level. So if the boys can't do something the girls laugh. If they make a messup, we laughs. . . . That's the only thing I reckon that separates us from the girls and that's standard.

BH: What do you mean standard? Skill or what?

Dave: Skill and—you know—fitness and strength. You don't see girls lifting up weights do you? I mean bodybuilding?

BH: Not often, sometimes.

Dave: Sometimes, yeh. They're not built for it. They're built for other things.

BH: What sort of things?

Dave: [indecipherable] Tennis, the nonphysical games, if you know what I mean. Because everything demands a lot of work, but some are more physical than others. The boys' sports—mostly you have to be very physical or otherwise the game won't be enjoyable.

BH: But here, given the chance, don't you think the girls could be as good or—

Dave: Definitely, sure they can, 'cause we don't do it anyway. So I mean there's a girl good at skiing, I think it's Gayle. She's rather good, she's better than me anyway. I falls over. I can't roller skate [either]. Yeh, the girls are better than us at roller skating.

Dave's stereotypical views in part flow from his life-historical immersion in the cultural milieu of the soccer field. It was also evident that his traditional PE experiences reinforced stereotypical notions about appropriate male and female behaviours and abilities (i.e., physical sports or attitudes are for boys).

More significantly, however, Dave highlights the ways in which boys' and girls' insufficient skill levels are differently received and evaluated by the peer group within Shotmoor and within the school. The curriculum offered at the outdoor-adventure centre provides opportunities for both girls and boys to learn new skills, skills that have physical, personal, and social components and are not merely individual but are also corporate. These experiences form the basis of physical activities to which boys are attracted, because adventure and risk taking are conventionally considered masculine activities. Lack of skill and experience is acceptable at Shotmoor. However, in contexts that celebrate macho masculinity, such as traditional school PE programmes, girls' aptitudes appear to be inappropriate and of a lesser standard, and girls' mistakes (and perhaps those of boys also) provoke anger. Furthermore, games conventionally considered female are seen as requiring different skills and as inappropriate for boys and are thus rated second.

> *BH:* Do you reckon it works well, working in the group with the girls then, or—
>
> *Dave:* Depends what activity it is. When you're playing something—and the girls don't usually play it and they muck something up—you get all angry and cross then. 'Cause you don't really think about when they don't really play the sport. You know. Say, if I wanted to play netball I'd mess everything up, wouldn't I? 'Cause I couldn't play netball to save my life.
>
> *BH:* But probably if it [netball] had been a boy's game which you'd learnt earlier on, you'd probably been alright, wouldn't you?
>
> *Dave:* Yeh, but you still wouldn't be accepted 'cause you'd be a girl—that's the only thing.

Perceptions of Girls' Abilities

Dave interprets girls' nonparticipation in masculine activities as evidence of girls' lack of the prerequisite skills that would enable them to successfully participate in sport. Ultimately, for Dave, the most damaging attribute is that of being a girl! These perceptions of girls' abilities can be juxtaposed with the ruling made by Lord Denning in 1978 (Pannick, 1983) in which a girl, whose ability to play league soccer was not in question, was legally barred from participation because of her sex. Here we see the subtle ways in which, over time, hegemonic control is accomplished by boys' internalization of the dominant group's official view. The ruling neatly, albeit crudely, exemplifies the double-bind situation experienced by girls and women in all spheres of male-dominated society but most visually evident in the realm of traditional sport. The ruling also highlights the ways in which this androcentric philosophy "logically" shapes and structures what are considered women's abilities and so can prevent women's access to those areas that are valued and perceived as exclusively masculine. Consequently, this internalization denies men and boys access to more humane behaviours.

In the following brief discussion between two 13-year-old white boys, Jim and Duncan, the differing underlying assumptions about girls' abilities, attributes, and attitudes are evident. Importantly, the discussion highlights the emergence of a challenge to hegemonic versions of gender relations arising out of the boys' experiences of the Shotmoor curriculum. We see that the boys feel that starting from similar experiences is important in countering misconceptions over apparent differences in behaviour between boys and girls.

Interestingly, Duncan, who celebrated maleness but recognised successful collaboration between boys and girls in this appropriately masculine context, elevates the girls to positions of honorary boys. However, we see that Jim questions this view, positing that boys and girls behave similarly, but such behaviour is unrelated to concepts of sex.

> *BH:*   What about your group?
>
> *Jim:*   Yeh, I think we've got quite a good group. I mean we work together well.
>
> *BH:*   How do you get on with the girls?
>
> *Jim:*   We get on fine. We just get on like a team; there's no —.
>
> *Duncan:* They act as though they are boys, same as us.
>
> *Jim:*   No, they act as though we're all the same.
>
> *BH:*   Why is that, do you think?
>
> *Jim:*   I don't know—'cause we're all doing the same sort of thing and you've got to act the same.

Jim later, in an extract not included here, challenges Duncan's assumption that climbing is an activity less appropriate for girls than boys, and Willy (another member of the group) suggests that girls do possess adequate physical strength to enable them to climb. Changes in attitude seemed to issue following sessions of climbing and other risk-taking activities in which the boys were able to see girls participating and in which all pupils were enabled to work cooperatively together.

The preceding discourses identify deep-seated, pervasive notions by which boys are rated superior to girls in sport. However, the form of physical education made available at Shotmoor, I would suggest, allows for more informed, contextual views to emerge concerning the status of boys vis-à-vis girls. Consequently, although most boys perceived the physical activities made available at Shotmoor as appropriate for them, few thought the activities were exclusively male, especially by the end of their stay.

Teacher Characteristics

Very few of the male centre staff set out to consciously challenge boys' conventional assumptions about girls' appropriate places and capabilities. In one case, however, an alternative view was made explicit. One boy, on first arriving at the institute, asked a male centre teacher, "What will the girls be doing while we are climbing and skiing?" The boy received the immediate and pointed, yet humorously conveyed, response, "I expect they will be leading you up the climbing wall and down the ski slope!" On no occasion did teachers denigrate, ignore, or marginalize girls, nor for that matter boys. Certainly, no boy was made to feel humiliated. The majority of male teachers and the one woman teacher whom I observed did explicitly recognize girls' lack of confidence and gave them positive support and encouragement. But the teachers recognised lack of self-esteem in boys and attempted to build their confidence also. Particularly significant for both boys and girls were the ways in which teachers interacted and talked with them. Certainly, the teaching approach that most teachers adopted conveyed messages significantly different from those perpetuated by the stereotypical aggressive, dominating, macho PE teacher. The particular forms of communication that pupils encountered were fundamentally different from the oppressive type that some pupils apparently experienced in school.

With few exceptions, the characteristics attributed to the Shotmoor teachers by the pupils closely matched those that constituted a "good" teacher for the pupils of Gannaway's study (1976). There was, however, one fundamental difference: Whereas Gannaway's pupils acknowledged strictness as a property of a good teacher, the pupils at Shotmoor did not recognise strictness as a feature of the majority of the Shotmoor teachers' approaches. In other studies (Beynon, 1985; Marsh, Rosser, & Harre, 1978), lack of strictness was perceived by boys to be a "bad" characteristic, reflecting "softness." This attribute, associated with femininity and thus with apparent lack of strength, was generally denigrated. Not so at Shotmoor, where teachers were "a lot more soft" than schoolteachers: "They don't shout at you as much!" This appreciation of a less oppressive form of pedagogy was echoed by many of the boys:

Andrew: It's fun, the teachers at school—right—half of 'em rise above you.

Sid: I don't like being disciplined much, see.

BH: Don't you think you're disciplined here?

Sid: Yeh, you are a bit. You don't feel so sort of trapped in.

BH: Why do you think that?

Sid: Well, you can talk to your teacher more freely than you can to a teacher [in school]. If it's a [school] teacher you've got to crawl to them.

The more caring, sensitive teaching approach evidenced at the centre was found to be a strong motivational feature for all the pupils, regardless of sex. Importantly, this form of pedagogy evinced by the male teachers who were both liked and respected provided male role models that contradicted the stereotypical images of the aggressive, egotistical sportsmen who celebrate machismo and expect feminine incompetence in physical activity. Consequently, boys not only received messages about the valid inclusion of girls and recognition of girls' capabilities, but also boys were generally able to acknowledge their own emotional feelings of fear, apprehension, and concern for others.

This ambience of encouragement engendered by the teachers for both boys and girls within a mixed-sex environment, with small numbers in the classes, encouraged collaboration between boys and girls and also enabled boys to gain respect for and greater understanding not only of girls but also of other boys and of themselves. Boys had the opportunity to experience nontraditional forms of physical activity, activities that did not identify winners or losers but rather enabled boys to experience personal and group success not at the expense of other boys or girls.

Howard: I think I've got courage, 'cause I didn't like to go up high—like on the climbing and that. When I climbed up, I looked down and thought—did I climb that? You know I don't really like heights. So when I abseiled down I was pleased with myself.

DISCUSSION

Girls' and boys' more sensitive understanding of themselves and each other was a consequence of the contextual and ideological features characteristic of the outdoor-adventure centre. This change in awareness was concomitant not only upon features such as mixed-sex grouping and high teacher-pupil ratio but also upon the ways in which pupils were positioned centrally in their learning and more importantly upon the ways in which affective communication was acknowledged. The particular PE curriculum and the ways in which it was made available at Shotmoor provided boys with contextual experiences of sport and gender. Behaviours demonstrating collaboration, responsibility, and group support were valued and encouraged rather than those expressing aggressive, competitive individualism. The experience provided the opportunity for boys to rethink their views about girls' physical potentials and competences. New, cooperative, yet challenging forms of activities replaced traditional competitive sports. The curriculum and pedagogy at the outdoor-adventure centre thus created a structural context in which alternative versions of gender identities and relations could be experienced and constructed. The programme visibly challenged both stereotypical assumptions about gender and everyday notions of physicality. This was largely a consequence of the regular programme that was designed to enable girls and boys to realise their full potentials through the process of learning the new skills associated with adventure activities.

Boys' rethinking of gender was an unintentional consequence of the programme. PE experiences of these types could form a developmental basis for alternative masculine identities that neither celebrate the warrior ethos nor identify cooperative endeavour, caring, and emotional expression as "wimpish" weaknesses.

These findings have considerable implications for those committed to reconstructing PE in a more humane way. Certainly, single-sex PE is limited in the ways it can provide boys with the opportunities to reconsider their stereotypical assumptions about girls. Coeducational PE alone cannot challenge these assumptions. Careful and sensitive innovations in mixed-sex PE programmes that draw upon caring, cooperative, and challenging forms of physical activities may create change. But, such innovations need to be supported and mediated by both women and men who are consciously committed to overcoming the macho image of sport and the inherent sexism in PE. Adequately resourced PE programmes with these underlying commitments could prove to be highly successful in empowering boys to identify with nonhegemonic models of masculinity. And such programmes might also pave the way toward a more humane, caring, and liberated society.

Chapter 17

Addressing Homophobia in Physical Education: Responsibilities for Teachers and Researchers

Pat Griffin
James Genasci

Homophobia is the irrational fear or intolerance of homosexuality, gay men or lesbians, and even behavior that is perceived to be outside the boundaries of traditional gender role expectations. Heterosexism is the societal assumption that heterosexuality is the only acceptable, sanctioned, and normal sexual orientation. Homophobic behavior ranges from the seemingly innocuous telling of "queer" jokes to verbal harassment of or physical violence to gay and lesbian people. For example:

Rumors are floating around school that one of the women physical education teachers is a lesbian. A small group of parents demand that she be fired.

One of the boys in the third period gym class refuses to take gymnastics because he says it's for fairies and girls.

During a health unit, a physical educator is teaching about AIDS. One of the students asks, "AIDS is a gay disease that they deserve anyway, so why do we have to talk about it?"

A junior high school girl confides to her physical education teacher that she thinks she, the student, might be gay; the teacher is extremely uncomfortable and has no idea what to say to the student.

Queer jokes are a staple part of faculty-room conversation in a high school.

Several high school boys beat up a classmate after school because they think he looks gay. The counselor suggests to the victim that he change his appearance to avoid future trouble.

A teacher who prides herself on her commitment to interrupting sexist or racist name-calling in her classes feels paralyzed when students call classmates "fags" or "lezzies."

A doctoral student expresses an interest in doing a dissertation on gay athletes and physical education teachers. His faculty committee refuses to approve the topic.

Each of the incidents described is an example of how homophobia is acted out in education. Most of these or similar situations are familiar to experienced educators. Yet few of us are in any way prepared to address such situations effectively and compassionately. Because of the extreme negative stigma attached to homosexuality in our culture, many, perhaps most, gay and lesbian people live double lives and are invisible members of our schools and communities. Even if there were no gay or lesbian people in a school, homophobia would still be present and would act to constrain and control the behavior of heterosexual people as they attempt to avoid the stigma of being called gay.

The intention of this chapter is to encourage an open professional dialogue about homophobia in education in general and in physical education in particular. The following assumptions are basic to our discussion in this chapter:

• We are all homophobic regardless of our sexual orientation because we live in a culture that teaches us to fear and condemn gay men and lesbians, and that stands in our way of learning accurate information about homosexuality.

• Homophobia has negative effects on all of our lives regardless of our sexual orientation.

• No sexual orientation—gay, lesbian, bisexual, heterosexual, or asexual—is inherently any more normal, natural, or acceptable than any other.

• Not everyone will agree with our first three assumptions.

The social taboo surrounding the serious discussion of homophobia and homosexuality in physical education results in the perpetuation of ignorance, fear, violence, isolation, and psychological stress. When we remain silent, the legacy of misinformation and homophobia is passed on to the next generation. Both teachers and researchers have a responsibility to open a professional dialogue about gayness, oppression, and homophobia if we are to break the silence and function in positive and informed ways.

NECESSITY OF OPEN COMMUNICATION

There are many reasons why it is important for physical educators to begin a professional dialogue about homophobia. We either are gay/lesbian ourselves or we have gay/lesbian colleagues. We have gay and lesbian students in our classes whose school experiences are often characterized by isolation, peer rejection, and self-hatred. Homophobic name-calling is a staple and, in some cases, an accepted part of school life as students (and some teachers) use slurs like fag, queer, or lezzie to put down classmates and teachers.

Women in physical education and athletics are often stereotyped as lesbians and as a result are sometimes regarded with suspicion, are harassed, or are discriminated against by homophobic administrators, parents, colleagues, and students. Unless a woman in physical education can provide tangible proof of her heterosexuality, in the form of children, a husband or boyfriend, or even a former marriage, her sexual orientation is suspect. In contrast, gay men in physical education are invisible. Because the stereotyped image of gay men as effeminate and unathletic clashes with the image of athletic men as masculine and physically competent, the concept of gay male athletes or physical educators is a contradiction in terms to many uninformed people. People expect male physical educators to be macho, masculine, and heterosexual. Additionally, most male physical educators are socialized into a subculture that is often rabidly homophobic and misogynist—not a comfortable or safe place for a gay man to spend a lot of time. Consequently, many gay men are discouraged from pursuing their athletic interests or developing their athletic talents because of this hostile environment. Both lesbians and gay men in the physical education profession typically live closeted, double lives in which they carefully separate their professional and personal lives lest they lose their jobs, the respect of their students and colleagues, or even their own self-esteem.

Homophobia is so strong among adolescent males, the age group many of us are responsible for educating, that young men are the most frequent perpetrators of violence against gay men and lesbians or those they suspect to be gay or lesbian. The extreme fear of homosexuality that motivates these young people to lash out with violence needs to be addressed. In addition, as physical educators many of us will be responsible for health units in which we must teach students about sex education and AIDS in nonhomophobic and nonheterosexist ways.

All forms of oppression thrive on ignorance, misunderstanding, and fear. It is often difficult for members of dominant social groups (men, white people, heterosexuals) to listen to the experiences and demands of oppressed social groups (women, people of color, gay men and lesbians) without feeling anger, guilt, and defensiveness. Yet there is something to gain for all people in the elimination of oppression and celebration of diversity. The relationship of homophobia and heterosexism to gender equity and sexism is especially interconnected. In fact, our efforts to address sexism in our profession and our society will be unsuccessful unless we are also willing to address homophobia. Homophobia is the glue that holds sexism together. Until the sting is taken out of homophobic name-calling, it will be difficult for boys and men to freely choose behavior they have been taught to associate with the feminine gender role. Until the power of accusations of homosexuality to intimidate is defused, girls and women who choose to challenge sexist assumptions in personal or political action will be forced to contend with rude questions and innuendos about their sexual orientations. Girls or women who participate seriously and competently in sport as athletes or coaches will be called "dykes" or the pejorative "tomboy." Boys who choose to participate in physical education or sport activities associated with the feminine gender role (e.g., dance, gymnastics, aerobics) will be called fags or fairies. It takes a young man of rare courage and self-assurance to stand up to such peer or teacher condemnation.

Most efforts, teacher workshops, and written curriculum guides designed to encourage gender equity in physical education and athletics have avoided any reference to homophobia and its relationship to gender equity and sexism. Until we can confront our own homophobia as professional educators and then help our students confront theirs, fear of and ignorance about sexual orientation and gender roles will be major obstacles to eliminating gender inequity in physical education and sport. Discussions of gender equity are incomplete and inadequate unless they address homophobia. Likewise, it is incomplete to address homophobia without discussing gender roles and sexism.

For these reasons, it is important that we open a dialogue in our profession about homophobia and homosexuality. Reasoned dialogue must be based on the informed understanding provided by education and research. We have all learned a lot about homosexuality from jokes, television, third-hand stories whispered in locker rooms, innuendos, and speculation about colleagues or students. These sources are often uninformed and typically do not encourage understanding; they have not served us or our students well. If physical education professionals, teachers, and researchers are to adequately address homophobia in our work and personal lives, we need to consider more effective and systematic learning strategies.

SUGGESTIONS FOR TEACHERS

Because homophobia is pervasive in our culture, failing to act against homophobia allows its effects to continue in the same way that failing to speak and act out against racism or sexism indicates silent tolerance of prejudice and discrimination based on color or sex. Inaction signals acceptance. Taking action against homophobia is the responsibility of all physical educators regardless of sexual orientation.

There are many ways we can act to prevent the incidents described in the beginning of this chapter from repeating in the next generation of teachers and students. The first step is to educate ourselves so we can separate myth from reality in understanding sexual orientation and gender. Then we must be willing to act on our beliefs to help educate colleagues and students. We can read books and other educational material that provide accurate and up-to-date information about homophobia and homosexuality (the reading list in the appendix to this chapter includes several suggestions). We can attend workshops on homophobia and heterosexism. There are resources available for educators who want to arrange for staff development programs on homophobia in schools (see the Campaign to End Homophobia reference at the end of this chapter). We must learn to recognize and change our own homophobic attitudes and actions. Specifically, we must

- stop assuming that all our colleagues and students are heterosexual, or should be;
- stop using homophobic slurs;
- stop telling or laughing at jokes about gay people;
- identify stereotypical assumptions made about gay men, lesbians, or people thought to "look" gay or lesbian;
- identify how homophobia affects our own choices of clothing styles, physical activity interests, teaching competencies, mannerisms, same-sex friendships, and family relationships; and
- be alert to different forms of oppression (racism, sexism, heterosexism). Learn to understand heterosexism through our understanding of the dynamics of racism or sexism.

Additionally, we must stop providing tacit support and consent for the homophobic actions of colleagues and students by remaining silent. We must establish and enforce class guidelines for name-calling, harassment, and teasing that treat homophobic interactions as seriously as racist or sexist interactions. We can also let colleagues know that homophobic innuendos, jokes, and teasing are as unacceptable as racist and sexist comments.

With regard to educational resources and materials, we can monitor school curriculum and policy for homophobic bias by

- including accurate information about homosexuality in sex education classes and addressing student homophobia in AIDS education;
- checking the school library for accurate and age-appropriate material about homosexuality;
- including a consideration of gay men and lesbians in social diversity awareness programs about different racial, religious, or ethnic groups; and
- identifying local or regional resources that can provide ongoing assistance in addressing homophobia among all students and support for gay and lesbian students (e.g., gay/lesbian organizations, nonhomophobic counseling services, social issues educational consulting groups, women's centers, Parents and Friends of Lesbians And Gays (PFLAG), and progressive churches).

Overcoming the strict social taboo surrounding reasoned discussions of homosexuality and homophobia in schools requires both personal courage and a commitment to establishing a safe and affirming climate for all members of the educational community. Teachers can use these suggestions to begin to create this acceptance of difference in their classes and in their schools.

SUGGESTIONS FOR RESEARCHERS

In addition to these practical teacher strategies, we must begin to address how homophobia restricts and prevents research on topics related to homophobia in physical education and sport. We have little research-based information about homophobia and homosexuality in physical education. Homophobia among researchers, doctoral dissertation committees, and university graduate programs can be a powerful impediment to the conduct of research on these controversial topics. Additionally, doing research on homophobia and homosexuality calls for much self-reflection on the part of the researcher. The contention that a researcher can achieve objectivity by standing outside personal sociohistorical context and separating himself or herself from personal history, values, and beliefs to identify some fixed human reality receives a severe test when the researcher studies controversial topics. Homosexuality and homophobia as controversial topics can encompass issues of sexuality, morality, human relationships, and social justice, discussions that guarantee a spirited debate with many different perspectives. By claiming to be objective, value free, and context free, researchers become invisible in their research reports. The researchers' values, however, are implicit and hidden rather than absent, and the sociohistorical events that shape our values are ignored, not transcended.

Researchers must name and reflect on their values and on how their value commitments affect their work. With this perspective, the researcher's focus changes from achieving "objectivity" to understanding personal ideology. Ideology is the system of knowledge, beliefs, and values that guide a researcher's work: intentions in conducting research, choices of topics, methods, interpretations of data, interactions with participants, and data analysis. Even the decision to conduct controversial research implies some strongly held ideology about the topic, an ideology that accounts for the risk taken in conducting research that will likely engender a range of positive and negative reactions among colleagues, friends, and family.

Trustworthy research on controversial topics must be open-ended and nondogmatic; must speak to and be grounded in the circumstances of everyday life; must have a deep respect for the capacities and integrity of the participants in the study; must be skeptical of appearances and dominant cultural understandings; and must be open to changes in a priori values. Both the researcher and the participant become the changer and the changed as a result of the research encounter.

Identifying and consciously monitoring researcher ideology throughout the research process have specific implications for research on homosexuality and homophobia in sport and physical education. What a researcher believes about homosexuality, his or her degree of homophobia, and what he or she knows about gay men and lesbians all interact to color decisions made during the research project. A researcher interested in studying homosexuality or homophobia must address three questions before undertaking the project: What does the researcher believe about homosexuality? How will the researcher's sexual orientation affect the research? What does the researcher know about homosexuality?

What Do Researchers Believe?

We have all grown up in a culture that has taught us, with varying degrees of intensity, that homosexuality is sinful, sick, criminal, disgusting, shameful, and perverted. Regardless of our sexual orientations—heterosexual, bisexual, or homosexual—we internalize these values. The intensity of our negative feelings depends on our personal history within this cultural context. For example, fundamentalist Christians who have never, to their knowledge, personally known a gay person, and who have derived all of their knowledge and values about homosexuality from television evangelists, probably will be intolerant. A parent whose lesbian daughter has recently expressed her sexual orientation and who has read recent books about homosexuality, met her daughter's friends, and perhaps joined a Parents of Gays group will probably be more tolerant. The point is that because of our embeddedness in our sociohistorical contexts, we are all homophobic to some degree, from the most condemning fundamentalist Christian to the most "out" gay or lesbian activist. Further, homophobia affects all of us regardless of our sexual orientations. Whether we are only monitoring our appearance, mannerisms, and companions to avoid being called gay or are targets of homophobic slurs and violence, we are all constrained by a fear of homosexuality.

Anyone undertaking research on homosexuality or homophobia must be willing to acknowledge his or her own homophobia and continually monitor how, not if, it affects the research process. Homophobia will affect not only decisions about participant selection, methodology, and data interpretation, but also the researcher's informal discussions of the research topic with friends, colleagues, and family. Breaking into a cold sweat each time someone asks about one's research topic or silently enduring jokes or innuendos about lesbians or gay men are reactions that reflect our own homophobia. In the end, no matter what a researcher believes about homosexuality, homophobia will be a factor in any research on homosexuality or homophobia. This must be acknowledged and confronted throughout the research process.

What Is the Researcher's Sexual Orientation?

The question of a researcher's sexual orientation is less important to the conduct of trustworthy research on homosexuality or homophobia than what she or he believes and knows about homosexuality and homophobia. Although heterosexual, homosexual, and bisexual researchers bring different personal perspectives to the process, all can provide important understandings from their own particular perspectives. The researcher's social identities will have effects on interactions with participants. Not only sexual orientation, but also sex, race, and other social group memberships will affect the nature of the researcher-participant relationship and, consequently, the information and experiences shared as part of the project. This is not a methodological deficiency. It is the nature of human interaction, not to be ignored, but acknowledged and accounted for in the research process.

All researchers are biased in different ways, but predicting bias on the basis of sexual orientation can be misleading. There are dilemmas, however, for researchers no matter what their sexual orientations. Gay or lesbian researchers may be accused of being too personally involved to be objective. Gay and lesbian researchers also must confront the decision of coming out to participants in the study and in research presentations when the study is completed. There is also the possibility that other more closeted gay and lesbian colleagues will feel threatened by public discussion of homosexuality in the profession and will work to prohibit such research from publication or presentation. Some heterosexual colleagues might share these feelings and work toward the same end: colluding in silence. Heterosexual researchers may be accused of being homophobic or ignorant about the lives of gay men and lesbians. Most probably, heterosexual researchers will have to contend with the assumption that they are gay or lesbian because of their choice of research topic.

In the end, sexual orientation alone is neither a qualification nor a disqualification for conducting research on homosexuality and homophobia. The important point is to acknowledge that a researcher's identity is a salient factor in the research process and must be accounted for as carefully as the researcher's beliefs.

What Does the Researcher Know?

What the researcher knows about homosexuality and where she or he learned this information is also important. Getting accurate information about gay men and lesbians is difficult. Because of the stigma associated with homosexuality, researching this topic requires that investigators overcome internal and external barriers to gaining access to trustworthy information. Buying books with the words *gay* or *lesbian* on the cover, asking a reference librarian to help with a computer search on "homosexuality in education," or even attending a presentation on the topic can present daunting internal obstacles to the potentially interested researcher. These barriers are built over many years of internalizing homophobic messages about gay men and lesbians that make personal interest in the topic threatening.

Researcher's Research. Even for investigators who are able to overcome these internal barriers to pursuing a review of the literature on homosexuality and homophobia, there are complications. Much of the research and professional writing about homosexuality and gay men and lesbians completed before the early 1970s is suspect. Research until then was completed primarily on male prisoners and male psychiatric patients and was then compared to male heterosexuals in the general population—hardly a representative sample of gay men or a fair comparison with heterosexuals. This research reveals the prevailing researcher ideology at the time: Male homosexuals are sick or criminal. The concept of a well-adjusted homosexual was a contradiction in terms. Lesbians, of course, were not studied (as was the case with women in general).

Research about gay and lesbian physical education teachers, coaches, athletes, and students or about homophobia among sport participants is practically nonexistent. Though numerous studies focus on sex-role orientation (femininity, masculinity, and androgyny), it is rare to actually see the words *gay, lesbian*, or *homophobia* in our professional literature. Two early studies of women in physical education illustrate the reluctance of researchers to use the "L-word." Locke and Jensen (1970) published a study with the intriguing title "Heterosexuality of Women in Physical Education," which reflected the homophobia of the early 1970s. Six years later, B. Beck (1976) studied the "lifestyles of never married women physical educators." In contrast, Guthrie's (1982) study of homophobia among college women athletes, nonathletes, and physical education majors represents a more open and informed examination of attitudes about lesbians in the physical education context. More recently, M.A. Hall (1987a) edited a special issue of *Women's Studies International Forum* devoted entirely to the topic of gender in sport, physical education, and leisure. Several of the articles included in this collection address either homophobia or heterosexism in sport. Woods's (1987) study of the experiences of lesbian physical education teachers in grades K-12 is the most out-of-the-closet study thus far and promises to provide an in-depth description of how homophobia affects the lives of lesbian physical educators in the public schools.

The dearth of research-based information about homophobia and homosexuality in physical education and sport is a reflection of our homophobic professional climate. For a researcher, especially a doctoral student or untenured faculty member, to choose this topic requires personal and professional risk taking that few have been willing to assume. Fear of stigma, suspect early research, and the lack of research in our own field combine to make gathering knowledge about gay men and lesbians difficult.

Researcher's Personal Knowledge.   In addition to what a researcher knows about homosexuality from research and professional readings, personal knowledge of gay men and lesbians is also a factor in determining researcher ideology. To the extent that a researcher has no regular personal contacts with a variety of "out" individual gay men and lesbians or accurate descriptions of the lives of gay men and lesbians, the researcher must operate, often unconsciously, on the basis of stereotypical beliefs learned in a homophobic society. The invisibility of most gay men and lesbians in our culture allows stereotypes perpetuated by the popular media and reinforced by the virulent attacks of the conservative religious far right to flourish. In the absence of an awareness of the diversity among gay men and lesbians, heterosexuals only identify gays as those who fit a one-dimensional stereotype of what a gay person looks and acts like; these heterosexuals are unaware that any number of the perfectly average-looking people who work with them, sell them insurance, teach their children, or share the same parents with them are lesbians and gay men.

In the absence of trustworthy research and "out" gay and lesbian colleagues, there is the potential for a great deal of misinformation in what a researcher may "know" about gay men and lesbians and homosexuality. To the extent that a researcher has not evaluated what she or he knows about homosexuality and where this information was learned, it is likely that her or his research will be compromised. This problem is not limited to heterosexual researchers. It is often just as difficult for gay men and lesbians to get accurate information and research about gay and lesbian life. If a library only has outdated material or defines any information about gay men and lesbians as obscene, all researchers are handicapped. In addition, many gay men and lesbians live isolated lives out of touch with gay or lesbian culture. Their lives are as impoverished as those of their heterosexual colleagues in terms of access to information and research about homosexuality. In the absence of information to counteract the stereotypes, homophobic beliefs are internalized by lesbians and gay men just as racist beliefs are internalized by people of color and sexist beliefs are internalized by women.

Researcher's Ideology.   Doing controversial research requires that the researcher be willing to acknowledge the importance of personal ideology in the research process. The researcher must be willing to engage in extensive self-examination and reevaluation during the project. Answering the questions What do I believe about homosexuality? How does my sexual orientation affect the research process? and What do I know about homosexuality? can help researchers focus this self-reflection.

CONCLUSION

We have been silent about homosexuality and homophobia in physical education for too long. If we are to openly acknowledge and promote an understanding of the diversity among us, we need to begin a professional dialogue. Teachers and researchers have important responsibilities in initiating and nurturing this dialogue. We need research that is self-conscious, rooted in openly acknowledged values, open ended, nondogmatic, and grounded in the experiences and dignity of the participants. We need teachers who will educate themselves and then be willing to educate colleagues and students through both interpersonal interactions and curriculum. The combined work of teachers and researchers in physical education can begin to change the oppressive nature of the silence imposed by homophobia that keeps some of us invisible, others of us ignorant, and all of us afraid.

APPENDIX

Suggested Readings About Homosexuality

Barnett, W. (1979). *Homosexuality and the Bible*. Wallingford, PA: Pendle Hill.
Beam, J. (Ed.) (1986). *In the life: A black gay anthology*. Boston: Alyson.

Beck, E. (1982). *Nice Jewish girls: A lesbian anthology.* Trumansburg, NY: Crossing Press.

Bell, A., Weinberg, M., & Hammersmith, S. (1981). *Sexual preference: Its development in men and women.* Bloomington: Indiana University Press.

Boswell, J. (1980). *Christianity, social tolerance, and homosexuality.* Chicago: University of Chicago Press.

Campaign To End Homophobia, P.O. Box 819, Cambridge, MA 02139.

Clark, D. (1987). *Loving someone gay.* New York: New American Library.

Cobhan, L. (1982). Lesbians in physical education and sport. In M. Cruikshank (Ed.), *Lesbian studies: Present and future.* Old Westbury, NY: Feminist Press.

Cornwell, A. (1983). *Black lesbian in white America.* Minneapolis: Naiad Press.

Council on Interracial Books for Children. (1983). Homophobia in education. *Bulletin.* (Available from CIBC, 1841 Broadway, NY 10023, $3.50 prepaid)

DeCecco, J. (1985). *Homophobia in American society: Bashers, baiters, and bigots.* New York: Harrington Park Press.

Gondola, J., & Fitzpatrick, T. (1985). Homophobia in girls' sport: Names that can hurt us. *Equal Play, 5*(2), 18-19.

Griffin, C., Wirth, M., & Wirth, A. (1986). *Beyond acceptance: Parents of lesbians and gays talk about their experiences.* Englewood Cliffs, NJ: Prentice-Hall.

Griffin, P. (1987, August). *Homophobia, lesbians, and women's sport: An exploratory analysis.* Paper presented at the American Psychological Association Annual Meeting, New York. (Available from the author: 105 Totman Building, University of Massachusetts, Amherst, MA 01003)

Heron, A. (Ed.) (1983). *One teenager in ten: Writings by gay and lesbian youth.* Boston: Alyson.

Human Rights Foundation, Inc. (1984). *Demystifying homosexuality: A teaching guide about lesbians and gay men.* New York: Irvington.

Katz, J. (1976). *Gay American history.* New York: Avon.

Klein, F., & Wolf, T. (Eds.) (1985). *Two lives to lead: Bisexuality in men and women.* New York: Harrington Park Press.

Chapter 18

How Should We Theorize Gender in the Context of Sport?[1]

M. Ann Hall

There is one thing we know for certain: Gender can no longer be treated as a simple, natural fact (Flax, 1983). Feminist theory has put gender front and center, and there are some who claim that feminist theory, along with neo-Marxism, psychoanalysis, and poststructuralism, is having a profound yet little-understood influence on Western culture and intellectual thought.[2] My focus here (as always) is on feminist theory, yet it becomes increasingly clear that all four discourses are interrelated in complex and as yet unraveled ways.

To understand the goals of feminist theory, we must consider first its central subject matter—gender. As will become clear, gender can no longer be treated as one of a number of variables that may affect performance (like age, height, and weight), or as an issue of sex differences in performance capabilities, or even as a problem of the inequitable distribution of resources, opportunities, and experiences among females and males. Gender is a socially and historically constructed set of power relations, yet it is becoming increasingly difficult to sort out what precisely this means. To enter the now-vast gender literature is, as Flax (1983) puts it, to "immediately plunge into a complicated and controversial morass" (p. 627). To help make sense of this conceptual and theoretical mess, let us back up a little and review some of our intellectual history both in feminist theory and in the social analysis of sport. I begin with some of the definitional dilemmas apparent in recent discussions of sex, gender, and gender relations.

SEX, GENDER, AND GENDER RELATIONS: DEFINITIONAL DILEMMAS

Of the two terms *sex* and *gender*, by far the most common and familiar, certainly in the English language, is *sex*. There are, however, two common usages of the word *sex* that I want to eliminate from consideration here: first, as it is used in the sense of physical relations between the sexes, and second, the specialization of the word toward women, as in the "gentler sex," "weaker sex," "fairer sex," and so forth (Williams, 1983).

Sex *Versus* Gender

In the late 1960s, and originally in the United States, the terms *sexism* and *sexist* came into general use as critical descriptions of attitudes and practices discriminatory toward women and of a social relationship in which males have authority over females. As the authors of *A Feminist Dictionary* point out, "It is an illustration of a concept, central to women's lives, which was wordless for many years" (Kramarae & Treichler, 1985, p. 411). These terms were later expanded as a critique of all or most of the extended characteristics, be they psychological, cultural, or social, of the distortion between the sexes (Williams, 1983). Despite this new meaning associated with the word *sex*, it was difficult to shake the association with its most common meaning, that of physical relations between the sexes. Terms such as *sex object*, *sexy*, *sex appeal*, and *sex life* made that clear.

For these reasons, some writers began using the colloquial alternative to *sex*, namely *gender*. It was used to designate the psychological, cultural, and social dimensions of maleness and femaleness, whereas *sex* was used to designate the dichotomous distinctions between females and males based on physiological characteristics that are genetically determined. The distinction, therefore, between *sex* and *gender* was meant to clarify the biological versus the cultural. This distinction, unfortunately, never did work very well. Kessler and McKenna (1975) perhaps said it best: "The cultural/biological distinction traditionally associated with usage of gender versus sex is a technical one, applicable to scientists in the laboratory and some textbooks, but little else" (p. 7).

What social scientists failed to recognize, until the last decade or so, were two interrelated problems. One is that biology itself provides no clear justification for a dichotomous view of sex. In the context of sport, and specifically the so-called sex or femininity test (now called "gender verification") given to all international athletes who wish to compete as females, science provides evidence of a biological continuum. Identified by this "test" are those individuals with certain types of congenital chromosome "abnormalities" who, paradoxically, often have body builds and muscularities culturally defined as female.[3] What we often forget is that so-called sexual dualism or dimorphism is socially constructed in such a way that it appears to be an immutable fact. We often construct sex as a dichotomy (as in the sex test) when, in fact, there is a continuum.

The second problem is that there is a constant, complex, and often unrecognized interaction between biology and culture. We know now that the meaning of a biological sex difference (e.g., greater physical strength among males) varies according to the culture through which it is mediated (Eichler, 1980). We know also that some sex differences, for example facial expressions and bodily postures/gestures of men and women, illustrate clearly the interaction between the cultural and the anatomical, even though these differences often become socially defined as biological differences (D.H.J. Morgan, 1986). These issues certainly cannot be avoided in the context of sport, where it is still unclear how the differing biological and physiological capacities of males versus females are products of the innate and/or the social. Social construction explanations of gender are often placed in direct opposition to biological explanations because biology is seen as fixed and therefore unchanging, whereas the social can be resisted and changed. Birke and Vines (1987) argue that biology itself can be changed and that a truly feminist understanding of women in sport must take the possible transformation of physiology into account.

Nonetheless, the notion of gender as a social construct is now the dominant view, certainly in current theorizing. To make this clear, the term *gender* is now much preferred over its sister term *sex*. Most of this new theorizing concerns the process (or processes) by which the social construction of gender occurs. A plethora of new terms have emerged that attempt to capture this process, such as *gendered, gendering, genderic, genderization*, and *intragenderly*.[4] As might be expected, there is little consensus on what these terms actually mean.

Gender Relations

Progress has been made, however, in moving the analysis of gender, whatever the terminology, away from questions of distribution to questions of relation. There is nothing particularly new about this distinction, because it has a long history in the theoretical analysis of social class, and less so in the analysis of race and ethnicity. Within a distributive approach we have asked (and still ask), for instance, what factors, what barriers prevent women from achieving full equality in sport? Our work has documented these barriers, and we have shown, in Western nations at any rate, that it is men who control sport. To be more precise, it is white, generally privileged men who control sport. Males still have access to more than twice the opportunities and public resources available for sport; moreover, there is little evidence that the men who control sport are genuinely interested in or committed to redressing the balance (B. Kidd, 1987).

Although it is certainly useful to document the distributive problem of unequal allocation of resources, it is crucial to understand the nature of the social relations between females and males, both in the past and present, that determine gender inequality. Here we would take a relational approach and pose different questions: How, for example, did sport come to embody and recreate male power and domination? What are the connections between women's sporting practice and the broader ensemble of patriarchal relations? Does women's sport have the potential to take on a set of oppositional meanings within a patriarchal ideology, and could it become a site of resistance to a specifically patriarchal social order? What is the relationship between power and physicality in countering the long-standing hegemonic control men have had over women's bodies? These are the kinds of relational questions taken up by the contributors to this book.

Gender relations is probably the most common term used to describe this system of relations structured by gender. Gender here is used as a modifier to mean a complex set of social relations that are historically variable (Flax, 1983). In the same way that class or race relations are relations of domination and subordination, so too are gender relations, because they are characterized by male dominance and female subordination. The term gender relations is relatively new, being preceded by concepts like sexual politics, patriarchy, and the sex/gender system. More terms are also coming to the fore, like the "relations of ruling" (D. Smith, 1987) and the "gender order" (Connell, 1987b). What these formulations have in common is that they define gender as a set of power relations, whereby men, as a social group, have more power over women than women have over them; they are socially constructed, not biologically given; and they are not fixed, but rather are subject to historical change and can be transformed.

Therefore, in the space of some 20 years, we have traveled from important though simplistic determinations of sex and gender, in order to sort out the biological versus the cultural, to theoretically sophisticated yet still-confused concepts like gender relations, which form the basis of new theories of gender. We have now reached a point, as Connell (1987b) points out, where there are two possibilities in the ultimate goal of transforming gender relations: One is the abolition of gender altogether, and the other is its reconstitution on new bases. What role has sport played in all this? Let us now turn to the sociology of sport and examine how gender has been (and is) theorized in that context.

GENDER AND THE PARADIGMS OF SPORT SOCIOLOGY

Most of the theorizing and empirical research about gender, within the context of sport, take place in North America in the subdiscipline of physical education known as the sociology of sport. What are the major theoretical paradigms influencing the field, and more important, how have questions of gender been discussed and analyzed?[5] In Figure 18.1, I have sketched the major theoretical paradigms or perspectives that I believe currently influence research within North American sport sociology. Some have been in existence longer than others, as indicated by the time line at the top of the chart. I have also tried to indicate their interconnections, which I will discuss in more detail.[6]

Idealist/Positivist Paradigm

The sociology of sport, which emerged in the 1960s in the United States, primarily in university physical education curricula, took the position that sociology should be as much like the natural sciences as possible, hence the label "positivist."

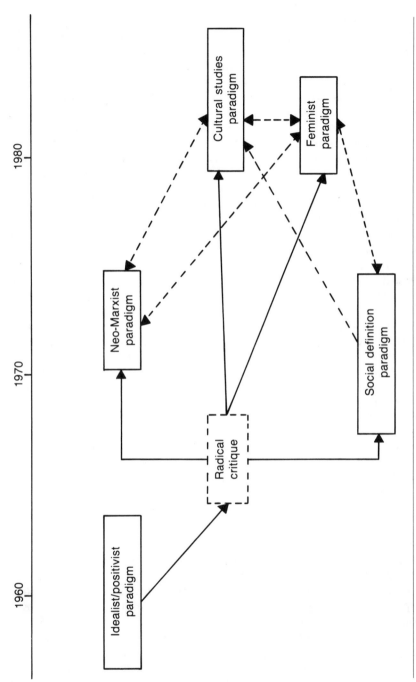

Figure 18.1 Major theoretical paradigms influencing the sociology of sport in North America.

In terms of research, this meant the search for formal propositional theory that included the creation of deductive theoretical systems whose predictions could be empirically verified. Within this view, society, and by implication sport, is best studied using a systems model whereby each interrelated part is seen as somehow contributing to the smooth operation of the whole. Sport, as one system part, is studied to assess how it contributes to individual personal growth and the maintenance of social order (Coakley, 1986). In this sense, sport is seen abstractly and ideally as nonproblematic, and social research about sport is divorced from a concern for social issues (e.g., sexism and racism) outside the world of sport. Although the idealist/positivist paradigm has, over the years, become less functionalist and certainly less reliant on positivist tendencies and methodologies, it is still, in my view, the dominant paradigm, particularly in the United States.

Gender, or sex as it was called then, was sometimes taken into account, because much of the early work within this paradigm focused on the process of socialization into sport from a social-system/social-role approach. In other studies, females were sometimes slotted in as an "independent variable," but more often than not the assumption was that findings derived from males also applied to females.[7]

With the proliferation of "sex roles" and "sex-identity" research in the 1970s, a considerable literature grew within the psychology and sociology of sport whose purpose was to settle the controversy as to whether or not competitive sport masculinizes the female athlete either psychologically or behaviorally. Also central was the concept of "role conflict" and the unquestioned assumption of some incompatibility between the role of woman and that of athlete. Inherent in this research was a very functionalist conception of gender. The language itself made the point clearly. Researchers spoke (and still speak) of sex-role or gender-role stereotyping; role socialization and role orientation with the emphasis on consensus; and stability and continuity (Stacey & Thorne, 1985). What all this fails to recognize is that femininity and masculinity are socially constructed, historically specific, and mediated by social class, race, and ethnicity. The unavoidable reification in this research has hindered political attempts to critique the cultural ideologies that maintain the stereotypes in the first place.[8]

The Radical Critique

From the mid- to late 1960s, and again primarily in the United States, there emerged an increasing volume of criticism aimed at the place, structure, and processes of sport in North American society. Critics struck out at the racism, sexism, militarism, commercialism, and excesses inherent in a corrupt system of sport, the product of postindustrial monopoly capitalism.[9] In part, this "jock-raking" literature was a reaction to an idealist and romanticized view of sport as a relatively stable system held together by common values and consensus. This literature also emerged during a decade of New Left politics, cynicism, and confrontation. Its importance, especially in challenging the dominant idealist/positivist perspective on sport, cannot be denied, and the subsequent paradigms that emerged were no doubt influenced by it. This literature was, however, as Ingham (1976) suggested, "social criticism without social theory," or as Gruneau (1978) put more succinctly, "commitment without content." There was, as Gruneau observed correctly, little point in polemics that were theoretically naive and failed to suggest an effective praxis.

In the early analysis of gender, however, this critique was very useful. It was, I think, among the first attempts to expose the rampant sexism inherent in American sport. It was also an attack on sexism in American society, which critics saw simply mirrored in sport. But in the same sense that the radical critique seemed unaware of a long tradition of classical sociological theory and analysis, it also took no account of the then nascent feminist theoretical analysis.

The radical analysis of sport, despite its limitations and naiveté, represented an ideological critique of the idealist, positivist, functionalist view of sport. Others, also critical, responded to the scientism and abstract empiricism inherent in positivism with a methodological critique. Like all critiques of positivism, it decried the inappropriateness of causal, mechanistic, and measurement-oriented models of human social behavior. The plea was to put more faith in methodologies reinforcing the epistemological assumption that the only way of knowing a socially constructed world is from within. This was certainly a useful beginning, and research utilizing a reflexive sociology (e.g., symbolic interactionism, phenomenology, ethnomethodology) became eventually a paradigm of its own. Unfortunately, the early analyses were, as Gruneau (1983) suggests, "crude decontextualized discussions of the meaning of the sporting experience" (p. 18). In the extreme, they were so apolitical as to be meaningless. More recent discussions of what constitutes a feminist methodology (M.A. Hall, 1985) reexamined these issues, but at the time the application of these ideas to research about gender was some years away.

The Neo-Marxist Paradigm

This particular paradigm emerged as a direct, critical response to the "commitment without content" critique of the late 1960s and early 1970s. I have labeled it "neo-Marxist" because all theorists who would be comfortable within this paradigm owe a debt to Karl Marx. Moreover, contemporary Marxism has many variants, and they are all in some way represented in this paradigm. It has developed in Canada (and Britain) much more than in the United States, because Canadian sociology has traditionally incorporated a strong emphasis on political economy that is both materialist and socialist (Marchak, 1985; Morrow, 1985).

The focus of the neo-Marxist paradigm in sport sociology was and is clear—the relationship of sport to the emergent features of industrial capitalism. Much of the work has been historical, tracing the emergence of sport primarily in Canadian and British society as the history of cultural struggle, whereby groups within our societies have actively constituted and reworked their relationships to each other. The theoretical debates have focused primarily on the relative autonomy of cultural forms like sport and the role of human agency in the social development of a nation's sport.[10]

Although it is recognized that a range of social relations—class, race, gender, ethnicity, and religion—influences how individuals structure their play, games, and sports, there is within this paradigm one central consideration, and it is social class. Here, in my opinion, lies its greatest weakness. Elsewhere (M.A. Hall, 1987b) I have argued that although materialist analyses of sport have been helpful, insofar as they address the intricacies of social class, they have been of much less assistance in discussions of gender. The problem is that all this work, useful as it is, still sees the class struggle as the motor of history and, to reference Connell again (1983), as its transmission, gears, steering, and stereo system as well. It relies on a prefeminist historical materialism whereby the sphere of production is given analytic primacy, with the result that a structuralist model of capitalist production relations is used as the context within which gender relations are examined (Connell, 1983).

More recently, a few sport sociologists working from within a materialist and feminist framework are attempting to work through the articulation of class and gender in the context of sport, and I will discuss their work under the feminist paradigm.

The Social Definition Paradigm

As discussed earlier, the radical analysis of the 1960s included a methodological critique that decried the scientism and abstract empiricism of positivism. The social definition paradigm was an extension of that critique. I have used the term "social definition" because it best describes the subject matter of this paradigm: how individuals define their social situations and the meanings they attach to their actions (Ritzer, 1975). In the context of sport, this has meant a focus on research into small groups, teams, and subcultures. The emphasis has been on qualitative methodologies (e.g., ethnographies, participant observation, life histories, and case studies) and less on the theory that should inform these methods (e.g., phenomenology, symbolic interaction, and ethnomethodology).

There has been little emphasis on gender in the social definition paradigm either as a key variable or as a theoretical category. Part of the problem, I believe, is some confusion over the use of gender. Some feminist sociologists (e.g., Matthews, 1982) argue that gender is not a good index to understand the social world. The argument here, presumably, is that functionalist conceptions of gender (e.g., sex roles and sex identity) reproduce and perpetuate notions of gender differences, when in fact the nonsignificant differences remain obscure. Another problem is that gender often translates to mean "women," so that, for example, men's behaviour in certain social situations is understood as having something to do with class, whereas women's behaviour in the same situation is understood as having something to do with gender (D.H.J. Morgan, 1986). Therefore, women are seen as deviating from a standard of normal behaviour, namely men's. It has been extremely difficult to rid our research in the sociology of sport of the perspective that women's experiences are somehow variations on men's. Birrell (1984) analyzed all issues of several research journals and conference proceedings in the field, and based on the research reported there came to the following conclusion:

> These research strategies imply that women are different from men, but are men different from women? Lamentably, we cannot answer because we use

male experiences as our reference points and male behaviors as our standards: we know women only in relation to men. (p. 128)

Given that the social definition paradigm, no matter what the theoretical orientation, has as its focus the understanding of the social world and specifically how individuals view their situations within that world, this paradigm seems ideally suited to a view of research that takes as its starting point women's unique experiences in the sporting world. Regrettably, this has not been the case, and the best ethnographic work thus far has been primarily about boys' and men's sport, such as Janet Lever's study of Brazilian soccer, Gary Alan Fine's symbolic interaction analysis of Little League baseball and preadolescent culture, and the studies by Alan Klein on the bodybuilding subculture and Charles Gallmeier on professional ice hockey. There are, however, some very useful ethnographic accounts of girls' leisure and subcultures, undertaken in Britain as part of the early work of the Centre for Contemporary Cultural Studies, which I will discuss in the cultural studies paradigm.

Cultural Studies Paradigm

The cultural studies perspective within sport sociology is closely aligned with (especially in Canada) an outgrowth of the earlier neo-Marxist paradigm. The focus is very much the same: the ways in which culture and ideology are relatively autonomous in relation to economic and political processes, and perhaps more importantly, the mediating role of human agency in the making of culture. Play, games, and sports within the cultural studies paradigm are considered to be real social practices, unlike the abstractions of the idealist/positivist framework or the simple products of material conditions as some neo-Marxists insisted. They are, as Gruneau (1983) puts it, "constitutive social practices whose meanings, metaphoric qualities, and regulatory structures are indissolubly connected to the making and remaking of ourselves as agents (individual and collective) in society" (p. 50). Play, games, and sports are forms of cultural production and as such they are creations of human agency, able to be transformed.

Cultural studies as an autonomous field of study has a much earlier genesis. It originates from changes in the social and cultural milieu of postwar British society in the mid-1950s and as such is closely linked to British working-class historiography and literary criticism (Baron, 1985). Put simply, it is a field of study in which different disciplines intersect in the analysis of cultural aspects of society. It draws upon sociology, politics, literary and communication studies, philosophy, semiotics, history, and more recently feminist theory, for its study of cultural forms, practices, and institutions. Its theoretical debates, often about the relative significance of hegemony and structuralism and culturalism, define a "radically new problematic concerned with the active role played by cultural and ideological practices in the processes whereby existing social formations are reproduced, or more exceptionally, transformed" (Bennett, 1981, p. 13).

What all this means for the cultural analysis of sport forms, institutions, and practices is to show, specifically and historically, how sports reproduce the dominant culture and in what ways they become transformed as women and men actively respond, within the context of sport, to the conditions of their social existence. More importantly, how will sports become transformed in the future?

Gender, as a significant social and theoretical category, is recognized within the cultural studies paradigm perhaps more than any other with the exception of the feminist paradigm. Stuart Hall in his survey of the work of the Birmingham, England University Centre for Contemporary Cultural Studies (1980), makes the point that feminism had a significant impact on the field, forcing a major rethink in every substantive area of work. "A theory of culture," he notes, "which cannot account for patriarchal structures of dominance and oppression is, in the wake of feminism, a non-starter" (p. 39).

In terms of concrete studies, the early work on gender at the Centre for Contemporary Cultural Studies produced some excellent scholarship on women's leisure and girls' subcultures, which not only has critiqued the consistent male bias of leisure studies and the sociology of youth, but has also extended our knowledge about girls' and women's culture ("Women take issue," 1978). The members of the early Women's Studies Group at the Centre have dispersed now, although a few published further work on women's and girls' leisure and culture. Unfortunately, the Centre itself has fallen victim to the economic and ideological constraints of Thatcherism and to all intents and purposes no longer exists. The tradition lives on, however, and I examine more recent work on gender within the feminist paradigm.

THE FEMINIST PARADIGM

Some would dispute the existence of a feminist paradigm, or perspective, within the sociology of sport. Nonetheless, I believe the time has come to state that North American sport sociology is no longer impervious to feminist challenges to its basic conceptual frameworks. Women and sport research and scholarship are less and less ghettoized, and we are beginning to see some admission that feminist theory is relevant to not only the study of gender but also to the epistemological and methodological foundations of the field itself. We still have a very long way to go, but that is why it is such an exciting time—there is so much to rethink, so much to do.

Resistance to Feminism

There is still substantial resistance to feminist scholarship, within sociology as well as its subfields. The feminist transformation of North American sociology has been contained in part by functionalism, which continues to exert a significant and inhibiting effect (Stacey & Thorne, 1985). The notion of *role*, for example, focuses more attention on the individual than on social structure, and depoliticizes the central questions of power and control in explaining gender inequality (as well as other forms of social inequality). As was pointed out in the description of the idealist/positivist paradigm of sport sociology, gender is more often treated as a variable than as a central, theoretical category. Gender is assumed to be a property of individuals and is conceptualized in terms of sex differences rather than as a principle of social organization.

Another form of resistance becomes apparent in the claim that feminism is a political activity and therefore devoid of scholarly "objectivity." Two of our founding fathers in the sociology of sport have recently made their views on this very clear. One is Gunther Luschen, in his public remarks as a keynote speaker representing the International Committee for the Sociology of Sport, at the Congress on Movement and Sport in Women's Life in Finland in August, 1987. The other is Eric Dunning, who states in a footnote to a recent article (Dunning, 1986), "Feminist writers, of course, have made a number of important advances in this regard but, on account of the strength of their ideological commitments, much of what they have written *appears*, at least, even to many who sympathize with their cause, to be lacking in object-adequacy" (p. 90).

Of course feminism and feminist scholarship are political. Whether through praxis or theory, the feminist project is to change the world, not merely to describe it. Debates about objectivity in social theory have a very long history, and they are central to all rejections of positivism. Elsewhere (M.A. Hall, 1985), I have argued that feminists challenge the notion of an objective reality that is "out there" and can be studied, grasped, and researched by anyone using universally applicable rules of inquiry. It is this sort of objectivism and the norm of objectivity that a feminist epistemology challenges. What the feminist challenge reaffirms, on the other hand, is that knowledge claims of women, at least those engaged in liberatory struggles, are indeed more objective because they place far more importance on moral and political truths than they do on scientific rationality. In this sense a feminist epistemology rejects objectivism and positivism but reaffirms a new concept of objectivity.

My final example of resistance to feminism concerns the neo-Marxist and cultural studies paradigms. Even though writers (mostly male) from within these two perspectives are usually sympathetic to feminism and incorporate gender (as well as race and ethnicity) into their class-based analyses, they have refused to utilize, sometimes even read, feminist theory and research. Rosemary Deem (1988), for example, has shown how current work in British sociology of sport and leisure (Weberian/figurational, neo-Marxist, and cultural studies) is still dominated by the view that class is the really important struggle and that gender is something women worry about. Those who are willing to take gender (race, age, ethnicity) on board do so providing it can be accommodated without shifting the ground and debate too far from class. In the Canadian context, Richard Gruneau (1983) is equally guilty of dismissing the now-vast literature on socialist feminist theory:

Much more could be said about different theoretical frameworks within which to analyse the emergence of "modern" sport. For example, the issue of patriarchy—domination of women by men—has scarcely been touched in this chapter. Yet, clearly there is an important story to be told here. One cannot examine the social development of sport and not be struck by the centrality of hegemonic conceptions of masculinity throughout western sport. Indeed, there is a continuity to this masculine hegemony which cuts across other fundamental social transitions in economic and cultural life. There is little in the theory of industrial society to aid in the understanding of this continuity. *And, while the Marxist tradition alerts us to sources of domination and their continuity in social life, Marxist writing, with few exceptions, has tended to maintain a huge silence on the question of gender relations.* [italics added] (p. 31)

Male sport sociologists can no longer avoid feminist theory and research. They have to begin reading this work: not just feminist analyses of gender and sport, but feminist social theory in general. However, as Jeff Hearn (1987) points out, one of the hardest things for men to do is to take feminism seriously because to do so can seriously change their lives.

Beyond "Women in Sport"

Birrell (1988a) traces the development of primarily American "women-in-sport" research and scholarship from their beginnings in the 1960s through to what she believes to be their current status and themes. As she points out,

The field has transformed itself from often angry, always well-intentioned, but generally atheoretical investigations of the patterns of women's involvement and the psychological factors that kept women from full participation, to a theoretically informed, critical analysis of the cultural forces that work to produce the ideological practices that influence the relations of sport and gender. (p. 492)

Over a 25-year period, there has been an evolution from what we used to call "women in sport" to what we now call "gender and sport." Yet gender, by and large, still translates as women, not men. Courses, symposia, conferences, and texts with the label gender and sport are considered for women only, and the issues discussed are thought relevant only to women, rarely to men. The fact that gender is an important conceptual tool to understanding the social world (as are class, race, and ethnicity) as well as a theoretical construct that requires careful, sustained analysis is simply not always accepted. This is why the major themes in the gender and sport area still place more emphasis on the analysis of women and femininity than they do on men and masculinity. However, as the articles in this book attest, there is now a growing interest in the feminist analysis of men in sport, which I will address in the next section.

Aside from the very new focus on men, masculinity, and sport, what are some of the current trends in research and scholarship in the feminist paradigm?[11] I will restrict my comments to themes that engage not only feminism but also some sort of "critical" social theory or sociology such as neo-Marxism and cultural studies. I do this because feminism, like critical theory, is an emancipatory theory in that it seeks to connect theory and experience. By its very nature, it has a critical dimension, and even though neo-Marxism and cultural studies have often failed to take gender seriously, they have been challenged, and to a certain extent transformed, by feminism. The social analysis of sport and leisure is but one site, a contested terrain if you like, for that transformation. More specifically, Deem (1988) has outlined the similarities between the critical and feminist approaches in the context of sport and leisure.

- A shared assumption that sport and leisure are practices that are struggled over and connected to the exercise of power
- A recognition that radical strategies involving sport and leisure are as important for social and economic changes as are strategies for the economy
- A shared belief that it is possible to transform sport and leisure from practices that help subordinate and oppress disadvantaged social groups into practices that can overcome exploitation

Themes of the Feminist Paradigm. With this in mind, there appear to be three major themes emerging within the feminist paradigm at present. The first is the role of sport, physical activity, and physical education in the social reproduction of gender and gender relations. The work here includes the production of media images (usually negative) of women in sport (Duncan & Hasbrook, 1988; Hilliard, 1984; MacNeill, 1988; Rintala & Birrell, 1984; Theberge & Cronk, 1986); the social reproduction of gender in physical education programs and curricula (Dewar, 1986, 1987a, 1987b; Leaman & Carrington, 1985; Scraton, 1986; Sherlock, 1987); the relationship of sport and physical education to young women's subcultures (Scraton, 1987; Varpalotai, 1987) and the ways in which sport is an important cultural sphere where meanings of masculinity and femininity are produced, reproduced, presented, and acted upon (J. Hargreaves, 1986; Messner, 1988).

The second theme focuses attention on the empowering of women through the empowerment of their bodies (Lenskyj, 1986; MacKinnon, 1987; Theberge, 1987). This theme ranges over several topics including power, physicality, and sexuality. It is not very extensive as yet, but it is extremely important because of the very-long-standing hegemonic control men have had over women's bodies. Moreover, and as I have argued elsewhere (Hall, 1985a), the body as subject underlies all human physical activity including sport. Unlike other physical activities with more utilitarian purposes, sport "calls upon the body's capacities and skills merely for the sake of determining what they can achieve" (I. Young, 1979, p. 46). Sport, therefore, is the paragon of body-subject. Patriarchal culture, on the other hand, has defined woman as other or object, more specifically body-object. What follows for women and sport is that a culture that defines sport as body-subject and woman as body-object forces an incompatibility between women and sport. This means either that women have been excluded from the symbols, practices, and institutions of sport, or, when they do participate, what they do is not considered true sport, nor in some cases are they viewed as real women. More specifically, they must always prove their heterosexuality (Lenskyj, 1986). Sport, exercise, and physical activity can be empowering for women, whether the purpose is to challenge the objectification of their bodies or to resist compulsory heterosexuality. Regardless, we need to understand the processes whereby the female body becomes sexualized, controlled, and oppressed, and more importantly the potential in sport, exercise, and physical activity for strategies of resistance and opposition.

The linkage between theory, policy, and practice is the third theme. The work at present is pluralistic but obviously important, because unless we can spell out the relationship between our theory and our policies, both public and private, we will make little progress toward transforming sport and leisure. The studies in this area are too numerous to mention, but Lenskyj (1986) is a good source for work in the Canadian contest, Birrell (1988) for the American, and Deem (1988) for the British.

There are also areas where the research is sparse and the theoretical analysis lacking. Whereas the neo-Marxists and cultural studies scholars have focused on class, and the feminists on gender, there is very little socialist feminist analysis of sport with the exception of the work of Cathy Bray (1983, 1984, 1985), who has consistently argued for an analysis that takes the existence of class oppression in a patriarchal society as a given. There should be more Canadian work in this regard because of a flourishing socialist feminist tradition that for some time has confronted the patriarchal dimensions of capitalist society (Hamilton & Barrett, 1987). Also lacking, as both Birrell (1988b) and Deem (1988) have pointed out, is any serious effort to incorporate race and ethnicity into our empirical and theoretical work. Regrettably, this is also an issue that feminist theory has yet to deal with adequately.

Women-Centered Research. One final comment concerns the obvious woman-centered nature of most feminist scholarship and research. It may seem that studies focus totally on women and that women are seen only in relation to a social universe constructed around females. This is a gynocentric model of social reality, as opposed to an androcentric one, and it has been an extremely useful and productive way to recognize and counter androcentric, sexist scholarship. It has also added immeasurably to our knowledge about women and their lives. There is no need to apologize for this intentionally women-centered focus; it must continue. But it is also useful to move beyond an exclusively woman-centered strategy to decipher how the patriarchal and gendered nature of modern sport has shaped men's lives as well. It is men, however, who should do this, not women.

Men, Masculinity, and Men's Studies

Jeff Hearn, a British sociologist, has written a fascinating critique of men and masculinity from a Marxist perspective (Hearn, 1987). Throughout his analysis, he is extremely sensitive to the role of men in feminism. He suggests that four possibilities exist for men in the social sciences who wish to engage with feminism: pretending to be "male feminists," becoming "experts" on women's studies, promoting gender studies as a discipline that encompasses both the new men's studies and the older women's studies, and finally, developing the study of men and masculinity. He argues strongly in favour of the last one, and I am in complete agreement with him.

He suggests further that the "most drastic action that men can take politically, personally, or academically is not to try and solve the problems of women for women, but to recognize our love and responsibility for each other, to change our relationship with each other'' (p. 180). He is not, incidentally, advocating a form of male academic separatism, and his own work (with Wendy Parkin) on the dynamics of sexuality within organizations is a clear indication of his belief in the need for collaboration (Hearn & Parkin, 1987). He does argue for the need for male social scientists to clarify what they are doing in relation to feminism, women's studies, and the study of gender. Men's studies, as he points out, has only arisen because of the establishment of women's studies as a separate and identifiable area (some would claim a discipline).

The contributions to this book represent a small but growing interest among primarily male theorists utilizing a feminist analysis to examine the complex relationships between masculinity and sport. Given the importance of sport in the reproduction of masculinity, particularly in Western cultures, presumably there is much more such analysis to come. I welcome it, because in the end we will understand much more about how men's power is reproduced and the role sport has played in this reproduction. Presumably also, men will begin to understand how and why they oppress each other.

Theorizing Gender

The feminist theoretical project has been to theorize gender and more specifically to understand the determinants of women's oppression. This theory is extremely diverse, and there is little consensus on which, if any, theory is "best." The scholarship is alive with more or less the same debates and issues that have occupied all critical social theorists: the analytic primacy of the mode of production, the autonomy of the political and ideological, and the tension between economism and voluntarism (B.L. Marshall, 1988).

Connell (1987b) argues that an adequate social theory of gender must be autonomous. In other words, "it cannot derive its logic from a source outside itself " (p. 91) such as natural difference, biological reproduction, the functional needs of society, or the imperatives of social reproduction. He is critical of much feminist theory, categorizing it as either extrinsic (class first through social reproduction to dual system theory), categorical (a blend of cultural and socialist theory), a sex role theory, or practice-based theory. He then sets out to suggest his own theory, which encompasses the major structures of gender relations (labour, power, and cathexis), femininity and masculinity in gender formation, and the patterns of sexual politics. Here, Connell, a male sociologist, is engaging with feminist theory on its own terms, a project I find highly problematic and one I discuss further in the next section.

THE IMPLICATIONS FOR
POLITICS AND PRACTICE

Quite clearly, this section could be a chapter, even a book, in itself. What I can do, if only briefly, is point to some of the implications of this discussion for both the politics and practice of feminism in sport. By *politics* I mean the struggle for control of women's sport, the structures and mechanisms required, and the debates over policy. By *practice* I mean specifically feminist practice normally engaged in by women. The other important point is that our theory, politics, and practice are inextricably linked so that those working in academe, who focus on research and scholarship, should be working hand in hand with those on the front line—be they participants, competitors, teachers, coaches, professional and volunteer leaders, policymakers, or activists. Feminists have always been concerned about the unification of theory and practice, the personal and the political, and it should be no different in sport.

Feminist practice in sport is as diverse as it is in other areas of struggle. There are, for example, considerable political differences between those who are working from within the male-dominated governing structures of sport and those who are resisting this domination by creating totally women-centered sport forms and structures. I have my students examine and discuss examples of these two seemingly contradictory approaches. One example is any "women and sport" policy statement. In Canada, these have been developed by our federal government, a few of our 10 provincial governments, and by a very small minority of the 70 or so national sport organizations. These statements all address issues of structures and systems, allocation of resources, opportunities for participation and competition, leadership opportunities, as well as promotion and public education. Governments, or government-funded bodies, promise to initiate, assist, support, provide, and encourage equality (meaning access to the fullest opportunity for individuals to exercise their potential) and equity (meaning justice and fairness in providing for the physical activity and sport needs of girls and women). We have come to call this a liberal feminist strategy, and those who promote it make extensive use of the state to bring about the abolition of sex discrimination. However, as Nancy Theberge (in press) has shown in the United States, these strategies have won women unprecedented admission to the world of sport but in terms very different from the ideals envisioned by earlier women's sport leaders, who fought against integration into a male-defined and -controlled institution.

In contrast, I have my students read Susan Birrell's and Diana Richter's (1987) discussion of a women's summer recreational softball league in the United States within which a group of feminists tried to transform their sport by making it more process-oriented, collective, inclusive, supportive, and enfused with an ethic of care. Through conscious intervention and counterhegemonic practices, they transformed their game into an experience that had meaning within their own lives. This approach is both radical and separatist, providing an opportunity for women to use sport as a site of resistance to patriarchal domination and control.

Whereas the liberal strategy is to ensure that women have just as much of the resource pie as do men, the radical perspective wants as little as possible to do with men's sport in order to create their own, women-centered activities. Private-sector advocacy groups such as the Canadian Association for the Advancement of Women and Sport must continually negotiate a fine line between liberal, system-oriented interests and radical, separatist strategies. A theory of gender, however, that recognizes the patriarchal dimensions of a capitalist society would be useful to both liberal and radical feminists, because as Rosemary Deem (1988) warns, "If sport and leisure are crucial ways in which forms of classed and gendered hegemony are maintained, and if sport and leisure industries are vital to capitalist economies, then the present conditions for transformation are far from ideal."

Feminist activists and scholars outside the sports world often characterize sport as having distinctly nonfeminist values: fierce competition, a hierarchy of authority, an overemphasis on winning, the dominance of the highly skilled, aggression, and violence, to mention just a few. Sport can be and often is brutal, dangerous, and anything but humane. It is, to many feminists, a world that repulses, one which they usually ignore. What feminists cannot ignore, however, is that despite reform that has considerably improved access to sport for highly skilled females, the vast majority of girls and women are still systematically denied opportunities to develop physical competences. Feminists cannot turn a blind eye to the fact that play, games, and sport are highly institutionalized aspects of our culture that help to maintain male hegemony. However, feminists do ignore this fact, and this accounts, I believe, for the noticeable absence of sport studies (and physical education and leisure studies) within women's studies curricula. In its attempt to be recognized as a legitimate and scholarly discipline, women's studies, like the traditional disciplines, has devalued the *body* side of the mind/body dualism, and as a result sees serious scholarship on sport as marginal. To be fair, however, physical educators, certainly in North America, have also shown little interest in women's studies and have not always comprehended the importance of feminism for both theory and practice.

Finally, I want to say a word about the new interest by men in the feminist analysis of sport. Like Jeff Hearn (1987) I believe that the "major task of the new 'men's studies' is the development of a critique of men's practice, partly, in the light of feminism, not the development of a critique of feminism" (p. 182). The critical target, he suggests, is men and men's discourse, not women or feminism. Although men, and certainly those wishing to critique the ideology of masculinity in sport, must recognize and utilize feminist work, it is not their concern to engage feminism on its own terms. Most of the male authors I read who write about feminism state emphatically that men must not seek to appropriate feminism or feminist theory. They respect the autonomy of feminism and women's studies; they do not wish to stand in judgment of its theoretical work or political debates. Stephen Heath (1987), in a fascinating article about male feminism in the context of literary criticism, has summed it all up so well:

What is difficult for men aware of feminism to realize is not to imagine equality for women but to realize the inequality of their own position: the first is abstract and does not take me out of my position (naturally women should be equal with me); the second is concrete and comes down to the fact that my equality is the masking term for their oppression (women are not equal with me and the struggle is not for *that* equality). (p. 25)

Epilogue

Carole Oglesby

The dictionary at my home describes an epilogue as either a valedictory, the concluding part of a discourse, a section added at the end, or the last word. In this particular instance, the editors wanted me to provide Number 3 on the list and I'm assuming Number 4 as well. (If, in regard to having the last word, you are saying to yourself, "Isn't that just like a woman," you may have missed the message here.)

Since first learning about the development of this book I've been excited by its possibilities, and I was pleased to be asked to review it for Human Kinetics Publishers. When I finished my reading, I was still absolutely sure about its importance, but my delight was tempered by the sense of a looming flaw—not a simple, objective omission or an analytic technicality that could be distanced and discoursed with safety. This was a perception of an "empty space" seen perhaps by only a few (crucially me at that moment) in a personal existential zone that cut to the core.

I spent one long jog thinking, "How can I tell Human Kinetics?" The inner dialogue ran along the lines (a) I might be wrong and appear stupid, or (b) I might be right and they might decide not to publish. The second long jog was filled with, "How can I tell the editors?" This whole line of thinking took me back to adolescence and earlier, when I was carefully schooled that girls cannot tell boys their truths—male egos, and all that. It was very powerful to see that all I know and all I have studied impacts little on cognitive/emotional structures about gender issues that are called forth at critical times. The end of this story, which is the beginning of the "last word," is that I wrote the review, the publishers still loved the book, and Don and Mike gave me the opportunity to explore this perceived empty space with the brave souls who have taken on this book.

J.C. Pearce (1971) most vividly clarified for me the arbitrariness of cultural realities in his delineation of each individual's worldview (cosmic egg) as a "circle of reason imposed by us on a random possibility" (p. 15). The whole of civilization as we know it was posited as a small clearing in a great, dark, and fearful forest: the unknown, the empty category. A wondrous process was also described whereby total attention and passionate commitment to a question or problem can lead to conversion, a crack in the cosmic egg through which imagination creates a new form, a new worldview.

Feminism has been a rich breeding ground for just such conversions. Friedan's "it changed my life" motif has been pervasively experienced and repeated. The writers of this text have effectively presented a new worldview explicating a radical and/or socialist feminism. Their analysis and dialogue revealed a gendered sport interacting continuously with its agent/participants, whether female or male. The work enlightened me and troubled me by an omission. I felt a lack of recognition of another wing of sport feminist thought. In this discussion and following the lead of Mary Daly (1984), I will call this line of thought Elemental Radical Sport Feminism. The authors of this book deal very effectively with what might crudely be called androgen poisoning, but they do not deal with the natural anecdote, the elements of the traditional feminine.

The authors legitimately rail against racism, classism, heterosexism, compulsory heterosexuality, patriarchal institutions, and the social reproduction of gender inequality for material gain. But where is the celebration of the feminine in feminism? Where is the call for males to not only set aside the hegemonic masculine, but to expand, elaborate, accentuate the expressive elements of personality? To demand such a stance is not without a firm basis in feminist theory and scholarship. Simone deBeauvoir (1952) was consistent about the contribution of the feminine to positive cultural forms, as was Margaret Mead (1949) and Jessie Bernard (1975), to whose work I shall return. Sally Gearhart's *The Wanderground* (1978) and other feminist allegories paint the beauty of the fullest elaboration of the feminine as it might be embodied in radical separatist societies. But what about the promise that the traditional feminine holds for all?

I have attempted to analyze and refine the definitional characteristics of a "sport-for-women," provided in history as a singularly female cultural form and trivialized as such, but possessing the same integrating forces that Bernard has demonstrated are the core of human culture (Holland & Oglesby, 1979). The parallel recognition of both the contributions of sport-for-women and men's traditional sport forms a basis for *transformed sport*, a new cultural form that might serve as a vehicle for self-expression as well as an instrument of socialization for the new beings I hope will one day walk this planet (Oglesby, 1988). In *Pure Lust*, Daly (1984) writes to bring women back to consciousness of their Elemental origin:

> For we are rooted, as are animals and trees, winds and seas, in the Earth's substance. Our origins are in her elements. Thus when true to our Originality, we are Elemental, that is of, relating to or caused by the great force of nature. . . . Many women sense that we have been physically, mentally, and emotionally separated from our Original, Elemental Race—made free, that is purified—of our own native characteristics and influence. We sense we are "migrants from another country." (pp. 5,6)

The *men* who write in this book seem to speak of their own alienation from self, from their own elements. Part of what is hidden, in them and from them, is their own feminine. How can we each claim the Other who resides within? At times, including sporting times, we will need to be among our own, at times men and women together, and at times alone. For men, to whom this book is primarily directed, a new consciousness must be recognized and raised in celebration of the feminine, which is, according to a Native American aphorism, the name of those "forces that hold up half the sky." Some principles woven into the feminine force in sport include (Oglesby, 1988) the following:

Passive—I will rest; I will wait; as in Aikido I will let her move me.

Subordinate—My advancement is not as important as our advancement.

Cooperation—The challenge we provide each other by performing the best we can perform will raise the level of the game to a personal best for each.

Dependent—Without his/her effort, none of us will succeed.

Chaotic—Strategically, I will do this now, for no one could possibly expect it.

Nonviolence—I care for my teammates, my opponents, and myself, and thus my intent is not to inflict pain but rather,

Nurturance—to show my care.

These defining characteristics of "sport-for-women" are yet another expression of "women's world of the past," which Jessie Bernard (1975) has called the "integry," the primary social function of which was integration, solidarity, and community. In the past, these functions were seen as women's tasks and were massively undervalued. Certainly as defining characteristics of the sporting experience, they go virtually unrecognized today. Feminist scholarship in sport studies must recognize Elemental Radical Sport Feminism as an additional sport feminist stance.

If the Elemental-Radical stance had been more prominent in the thoughts of the authors of this text, certain subtle and important changes might have been seen. For example, the authors use the word *sport* as if there were one universal meaning to the word, even in a gender context. This usage ignores what I have called sport-for-women, an invention of English and American women physical educators of the late 19th and early 20th centuries. This "sport" has been heavily criticized from a feminist perspective, though I think many have not bothered to really examine it. This orientation to sport was little known to any but those girls and women who were involved in it. I do not defend it here, but I do maintain that a complete sociology of gendered sport must be cognizant of at least two sports—traditional sport and sport-for-women. When Messner and Sabo state in the introduction that it is argued that sport is an institution created by and for men, the focus is entirely on men's sport or traditional sport. The sport of women is not even important enough to mention.

This kind of omission occurs in other chapters as well. Pronger writes, "The world of athletics is a gymnasium of heterosexual masculinity" (p. 143). This refers to men's athletics, not to athletics in general. The whole discussion of "gay irony" (the fluidity of gay male athletes passing) is premised on the traditional assumption that the male athlete is straight. The situation of a female athlete is quite different, because the traditional assumption is that she is lesbian. It seems to me that a feminist analysis requires a "passing" reference (pardon the pun) to the difference. The reality of women's traditions also seems to be overlooked by Davis, who ignores the role of male/female cheerleading that accompanies Division I

Women's Basketball in the United States. Likewise, Humberstone's discussion of traditional physical education for boys disregards the fact that traditional girls' physical education is quite different.

A second general criticism is that try as they have, these scholars still communicate to me at times an ambivalent stance about men and traditional masculinity. In many ways, especially in their "scholarly mind work," they push men to go beyond the conventional. In the more literary selections, however, and in some of the vivid imagery of past socialization, the collective gut seems to ache longingly for "the good old days." For example, the volume calls for an end to sexual inequality, and I believe this means, among other things, the end to men's traditional resistance to the expression of the feminine qualities. Although the editors stand foursquare for renouncing unrelieved masculinity (i.e., pain is good for you and inevitable), they do not explicitly call for the resurrection of the feminine-expressive self that childhood and adolescent experiences have crucified within many. Kimmel's chapter seems to me to be virtually a lyric poem in honor of "the way sport was" for boy-building. Whitson's chapter is also ambivalent; see the concluding comments regarding the "painful" readjustments required. Undoubtedly the pain is real, but the article communicates a question about whether the pain is justified by the solution. Even Sabo and Panepinto detail "the way it is" but stop well short of a repudiation of the training practices in football. Although feminists disagree on many points, the need for transformations beyond traditional stereotypes is a common ground. Hence, I think that the book would have benefited from a clearer stance on this issue.

Adrienne Rich (1978), the poet laureate of feminism to my eye and ear, can be here cited. In *Dream of a Common Language*, she speaks of "a whole new poetry beginning here" (p. 39). Likewise, I believe a whole new poetry on men and sport has begun here and begins anew with every man who, replete in his chosen athletic attire, looks at only himself in the mirror and asks the question from his depths, Who am I and what am I doing here, really?

This is the existential question that the authors and editors have posed on every page of this work. The daring of their effort can all too easily be dismissed. The men and women who write here have identified a domain of knowledge (both common and scientific) that I will label as the domain of men, women, and their sports. This domain is widely believed to be part of our clearing in the forest. The authors have proclaimed that the traditional notions about this domain are inaccurate, misguided, limiting, and illusory. Columbus declared that the notion of the flat earth was similarly inadequate. G.W. Carver dispatched the idea that the peanut was worthless, and Sojourner Truth pointed out the flaws of the notion that people of color were satisfied with their lot as slaves. The authors see the sport/gender clearing in the forest in a light different from that which has existed, and through the action of research, writing, and publishing, they seek to share their alternative visions with others.

We feminists speak, and have long been speaking, about massive social conversion, and perhaps the urgency and importance of our politics have at times pushed both speakers and listeners too far into polarities and camps. Are you a feminist or not? Are you liberal or radical? As a Black woman, are you more oppressed as a Black or as Woman? Human and humane processing proceeds best, I believe, from a balanced inquiry: analysis/synthesis, dialogue/contemplation, experiencing particularities/abstracting universals. My hope for the feminist sport scholarship that will flow from this book is that we can better weave the inclusiveness and synthesis aspects of our thinking into our analytic work. This can provide the common language, common ground, and solidarity that in turn will give us the strength and courage needed to reformulate our work and lives.

Notes

Introduction: Toward a Critical Feminist Reappraisal of Sport, Men, and the Gender Order

1. The Wheel Model is intended as a preliminary conceptualization of varied forms of social domination and resistance, not as a full-blown theory. We recognize that the model has limitations and tends to oversimplify reality in important ways. For instance, the way that the various spokes connect to a single hub tends to suggest that all forms of social oppression are connected to a single dynamic of constraint and agency, when in reality, each form of domination (e.g., class, age, and gender) has its own semiautonomous dynamic of constraint and agency. And as some of the articles in this book suggest, a form of resistance against one form of domination may not necessarily constitute resistance against all domination; for example, there are some racist feminists, classist gay liberationists, and sexist Black power activists. Rather than complicating the model by adding ball bearings at the axle to demonstrate these independent dynamics, we have chosen to stay with the simplified, if somewhat flawed, model in the belief that it still yields important insights into how to conceptualize power, resistance, and change.

Chapter 1   Sport in the Social Construction of Masculinity

1. Connell (1983) goes on to suggest that work (and, it can be suggested, the superior earning power attached to success in intellectual work), fatherhood, and success in adult sexual relationships are the typical ways in which nonphysical adult men establish masculinity. The converse of this last point is captured in Oriard's observation that the masculinity whose codes he and his football teammates were exploring was a peculiarly asexual kind, which depended upon the absence of women rather than on sexual attraction.

2. Canadian hockey fans, for example, are regularly subjected to CBC commentator (and former Boston Bruin coach) Don Cherry's praising "tough guys" and disparaging European players, players who wear visors, and generally any player whose game is based upon skill rather than force and intimidation.

3. Indeed Dunning (1986) has argued that the rugby club as a social institution was developed precisely as a male preserve, where upper- and middle-class men could meet to mock and objectify absent women. Dunning suggests that men of these classes were the first to feel threatened in their masculinity, because it was in these classes that intellectual prowess was already rendering physical prowess obsolete in job performance, and from these classes that the early suffragettes came.

4. We can compare these sanctions with the ostracism and the visceral hatred that European colonials often directed at members of their own kind whose departures from the norms of white behaviour made the structures of white authority more difficult to sustain. See "Tarzan is an Expatriate" in Theroux (1986).

Chapter 2   The Men's Cultural Centre: Sports and the Dynamic of Women's Oppression/Men's Repression

1. Many women contributed to the development of girls' rules. Atkinson (1978), Lenskyj (1986), and others have argued that in part this represented a tactically necessary defence against male control of women's institutions and a creative attempt to avoid the most brutalizing features of male sport, and that without these rules, girls and women would not have been allowed to play at all. Nevertheless, girls' rules confined most females interested in sports to a ghetto of inequality and left unchallenged the existing stereotypes about female frailty.

2. There are, of course, lots of cooperative games in which this does not necessarily occur. My favourite is the Mbuti tug-of-war from Zaire, where winning happens when, through the exchange of players, both teams achieve equal strength.

Chapter 3   Masculinity, Sexuality, and the Development of Early Modern Sport

1. The author would like to thank the following people for helpful comments and suggestions on earlier drafts of this paper: Kathy Barry, Mike Messner, Ann Hall, and Anne Richmond.

2. Social scientists of the 1950s, however, employed a Freudian psychology rather than a Spencerian biology to explain sport's male character (see Stone, 1973). The determinism of both approaches should not be overlooked.

3. The phrase "the great transformation" is taken from Karl Polanyi's classic book of the same title.

4. Although Marx overstated the power of capitalism, his analysis was essentially correct when he wrote,

[Capitalism] has put an end to all feudal, patriarchal, idyllic relations. It has pitilessly torn asunder the motely feudal ties that bound man to his "natural superiors" and has left remaining no other nexus between man and man than naked self-interest, than callous "cash payment." . . . The bourgeoisie has torn away from the family its sentimental veil and has reduced the family relation to a mere money relation. . . . Differences of age and sex have no longer any distinctive social validity for the working class. (Marx & Engels, 1964, p. 97)

5. Kate Millett notes that a similar reaction to power gains by women occurred in the middle of this century. She points out that in the United States, Germany, and the Soviet Union, liberal laws regarding divorce and abortion passed in the early 1900s were overturned a few decades later.

Chapter 4   Baseball and the Reconstitution
of American Masculinity, 1880-1920

1. I am grateful to several people for their criticism, support, and inspiration as I explored the relationship of baseball and masculinity: Norman Kent, Sandy Koufax, Mike Messner, George Robinson, Jackie Robinson, Don Sabo, and my father, for endless summer afternoons in the backyard.

2. The material in this section is from Kimmel, M., *Gender and Society,* (Vol. 1, Number 3) pp. 263-266, Copyright 1987 by Michael Kimmel. Adapted by permission of Sage Publications, Inc.

3. Of course, many masculinists were vigorously antifeminist. But the thrust of the masculinism was indifferent to the institutional gains for women and sought only the preservation of "islands" of masculinity.

4. Of course, the key term here is *organized*, and I will return to that aspect in the next section.

5. Such experiences of community are reproduced by baseball across generations, so that community with neighbors is linked with a relationship between father and son as fans. I recall vividly, for example, my first ride on the subway to Ebbets Field, when I knew everyone in the train was as adoring of the Dodgers as my father was—and, of course, as I was. I remember reaching up to hold his hand as we walked to that sagging building, and gasping as we entered the stands when I saw how bright and green the field itself was. One needn't be a psychoanalyst to understand how feeling so close to 46,000 neighbors was so intimately linked to feeling so close to that most special person. The memory of community is linked to the memory of family love for generations of American men. And the sinews of that community are the shared idols of boyhood—his Rube Walker and my Sandy Koufax. Such links may help explain my continued passion for the game, both as a player and as a spectator. And, perhaps, why I still root for the Dodgers, who, from my perspective, are simply on a very long road trip.

Chapter 6   An Iron Man: The Body and Some Contradictions
of Hegemonic Masculinity

1. My thanks to Norm Radican and Pip Martin, who did most of the fieldwork on this project; the Australian Research Grants Committee, which funded it; Marie O'Brien, who typed the paper; and the respondents, without whose willingness to bare their souls this kind of research and reflection would be impossible.

Chapter 7   Masculinities and Athletic Careers:
Bonding and Status Differences

1. This chapter previously appeared, in a slightly different form, in Messner, M., *Gender and Society,* (Vol. 3, Number 1) pp. 71-88, copyright 1989 by Sociologists for Women in Society. Adapted by permission of Sage Publications, Inc. This work is based upon research that will appear in a book tentatively entitled *Masculinity and Sports: The Lives of Athletes*, Beacon Press, 1990. Parts of this chapter were presented as papers at the American Sociological Association

meetings in Chicago in August 1987 and at the North American Society for the Sociology of Sport meetings in Edmonton, Alberta, in November 1987. I thank Maxine Baca Zinn, Bob Blauner, Bob Dunn, Pierrette Hondagneu-Sotelo, Carol Jacklin, Michael Kimmel, Judith Lorber, Don Sabo, Barrie Thorne, and Carol Warren for constructive comments on earlier versions of this paper.

2. "Mitch Harris" is a pseudonym.

Chapter 8   "Cool Pose:" Black Masculinity and Sports

1. I would like to thank Michael Messner and James T. Todd for their invaluable assistance in the development of this article. Thanks also to Glenn W. Martin and Emily Collias for their help. This article, which is based on the author's doctoral dissertation (Majors, 1987), is dedicated to Uncle Charles Hughes (who was my sport hero) and to my friend Eugene Scott, who together taught me how to use masculinity with sensitivity and grace.

2. For more discussion of what the author has termed "the problem of selective indiscrimination," see Majors (1987).

Chapter 9   Football Ritual and the Social Reproduction of Masculinity

1. The authors are indebted to Mike Messner and Richard Lapchick for their contributions to this paper. Special thanks are also owed to the theoretical work of Jean La Fountaine and to Todd Crosset (1986), whose pioneering research on male-coach/female-athlete relationships gave us fruitful directions to direct our inquiry and thinking.

Chapter 10   Little Big Man: Hustling, Gender Narcissism, and Bodybuilding Subculture

1. In sports one can cite a number of critical case studies (e.g., Brower, 1976) and a few case studies on men in sport (e.g., Messner, 1985b; Sabo, 1985; Sabo & Runfola, 1980).

2. Elliot Gorn's insightful study of bareknuckle fighting in 19th-century America also describes a form of gender narcissism he described as "bachelor subculture" (1986).

3. A 1965 Harris Poll ranked fear of homosexuality third behind fear of communism and atheism. One can only imagine that the recent AIDS outbreak has increased such fears. For studies done on the psychology of homophobia, see K. Smith (1971), and Shirrel (1974).

4. Only one case of a man hustling a woman was recorded during my field stays, and this was also by a man who hustled other men. Female bodybuilders do not have to hustle because they tend to have higher status jobs and more education. There is also no history of female hustling in the subculture, making it more difficult to start it up. Ironically, the outbreak of AIDS has brought hustling to a new crisis level that has enabled some people to discuss it more openly. On a related note, AIDS has curbed hustling somewhat. However, the more enterprising hustler/bodybuilders have begun making videos of themselves posing sug-

gestively either nude or seminude. Some sell these videos in place of sex acts.

5. I didn't get a direct interview with a hustler until I had been in the subculture for over a year, and even then it was only after testing my attitudes toward hustling that people would open up.

6. Male bodybuilders tend to come from blue-collar backgrounds. Their educational levels are significantly lower than those of female bodybuilders. Sixteen percent of the men in my sample (n=40) graduated from college, as compared to 40% (n=38) of the women. This translates into work histories that consistently show men in menial jobs whereas women have professionally oriented careers. Certain jobs do run in the gym community, getting passed around. Bouncers in bars, bodyguards, and bill collectors are all jobs that make use of the large size of the bodybuilder and allow for his need for flexible hours.

Chapter 11   Gay Jocks: A Phenomenology of Gay Men in Athletics

1. An earlier version of this paper was presented to the Canadian Sociology and Anthropology Association on June 3, 1987, at the Learned Societies Conference at McMaster University, Hamilton, ON.

2. Gay men are involved in both mainstream and gay community athletic milieux. Gay athletic clubs, which can be found in major cities across North America (Rowland, 1986), constitute a major aspect of gay community life. These clubs offer gay men and lesbians a unique experience of athletics. Because space here is limited, I will devote this paper to the experience of gay men in mainstream athletics.

The phenomenology of gay men in athletics is an entirely new field of enquiry, both in regards to its approach and its subject. This paper is a simplified and brief outline of a complex and extensive phenomenon.

3. My approach to phenomenology is drawn from Martin Heidegger (1926, pp. 49-62). He says, that the term *phenomenology* refers to a method of enquiry, whereas *sociology*, *anthropology*, and *psychology* refer to what is to be studied. Phenomenology, he says, directs us to the "how" of an investigation; it is the study of the way in which things appear to us.

4. I am not suggesting that all gay men behave effeminately. In fact, nowhere in this paper do I suggest that gay men behave in a uniform fashion. As the reader will see, the fluidity of being gay precludes such a notion.

5. The fluidity of being gay should be kept in mind here; that is, there are men who may practice homosexuality who see their masculine behaviours not in this gay context but in a traditional patriarchal one. Moreover, they may switch from a traditional context to a gay one from time to time, depending on the situation.

Chapter 12   Male Cheerleaders and the Naturalization of Gender

1. I would like to thank Susan Birrell for suggesting the label "feminine preserve" to describe modern cheerleading.

Chapter 13   Women Coaching Male Athletes

1. The author would like to express her deep appreciation to Dr. Carole Oglesby for her assistance and direction with this project.

2. Coaches were selected from the northeast sector of the country in part to facilitate recruitment and to cut back on travel expenses.

3. Ms. Oates's confidence about her ability to forge a winning team was grounded in the fact that she had established a winning reputation in Washington, DC, and was a multiple recipient of the coach-of-the-year award in basketball in Washington, DC. She also consistently produced winning records in track, volleyball, and softball. Moreover, she had never participated in any of the sports she coached.

Chapter 14   Challenges to Male Hegemony in Sport

1. For this and a number of other reasons (e.g., its shorter history as a highly symbolic national sport and its close association with its female form), I do not see tennis to have a pivotal role in the construction and maintenance of hegemonic masculinity. This is despite considerable public interest in the sport. In fact, it is the top-rating sport as far as women's interests are concerned (68%) and third for men (60%) (Brian Sweeney and Associates, 1986).

Chapter 15   Women of Color, Critical Autobiography, and Sport

1. This paper marks the beginning of an attempt to come to terms with complex and significant issues in sport studies and in critical theory. In arriving at this point of departure, I have been fortunate to have participated in a variety of learning experiences. I have benefited from the many sessions and experiences offered through the Women Against Racism conferences at the University of Iowa from 1983 to the present. I have learned a great deal about the criticisms and impatience of women of color through our dialogues in the classroom and in the session on "Diversity in Feminist Theory" in the 1988 Women as Leaders conference sponsored by the University of Iowa Department of Physical Education and Sports Studies.

I would like to thank Rusty Barcelo for sharing several important sources on Chicano and Chicana scholarship with me, and Carol Jasperson and Mary June Harris for a good deal of retyping. A thorough review by Mike Messner of an earlier draft of this paper prompted me to rethink my position on a number of points, for which I am very grateful. Finally, I wish to thank Cheryl Cole for continually bringing new materials to my attention, for critical feedback on several drafts, and for sharing my intellectual excitement in this project.

The final stage of this manuscript was prepared with the support of a developmental assignment at University House at the University of Iowa.

2. Exceptions include Chicana scholar Baca Zinn (1979, 1981) and Black scholars Hooks (1981, 1984) and A. Davis (1981).

3. In this review, attention is primarily directed to the work of Black and Chicano scholars. A more inclusive analysis examining the writing of Asian Americans and Native Americans awaits our attention.

4. The dialogue about theory is underscored by a fundamental ambivalence of women of color about the value of theory itself. One can read both antitheory positions and countertheory positions into their critiques. The former is a dismissal of theory as a useless enterprise; the latter acknowledges some value of theory but disputes the form and content of dominant theoretical practices. The antitheorist would make no claims to theory in relation to her own work; the countertheorist would argue for a reconstruction of theory along more inclusive lines that would acknowledge her work as theory.

5. The primary works in this tradition include *I Know Why the Caged Bird Sings* (Angelou, 1969); *The Bluest Eye* (Morrison, 1970); *But Some of Us Are Brave* (Hull, Bell, & Smith, 1982); *This Bridge Called My Back* (Moraga & Anzaldua, 1983); *Cuentos* (Gomez, Moraga, & Romo-Carmona, 1983); *Common Differences* (Joseph & Lewis, 1981); *Sister Outsider* (Lourde, 1984); *Loving in the War Years* (Moraga, 1983); *Yours in Struggle* (Bulkin, Pratt, & Smith, 1984); and most recently *Borderlands/La Frontera* (Anzaldua, 1987) and *Tight Spaces* (Scott, Muhanji, & High, 1987).

6. The choice of the term "minority discourse" is an unfortunate one, for regardless of its intended connotation, it carries a complacent and patronizing tone. Christian (1987) has also objected to the term.

7. The texts C. Kaplan (1987) analyzes are Pratt (1984), Cliff (1980), and Anzaldua's essay "Speaking in Tongues" (Moraga & Anzaldua, 1983).

Chapter 16 Warriors or Wimps? Creating Alternative Forms of Physical Education

1. Gender is learned behaviour, and as Connell et al. (1982) point out, it is "a pattern of relation among people . . . an extensive and complex pattern woven through all institutions they live in . . . and shapes their lives at every level" (pp. 33-34).

2. This "choice" can be viewed in more general terms in Giddens's (1976, 1984) concept of structuration, which allows for the metaphysical conceptualisation of the dynamic processes whereby social structures are both constituted by individual or group agency and may also be the very medium of that constitution. He does not, however, identify the centrality of gender in his theorizing.

3. See J. Evans (1986), a critical discourse on British PE, which from a largely socialist perspective explores the possibilities of recent innovations in British school PE programmes for providing equality of opportunity.

4. Shotmoor is a pseudonym for the outdoor education institute. A more detailed description of the institute can be found elsewhere (Humberstone, 1986).

5. An abseil is a technique by which a climber uses a rope and a device called a descender to travel downward.

6. At the time of the study, there was regrettably only one woman teacher fully involved in teaching the activities.

Chapter 18   How Should We Theorize Gender in the Context of Sport?

1. I originally gave a much shorter version of this paper at the Sport, Sex, and Gender Conference in Lillehammer, Norway, in November 1986. Since then I have rethought my position on several issues and have expanded the paper substantially. I want to thank Jane Haslett, Nancy Theberge, and the editors of this volume for their assistance in this process.

2. Although the point is Jane Flax's (1987), she would not include Marxism in this list. See also Alcoff (1988) and articles in the relatively new journal *Cultural Critique*.

3. Sex chromatin screening will not identify "normal" females who have taken hormones or steroids that may increase muscular strength (see Chapelle, 1986, for a useful exposé of this ridiculous test).

4. See the editorial and many of the articles in *Signs: Journal of Women in Culture and Society*, **13**(3), 1988. I used the term *gendering* (of sport, leisure, and physical education) in the title of a special issue of *Women's Studies International Forum*, **10**(4), 1987, but unfortunately I did not define it.

5. I have limited my review primarily to North American sport sociology, more specifically to developments in Canada, and more specifically still to anglophone Canada. However, given the English Canadian academic tradition, which is influenced not only by our neighbours to the south but also from across the Atlantic and particularly by developments in Britain, the description here is somewhat broader than what is present within our national boundaries. Still, this does not recognize the enormous debt we owe to European sociological traditions and current scholars, especially in France and Germany. Neither does it take cognizance of the work in communist nations nor in Third World countries. In addition to my summary here, the reader would benefit from two recently published essays that complement my analysis. One is by George Sage (1987a), written primarily for nonspecialists in the sociology of sport, in which he describes the rise of the field within North American academe and its relationship to physical education. The other is Susan Birrell's (1988a) excellent historical analysis of the field known as "women-in-sport" and its maturation to the study of gender relations.

6. It is also important to note that this represents my personal view of a subfield and that not everyone would agree with this assessment. For instance, see Rees and Miracle (1986), which purports to offer an overview of the various theoretical perspectives within North American sport sociology. Here, there is no mention of work within a neo-Marxist, cultural studies, or feminist paradigm. Moreover, there is not a single contribution from a female (let alone feminist) sport sociologist.

7. Birrell (1984) presents some interesting data on this point: In an analysis of journals and proceedings on research in the sociology of sport, 50% of the studies made no mention of gender, 22% focussed only on males, and 6% focussed

only on females. Therefore, as she suggests, "There is a strong possibility that 72 percent of the articles do not speak at all to the female experience in sport and thus do not take gender into account in any meaningful way" (p. 133).

8. Elsewhere, I have reviewed and critiqued this literature extensively (M.A. Hall, 1981).

9. For an overview and critique of this literature, see Theberge (1981).

10. The major Canadian theorists in this particular paradigm are Rob Beamish, Hart Cantelon, Richard Gruneau, Jean Harvey, Bruce Kidd, and David Whitson. Some, however, may feel a little more comfortable being identified with the cultural studies paradigm. See also Harvey and Cantelon (1988) for a recent collection of essays in Canadian sport sociology.

11. For an up-to-date summary and bibliography of research into all aspects of women, sport, and physical activity, see Lenskyj (1986).

CHESTER COLLEGE LIBRARY

References

Abigail, J. (1985). Girls and physical education. *New Zealand Journal of Health, Physical Education and Recreation*, **17**(1), 1-4.

Abney, R. (1988). *The effect of role models and mentors on the careers of Black women athletic administrators and coaches in higher education*. Unpublished doctoral dissertation, University of Iowa, Iowa City.

Acosta, V., & Carpenter, L. (1985). Status of women in athletics: Changes and causes. *JOPERD*, **56**(6), 30-37.

Adelman, M. (1986). *Long time passing: Lives of older lesbians*. Boston: Alyson.

Adelman, M.L. (1986). *A sporting time: New York City and the rise of modern athletics, 1820-1870*. Urbana: University of Illinois Press.

Adorno, T. (1950). *The authoritarian personality*. New York: Wiley.

Alcoff, L. (1988). Cultural feminism versus poststructuralism: The identity crisis in feminist theory. *Signs: Journal of Women in Culture and Society*, **13**(3), 405-436.

Alexander, A. (1978). *Status of minority women in the AIAW*. Unpublished master's thesis, Temple University, Philadelphia.

Alison, L. (1980). Batsman and bowler: The key relationship of Victorian England. *Journal of Sport History*, **7**, 5-20.

Althusser, L. (1971). Ideology and ideological state apparatuses. *Lenin and philosophy and other essays*. London: New Left Books.

Alyson, S. (Ed.) (1981). *Young, gay, and proud*. Boston: Alyson.

Angell, R. (1982). *Late innings: A baseball companion*. New York: Simon & Schuster.

Angelou, M. (1969). *I know why the caged bird sings*. New York: Bantam.

Anzaldua, G. (1987). *Borderlands/La frontera*. San Francisco: Spinsters/Aunt Lute Press.

Aschenbrenner, J. (1975). *Lifelines: Black families in Chicago*. New York: Holt, Rinehart, & Winston.

Askew, S., & Ross, C. (1988). *Boys don't cry: Boys and sexism in education*. New York: Open University Press.

Atkinson, P. (1978). Fitness, feminism and schooling. In S. Delamont & L. Duffin (Eds.), *The nineteenth century woman: Her physical and cultural world* (pp. 92-133). London: Croom Helm.

Baca Zinn, M. (1979). Field research in minority communities: Ethical, methodological, and political observations of an insider. *Social Problems*, **27**, 209-219.

Baca Zinn, M. (1981). Sociological theory in emergent Chicano perspectives. *Pacific Sociological Review*, **24**, 255-272.

Baca Zinn, M. (1982). Chicano men and masculinity. *Journal of Ethnic Studies*, **10**, 29-44.

Baca Zinn, M., Weber Cannon, L., Higginbotthen, E., & Thornton-Dill, B. (1986). The costs of exclusionary practices in women's studies. *Signs: Journal of Women in Culture and Society*, **11**, 290-303.

Ball, D. (1986). The outdoors and gender adventure education. *Journal of the National Association for Outdoor Education*, **3**(2), 28-30.

Barclay, V.M. (1979). *Status of black women in sports among selected institutions of higher education*. Unpublished master's thesis, University of Iowa, Iowa City.

Barker-Benfield, G.J. (1976). *The horrors of the half-known life*. New York: Harper & Row.

Baron, S. (1985). The study of cultural studies and British sociology compared. *Acta Sociologica*, **18**(2), 71-85.

Barrett, M. (1987). The concept of difference. *Feminist Review*, **26**, 29-41.

Barth, G. (1980). *City people: The rise of modern city culture in nineteenth century America*. New York: Oxford University Press.

Beck, B. (1976). *Lifestyles of never married women physical educators in institutions of higher learning in the United States* (Doctoral dissertation, University of North Carolina, Greensboro). *Dissertation Abstracts International*, **37**, 2715A.

Beck, B. (1980). The future of women's sport: Issues, insights, and struggle. In D. Sabo & R. Runfola (Eds.), *Jock: Sports and Male Identity* (pp. 299-314). Englewood Cliffs, NJ: Prentice-Hall.

Benedict, R. (1959). *Patterns of culture*. Boston: Houghton Mifflin.

Benjamin, J. (1988). *The bonds of love: Psychoanalysis, feminism, and the problem of domination*. New York: Pantheon Books.

Bennett, T. (1981). Editor's introduction. In T. Bennett (Ed.), *Culture, ideology and social process* (pp. 9-15). London: Batsford.

Berger, J., Blomberg, S., Fox, C., Dibb, M., & Hollis, R. (1985). *Ways of seeing*. London: British Broadcasting & Penguin Books.

Berghorn, F. J., Yetman, N.R., & Hanna, W.E. (1988). Racial participation in men's and women's intercollegiate basketball: Continuity and change, 1958-1985. *Sociology of Sport Journal*, **5**, 107-124.

Bernard, J. (1975). *Women, wives, and mothers: Values and options*. Chicago: Aldine Press.

Beynon, J. (1985). *Initial encounters in the secondary school: Sussing, typing, and coping*. London: Falmer Press.

Birke, L., & Vines, G. (1987). A sporting chance: The anatomy of destiny. *Women's Studies International Forum*, **10**(4), 337-347.

Birmingham, England University Centre for Contemporary Cultural Studies. (1980). *Women take issue: Aspects of women's subordination*. London: Hutchinson.

Birrell, S. (1978). Achievement related motives and the woman athlete. In C. Oglesby (Ed.), *Women and sport: From myth to reality*. Philadelphia: Lea & Febiger.

Birrell, S. (1984). Studying gender in sport: A feminist perspective. In N. Theberge & P. Donnelly (Eds.), *Sport and the sociological imagination* (pp. 125-135). Fort Worth: Texas Christian University Press.

Birrell, S. (1987/1988). The woman athlete's college experience: Knowns and unknowns. *Journal of Sport and Social Issues*, **11** (Fall/Winter), 82-96.

Birrell, S. (1988a). Discourses on the gender/sport relationship: From women in sport to gender relations. *Exercise and Sport Science Reviews*, **16**, 459-502.

Birrell, S. (1988b). *Racial relations theory and sport*. Unpublished manuscript, University of Iowa, Iowa City.

Birrell, S., & Cole, C. (1986, July). *The body as political territory*. Paper presented at Women on the Cutting Edge, Women as Leaders Conference, University of Iowa, Iowa City.

Birrell, S., & Richter, D.M. (1987). Is a diamond forever? Feminist transformations of sport. *Women's Studies International Forum*, **10**(4), 395-409.

Bloom, B.S. (1964). *Stability and change in human characteristics*. New York: Wiley.

Booth, W. (1974). *A rhetoric of irony*. Chicago: University of Chicago Press.

Bourdieu, P. (1977). Cultural reproduction and social reproduction. In J. Karabel & A. H. Halsey (Eds.), *Power and ideology in education*. New York: Oxford University Press.

Bourdieu, P. (1978). Sport and social class. *Social Science Information*, **18**(6).

Boutilier, M., & SanGiovanni, L. (1983). *The sporting woman*. Champaign, IL: Human Kinetics.

Bouton, J. (1971). *I'm glad you didn't take it personally*. New York: Dell.

Bowlby, J. (1969). *Attachment and loss: Vol. 1. Attachment*. London: Hogarth Press.

Bray, C. (1983). Sport, capitalism and patriarchy. *Canadian Woman Studies*, **4**(3), 11-13.

Bray, C. (1984). Gender and political economy of Canadian sport. In N. Theberge & P. Donnelly (Eds.), *Sport and the sociological imagination* (pp. 104-124). Fort Worth: Texas Christian University Press.

Bray, C. (1985). *Sport, patriarchy and capitalism: Socialist feminist analysis*. Unpublished doctoral dissertation, University of Alberta, Edmonton.

Brian Sweeney and Associates. (1986). *Australians and sport: An annual survey of sporting participation, attendance and media habits*. South Melbourne. Author.

Brod, H. (1983/1984). Work clothes and leisure suits: The class basis and bias of the men's movement. *M: Gentle Men for Gender Justice*, **11**, 10-12, 38-40.

Brod, H. (1987) (Ed.) *The making of masculinities: The new men's studies*. Winchester, MA: Allen & Unwin.

Brower, J. (1976). *Little League baseball and Little Leaguism: A critique of sport*. Paper presented to the annual meeting of the Pacific Sociological Conference, San Francisco.

Brown, B., & Adams, P. (1979). The feminine body and feminist politics. *m/f*, **3**, 35-50.

Brown, D.W. (1987). Muscular Christianity in the antipodes: Some observations on the diffusion and emergence of a Victorian ideal in Australian social theory.

Sporting Traditions: The Journal of the Australian Society for Sports History, **3**(2), 173-187.

Brownmiller, S. (1975). *Against our will: Men, women and rape*. New York: Simon & Schuster.

Bryson, L. (1983). Sport and the oppression of women. *Australia and New Zealand Journal of Sociology*, **19**(3), 413-426.

Bryson, L. (1987a). Sport and the maintenance of masculine hegemony. *Women's Studies International Forum*, **10**, 349-360.

Bryson, L. (1987b). Women and management in the public sector. *Australian Journal of Public Administration*, **XLVI**(3), 259-272.

Bulhan, H. (1985). Black Americans and psychopathology: An overview of research and therapy. *Psychotherapy*, **22**, 370-378.

Bulkin, E. (1984). Hard ground: Jewish identity, racism, and anti-Semitism. In E. Bulkin, M.B. Pratt, & B. Smith (Eds.), *Yours in struggle: Three feminist perspectives on anti-Semitism and racism* (pp. 89-128). Brooklyn: Long Haul Press.

Bulkin, E., Pratt, M. B., & Smith, B. (1984). *Yours in struggle: Three feminist perspectives on anti-Semitism and racism*. Brooklyn: Long Haul Press.

Burstyn, V. (1986). Play, performance, and power—the men (*CBC Radio Ideas*, October 2). Toronto: CBC Transcripts.

Butts, D. S. (1976). *The psychology of sport*. Toronto: Van Nostrand Reinhold.

Carby, H. (1982). White woman listen! Black feminism and the boundaries of sisterhood. In Centre for Contemporary Cultural Studies (Ed.), *The empire strikes back: Race and racism in 70's Britain* (pp. 215-235). London: Hutchinson.

Carrigan, T., Connell R., & Lee, J. (1985). Toward a new sociology of masculinity. *Theory and Society*, **14**(5), 551-604.

Carrigan, T., Connell, R., & Lee, J. (1987). Toward a new sociology of masculinity. In H. Brod (Ed.), *The making of masculinities: The new men's studies* (pp. 63-100). Boston: Allen & Unwin.

Carroll, J. (1986). Sport: Virtue and grace. *Theory and Society*, **3**(1), 91-98.

Case, C. (1906). *The masculine in religion*. Philadelphia: American Baptist Publication Society.

Cashman, R. (1984). *"Ave a go, yer mug!" Australian cricket crowds from Larrikin to Ocker*. Sydney: Collins.

Cavello, D. (1981). *Muscles and morals: Organized playgrounds and urban reform: 1880-1929*. Philadelphia: University of Pennsylvania Press.

Cazenave, N. (1984). Race, socioeconomic status, and age: The social context of American masculinity. *Sex Roles*, **11**, 639-657.

Centre for Contemporary Cultural Studies. (1982). *The empire strikes back: Race and racism in 70's Britain*. London: Hutchinson.

Centre for Contemporary Cultural Studies. (1978). *Women take issue*. University of Birmingham. London: Hutchinson.

Chambliss, D.F. (1988). *Champions: The making of Olympic swimmers*. New York: Morrow.

Chapelle, A. (1986). The use and misuse of sex chromatin screening for 'gender identification' of female athletes. *Journal of the American Medical Association*, **256**, 1920-1923.

Chesler, P. (1972). *Women and madness*. Garden City, NY: Doubleday.

Chodorow, N. (1978). *The reproduction of mothering: Psychoanalysis and the sociology of gender.* Berkeley: University of California Press.

Christian, B. (1987). The race for theory. *Cultural Critique,* **6,** 51-63.

Clell Wade coaches directory for 1987-1988. Cassville, MO: Clell Wade.

Cliff, M. (1980). *Claiming an identity they taught me to despise.* Watertown, MA: Persephone Press.

Coakley, J. (1986). *Sport in society: Issues and controversies.* St. Louis: Times/ Mirror Mosby.

Cohen, J., & Manion, T. (1981). *Perspectives on classrooms and schools.* London: Holt, Rinehart, & Winston.

Cohen, S.D. (1980). *More than fun and games.* Unpublished doctoral dissertation, Brandeis University, Waltham, MA.

Cole, C., & Birrell, S. (1986, October). *Resisting the canon: Feminist cultural studies and sport.* Paper presented at the meeting of the North American Society for Sociology of Sport, Las Vegas, NV.

Combahee River Collective. (1981). Black feminist statement. In C. Moraga & G. Anzaldua (Eds.), *This bridge called my back* (pp. 210-218). New York: Kitchen Table/Women of Color Press.

Connell, R.W. (1983). *Which way is up? Essays on class, sex and culture.* Sydney, Australia: Allen & Unwin.

Connell, R.W. (1987a). *Gender and power.* Sydney, Australia: Allen & Unwin.

Connell, R.W. (1987b). *Gender and power: Society, the person and sexual politics.* Stanford, CA: Stanford University Press.

Connell, R.W., Ashenden, D.J., Kessler, S., & Dowsett, G.W. (1982). *Making the difference: Schools, families and social division.* Sydney, Australia: Allen & Unwin.

Coopersmith, S. (1967). *The antecedents of self-esteem.* San Francisco: Freeman.

Cordes, C. (1985, January). Black males at risk in America. *APA Monitor,* **9-10,** 27-28.

Cott, N. (1984). *In the bonds of womanhood.* Unpublished doctoral dissertation, Brandeis University, Waltham, MA.

Craib, I. (1987). Masculinity and male dominance. *Sociological Review,* **35**(4), 721-743.

Crawford, R. (1984). Sport for young ladies: The Victorian independent schools 1875-1925. *The Journal of the Australian Society for Sports History,* **1**(1), 61-82.

Crisp, Q. (1968). *The naked civil servant.* London: Jonathon Cape.

Crosset, T. (1986). *Male coach/female athlete relationships.* Paper presented at the First Multidisciplinary Conference for Sport Sciences, November 13, Lillehammer, Norway.

Curtis, J., & Loy, J. (1978). Positional segregation in professional baseball: Replications, trend data and critical observation. *International Review of Sport Sociology,* **4**(13), 5-21.

Daly, M. (1978). *Gyn-Ecology: The metaethics of radical feminism.* Boston: Beacon Press.

Daly, M. (1984). *Pure lust: Elemental feminist philosophy.* Boston: Beacon Press.

Davis, A. (1981). *Women, race and class.* New York: Vintage.

Davis, N. (1971). The prostitute: Developing a deviant identity. In J. Henslin (Ed.), *Studies in the sociology of sex.* New York: Appleton-Century-Crofts.

deBeauvoir, S. (1952). *The second sex*. New York: Knopf.

Deem, R. (1988). "Together we stand, divided we fall": Social criticism and the sociology of sport and leisure. *Sociology of Sport Journal*, **5**(4), 341-354.

Delamont, S. (1980). *Sex roles and the school*. London: Methuen.

Deleuze, G., & Guattari, F. (1986). *Kafka: Towards a minor literature* (D. Polan, Trans.). Minneapolis: University of Minnesota Press.

Dewar, A. (1986). *The social construction of gender in a physical education programme*. Unpublished doctoral dissertation, University of British Columbia, Vancouver.

Dewar, A. (1987a). Knowledge and gender in physical education. In J. Gaskell & A.T. McLaren (Eds.), *Women and education: A Canadian perspective* (pp. 265-288). Calgary, AB: Detselig.

Dewar, A. (1987b). The social construction of gender in physical education. *Women's Studies International Forum*, **10**(4), 453-465.

Dinnerstein, D. (1976). *The mermaid and the minotaur: Sexual arrangements and human malaise*. New York: Harper & Row.

Donnelly, P., & Young, K. (1985). Reproduction and transformation of cultural forms in sport: A contextual analysis of rugby. *International Review for the Sociology of Sport*, **20**(1), 19-38.

Donovan, A.J. (1987). *Fatso: Football when men were really men*. New York: Morrow.

Donovan, J. (1985). *Feminist theory: The intellectual traditions of American feminism*. New York: Ungar.

Dubbert, J. (1979). *A man's place: Masculinity in transition*. Englewood Cliffs, NJ: Prentice-Hall.

Duncan, M. (1985). *The ethnographic investigation of curriculum innovation involving mixed physical education within a secondary school*. Unpublished master's thesis, University of Southampton, England.

Duncan, M.C., & Hasbrook, C.A. (1988). Denial of power in televised women's sports. *Sociology of Sport Journal*, **5**(1), 1-21.

Dundes, A. (1985). The American game of 'smear the queer' and the homosexual component of male competitive sport and warfare. *Journal of Psychoanalytic Anthropology*, **8**(3), 115-131.

Dunkle, M. (1985). Minority and low-income girls and young women in athletics. *Equal Play*, **5**, 12-13.

Dunning, E. (1986). Sport as a male preserve: Notes on the social sources of masculine identity and its transformation. *Theory, Culture & Society*, **3**(1), 79-90.

Dunning E., & Sheard, K. (1979). *Barbarians, gentlemen and players*. New York: New York University.

Duquin, M. (1978). The androgynous advantage. In C.A. Oglesby (Ed.), *Women and sport: From myth to reality*. Philadelphia: Lea & Febiger.

Duquin, M. (1984). Power and authority: Moral consensus and conformity in sport. *International Review for Sociology of Sport*, **19**, 295-304.

Dworkin, A. (1981). *Pornography: Men possessing women*. London: Women's Press.

Dwyer, T., & Dyer, K.F. (1984). *Running out of time*. Sydney, Australia: University of New South Wales Press.

Dyer, K.F. (1982). *Challenging the men.* New York: University of Queensland.

Edwards, H. (1969). *The revolt of the black athlete.* New York: Free Press.

Edwards, H. (1971, November). The myth of the racially superior athlete. *The Black Scholar,* **3**, 56-68.

Edwards, H. (1973). *The sociology of sport.* Homewood, IL: Dorsey.

Edwards, H. (1982). Race in contemporary American sports. *National Forum,* **62**, 19-22.

Edwards, H. (1984). The collegiate athletic arms race: Origins and implications of the 'Rule 48' controversy. *Journal of Sport and Social Issues,* **8**, 4-22.

Effron, A. (1971). *Don Quixote and the Dulcineated world.* Austin, TX: University of Texas Press.

Ehrenreich, B., & English, D. (1978). *For her own good: 150 Years of the experts' advice to women.* New York: Anchor Press.

Eichler, M. (1980). *The double standard: A feminist critique of feminist social science.* London: Croom Helm.

Eichler, M. (1989). *Nonsexist research methods: A practical guide.* New York: Unwin Hyman.

Eisenstein, Z.R. (Ed.) (1979). *Capitalist patriarchy and the case for socialist feminism.* New York: Monthly Review.

Eisenstein, Z.R. (1981). *The radical future of liberal feminism.* Boston: Northeastern University Press.

Eitzen, D.S. (1984). *Sport in contemporary society: An anthology.* New York: St. Martin's Press.

Eitzen, D.S., & Purdy, D.A. (1986). The academic preparation and achievement of black and white college athletes. *Journal of Sport and Social Issues,* **10**, 15-29.

Eitzen, D.S., & Tessendorf, I. (1978). Racial segregation by position in sports. *Review of Sport and Society,* **3**, 109-128.

Eitzen, D.S., & Yetman, N.B. (1977). Immune from racism? *Civil Rights Digest,* **9**, 3-13.

Elias, N. (1971). The genesis of sport as a sociological problem. In E. Dunning (Ed.), *The sociology of sport: A selection of readings* (pp. 85-115). Toronto: University of Toronto.

Elias, N., & Dunning, E. (1986). *Quest for excitement: Sport and leisure in the civilizing process.* New York: Blackwell.

Evans, J. (Ed.) (1986). *PE, sport and schooling: Studies in sociology of PE.* London: Falmer Press.

Evans, M. (1985). *An action approach to the innovation of mixed physical education in a secondary school.* A paper written for the Advanced Diploma, Kingston Polytechnic, England.

Farr, K.A. (1988). Dominance bonding through the good old boys sociability group. *Sex Roles,* **18**(5/6), 259-278.

Farrell, W. (1974). *The liberated man: Freeing men and their relationships with women.* New York: Random House.

Fasteau, M.F. (1974). *The male machine.* New York: McGraw-Hill.

Felshin, J. (1974). The triple option...for women in sport. *Quest* (January) **17**, pp. 36-40.

Filene, P. (1986). *Him/her self: Sex roles in America* (2nd ed.). Baltimore: Johns Hopkins University Press.

Fine, G.A. (1987). *With the boys: Little League baseball and preadolescent culture*. Chicago: University of Chicago Press.

Finlay, M.I., & Pleket, H.W. (1976). *The Olympic games: The first thousand years*. London: Chatto & Windus.

Flax, J. (1983). Postmodernism and gender relations in feminist theory. *Signs: Journal of Women in Culture and Society*, **12**(4), 621-643.

Fletcher, S. (1984). *Women first: The female tradition in English physical education 1880-1980*. London: Louds.

Foucault, M. (1978). *The history of sexuality: Vol. 1. An introduction* (R. Hurley, Trans.). New York: Vintage.

Franklin, C.W. (1984a). *The changing definition of masculinity*. New York: Plenum.

Franklin, C.W. (1984b, November). The male sex drive. *Essence*, pp. 79-80, 154-158.

Franklin, C.W. (1986). Surviving the institutional decimation of black males: Causes, consequences, and intervention. In H. Brod (Ed.), *The making of masculinities: The new men's studies* (pp. 115-170). Winchester, MA: Allen & Unwin.

Freeman, J. (1989). *Women: A feminist perspective* (4th ed.). Mountainview, CA: Mayfield.

Freud, S. (1940). An outline of psychoanalysis. *The complete works of Sigmund Freud Vol. 3*. London: Hogarth Press.

Friedan, B. (1981). *The second stage*. New York: Summit Books.

Gannaway, H. (1976). Making sense of school. In M. Stubbs & S. Delamont (Eds.), *Exploration in classroom observation*. Chichester, England: Wiley.

Garcia, A.M. (1986). Studying Chicanas: Bringing women into the frame of Chicano studies. In T. Gordova, N. Cantu, G. Cordenas, J. Garcia, & C. Sierra (Eds.), *Chicana voices: Intersections of class, race and gender* (pp. 19-29). Austin, TX: Center for Mexican American Studies. Proceedings of the 1984 National Association for Chicano Studies.

Gathorne-Hardy, J. (1977). *The old school tie*. New York: Viking Press.

Gearhart, S. (1978). *The wanderground: Stories of the hill women*. Watertown, MA: Persephone Press.

Geertz, C. (1973). *The interpretation of cultures*. New York: Basic Books.

Gerber, E.R., Felshin, J., Berlin, P., & Wyrick, W. (1974). *The American woman in sport*. Reading, MA: Addison-Wesley.

Gerson, K. (1986). What do women want from men? *American Behavioral Scientist* **29**, 619-634.

Gibbs, J.T. (1988). Young black males in America: Endangered, embittered, and embattled. In J.T. Gibbs (Ed.), *Young, black, and male in America: An endangered species* (pp. 1-36). Dover, MA: Auburn House.

Giddens, A. (1976). *New rules of sociological method*. London: Hutchinson.

Giddens, A. (1979). *Central problems in social theory*. London: Macmillan.

Giddens, A. (1984). *The constitution of society*. London: Polity Press.

Gilligan, C. (1982). *In a different voice: Psychological theory and women's development*. Cambridge, MA: Harvard University Press.

Girl wins appeal to play boy's hockey. (1987, December 5). *Calgary Herald*.

Gite, L. (1985, November). Black men and stress. *Essence*, pp. 25-26, 130.

Godelier, M. (1986). *The making of great men: Male domination and power among the New Guinea Baruya*. Cambridge England: Cambridge University Press.

Gomez, A., Moraga, C., & Romo-Carmona, M. (1983). *Cuentos: Stories by Latinas*. New York: Kitchen Table/Women of Color Press.

Gonzales, A.F. (1956, November). The first college cheer. *The American Mercury*, **83**, 101-104.

Gorn, E. (1986). *The manly art: Bare knuckle fighting in the 19th century America*. Ithaca, NY: Cornell University Press.

Gould, D., & Martens, R. (1979). Attitudes of volunteer coaches toward significant youth sport issues. *Research Quarterly*, **50**(3), 369-380.

Gramsci, A. (1971). *Selections from the prison notebooks*. London: Lawrence & Wishart.

Graydon, J. (1983). But it's more than a game. It's an institution. *Feminist Review*, **13**, 5-16.

Green, G. (1953). *The history of football association*. London: Naldrett Press for the Football Association.

Green, H. (1986). *Fit for America: Health, fitness and sport in American society*. New York: Pantheon Books.

Green, T.S., Oglesby, C.A., Alexander, A., & Franke, N. (1981). *Black women in sport*. Reston, VA: American Alliance for Health, Physical Education, Recreation, and Dance.

Greendorfer, S.L. (1974). *The nature of female socialization into sport: A study of selected college women's sport participation*. Doctoral dissertation, University of Wisconsin, Madison.

Greendorfer, S.L. (1978). The role of socializing agents in female sport involvement. *Research Quarterly*, **48**, 304-310.

Greendorfer, S.L., & Ewing, M. (1981). Race and gender differences in children's socialization into sport. *Research Quarterly*, **52**, 301-310.

Griffin, C., Wirth, M., & Wirth, A. (1986). *Beyond acceptance: Parents of lesbians and gays talk about their experiences*. Englewood Cliffs, NJ: Prentice-Hall.

Griffin, P. (1983). Gymnastics is a girl's thing. In T. Templin & J. Olson (Eds.), *Teaching in physical education* (pp. 71-85). Champaign, IL: Human Kinetics.

Griffin, P. (1989). Homophobia in physical education. *Canadian Association for Physical Education and Recreation,* **11**(2), 333-346.

Grimkè, S. (1970). *Letters on the equality of the sexes and the condition of women*. New York: Burt Franklin. (Original work published 1838)

Grow, R. (1986). Nineteenth century football and the Melbourne press. *Sporting Traditions: The Journal of the Australian Society for Sports History*, 3(1), 23-37.

Gruneau, R.S. (1978). Conflicting standards and problems of personal action in the sociology of sport. *Quest*, **30**, 80-90.

Gruneau, R.S. (1983). *Class, sports, and social development*. Amherst: University of Massachusetts Press.

Guthrie, S. (1982). *Homophobia: Its impact on women in sport and physical education*. Unpublished master's thesis, California State University, Long Beach.

Guttmann, A. (1978). *From ritual to record*. New York: Columbia University.

Hall, D. (1985). *Fathers playing catch with sons*. San Francisco: North Point Press.

Hall, M.A. (1972). A 'feminine woman' and an 'athletic woman' as viewed by female participants and non-participants in sport. *British Journal of Physical Education*, **3**.

Hall, M.A. (1978). *Sport and gender: A feminist perspective on the sociology of sport.* Ottawa: Canadian Association of Health, Physical Education, and Recreation Sociology of Sport Monograph Series.

Hall, M.A. (1981). Sport, sex roles and sex identity. *CRIAW Papers/Les Documents de 1kl'CRAF, 80-81.* Ottawa: The Canadian Research Institute for the Advancement of Women.

Hall, M.A. (1984). Towards a feminist analysis of gender inequality in sport. In N. Theberge & P. Donnelly (Eds.), *Sport and the sociological imagination.* Fort Worth: Texas University.

Hall, M.A. (1985). How should we theorize sport in a capitalist patriarchy? *International Review for Sociology of Sport,* **1**, 109-113.

Hall, M.A. (Ed.) (1987a). The gendering of sport, leisure, and physical education [Special issue]. *Women's Studies International Forum,* **10**(4).

Hall, M.A. (1987b). *Masculinity as culture: The discourse of gender and sport.* Paper presented at the Congress on Movement and Sport in Women's Life, Jyväskalä, Finland.

Hall, M.A. (1988). The discourse on gender and sport: From femininity to feminism. *Sociology of Sport Journal,* **5**(4), 330-340.

Hall, M.A., & Richardson, D.A. (1982). *Fair ball: Towards sexual equality in Canadian sport.* Ottawa, ON: The Canadian Advisory Council on the Status of Women, Ottawa.

Hamilton, R., & Barrett, M. (Eds.) (1987). *The politics of diversity: Feminism, Marxism, and nationalism.* Montreal: Book Center.

Hammersley, M. (Ed.) (1983). *The ethnography of schooling.* Driffield, England: Nafferton Books.

Hantover, J.P. (1980). The Boy Scouts and the validation of masculinity. In E. Pleck & J. Pleck (Eds.), *The American man,* (pp. 285-301). Englewood Cliffs, NJ: Prentice-Hall.

Haraway, D. (1983). Animal sociology and a natural economy of the body politic: Part I. A political physiology of dominance. In E. Abel & E.K. Abel (Eds.), *The Signs reader: Women, gender and scholarship* (pp. 123-138). Chicago: University of Chicago Press.

Haraway, D. (1985). A manifesto for cyborgs: Science, technology, and socialist feminism in the 1980's. *Socialist Review,* **15**, 65-107.

Harding, S. (1986). *The science question in feminism.* Ithaca, NY: Cornell University Press.

Hare, N., & Hare, J. (1984). *The endangered black family: Coping with the unisexualization and coming extinction of the black race.* San Francisco: Black Think Tank.

Hargreaves, J. (1986). *Sport, power and culture: A social and historical analysis of popular sports in Britain.* New York: St. Martin's Press.

Hargreaves, J.A. (Ed.) (1982). *Sport, culture and ideology.* London: Routledge & Kegan Paul.

Hargreaves, J.A. (1986). Where's the virtue? Where's the grace? A discussion of the social production of gender relations in and through sport. *Theory, Culture & Society,* **3**(1), 109-121.

Harris, D.S., & Eitzen, D. S. (1978). The consequences of failure in sport. *Urban Life,* **7**, 177-188.

Harris, D.V. (1972). *Women and sport: A national research conference.* Proceedings from the National Research Conference, Women and Sport. (Penn State HYPER Series No. 2), Pennsylvania State University, August 13-18.

Hartman, H. (1979). Capitalism, patriarchy and job segregation by sex. In Z. Eisenstein (Ed.), *Capitalist patriarchy and the case for socialist feminism.* New York: Monthly Review Press (pp. 206-247).

Hartman, H. (1981). The unhappy marriage of Marxism and feminism. In L. Sargent (Ed.), *Women and revolution: A discussion of the unhappy marriage of Marxism and feminism* (pp. 1-41). Boston: South End Press.

Hartman, M. (1984). *Sexual crack-up: The role of gender in western history.* Unpublished paper, Rutgers University, New Brunswick, NJ.

Hartsock, N. (1983). The feminist standpoint: Developing the ground for a specifically feminist historical materialism. In S. Harding & M.B. Hintikka (Eds.), *Discovering reality: Feminist perspectives on epistemology, metaphysics, methodology, and philosophy of science* (pp. 283-310). Boston: D. Reidel.

Hartsock, N. (1987). Rethinking modernism: Minority vs. majority theories. *Cultural Critique*, **7**, 187-206.

Harvey, J., & Cantelon, H. (Eds.) (1988). *Not just a game: Essays in Canadian sport sociology.* Ottawa, ON: University of Ottawa Press.

Hatton, C.T., & Hatton, R.W. (1978). The sideline show. *Journal of the National Association for Women Deans, Administrators, & Counselors*, **42**(1), 23-28.

Haug, F. (Ed.) (1987). *Female sexualization.* London: Verso.

Hearn, J. (1987). *The gender of oppression: Men, masculinity and the critique of Marxism.* Brighton, England: Wheatsheaf.

Hearn, J., & Parkin, P.W. (1987). *'Sex' at 'work': The power and paradox of organisation sexuality.* Brighton, Eng: Wheatsheaf.

Heath, S. (1987). Male feminism. In A. Jardine & P. Smith (Eds.), *Men in feminism* (pp. 1-32). New York: Methuen.

Heckler, M. (1985). *Report of the secretary's task force on black and minority health.* Bethesda, MD: U.S. Department of Health and Human Services.

Heidegger, M. (1926). *Being and time* (J. Macquarrie & E. Robinson, Trans.). New York: Harper & Row.

Herdt, G.H. (1982a). Fetish and fantasy in Sambia initiation. In G.H. Herdt (Ed.), *Rituals of manhood: Male initiation in Papua New Guinea* (pp. 44-98). Berkeley: University of California Press.

Herdt, G.H. (Ed.) (1982b). *Rituals of manhood: Male initiation in Papua New Guinea.* Berkeley: University of California Press.

Hill, P., & Lowe, B. (1978). The inevitable metathesis of the retiring athlete. *International Review of Sport Sociology*, **9**, 5-29.

Hilliard, D.C. (1984). Media images of male and female professional athletes: An interpretive analysis of magazine articles. *Sociology of Sport Journal*, **1**(3), 251-262.

Hobbes, T. (1968). *Leviathan.* C. MacPherson (Ed.). Harmondworth, England: Penguin Books. (Original work published in 1651)

Hoberman, J. (1984). *Sport and political ideology.* Austin, TX: University of Texas Press.

Hoch, P. (1972). *Rip off the big game.* New York: Anchor Press.

Holland, J., & Oglesby, C. (1979). Women and sport: The synthesis begins. *Annals*, AAPSS, 445.

Hooks, B. (1981). *Ain't I a woman? Black women and feminism*. Boston: South End Press.

Hooks, B. (1984). *Feminist theory: From margin to center*. Boston: South End Press.

Hopkins, E.M. (1950). *This our purpose*. Hanover, MA: Dartmouth Publications.

Horney, K. (1932). The dread of women. *International Journal of Psychoanalysis*, **13**, 348-360.

Houzer, S. (1974). Black women in athletics. *Physical Educator*, **31**, 208-209.

Howell, R. (Ed.) (1982). *Her story in sport*. West Point, NY: Leisure Press.

Hubbard, R., Henifen, M.S., & Fried, B. (1982). *Biological woman—The convenient myth: A collection of feminist essays and a comprehensive bibliography*. Cambridge, MA: Schenkman.

Hughes, T. (1979). *Tom Brown's schooldays*. London: Macmillan. (Original work published 1867)

Hughes, T. (1880). *The manliness of Christ*. Boston: Houghton, Osgood.

Huizinga, J. (1950). *Homo ludens: A study of the play element in culture*. Boston: Beacon Press.

Hull, G.T., Bell, P., & Smith, B. (Eds.) (1982). *But some of us are brave: Black women's studies*. Old Westbury, NY: Feminist Press.

Humphreys, L. (1970). *Tearoom trade: Impersonal sex in public places*. Chicago: Aldine.

Ingham, A. (1976). Sport and the 'new left': Some reflections upon opposition without praxis. In D.M. Landers (Ed.), *Social problems in athletics* (pp. 238-248). Champaign, IL: University of Illinois Press.

Inglis, F. (1977). *The name of the game*. London: Heinemann.

Jackson, K. (1985). *Crabgrass frontier: The suburbs in American history*. New York: Oxford University Press.

James, C.L.R. (1963). *Beyond a boundary*. New York: Pantheon Books.

JanMohamed, A. J., & Lloyd, D. (1987). Introduction: Toward a theory of minority discourse. *Cultural Critique*, **6**, 5-12.

Jhally, S. (1984). The spectacle of accumulations: Material and cultural factors in the evolution of the sports media complex. *The Insurgent Sociologist*, **12**, 41-57.

Joseph, G., & Lewis, J. (1981). *Common differences: Conflicts in black and white feminist perspectives*. Garden City, NJ: Anchor Press.

Kaiser, L. (1979). *The vice lords: Warriors of the streets*. New York: Holt, Rinehart, & Winston.

Kandiyoti, D. (1988). Bargaining with patriarchy. *Gender and Society*, **2**(3), 274-290.

Kaplan, C. (1987). Deterritorializations: The rewriting of home and exile in western feminist discourse. *Cultural Critique*, **6**, 187-198.

Kaplan, E. A. (1983). Is the gaze male? In A. Snitow, C. Stansell, & S. Thompson (Eds.), *Powers of desire: The politics of sexuality* (pp. 309-327). New York: Monthly Review.

Kaplan, J. (1979). *Women and sports*. New York: Avon Books.

Katz, J. (1983). *Gay/lesbian almanac: A new documentary*. New York: Harper & Row.

Kaufman, M. (1986). *Beyond patriarchy: Essays by men on pleasure, power, and change*. New York: Oxford University Press.

Kernberg, O. (1975). *Borderline conditions and pathological narcissism*. New York: Science House.

Kessler, S.J., & McKenna, W. (1975). *Gender: An ethnomethodological approach.* New York: Wiley.

Kett, J. (1977). *Rites of passage.* New York: Basic Books.

Kidd, B. (1983). Getting physical: Compulsory heterosexuality in sport. *Canadian Woman Studies*, **4**, 62-65.

Kidd, B. (1984). The myth of the ancient Olympic games. In A. Tomlinson & G. Whannel (Eds.), *Five ring circus: Money, power, and politics at the Olympic games* (pp. 71-83). London: Pluto.

Kidd, B. (1987). Sports and masculinity. In M. Kaufman (Ed.), *Beyond patriarchy: Essays by men on pleasure, power, and change* (pp. 250-265). Toronto: Oxford University Press.

Kimmel, M. (1986). Toward men's studies. *American Behavioral Scientist*, **29**(5), 517-529.

Kimmel, M. (Ed.) (1987a). *Changing men: New directions in research on men and masculinity.* Newbury Park, CA: Sage.

Kimmel, M. (1987b). Men's responses to feminism at the turn of the century. *Gender and Society*, **1**(3), 261-283.

Kinsman, G. (1987). Men loving men: The challenge of gay liberation. In M. Kaufman (Ed.), *Beyond patriarchy: Essays by men on pleasure, power, and change* (pp. 103-119). Toronto: Oxford University Press.

Kirkham, G. (1971). Homosexuality in prison. In J. Heslin (Ed.), *Studies in the sociology of sex* (pp. 65-78). New York: Apple-Century-Crofts.

Klein, A.M. (n.d.). *No pain, no gain: The ethnography of bodybuilding.* Unpublished manuscript.

Klein, A.M. (1985a). Muscle manor: The use of sport metaphor and history in sport sociology. *Journal of Sport and Social Issues*, **9**(1), 4-17.

Klein, A.M. (1985b). Pumping iron. *Society*, **22**(6), 68-76.

Klein, A.M. (1987). Fear and self-loathing in Venice: Narcissism, fascism, and bodybuilding. *Journal of Psychoanalytic Anthropology*, **10**(2), 117-137.

Kleinberg, S. (1987). The new masculinity of gay men and beyond. In M. Kaufman (Ed.), *Beyond patriarchy: Essays by men on pleasure, power, and change* (pp. 120-138). Toronto: Oxford University Press.

Kohut, H. (1971). *The analysis of the self: A systemic approach to the treatment of the narcissistic personality.* New York: International University Press.

Kopay, D., & Young, P. (1977). *The David Kopay story: An extraordinary self revelation.* New York: Arbor House.

Kramarae, C., & Treichler, P.A. (1985). *A feminist dictionary.* Boston: Pandora Press.

La Fountaine, J. S. (1985). *Initiation: Ritual drama and secret knowledge across the world.* New York: Penguin Books.

Lamb, G. (1959). *The happiest days.* Toronto: Collins.

Lambert, R. (1966). *The state and boarding education.* New York: Barnes & Noble.

Larson, T.E. (1988). Employment and unemployment of young black males. In J.T. Gibbs (Ed.), *Young, black, and male in America: An endangered species* (pp. 97-128). Dover, MA: Auburn House.

Lasch, C. (1979). *The culture of narcissism: American life in an age of diminishing expectations.* New York: Norton.

Leach, E.R. (1976). *Culture and communication.* London: Cambridge University Press.

Leaman, O., & Carrington, B. (1985). Athleticism and the reproduction of gender and ethnic marginality. *Leisure Studies*, **4**, 205-217.

Lebsock, S. (1984). *The free women of Petersburg: Status and culture in southern town, 1784-1860*. New York: Norton.

Lehne, G. (1976). Homophobia among men. In D. David & R. Brannon (Eds.), *The forty-nine percent majority: The male sex role* (pp. 120-132). Reading, MA: Addison-Wesley.

Lenskyj, H. (1986). *Out of bounds: Women, sport and sexuality*. Toronto: Women's Press.

Leonard, W.M., II, & Reyman, J.M. (1988). The odds of attaining professional athlete status: Refining the computations. *Sociology of Sport Journal*, **5**, 162-169.

Lever, J. (1976). Sex differences in the games children play. *Social Problems*, **23**, 478-487.

Levine, M. (1979). Gay ghetto. In M. Levine (Ed.), *Gay men: The sociology of male homosexuality* (pp. 183-203). New York: Harper & Row.

Levinson, D. J. (1978). *The seasons of a man's life*. New York: Ballantine.

Locke, L., & Jensen, M. (1970). Heterosexuality of women in physical education. *The Foil*, Fall, 30-34.

Lopez, S. (1985). *An innovation in mixed gender PE*. Master's thesis. University of Southampton.

Lourde, A. (1984). *Sister outsider*. Trumansburg, NY: Crossing Press.

Lukes, S. (1975). Political ritual and social integration. *Sociology*, **9**, 289-308.

MacAloon, J. J. (1981). *This great symbol: Pierre de Coubertin and the origins of the modern Olympic games*. Chicago: University of Chicago.

MacAloon, J.J. (1987). An observer's view of sport sociology. *Sport Sociology Journal*, **2**, 103-115.

MacKinnon, C. (1987). *Feminism unmodified: Discourses on life and law*. Cambridge, MA: Harvard University Press.

MacLeod, D. (1986). *Building character in the American boy*. Madison, WI: University of Wisconsin.

MacLeod, J. (1987). *Ain't no makin' it*. Boulder, CO: Westview Press.

MacNeill, M. (1988). Active women, media representations, and ideology. In J. Harvey & H. Cantelon (Eds.), *Not just a game: Essays in Canadian sport sociology* (pp. 195-211). Ottawa, ON: University of Ottawa Press.

Mailer, N. (1968). *The armies of the night*. New York: New American Library.

Majors, R. (1986). Cool pose: The proud signature of black survival. *Changing Men: Issues in Gender, Sex and Politics*, **17**, 5-6.

Majors, R. (1987). *Cool pose: A new approach toward a systematic understanding and study of black male behavior*. Unpublished doctoral dissertation, University of Illinois, Urbana.

Mandle, W. (1976). Cricket and Australian nationalism in the nineteenth century. In T.D. Jacques & G.R. Pavia (Eds.), *Sport in Australia* (pp. 46-72). Sydney, Australia: McGraw-Hill.

Manfredi, J. (1983). Peptalk: The history of cheerleading. *Seventeen*, **42**, 94.

Mangan, J. A. (1981). *Athleticism in the Victorian and Edwardian public schools*. Cambridge, England: Cambridge University Press.

Mangan, J. A. (1987). *The games ethic and imperialism*. New York: Viking Press.

Marchak, P. (1985). Canadian political economy. *The Canadian Review of Sociology and Anthropology*, **22**(5), 673-709.

Marlow, J. (1982). Popular culture, pugilism, and Pickwick. *Journal of Popular Culture*, **15**, 6-21.

Maroney, J.J., & Luxton, M. (1987). *Feminism and political economy: Women's work, women's struggles*. Toronto: Methuen.

Marsh, P., Rosser, E., & Harre, R. (1978). *The rules of disorder*. London: Routledge & Kegan Paul.

Marshall, B.L. (1988). Feminist theory and critical theory. *Canadian Review of Sociology and Anthropology*, **25**(2), 208-230.

Marshall, J. (1981). Pansies, perverts and macho men: Changing conceptions of male homosexuality. In K. Plummer (Ed.), *The making of the modern homosexual* (pp. 133-154). London: Hutchinson.

Martin, B., & Mohanty, C.T. (1986). Feminist politics: What's home got to do with it? In T. deLauretes (Ed.), *Feminist studies/critical studies* (pp. 191-212). Bloomington: Indiana University Press.

Marx, K., & Engels, F. (1964). *The communist manifesto* (P. Sweezy, Trans.). New York: Pocket Books. (Original work published 1848)

Matthaei, J.A. (1982). *An economic history of women in America: Women's work, the sexual division of labor and the development of capitalism*. New York: Schocken Books.

Matthews, S.W. (1982, February). Rethinking sociology through a feminist perspective. *American Sociologist*, **17**, 29-35.

Matza, D. (1964). *Delinquency and drift*. New York: Wiley.

Matza, D. (1969). *Becoming deviant*. Englewood Cliffs, NJ: Prentice-Hall.

McKeever, W. (1913). *Training the boy*. New York: Macmillan.

McLoughlin, W. G. (1955). *Billy Sunday was his real name*. Chicago: University of Chicago Press.

Mead, M. (1949). *Sex and temperament in three primitive societies*. New York: Dell.

Melnick, M.J., & Sabo, D. (1987). Analysis of free communications presented at the first seven NASSS annual meetings: Some patterns and trends. *Sociology of Sport Journal*, **4**, 289-297.

Merleau-Ponty, M. (1962). *The phenomenology of perception*. New York: Humanities Press.

Messner, M. (1985a). The changing meaning of male identity in the lifecourse of the athlete. *Arena Review*, **9**, 31-60.

Messner, M. (1985b). *Masculinity and sports: An exploration of the changing meaning of male identity in the lifecourse of the athlete*. Unpublished doctoral dissertation, University of California, Berkeley.

Messner, M. (1987a). The life of a man's seasons: Male identity in the lifecourse of the athlete. In M. Kimmel (Ed.), *Changing men: New directions in research on men and masculinity* (pp. 53-67). Newbury Park, CA: Sage.

Messner, M. (1987b). *Masculinity, ethnicity, and the athletic career: Motivations and experiences of white men and men of color*. Paper presented at the North American Society for the Sociology of Sport meetings, Edmonton, AB.

Messner, M. (1987c). The meaning of success: The athletic experience and the development of male identity. In H. Brod (Ed.), *The making of masculinities: The new men's studies* (pp. 193-209). Boston: Allen & Unwin.

Messner, M. (1988). Sports and male domination: The female athlete as contested ideological terrain. *Sociology of Sport Journal*, **5**(3), 197-211.

Mill, J.S. (1970). The subjection of women. In A.S. Rossi (Ed.), *John Stuart Mill and Harriet Taylor Mill: Essays on sex equality*. Chicago: University of Chicago Press.

Millett, K. (1970). *Sexual politics*. Garden City, NY: Doubleday.

Mirande, A. (1985). *The Chicano experience: An alternative perspective*. Notre Dame, IN: University of Notre Dame Press.

Mirande, A., & Enriquez, E. (1979). *La Chicana: The Mexican American woman*. Chicago: University of Chicago Press.

Mitchell, J. (1973). *Women's estate*. New York: Vintage.

Mix, R. (1987). So little gain for the pain. *Sports Illustrated*, **67**(17), 54-56, 69.

Moore, H. L. (1986). *Space, text and gender: An anthropological study of the Marakwet of Kenya*. Cambridge, England: Cambridge University Press.

Moraga, C. (1983). *Loving in the war years*. Boston: South End Press.

Moraga, C., & Anzaldua, G. (1983). *This bridge called my back*. New York: Kitchen Table Press.

Morgan, D.H. J. (1986). Gender. In R.G. Burgess (Ed.), *Key variables in social investigation* (pp. 3-53). London: Routledge & Kegan Paul.

Morgan, W.J. (1983). Towards a critical theory of sport. *Journal of Sport and Social Issues*, **7** (Winter/Spring), 24-34.

Morrison, T. (1970). *The bluest eye*. New York: Holt, Rinehart & Winston.

Morrow, R.A. (1985). Critical theory and critical sociology. *The Canadian Review of Sociology and Anthropology*, **22**(5), 710-747.

Morton, C.W. (1952). Accent on living. *Atlantic Monthly*, **189**, 92-93.

Mrozek, D.J. (1983). *Sport and American mentality: 1880-1910*. Knoxville: University of Tennessee Press.

Muecke, D. (1982). *Irony and the ironic*. London: Methuen.

Mulvey, L. (1985). Visual pleasure and narrative cinema. In G. Mast & M. Cohen (Eds.), *Film theory and criticism: Introductory readings* (3rd ed.) (pp. 803-816). New York: Oxford University Press.

Murphy, M.D. (1980). *The involvement of blacks in women's athletics in member institutions of the AIAW*. Unpublished doctoral dissertation, University of Florida, Gainesville.

Naison, M. (1972, July/August). Sports and the American empire. *Radical America*, pp. 95, 96, 107-110.

Oakley, A. (1981). *Subject women*. Oxford, England: Martin Robertson.

Oglesby, C.A. (1978). The masculinity/femininity game: Called on account of . . . In C.A. Oglesby (Ed.), *Women and sport: From myth to reality* (pp. 75-87). Philadelphia: Lea & Febiger.

Oglesby, C.A. (1984). Interaction between gender, identity, and sport. In J.M. Silva & R.S. Weinberg (Eds.), *Psychological foundations of sport* (pp. 387-399). Champaign, IL: Human Kinetics.

Oglesby, C.A. (1988). Women and sport. In J. Goldstein (Ed.), *Sport games and play: Social and psychological viewpoints*. Hillsdale, NJ: Lawrence Erlbaum Associates.

Olson, M. (1986). *From closet to classroom: A perspective on gay and lesbian individuals in U.S. schools*. Grand Forks, ND: University of North Dakota Press. (Available through the UND Bookstore, Box 8197, University Station, Grand Forks, ND 58201)

Omi, M., & Winant, H. (1986). *Racial formation in the United States*. New York: Routledge & Kegan Paul.

Oriard, M. (1984). *The end of autumn*. Garden City, NJ: Doubleday.

Orozco, C. (1986). Sexism in Chicano studies and the community. In T. Cordova, N. Cantu, G. Cordenas, J. Garcia, & C. Sierra (Eds.), *Chicano voices: Intersections of class, race, and gender* (Proceedings of the 1984 National Association for Chicano Studies, pp. 11-18). Austin, TX: Center for Mexican American Studies.

Oxendine, J. (1988). *American Indian sports heritage*. 22-. Champaign, IL: Human Kinetics.

Palmer, B. (1979). *A culture in conflict*. Montreal: Queen's-McGill.

Pannick, D. (1983). *Sex discrimination in sport*. London: Equal Opportunities Commission.

Pearce, J.C. (1971). *The crack in the cosmic egg*. New York: Julian Press.

Pearson, K. (1982). Conflict, stereotypes and masculinity in Australian and New Zealand surfing. *Australian and New Zealand Journal of Sociology*, **18**(2), 117-135.

Phillips, J. (1980). Mummy's boys: Pakeha men and male culture in New Zealand. In P. Bunkle & B. Hughes (Eds.), *Women in New Zealand society*. Auckland, New Zealand: Allen & Unwin.

Pleck, E. (1983). Feminist responses to crimes against women, 1868-1896. *Signs: Journal of Women in Culture and Society*, **8**(3), 451-470.

Pleck, J.H. (1982). *The myth of masculinity*. Cambridge, MA: MIT Press.

Plummer, K. (1981). Building a sociology of homosexuality. Homosexual categories: Some research problems in the labeling perspective of homosexuality. In K. Plummer (Ed.), *The making of the modern homosexual* (pp. 17-29, 53-75). London: Hutchinson.

Plummer, K. (1983). *Documents of life*. London: Allen & Unwin.

Polanyi, K. (1957). *The great transformation*. Boston: Beacon Press.

Pratt, M.B. (1984). Identity: Skin, blood, heart. In E. Bulkin, M.B. Pratt, & B. Smith (Eds.), *Yours in struggle* (pp. 11-63). Brooklyn: Long Haul Press.

Pringle, H.J. (1931). *Theodore Roosevelt: A biography*. New York: Harcourt Brace.

Rainwater, L. (1966). The crucible of identity: The lower class negro family. *Daedalus*, **95**, 172-216.

Rees, R.C., & Miracle, A.W. (Eds.) (1986). *Sport and social theory*. Champaign, IL: Human Kinetics.

Reiss, D. (1971). The social integration of peers and queers. In E. Rubington & M. Weinberg (Eds.), *Deviance: The interactionist perspective* (pp. 204-219). New York: Macmillan.

Rich, A. (1978). *The dream of a common language*. New York: Norton.

Rintala, J., & Birrell, S. (1984). Fair treatment for the active female: A content analysis of Young Athlete magazine. *Sociology of Sport Journal*, **1**(3), 213-250.

Ritzer, G. (1975). *Sociology: A multiple paradigm science*. Boston: Allyn & Bacon.

Roberts, R. (1976). The ramifications of the study of women. In J. Roberts (Ed.), *Beyond intellectual sexism: A new woman, a new reality* (pp. 3-13). New York: McKay.

Rogin, M. (1975). *Fathers and children*. New York: Pantheon Books.

Rowland, C. (1986, December 23). Games people play: The burgeoning world of gay athletics. *The Advocate*, **462**, 42-47, 108-109.

Rubin, L.B. (1985). *Just friends: The role of friendship in our lives*. New York: Harper & Row.

Rudman, W.J. (1986). The sport mystique in black culture. *Sociology of Sport Journal*, **3**(4), 305-319.

Ryan, M.P. (1975). *Womanhood in America*. New York: New Viewpoints.

Sabo, D. (1985). Sport, patriarchy, and male identity: New questions about men and sport. *Arena Review*, **9**, 1-30.

Sabo, D. (1986). Pigskin, patriarchy, and pain. *Changing Men: Issues in Gender, Sex and Politics*, **16**(Summer), 24, 25.

Sabo, D. (1987, November). *The football coach as officiant in patriarchal society: Conformity and resistance in the social reproduction of masculinity*. Paper presented at the meeting of the North American Society for the Sociology of Sport, Edmonton, AB.

Sabo, D. (1988, November). Title IX and athletics: Sex equity in schools. *Updating School Board Policies*, **19**(10), 1-4.

Sabo, D., & Runfola, R. (Eds.) (1980). *Jock: Sports and male identity*. Englewood Cliffs, NJ: Prentice-Hall.

Safilios-Rothschild, C. (1977). *Love, sex, and sex roles*. Englewood Cliffs, NJ: Prentice-Hall.

Sage, G.H. (1974). Value orientations of American college coaches compared to male college students and businessmen. In G.H. Sage (Ed.), *Sport and American society*. Reading, MA: Addison-Wesley.

Sage, G.H. (1987a). Pursuit of knowledge in sociology of sport: Issues and prospects. *Quest*, **39**, 255-281.

Sage, G.H. (1987b). The social world of high school athletic coaches: Multiple role demands and their consequences. *Sociology of Sport Journal*, **4**, 213-228.

Scarry, E. (1985). *The body in pain: The making and unmaking of the world*. New York: Oxford University Press.

Schafer, W.E. (1975). Sport and male sex role socialization. *Sport Sociology Bulletin*, **4**(Fall), 224-233.

Scott, J. (1971). *The athletic revolution*. New York: Free Press.

Scott, K., Muhanji, C., & High, E. (1987). *Tight spaces*. San Francisco: Spinsters/ Aunt Lute Press.

Scraton, S.J. (1986). Images of femininity and the teaching of girls' physical education. In J. Evans (Ed.), *Physical education, sport and schooling* (pp. 71-94). London: Falmer Press.

Scraton, S.J. (1987). ''Boys muscle in where angels fear to tread''-girls' subcultures and physical activities. In J. Horne, D. Jary, & A. Tomlinson (Eds.), *Sport, leisure and social relations* (pp. 160-186). London: Routledge & Kegan Paul.

Sears, R. (1970). Relation of early socialization experiences to self-concept and gender role in middle childhood. *Child Development*, **44**, 267-289.

Sheard, K., & Dunning, E. (1973). The rugby football club as a male preserve. *International Review of Sport Sociology*, **3/4**, 5-21.

Sherlock, J. (1987). Issues of masculinity and femininity in British physical education. *Women's Studies International Forum*, **10**(4), 443-451.

Sherril, J. (1974). Homophobia: A tentative personality profile. *Psychological Reports*, **1**, 9-27.

Silverman, D. (1985). *Qualitative methodology and sociology*. Gower, South Wales: Aldershot.

Silverman, E.L. (1973). *Theodore Roosevelt and women: The inner conflict of a president and the impact on his ideology*. Unpublished doctoral dissertation, University of California at Los Angeles.

Sipes, R.G. (1973). War, sports and aggression. *American Anthropologist*, **75**, 64-86.

Smith, B. (Ed.) (1983). *Home girls: A black feminist anthology*. NY: Kitchen Table/Women of Color Press.

Smith, D. (1987). *The everyday world as problematic: A feminist sociology*. Toronto: University of Toronto Press.

Smith, K. (1971). Homophobia: A tentative personality profile. *Psychological Reports*, **29**, 1091-1094.

Smith-Rosenburg, C. (1985). *Disorderly conduct: Visions of gender in Victorian America*. New York: Knopf.

Spalding, A. (1911). *America's national game*. New York: American Sports.

Spender, D. (Ed.) (1981). *Men's studies modified: The impact of feminism on the academic disciplines*. Oxford, England: Pergamon Press.

Spirit of Houston. (1978). *The first national women's conference: An official report to the President, the Congress, and the people of the United States*. Washington: National Commission on the Observance of International Women's Year.

Spivey, D., & Jones, T. (1975). Intercollegiate athletic servitude: A case study of the Black Illini student-athlete. *Social Science Quarterly*, **55**, 937-947.

Sprague, H. (1982). [Psychological testing on bodybuilders]. Unpublished raw data.

Stacey, J. (1979). When patriarchy kowtows: The significance of the Chinese family revolution for feminist theory. In Z.R. Eisenstein (Ed.), *Capitalist patriarchy and the case for socialist feminism* (pp. 199-348). New York: Monthly Review.

Stacey, J., & Thorne, B. (1985). The missing feminist revolution in sociology. *Social Problems*, **32**(4), 301-316.

Stanley, L., & Wise, S. (1983). *Breaking out: Feminist consciousness and feminist research*. London: Routledge & Kegan Paul.

Staples, R. (1982). *Black masculinity*. San Francisco: Black Scholar Press.

Staurowsky, E.J. (1987, April). *Women coaching male athletes: A new look at an old rite of passage*. Paper presented at the meeting of the American Alliance for Health, Physical Education, Recreation, and Dance, Las Vegas, NV.

Stevens, W. (1977). *Opus posthumous*. New York: Knopf.

Stewart, J., & Scott, J. (1978). The institutional decimation of Black American males. *Western Journal of Black Studies*, **8**, 82-93.

Stone, G. (1973). American sports: Play and display. In J.T. Talamini & C.H. Page (Eds.), *Sport and society* (pp. 65-84). Boston: Little, Brown.

Talbert, T. (1976). *The black athlete in the southwest conference: A study of institutionalized racism*. Unpublished doctoral dissertation, Baylor University, Waco, TX.

Terkel, S. (1974). *Working*. New York: Avon Books.

Theberge, N. (1981). A critique of critiques: Radical and feminist writings on sport. *Social Forces*, **60**(2), 341-353.

Theberge, N. (1987). Sport and women's empowerment. *Women's Studies International Forum*, **10**(4), 387-393.

Theberge, N. (1989). Social control and women in sport. In J. Freeman (Ed.), *Women: A feminist perspective* (4th ed.). Mountainview, CA: Mayfield.

Theberge, N., & Cronk, A. (1986). Work routines in newspaper sports departments and the coverage of women's sports. *Sociology of Sport Journal*, **3**(3), 195-203.

Theroux, P. (1986). Being a man. In *Sunrise with seamonsters: Travels and discoveries*. Boston: Houghton Mifflin.

Thirer, J., & Wright, S.D. (1985). Sport and social status for adolescent males and females. *Sociology of Sport Journal*, **2**(2): 164-171.

Thompson, J. (1984). *Studies in the theory of ideology*. Cambridge, England: Cambridge University Press.

Thompson, M. (1898, September 1). Vigorous men, a vigorous nation. *Independent*.

Titley, V., & McWhirter, R. (1970). *Centenary history of the rugby football union*. London: Pluto.

Tong, R. (1989). *Feminist theory: A comprehensive introduction*. Boulder, CO: Westview Press.

Townsend, R. (1977). The competitive male as loser. In D. Sabo & R. Runfola (Eds.) (1980), *Jock: Sports and male identity*. Englewood Cliffs, NJ: Prentice-Hall.

Turner, B. (1984). *The body in society*. New York: Blackwell.

Tutko, T.A., & Bruns, W. (1976). *Winning is everything and other American myths*. New York: Macmillan.

Twin, S. (1979). *Out of the bleachers: Writings on women and sport*. Old Westbury, NY: Feminist Press.

Tygiel, J. (1983). *Baseball's great experiment: Jackie Robinson and his legacy*. New York: Oxford University Press.

Uhler, G.A. (1987, July/August). Athletics and the university: The post-woman's era. *Academe*, **73**, 25-29.

Varpalotai, A. (1987). The hidden curriculum in leisure: An analysis of a girls' sport subculture. *Women's Studies International Forum*, **10**(4), 411-422.

Veblen, T. (1953). *Theory of the leisure class*. Boston: Houghton Mifflin. (Original work published 1899)

Weber, E. (1970). Pierre de Coubertin and the introduction of organized sport into France. *Journal of Contemporary History*, **5**(2), 3-26.

Weeks, J. (1981). Discourse, desire and sexual deviance: Some problems in a history of homosexuality. In K. Plummer (Ed.), *The making of the modern homosexual* (pp. 76-111). London: Hutchinson.

Weeks, J. (1985). *Sexuality and its discontents*. London: Routledge & Kegan Paul.

Weeks, J. (1986). *Sexuality*. Chichester, England: Ellis Horwood.

Wellman, D. (1986). The new political linguistics of race. *Socialist Review*, **87/88**, 43-62.

Whitehead, N., & Hendry, L.B. (1976). *Teaching physical education in England: Description and analysis*. London: Lepus.

Williams, R. (1983). *Keywords: A vocabulary of culture and society* (2nd ed.). London: Fontana Paperbacks.

Willis, P. (1982). Women in sport and ideology. In J. Hargreaves (Ed.), *Sport, culture and ideology* (pp. 117-135). London: Routledge & Kegan Paul.

Wilson, W.J., & Neckerman, K.M. (1986). Poverty and family structure: The widening gap between evidence and public policy issues. In S.H. Danzinger & D.H. Weinber (Eds.), *Fighting Poverty* (pp. 232-259). Cambridge, MA: Harvard University Press.

References 277

Wittig, M. (1982). The category of sex. *Feminist Issues, 2*(2), 63-68.
Wolf, D. (1972). *Foul: The Connie Hawkins story.* New York: Warner Books.
Wollstonecraft, M. (1975). *A vindication of the rights of woman.* Edited by C.H. Poston. New York: Norton. (Original work published 1792)
Woods, S. (August, 1987). *Studying the experiences of lesbian physical education teachers.* Paper presented at the annual meeting of the American Psychological Association, New York.
Working Group on Women in Sport. (1985). *Women, sport and the media: A report to the federal government from the Working Group on Women in Sport.* Canberra, Australia: Australian Government Publishing Service.
Wright, F.L. (1970). *The future of architecture.* New York: Dover. (Original work published 1953)
Yetman, N., & Eitzen, S. (1972). Black Americans in sport: Unequal opportunity for equal ability. *Civil Rights Digest, 5,* 20-34.
Young, D. (1985). *The myth of Greek amateur athletics.* Chicago: Ares.
Young, F. (1965). *Initiation ceremonies: A cross-cultured study of status dramatization.* Indianapolis: Bobbs-Merrill.
Young, I. (1979). The exclusion of women from sport: Conceptual and existential dimensions. *Philosophy in Context, 9,* 44-53.
Young, K. (1983). *The subculture of rugby players: A form of resistance and incorporation.* Unpublished master's thesis, McMaster University, Hamilton, ON.
Zaner, R.M., & Enggelhardt, H.T., Jr. (1974). *Structures of the lifeworld* (A. Schutz & T. Luckmann, Trans.). Evanston, IL: Northwestern University Press. (Original work published 1973)

Supplemental Readings

Beam, J. (Ed.) (1986). *In the life: A black gay anthology.* Boston: Alyson.

Beck, E. (1982). *Nice Jewish girls: A lesbian anthology.* Trumansburg, NY: Crossing Press.

Bernstein, B. (1977). *Class, codes and control.* London: Routledge & Kegan Paul.

Broun, H. (1939, May 6). The happy days of baseball. *Brown's Nutmeg.*

Brunt, S. (1986). In sync: Carolyn Waldo's crusade for recognition. *Globe and Mail,* p. C1.

DeCecco, J. (1985). *Homophobia in American society: Bashers, baiters, and bigots.* New York: Harrington Park Press.

Degler, C. (1980). *At odds.* New York: Oxford University Press.

Douglass, A. (1977). *The feminization of American culture.* New York: Knopf.

Dunning, E. (1981). Social bonding and the socio-genesis of violence: A theoretical-empirical analysis with reference to combat sports. In A. Tomlinson (Ed.), *The sociological study of sport: Configurational and interpretive studies* (pp. 1-35). Eastbourne, England: Brighton Polytechnic, Chelsea School of Human Movement.

Duquin, M. (1988, April 14-17). *Sportive pain: Pain as discourse.* Paper presented at the meeting of the North Central Sociological Association, Pittsburgh, PA.

Evans, J. (in press). Body matters: Towards a socialist PE. In H. Lauder & P. Brown (Eds.), *Education in decline, policies of reconstruction.* London: Falmer Press.

Fromm, E. (1948). The Oedipus complex and the Oedipus myth. In R.N. Aushen (Ed.), *The family its function and destiny* (Vol. V). New York: Harper.

Griffin, P. (in press). Homophobia in physical education. *CAHPER Journal* [Special issue on equity].

Gruneau, R.S. (1981). Cultural studies: Two paradigms. In T. Bennett (Ed.), *Culture, ideology and social process* (pp. 19-37). London: Batsford.

Heron, A. (Ed.) (1983). *One teenager in ten: Writings by gay and lesbian youth.* Boston: Alyson.

Hollands, R.G. (1984). The role of cultural studies and social criticism in the sociological study of sport. *Quest, 36,* 66-79.

Jansen, S.J. (1988). *Censorship: The knot that binds power and knowledge.* New York: Oxford University Press.

Kinsey, A.W., & Pomeroy, C.M. (1948). *Sexual behavior in the human male.* Philadelphia: Saunders.

Klein, A.M. (1986). Pumping irony: Crisis and contradiction in bodybuilding subculture. *Sociology of Sport Journal, 3*(1), 3-23.

Know baseball, know the American. (1913, September). *American Magazine*, p. 76.

Kuhn, T.S. (1970). *The structure of scientific revolutions* (2nd ed.). Chicago: University of Chicago Press.

Lipsyte, R. (1975). *Sportsworld: An American dreamland.* New York: Quadrangle Books.

Mandell, R.D. (1984). *Sport: A cultural history.* New York: Columbia University Press.

Mead, M. (1949). *Male and female.* New York: Morrow.

Messner, M. (1990). Boyhood, organized sports, and the construction of masculinities. *Journal of Contemporary Ethnography,* **18**(4), 416-444.

Morgan, W.J. (1987). 'Radical' social theory of sport: A critique and a conceptual emendation. *Sociology of Sport Journal,* **2**(1), 56-71.

Powell, E.H. (1988). *The design of discord: Studies of anomie.* New Brunswick, CT: Transaction.

Randall, M. (1987). It's only sexual terrorism. *Broadside,* p. 14.

Roszak, T., & Roszak, B. (1975). *Masculine/feminine.* New York: Harper & Row.

Sabo, D. (1986). *A feminist analysis of men and sport: Wrestling with the legacy of the plow.* Keynote address for the First Multidisciplinary Conference for Sport Sciences, November 14, Lillehammer, Norway.

Sabo, D. (1989). The myth of the sexual athlete. *Changing Men: Issues in Gender, Sex and Politics,* **20**(Winter/Spring), 38-39.

Sabo, D., with The Women's Sports Foundation (1989). *The Women's Sports Foundation report: Minorities in sports.* New York: Women's Sports Foundation.

Index

A

Adelman, M.L., 48, 52, 61
Adorno, T., 130
Aggression, ritualization of, 27-28, 39, 62, 68, 70-71, 93, 115, 121, 177-178, 202. *See also* Force; War
Alcohol, consumption of, 68, 71, 75, 76, 86
Ali, Muhammed, 112
Althusser, L., 125
Amateurism, 47, 92
Amin, Idi, 151
Anagnorisis, 149-150
Androcentrism. *See* Male domination; Patriarchy
Angell, Roger, 56
Anzaldua, G., 192, 193
Ashenden, D.J., 20
Auchincloss, Eva, 2

B

Baca Zinn, Maxine, 7, 106
Baden-Powell, Lord Robert, 61
Barth, G., 63
Baseball, and manliness, 52, 55-65
Beck, B., 219
Benjamin, J., 100
Bernard, Jessie, 242, 243
Birke, L., 225
Birrell, Susan, 2, 160, 181, 230, 234, 236, 238
Blainey, Justine, 38
Body. *See also* Physical prowess
  female, 35, 36, 50, 182, 235
  and gender identity, 22-23, 27, 239
  male, 21-24, 50, 52-53, 80, 84, 87, 89-92, 94, 129, 150-151, 157, 158, 175
Bodybuilding, 127-130, 132-135, 139
Booth, Wayne, 148
Bourdieu, P., 125
Bowlby, J., 75
Bray, Cathy, 236
Brod, H., 97
Brownmiller, Susan, 2, 174
Bruce, 64
Bruns, W., 41
Bryson, Lois, 25, 28, 121
Bulkin, E., 191
Butts, D.S., 129

C

Carlos, John, 112
Carrigan, T., 29, 143
Carroll, J., 202
Case, Carl, 58
Chadwick, Henry, 61
Chambliss, D.F., 116
Cheerleaders, 32, 80, 153, 154-161
Chodorow, Nancy, 38-39, 40, 74, 121, 180, 184

Christian, B., 189, 192-193
Class
  and athletic careers, 80, 97-108, 113-114
  and exclusion from sports, 34-35, 65, 109
  mingling through sports participation, 47-48, 64
  and oppression, 7, 8, 9, 62, 111, 236
  and overcoming discrimination through sports achievement, 104-106
Coaching
  and commercial sports, 85, 92-93
  in football, 116-117, 118-119
  of men by women, 80-81, 163-170
Cohen, J., 203
Cole, C., 160
Commercialism, in sport, 86, 92-93, 183
Compartmentalization, of sexuality, 136, 137-138, 139
Congress on Movement and Sport in Women's Life, 233
Connell, R.W., 11, 12, 18, 20, 22, 23, 28, 40, 80, 99, 103, 107, 108, 149, 158, 179, 184, 226, 230, 237
Craib, I., 21, 22, 27, 29
Cricket, 62-63, 174
Crisp, Quentin, 146
Critical autobiography, 192-195, 199
Crosset, Todd, 119
Cultural studies paradigm, 231-232, 233, 234

D

Daly, Mary, 2, 3, 174, 188, 242
Davis, N., 134
Dawkins, Darryl, 112
de Beauvoir, Simone, 2, 242
de Coubertin, Pierre, 21, 34, 35, 177
Deem, Rosemary, 233, 235, 236, 239
Delamont, S., 203
Deleuze, G., 196
Dickens, Charles, 37
Dinnerstein, Dorothy, 39, 40, 74, 180, 184
Discourse theory, 195-197
Donnelly, P., 71
Donoghue, Steve, 84-95
Donovan, Josephine, 3
Dowsett, G.W., 20
Du Bois, W.E.B., 192
Dunkle, M., 105
Dunning, Eric, 24, 26, 28, 36, 48, 70, 71, 77, 177, 233
Duquin, Mary, 2
Dworkin, Andrea, 174
Dyer, Ken, 38

E

Edwards, H., 12, 97, 113
Effeminacy, of gay men, 145-146, 151. *See also* Femininity
Effron, A., 116
Eisenstein, Zillah, 5
Elemental Radical Sport Feminism, 242-243

Equality, between the sexes, 181-182
Erving, Julius "Dr. J.," 112

F

Families, 49-50, 73-74
Farr, K.A., 102-103
Farrell, W., 12
Fasteau, M.F., 12
Felshin, Jan, 2
Femininity. *See also* Effeminacy
  changes in, 49
  of cheerleaders, 154-155, 159
  definition of, 144
  enhanced by certain sports, 36
  in feminism, 242-243
  and men's emotional development, 40, 69, 117, 179-180
  threatened by participation in sports, 35, 36, 50
Feminism
  challenge to male dominance by, 2, 5, 31, 43, 49, 57, 58, 71, 180-184, 244-245
  definition of, 1
  liberal, 3, 4-6, 185, 188
  male reaction to, 36
  among minorities, 187, 189-191
  politics and practice, 236, 237-239
  radical, 3, 4, 5, 107, 185
  resistance to, 232-234
  socialist, 3-4, 185
  and sociology of sport, 232-235
  types of, 3-6
  and women's sport history, 48
Fine, Gary Alan, 25, 26, 27, 48, 116, 120, 231
Fiske, G. Walter, 60
Flax, J., 223
Folk games, 34, 67, 68, 69, 70
Football
  and conformity, 117, 119-120
  and homophobia, 132
  interpersonal relationships developed through, 116-117, 118-119
  and male authority, 117, 121-122
  and masculinity, 115-116, 124-125
  and pain, 117, 122-124
  and rugby, 67, 69
  and social isolation, 117, 120-121
  socialization of boys through, 116-118
Force, development of, 23, 40, 68, 144, 173-174, 179
  See also Aggression, ritualization of; War
Foucault, Michel, 18, 50-51, 142-143, 146
Fowles, John, 150
Franklin, C.W., 105
Freud, Sigmund, 89
Friedan, Betty, 2, 241

G

Gallmeier, Charles, 231
Gannaway, H., 209
Gathorne-Hardy, J., 76
Gearhart, Sally, 242
Geertz, Clifford, 143
Gender, 224-225, 237
Gender confusion, 146
Gender identity, 22-23, 27, 39, 50, 68, 69, 73-74, 76-77, 100, 103-104, 115-116, 179-180, 228. *See also* Femininity; Homosexuality; Masculinity; Sexuality
Gender narcissism, 80, 94, 127, 128, 130, 131-132, 139
Gender order, 9-12, 99, 107, 226
Gender politics, 50-51

Gender relations, 225-226
Giddens, Anthony, 176
Gramsci, Antonio, 8
Greendorfer, Susan, 2
Gretsky, Wayne, 37
Griffin, P., 27
Grimkè, Sarah, 3
Grow, R., 178
Gruneau, Richard, 8, 34-35, 47, 98, 228-229, 231, 233
Guattari, F., 196
Guthrie, S., 219
Guttmann, Allen, 47
Gynocentrism, 236

H

Habermas, Jurgen, 172
Hall, Donald, 56
Hall, M. Ann, 2, 19, 163, 219
Hall, Stuart, 232
Harding, Sandra, 9-10, 18
Hare, J., 98
Hare, N., 98
Hargreaves, Jennifer A., 7, 163
Hargreaves, John, 8, 177
Harraway, D., 19
Harris, Dorothy, 2
Hartsock, N., 192, 197
Haug, F., 160
Hearn, Jeff, 202, 234, 236-237, 239
Heath, Stephen, 239
Hegemony, male, 8, 9, 12, 21, 24-27, 28, 29, 37, 71, 79, 80, 83, 93, 94, 99, 107-108, 114, 115, 124-125, 126, 171, 173, 174, 184, 201
Hill, Octavia, 61
Hobbes, Thomas, 151
Hoberman, John, 151
Hoch, Paul, 8, 12
Homophobia, 27, 37, 39, 42, 60, 68, 73, 75, 80, 94, 120, 127, 131-132, 137, 138, 139, 149, 172, 211-221
Homosexuality. *See also* Homophobia; Sexuality
  and gay athletes, 107, 141-152, 213
  and male cheerleading, 155
  and masculinity, 27, 60, 72, 75-76, 80, 144-145, 150
  research on, 216-220
Hooks, B., 188, 191, 192, 193, 194-195
Hopkins, E.M., 53
Hughes, Thomas, 35, 58
Humor, and sport, 26, 42, 149
Humphreys, L., 137
Hustling, by bodybuilders, 127-128, 130, 132-137, 138, 139
Hypermasculinity, 127, 130, 139

I

Idealist/positivist paradigm, 226-228, 232
Identity politics, 190-191, 192
Ingham, A., 228
Inglis, F., 25
Injury, 91, 122. *See also* Pain
Intimacy, and male development, 74-75, 76, 136
Iron men, 79, 83-95, 108
Irony, and gay sensibility, 147-151, 152

J

James, C.L.R., 198
JanMohamed, A.J., 195, 196
Jensen, M., 219
Johnson, Billy "Whiteshoes," 111
Johnson, Butch, 111

Johnson, Magic, 43
Jordan, Michael, 112
K
Kaplan, C., 190, 191, 194, 196
Kernberg, O., 130
Kessler, S.J., 20, 224
Kirkham, G., 137
Klein, Alan, 231
Kohut, H., 130
Kopay, David, 132, 149
L
La Fountaine, J.S., 116, 124
Leach, E.R., 116
Lebsock, Susan, 49
Lehne, G., 132
Lenskyj, H., 155, 236
Lever, Janet, 231
Levinson, D.J., 99, 100
Lloyd, D., 195, 196
Locke, L., 219
Lott, Ronnie, 103
Lourde, A., 188, 192
Lukes, S., 116
Luschen, Gunther, 233
M
McKeever, William, 61
McKenna, W., 224
Mailer, N., 120
Majors, Richard, 106, 108
Male domination. *See* Hegemony, male; Patriarchy
Mangan, J.A., 21, 45, 54, 202
Manion, T., 203
Manliness, 21, 45-46, 48, 51, 54, 67-78, 178
Marshall, Edward, 61
Martin, B., 194
Martin, Pip, 84
Marx, Karl, 8, 229
Masculinity. *See also* Hypermasculinity
    and boyishness, 60
    changes and crisis in, 57-59
    differences in, 19, 29, 33, 37-38, 52-53, 80, 83,
        93-94, 103, 107-108
    and domination, 26, 53-54, 69, 115-116, 143-144
    of gay men, 144-145, 150
    and male socialization, 19-29, 35
    among minorities, 106, 108, 109, 110-111
    revitalization of, 58, 59, 64-65
    study of, 12-13
Matza, D., 128, 134
May, Norman, 183
Mead, Margaret, 242
Merleau-Ponty, M., 23
Messner, Michael A., 76, 113
Mill, John Stuart, 3
Millett, Kate, 2, 3
Minorities
    in bodybuilding, 128
    domination of sports by, 109, 113
    and education, 105, 106-107, 113-114
    exclusion from mainstream theory, 188-189
    exclusion from sports, 64, 65, 109, 198
    military experiences of, 112
    oppression of, 7, 8, 9, 80, 110-111
    participation in sports, 97-98, 104-106, 108, 109-110,
        111-114, 172
    and women's interest in sports, 105, 185-186, 195,
        198, 199
Mirroring, 130-131

Mitchell, Juliet, 2
Mohanty, C.T., 194
Moraga, Cherrie, 187, 193
Morality, and physical prowess, 21-22, 45, 53, 60,
    61, 92
Muscular Christianity movement, 58-59, 177, 178
N
Naison, M., 12
Neo-Marxist paradigm, 229-230, 231, 233, 234
Nesterenko, Eric, 23, 25
New woman, 57
Nonviolence, 243
Nurturing
    as female responsibility, 39, 73, 74, 75, 180
    as feminine, 243
    by men, 89
    shared, 180, 184
O
Oates, Wanda, 166
Oedipal crisis, 68-69
Oglesby, Carole, 2, 163, 169, 170
Olympic Games, ancient, 33-34
Olympic Games, modern
    development of, 33, 34, 35, 41, 177
    male domination of, 36
    participation of women in, 182
    racism protest at, 112
    sexism at, 176
Oriard, M., 23, 25
P
Pain
    repression of, 39, 40, 93, 117-118, 122-124, 179
    in ritual, 117, 124
Parkin, Wendy, 237
Patriarchy. *See also* Feminism, challenge to male
        dominance by; Hegemony, male; Sport, and male
        domination
    definition of, 6-7
    and gay men, 145
    and male advantage, 24-25, 34, 49-50
    radical feminist perspective on, 3
    in ritual, 116
    socialist feminist perspective on, 4
Pearce, J.C., 241
Phillips, J., 202
Physical education
    alternatives for, 204-205, 208-210
    fostering sexist stereotypes in, 172, 201-204
    and homophobia, 172, 211-221
    for men, 45, 203-204, 205-210
Physical prowess. *See also* Aggression, ritualization of;
        Body; Bodybuilding; Force; Skill, perfection of
    and male cheerleading, 157, 158, 160
    and male superiority, 50, 158
    and morality, 21-22, 45, 53, 60, 61, 92
Playground movement, 21
Pleck, Joseph H., 103, 130
Pratt, M.B., 189, 190-191, 194
Pronger, Brian, 107
R
Racial relations theory, 186-187, 192, 199
Racism. *See* Minorities
Radical criticism, 228-229
Radican, Norm, 84
Recreation
    and competition, 42-43
    and diversion, 64
    rational, 34, 47, 53

Reiss, D., 128, 135, 137
Relationships, interpersonal, 85-86, 116-117, 118-119.
    See also Intimacy, and male development
Relations of ruling, 226
Reproduction, threatened by women's participation
    in sports, 35, 36, 50
Rich, Adrienne, 244
Richter, Diana, 181, 238
Role models. *See also* Coaching
    for blacks, 98, 106
    male, 87-88, 131, 166, 167, 170, 179-180
Role theory, 7-8, 22, 99, 228
Roosevelt, Theodore, 35, 59, 60-61
Rubin, L.B., 100
Rudman, W.J., 98
Rugby, 67-78, 177-178
Runfola, R., 12
Ryan, M.P., 49

S
Sabo, Donald F., 12, 26, 149
Sack, Allen, 42
Sargent, D.A., 60
Schools, sports in. *See also* Physical education
    boys' participation in, 51-52, 70
    girls' participation in, 4-5
Schutz, A., 148
Schwarzenegger, Arnold, 131
Scott, J., 12, 110
Seton, Ernest Thompson, 58
Sex, and gender, 224-225
Sexism. *See also* Sport, exclusion of women from
    definition of, 224
    ending, 42, 43, 180-184
    in rugby, 68, 71, 75, 77
Sex roles. *See* Role theory
Sexuality. *See also* Homosexuality
    and masculinity, 26, 46, 72-73, 91, 120, 136
    Victorian, 46, 50-51, 53
Sexual politics. *See* Gender politics
Sheard, Kevin, 36, 71, 77, 177
Sherlock, J., 202
Skill, perfection of, 23, 40, 68, 90, 121, 179
Smith, B., 187, 189, 193
Smith, Tommie, 112
Smith-Rosenberg, C., 49
Social definition paradigm, 230-231
Social practices, effect on sports, 26-27
Social reproduction theory, 125, 235
Somatic compliance, and masculinity, 89
Songs, and rugby, 68, 71, 75, 76, 77
Spalding, Albert G., 61, 63, 64
Spectatorship, 62-64, 154-155, 156, 159, 160-161, 174,
    177
Spermatic economy, 52
Sport
    and admiration, 88, 94, 100, 102, 130, 131, 134
    barriers to male development imposed by, 40-41,
        202, 213, 214
    careers in, 80, 97-108, 113-114
    as character building, 60, 178
    control of, 5, 182, 183, 225
    exclusion of women from, 24, 32, 33, 34, 35, 77, 78,
        85, 94, 109, 120-121, 122, 163, 165-166, 169,
        175-176, 177, 207-208, 239
    male companionship in, 25-26, 28, 40-41, 100,
        102-103, 116-117
    and male domination, 2, 4, 12, 18, 20, 32-33, 36-37,
        99, 103-104, 107, 163, 172, 173, 174-175

male socialization through, 14, 18, 19-29, 34-35,
    38-39, 60, 68, 72-77, 95, 99-101, 116-118,
    124-125, 175, 179-180, 201-204, 205-210
    masculinist bias in, 41-42, 205-207
    naturalness of, 19, 33-34
    participation of women in, 4-5, 24, 28, 36-37, 38,
        48, 154, 155, 176, 178, 182-183, 234-235, 238,
        243
    and rationality, 46-47, 53-54
    social function of, 47-48
    value changes needed in, 42
Sport sociology, critical, 8-9, 226-232
Sprague, H., 130
Stacey, J., 2
Stanley, L., 195
Staples, R., 98
Status. *See* Class
Stevens, Wallace, 150
Stewart, J., 110
Subordination, 243. *See also* Sport, and male domination
Sunday, Billy, 59
Symbolic interactionism, 27
T
Terkel, Studs, 25
Theberge, Nancy, 238
Thomas, Isiah, 43
Thompson, J., 26
Thorne, B., 2
Title IX, 4, 181
Tong, Rosemary, 3, 5-6
Townsend, R., 12
Transsexuals, 89
Transvestites, 89, 143
Truth, Sojourner, 198, 244
Turner, B., 25, 27
Tutko, T.A., 41
Twain, Mark, 55
V
Veblen, Thorstein, 45, 59, 60, 62
Vines, G., 225
W
War. *See also* Aggression, ritualization of
    and ancient Olympic Games, 33, 34
    and football, 124
    and military metaphors for sport, 42-43, 202
    and rugby, 67, 70
Weeks, Jeffrey, 11, 142-143
Wellman, D., 98
Williams, Doug, 113
Willis, Paul, 175
Winters, Barbara Mayer, 176
Wise, S., 195
Witt, Katerina, 176
Wolf, D., 112
Wollstonecraft, Mary, 3
Women
    bodybuilding by, 128
    changing role of, 49-50
    minority, 105, 185-186, 195, 198, 199
    relationships with gay men, 144
    rendered invisible by male sports domination, 32, 176
Woods, S., 219

Y
YMCA, 36, 58
Young, D., 116
Young, I., 24
Young, K., 71

About the Authors

Susan Birrell is an associate professor at the University of Iowa, U.S., where she teaches in the Department of Physical Education and Sports Studies and is active in the Women's Studies Program. She is a feminist whose recent publications include an intellectual history of the field of women and sport and an analysis of feminist resistance through sport. She is at work on a book about gender relations and sport and, with Cheryl Cole, an anthology on gender, sport, and culture.

Lois Bryson is an associate professor in the School of Sociology, University of New South Wales, Sydney, Australia. She is widely published in the areas of social policy and the welfare state, public administration, sport, and family, all with a consistent concern for issues of inequality, particularly gender inequality.

R.W. Connell is a professor of sociology at Macquarie University in Australia. He is the author of books in history, political science, and sociology—most recently *Gender and Power*, a general theory of gender and sexual politics, and *Staking a Claim: Feminism, Bureaucracy and the State* with co-authors Suzanne Franzway and Dianne Court. A long-time activist in the Australian labour movement and contributor to socialist and progressive journals, he is also a Wagner freak, a body surfer, and a pretty bad medium-paced bowler.

Todd Crosset is a PhD candidate in sociology at Brandeis University, Waltham, Massachusetts, U.S. He received an undergraduate degree in philosophy from the University of Texas, where he was an All-American swimmer and a member of the 1980 NCAA Championship Team. He received his master in sociology from Brandeis in 1985.

Laurel R. Davis currently lives in St. Paul, Minnesota, U.S., where she is working on a dissertation to complete a PhD in sport sociology from the University of Iowa. Her primary academic interests include feminist theory and practice, race analysis and politics, qualitative sociology, cultural studies, and body culture. Her sport involvement includes field hockey, softball, and jogging.

Jim Genasci is a professor of physical science at Springfield (Massachusetts) College and the co-coordinator of Parents and Friends of Lesbians and Gays, Pioneer Valley, with his wife, Jean. He conducts public education seminars on gayness/oppression/homophobia, participates on panels and in workshops, and directs symposia on the topic of gayness. He has related interests in homophobia in sports, athletics, and physical education. Jim has published and presented locally, regionally, and nationally. His work with Pat Griffin includes workshops at the AAHPERD National Conference on homophobia in physical education.

Pat Griffin is an associate professor in physical education teacher education at the University of Massachusetts, Amherst, U.S., and an adjunct professor in the School of Education. Pat has conducted research and published widely on racism, sexism, and homophobia in physical education and education. In addition, she is an experienced speaker and trainer, having conducted many workshops on homophobia and heterosexism, racism, sexism, and social diversity awareness for teachers, college students, and human service personnel. Pat has special interest in homophobia in sport, especially women's sport, and expertise in qualitative and empowerment research.

M. Ann Hall is a professor of physical education and sport studies at the University of Alberta, Edmonton, Canada, where she has taught since 1968. She has focused her research primarily on gender relations in sport, recreation, and leisure, and more recently on the gender structure of amateur organizations. Because of her interest in applying feminist epistemology and methodology to the social sciences and humanities, she also teaches in her school's Women's Studies Program. Active in the women's movement, Ann is a past president of the Canadian Research Institute for the Advancement of Women and a founding member of the Alberta Status of Women Committee and the Canadian Association for the Advancement of Women and Sport. An aging athlete who has recently taken up equestrianism, her most pressing challenge is to stay atop her horse.

Barbara Humberstone teaches physical and outdoor education and gender issues in education in the Department of Physical Education, Faculty of Educational Studies, University of Southampton, England. Her research has focused on the organization of teaching and learning in outdoor education and the implications of this sort of pedagogy to the construction of gender identities. She is editing a book on gender, physicality, and physical sciences and has published a number of articles related to her research. Barbara is president of a climbing club, sails both a board and a 24-foot racing catamaran, and was a runner in the all-woman team that finished seventh in the grueling Three Peaks Yacht Race.

Bruce Kidd is the coordinator of the Canadian studies and an associate professor of physical and health education at the University of Toronto, Ontario, Canada. A former Commonwealth champion in track and field, he has written extensively on the history of politics of sport. His publications include *The Death of Hockey* (with John McFarlane), *The Political Economy of Sport, Tom Longboat,* and *Athletes' Rights in Canada* (with Mary Eberts). Bruce is also chair of the Olympic Academy of Canada.

Michael S. Kimmel is an assistant professor of sociology at the State University of New York at Stony Brook, U.S., where he teaches courses on gender, sexuality, social change, and social movements. His books include *Changing Men: New Directions in Research on Men and Masculinity, Men Confronting Pornography,* and *Men's Lives* (with Michael Messner). Michael is at work on a documentary history of pro-feminist men in America and a book on the relationship of sexuality and gender. Shortstop on the National Writers Union softball team, he had been chosen the All-Star shortstop for the past three seasons.

Alan M. Klein is an associate professor of sociology-anthropology at Northeastern University in Boston, Massachusetts, U.S. He has conducted research on various Native American communities, bodybuilders in southern California, the Boston Red Sox baseball team, and most recently on baseball and cultures of resistance in the Dominican Republic. Alan's publications on gender include work on the impact of fur trade on 19th-century Plains Indian women, and a study of men and women in a competitive bodybuilding community in southern California.

Richard Majors is a National Institutes of Health postdoctoral fellow at Kansas University, Lawrence, Kansas, U.S., in the Department of Human Development and Family Life. His present research focuses on the psychosocial development of the black male, masculinity and gender development, coping processes, adolescent behavior, and nonverbal behaviors and communication styles among ethnic groups.

Michael A. Messner is an assistant professor of sociology in the Program for the Study of Women and Men in Society at the University of Southern California, U.S. He has written widely on masculinity and sports, including his forthcoming book, tentatively titled *Power at Play: Organized Sports and the Construction of Masculinity.* Michael is also coeditor (with Michael S. Kimmel) of *Men's Lives,* a book of readings on men and masculinity.

Carole A. Oglesby is chairperson of the Department of Physical Education and director of the graduate program in psychosocial interactions and movement at Temple University, Philadelphia, Pennsylvania, U.S. She has written a text, monographs for AAHPERD and UNESCO, and numerous articles in the area of gender identity and sport. Her interests include the worldwide development of both sport psychology and girls' and women's sport. Carole is a fellow of the Association for the Advancement of Applied Sport Psychology and a former president of the NASPE Sport Psychology Academy. She is on the research teams funded by the Women's Educational Equity Program and the National Ski Areas Association, and is a member of the USOC House of Delegates and the U.S. Collegiate Sports Council Executive Board.

Joe Panepinto graduated from Hamilton College, U.S., with a BA in psychology, where his honors thesis focused on the sex role orientation of male and female athletes. He later earned an MA in journalism at Boston University. Joe has been a reporter for the *Boston Herald,* writing about high school sports and the Boston public schools. He also served as the research coordinator at the Center for the Study of Sport in Society at Northeastern University. Joe is presently a reporter for a national computer newsmagazine based in Framingham, Massachusetts.

Brian Pronger is completing a book on the experience of homosexual men and boys in athletics, *Irony and Ecstasy: Gay Men and Athletics.* He is currently an associate researcher at the School of Physical and Health Education at the University of Toronto, Ontario, Canada. He is also doing graduate work on the phenomenological hermeneutics of the experience of well-being associated with physical exercise.

Donald F. Sabo is an associate professor of social sciences at D'Youville College in Buffalo, New York, U.S. He has coauthored (with Aleksander Gella and Susan Curry Jansen) *Humanism in Sociology* and coedited (with Ross Runfola) *Jock: Sports and Male Identity.* He is an Advisory Board member of the Women's Sports Foundation and has researched, written, and lectured widely on gender and sport issues.

CHESTER COLLEGE LIBRARY

Ellen J. Staurowsky is director of athletics and physical education at William Smith College in the U.S. She holds a master's degree in physical education from Ithaca College. After pursuing postgraduate work at Temple University, she enrolled in a doctoral program at Syracuse University. In her 10-year career, she has served as director of both men's and women's programs and has coached collegiate field hockey, women's lacrosse, and men's soccer. Ellen's main research area is the psychosocial aspects of sport, with an emphasis on issues of gender and sport.

Anne Vagi is a clinical psychologist at the Mississauga (Ontario) Hospital in Canada. She received her PhD from the University of Waterloo in 1984. Her professional activities and interests include individual and group psychotherapy with adults, women's issues, and psychological assessment.

David Whitson taught sociology of sport and leisure for 11 years at Dufermline College, Scotland, and earned his doctoral degree from the University of Queensland, Australia. He currently teaches in the Department of Recreation and Leisure Studies, University of Alberta, Edmonton, Canada. He has published articles on gender and sport in *Theory, Culture, and Society* and other academic journals.

Phil White is a teacher and researcher of the sociology of sport at McMaster University, Hamilton, Ontario, Canada. He received his PhD in sociology from the University of Waterloo in 1987. His intellectual interests include the sociology of sport, social stratification, Canadian society, and race and ethnic relations. Phil is the varsity rugby coach at McMaster and plays tennis, golf, and squash.